The Bible

The Bible

An Introduction, Second Edition

Jerry L. Sumney

Fortress Press
Minneapolis

for Diane Furlong Sumney

A prudent wife is from the LORD.
—Proverbs 19:14

The teaching of kindness is on her tongue.
—Proverbs 31:26

THE BIBLE
An Introduction, Second Edition

Cover image: blueenaylm/iStock/Thinkstock
Cover design: Erica Rieck
Book design: PerfecType, Nashville, TN

Library of Congress Cataloging-in-Publication Data
Print ISBN: 978-1-4514-6924-0
eBook ISBN: 978-1-4514-8433-5

The paper used in this publication meets the minimum requirements of American National Standard for Information Sciences — Permanence of Paper for Printed Library Materials, ANSI Z329.48-1984.

Manufactured in the U.S.A.

BRIEF TABLE OF CONTENTS

PART 1: WHAT IS THE BIBLE, AND HOW DID IT COME ABOUT?

PART 2: WHAT IS THE STORY OF THE HEBREW BIBLE?

PART 3: WHAT IS THE STORY OF THE NEW TESTAMENT?

CONTENTS

PART 3: WHAT IS THE STORY OF THE NEW TESTAMENT?

ILLUSTRATIONS AND BOXES

MAPS

ILLUSTRATIONS

BOXES

CHARTS

TIMELINE

World at Large	Date	Persons, Biblical World	Biblical World
	B.C.E. (Before the Common Era)		
	15000		
Lascaux cave paintings (France)			
	10000		
Ice Age ends (Pleistocene Era)			First settlements in Canaan
	9000		
			First permanent settlement in Jericho
	8000		
Pre-pottery Neolithic societies in Syria and Palestine			
	4000		
		Adam and Eve, according to Genesis (4000)	Creation of the world, according to Genesis (4000)

World at Large	Date	Persons, Biblical World	Biblical World
			First year of Jewish calendar (= 3760 B.C.E.)
Bronze Age begins (3400)			
	3000		
Sumerian city-states emerge (3000)			
Epic of Gilgamesh (or 1200?)			
Great Pyramids of Egypt (2800)			
	2000		
Stonehenge built in England (2000)			
		Abraham (circa 2000–1500)	
Hammurabi Code (1700)		Isaac, Jacob (circa 2000–1500)	
Upanishads written in India (Hinduism) (1500)			
			Hittites rule in eastern Asia Minor (1340–1200)
		Moses leads the exodus (circa 1250)	Israelites' exodus out of Egypt (1250–1200)
End of Bronze Age; Beginning of Iron Age (1200)			Emergence of Israel in the highlands of Canaan (1200); Philistines control coastal areas of Palestine (1200)
Trojan War (1194–1184)			Phoenicians arrive in the Levant (1200–1100)
		Samuel (circa 1100)	
		Saul anointed (1050)	

	1000		
		David becomes king (1000)	Beginning of monarchy in Jerusalem (established as capital) under King David (until circa 960)
		Solomon becomes king (960)	
			Yahwist document (J) of Pentateuch composed (950)
			Building begins on first temple in Jerusalem under King Solomon (until circa 922)
		Rehoboam, king of Judah (922–915)	Division of kingdom: Israel in north; Judah in South (922)
Rise of Neo-Assyrian Empire (911)		Jeroboam I (922–901)	
			Chaldeans settle in Ur (900)
	900		
Homer's *Iliad* and *Odyssey* (860 or 700?)		Elijah, Elisha (860–840)	
Etruscan civilization emerges (850)		Ahab (869–850); Jehu (842–815)	
	800		
		Uzziah (Azariah; 783–742)	
		Isaiah, Amos, Hosea (780–690)	
First Olympic games (776)			
Founding of Rome (753)			
			Elohist document (E) of Pentateuch composed (750)
			Destruction of Samaria, capital of Israel, by Assyrians; end of Israel's kingdom (722–721)

World at Large	Date	Persons, Biblical World	Biblical World
	700		
Building of Greek Acropolis (650)			
Rise of Neo-Babylonian Empire (626)		Nebuchadnezzar (630–562)	
		Josiah (640–609)	Reform of Jerusalem cult by King Josiah; promulgation of book of the law/ Deuteronomy (D) of Pentateuch (622)
Battle of Megiddo (609)		Pharaoh Neco (circa 615); Story of Judith (circa 600)	
	600		
		King Cyrus (600–529)	Capture of Jerusalem by Babylonians (597)
			Destruction of Jerusalem by Babylonians (King Nebuchadnezzar); beginning of Babylonian captivity of Judah (586)
Siddhartha Gautama (563); later becomes the Buddha		Story of Daniel (circa 570)	
Confucius (551–479); later articulates philosophy			
Rise of Persian Empire (550)			Priestly document (P) of Pentateuch composed (550)
Aesop's fables (550)		Darius I (549–486)	
		Nehemiah arrives in Judah (538)	Conquest of Babylon by Cyrus of Persia; Jews end exile and return to Judah; Judah now province of Persia (539)
			Rebuilding of (second) temple in Jerusalem (520–515)

Roman republic established (509)			
	500		
Emergence of Athenian (Greek) democracy (500)		Ahasuerus (Xerxes; 485–465)	
		Mordecai (circa 470)	
Parthenon built in ancient Athens, Greece (438)		Ezra in Judah (circa 460)	Compilation of the Torah (circa 460–445)
Peloponnesian Wars (431–404)		Story of Esther (circa 450)	
Plato (427–347)		Artaxerxes (465–425)	
	400		
Death of Socrates (399)			
Aristotle (384–322)			
Rise of Greek Empire; Alexander the Great conquers Persia (336–323)			
			Judea controlled by Ptolemies of Egypt (founded under Alexander) (312)
	300		
Early Maya civilization emerges (280)			
Punic Wars between Rome and Carthage (264–146)			
			Torah translated into Greek forming beginning of Septuagint Bible (250)

World at Large	Date	Persons, Biblical World	Biblical World
Great Wall of China construction begins (210)			
	200		
		Antiochus IV Epiphanes (175–164)	Jews persecuted by Syria; Maccabean Revolt in Judea (168–167)
		Maccabean leaders: Mattathias (167–166); Judas (166–161/60); John Hyrcanus (135/4–105/4)	Hasmonean (Maccabean) kings rule Judah (142–63)
	100		
			Conquest of Jerusalem by Pompey (Roman general) (63)
Establishment of Julian calendar (365 days/year) (46)			
Rise of Roman Empire; Julius Caesar assassinated (March 15) (44)			
		Last Hasmonean (Antigonus) defeated (37)	Herod captures Jerusalem; installed as king of Judea (37)
		Birth of John the Baptist (circa 7)	
		Birth of Jesus (circa 6)	
	C.E. (Common Era)		
	1		
			John the Baptist's ministry (26)
		Baptism of Jesus (circa 27/30)	Ministry of Jesus (27–30 or 30–33)
		Death of Jesus (circa 30/33)	Pentecost; first "Christian" community in Jerusalem (30/33)

		Martyrdom of Stephen (circa 31/34)	
		Death of Apostle James (44)	Missionary work of Paul (35–62)
Great Roman fire (64)		Death of Paul (ca. 62–64)	
			Persecution of Christians under Roman emperor Nero (64)
			Jewish revolts against Rome (66–73)
			Gospel of Mark, the first Gospel, is composed (66–70)
			Destruction of Jerusalem and the Temple during Jewish-Roman war (70)
			Establishment of Hebrew Bible (70–130)
Colosseum in Rome built (70)			
			Composition of Luke and Acts (80–90)
Mount Vesuvius erupts, destroying Pompeii and Herculaneum (79)			
			Gospel of Matthew is composed (80–85)
			Composition of Gospel of John (90–100)
	100		
			Irenaeus (130–202)
			Bar Kochba leads Jewish revolt against Romans (132)
			First collection of four canonical Gospels (150)
			Origen (185–250)

World at Large	Date	Persons, Biblical World	Biblical World
	200		
			Mishnah (which systematizes tradition and laws) is compiled (200)
	300		
			Christian persecution under Roman emperor Diocletian (303–305)
			Constantine succeeds Diocletian; makes Christianity legal in Roman Empire (313)
			Council of Nicea condemns Arianism heresy establishes Nicene Creed (325)
			Augustine (354–430)
			Council at Constantinople defines doctrine of the Trinity (381)
			Roman emperor, Theodosius I, makes Christianity the state religion (390)
	400		
			Jerome completes Vulgate (Latin Bible) (405)
	500		
			The Talmud is compiled (500)
Church of Hagia Sophia built in Constantinople (532)			
Emergence of Islam under Mohammed; Qur'an is dictated (570–632)			

	600		
Great library at Alexandria, Egypt destroyed by Arabs (641)			
	700		
Feudal society emerges (751)			
	800		
Charlemagne crowned as emperor of west by Pope Leo III (800)			
Charlemagne crowned as emperor of east by Byzantine emperor, Michael I (814)			
	1000		
First crusade to Holy Land (1095–1099)			
Martin Luther (1483–1546)			
Columbus arrives in America; beginning of Spanish colonialism (1492)			
Beginning of Protestant Reformation (1517)			
Beginning of Protestant Reformation (1517)			

PREFACE TO THE FIRST EDITION

My goal in these pages is, first, that those interested in the Bible for its own sake will gain deeper understanding of its contents, as well as an appreciation of the ways it has nourished faith through history; and second, that when this book presses beyond seeing problematic elements in the texts to asking why the authors would have thought such things were good, it will help provide people of faith with ways to better appropriate the biblical texts as a whole. My aim is to speak to students in an academic setting and to those in other settings as well who study the Bible for guidance in their lives. The separation between critical study that aims at understanding the Bible on its own terms and use of the Bible in the search for meaning in terms of understanding the will of God does not need to be as deep as it is often perceived. In fact, I hold that those who use the Bible for religious guidance should start with critical study and use its results to make better use of the Bible.

▶ Overview

This book introduces the content of the biblical texts and the ways scholars in the field of biblical studies approach them today. Understanding the Bible is an important element of one's education because it continues to be one of the most powerful shapers of our world culture. Thus, in our society one needs a basic understanding of the Bible so one can understand and evaluate the various ways different groups use it. Careful study of the Bible may also help a person engage in more informed conversation about the meaning of these texts when they are used in the public arena.

This text introduces the methods of biblical criticism that help clarify how these texts emerged and what they meant in their original settings. We will pay special attention to the historical settings and the literary types, or genres, of the individual books in the Bible. Without a clear understanding of and accounting for these two matters, we will not be able to understand the messages these texts conveyed to their initial audiences. The reading presented here will emphasize that these texts always intended to be theological interpretations of life and events, not objective historical or factual accounts of events such as we might look for in a newspaper account. That is, these texts always look to an explanation of events that attributes their happening to God rather than to social, political, or cultural settings or phenomena.

In our study of the biblical writings, we will encounter ideas, values, and assumptions that often are very different from our own. We will discover some disturbing things that receive implicit and explicit approval: for example, mass killings of an indigenous population, assigning people to experience torment in the afterlife, and the exclusion of some populations from positions of leadership in a community. We will examine not only what these texts advocate, but also why their original authors might have held the views expressed here.

▶ Features in the Book

Readers will find several features and elements to help enrich and extend their understanding of the sometimes complex material covered in these pages. Each chapter is carefully organized with numerous headings and subheadings to aid in comprehension and review. At the beginning of each chapter, a helpful preview alerts readers to the main topics and issues in that chapter. In addition, numbered *textboxes* appear frequently throughout the book to highlight an important point or to offer some clarification, definition, or helpful additional information. Some of these boxes focus on historical material, some on archaeology, and others on literary matters. Others invite reflection or discussion about specific biblical texts. Unless otherwise noted, the quotations of biblical texts are from the New Revised Standard Version.

The book also contains 18 *full-color maps* to help readers locate the places mentioned in the text. Knowing the locations of the cities, regions, and nations the biblical texts refer to can often help us understand the concerns and issues raised in those texts. A *comprehensive timeline* that includes what is happening on the cultural, political, social, and intellectual landscape of the ancient world helps us see how the things reported in the biblical texts relate to what is happening in the larger setting, Over 80 *vivid photographs* integrated throughout the text provide glimpses of the material culture of the various societies involved in the biblical stories and the kinds of natural settings found in those areas of the world, in addition to numerous artifacts and artistic representations of key biblical stories and events.

Each chapter ends with a brief summary, *Let's Review*. For a fuller summary of the contents of each chapter, readers may go to the Fortress Press website www.fortresspress.com/sumney. Additional end-of-chapter review is provided with a listing of *Key Terms* (all of which appear in the end-of-book glossary), a series of *Questions for Review*, and a list of other textual resources, *For Further Reading*. At the end of the book, a *comprehensive glossary* gives brief definitions of the important end-of-chapter key terms used in biblical studies. This tool is designed to help students find with ease important terms and concepts so they can more quickly attain the knowledge and skills that are needed when developing an understanding of the Bible.

▶ Pursuing Further Study of the Bible

The bibliographies that appear at the end of each chapter are intended to help readers take the next step in their study of the topics covered in that chapter. As students begin to explore parts of the Bible in more detail, they may find some material rather difficult. The best way to begin further study is to look up the topic or book of the Bible in a good Bible dictionary. Such a dictionary will introduce readers to the main issues related to the topic or book; longer entries will include the different positions taken by different scholars, and perhaps a few of the reasons for taking one view rather than another. The one-volume Bible dictionaries I would recommend are the *HarperCollins Bible Dictionary* or the *Mercer Bible Dictionary*. For more in-depth discussions, the good multi-volume dictionaries are the *New Interpreter's Dictionary of the Bible* and the *Anchor Bible Dictionary*.

After students consult such dictionaries, they are ready to move to nontechnical books, articles, and commentaries. Commentaries are books that give an introduction to a particular biblical book (or related group of books), discussing issues like authorship, date of composition, and literary and historical settings, and providing interpretive comments about each verse of that book. Some commentaries are quite accessible to beginning students; others are intended for professionals in the field. This book's companion website provides a list of commentary series that will help you identify the more and less technical commentary series.

Once you read the somewhat lengthier discussions of the topic or book you are researching, you can move to more technical resources. There may still be some things you will not understand, but much more of the argument will be accessible because you already know what the issues are and have been introduced to some of the vocabulary and ideas. By conducting your research in these steps, you will be able to use materials from scholars by the end of your study that you would not have understood at the beginning. Following this plan, you will know and understand much more about the topic.

▶ Companion Website

The companion website for this textbook provides resources for both students and professors, including the list of commentaries mentioned above. For students there are chapter summaries and helpful research aids. The website also includes links to other websites that will be valuable in further study and research. For professors there are sample syllabi, a sample test, and other instructional aids.

▶ Acknowledgments

This book takes the form that it has because of my experiences introducing the Bible in graduate and undergraduate classrooms and in places outside formal academic settings. Those interactions with students have reminded me of the questions I had when I began to learn the kinds of things discussed in this text and have helped me sharpen my own understanding of both the questions and the texts. I am grateful for the insights of those beginning readers, as well as for those scholars from whom I have learned.

I am pleased to thank Lexington Theological Seminary for the sabbatical during which I was able to write this book. Such institutional support not only made this book possible, but has also supported and nurtured the intellectual growth of all the faculty and thus of our students. I also thank editors of Fortress Press, and especially Neil Elliott, for their vision of the kind of book my manuscript could become. Their thought and creativity have added significantly to its usefulness. I owe a great debt of gratitude to Ross Miller of Fortress Press for his diligent work, good ideas, and wisdom as this book came together. His sharp, timely, and wise editorial work has enhanced this project greatly.

This book is dedicated to Diane Furlong Sumney, my wife. She has supported my work and remained continually helpful as I have thought through many of the questions that critical study of the Bible raises. Her valuable reminders to keep an ear tuned to what some things sound like when they are heard for the first time have strengthened my work overall, and this project in particular. She has also helped me balance family and professional life so that my life is richer in both settings. Her knowledge and acuity in contexts quite different from mine helpfully reminds me of the need to cultivate humility as I see what a small piece of the world I know about.

Jerry L. Sumney
Lexington, Kentucky

PREFACE TO THE SECOND EDITION

I am grateful that the reception of this book permits me to produce a second edition. Producing this new edition has allowed me to clarify some things and add others. This edition has updated bibliographies at the end of each chapter, including more online resources. I have also added an appendix on alternative reading strategies. Most of the quotations of Scripture passages have been removed from textboxes in favor of inserting questions and observations about passages that ask the student to read passages within the Bible with those questions or ideas in mind. Some higher order questions have also been added at the ends of chapters in the Questions For Review.

This new edition has also given us the opportunity to create several new pedagogical resources: a *Study Companion*, which is meant to accompany the print textbook, and an *Inkling interactive edition*, which is an interactive eBook alternative to the print textbook. The *Study Companion* includes resources to reinforce and expand student understanding, such as summaries and learning objectives for each chapter, key terms and themes, and a significant amount of primary text—from biblical and other ancient sources—with questions for reflection and discussion. The *Inkling interactive edition* includes all of the content from the print textbook, and is enhanced with interactive features and links to further resources on the web. More information about the inkling interactive edition can be found at www.inkling.com. I am grateful to all the people at Fortress Press who have contributed to the development of these new resources.

Jerry L. Sumney

PART 1

What Is the Bible, And How Did It Come About?

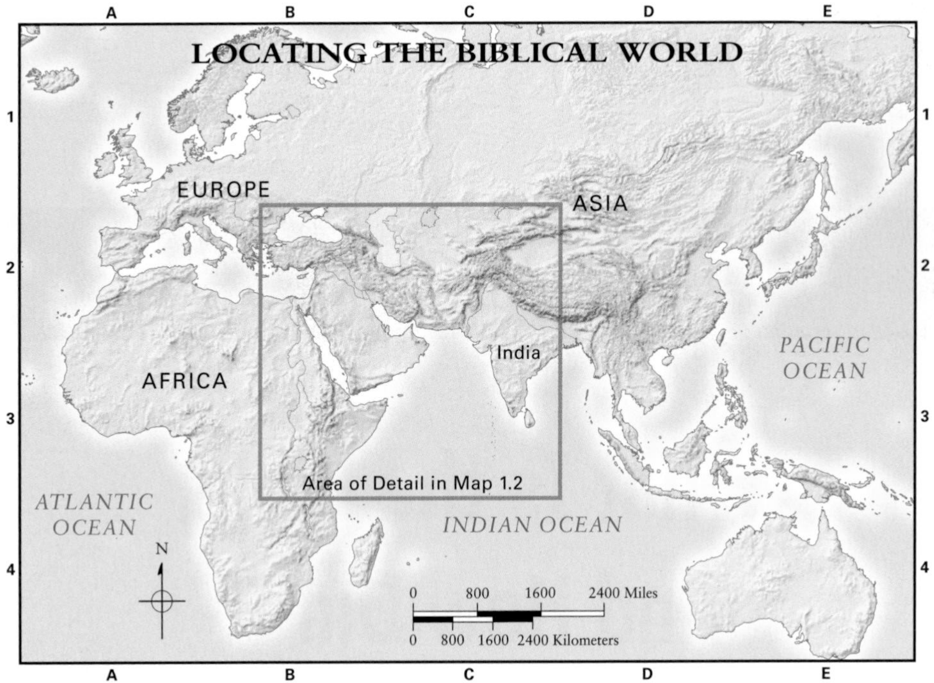

MAP 1.1

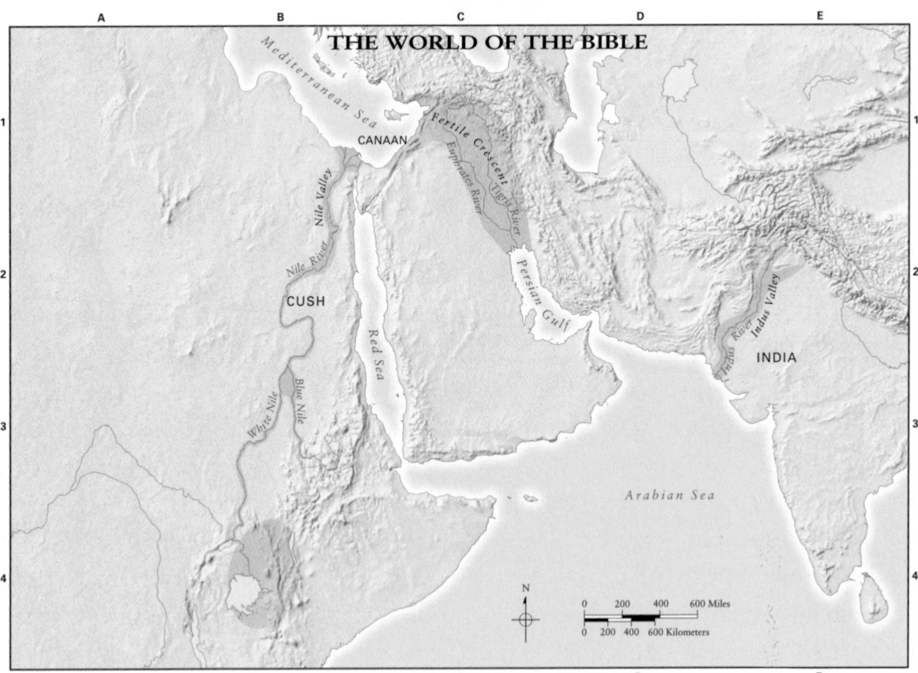

MAP 1.2

The "Fertile Crescent" is the name given to the rich arable land in Mesopotamia and the Nile Valley, where ancient civilizations first developed. The area shaded yellow around Lake Victoria is where the oldest known human fossils have been discovered.

1 The Bible
A Gradually Emerging Collection

IN THIS CHAPTER, YOU WILL LEARN ABOUT

- The process of canonization of the Bible
  - Hebrew Bible
  - New Testament
- Why communities need a canon
- The criteria writings needed to meet for admission to the New Testament

While most of us recognize a Bible when we see one, we often do not stop to consider just what it contains. What kinds of writings are in it? How did it get to us? Why are translations so different? We often hear questions of a different sort, questions about whether the Bible is true when it says the world was created in six days or that Jesus stopped a raging storm. What are those of us in a world dominated by a scientific outlook to think about such things in the Bible? How can an ancient book that seems to view the world so differently be valuable for understanding life in this technological age? These all-important questions deserve clear and careful answers.

The Bible has been and can be an extremely valuable resource as we try to understand our lives today and try to find meaning in a fragmented world. In this book I try to understand the Bible in its own context, coming to see what understandings of God, the world, humanity, and God's people the Bible contains. Only after we have done that can we decide whether those understandings have something to offer twenty-first-century readers.

▶ The Bible: A Collection

The Bible is not a single book, but a collection of over sixty different writings composed by many different authors over hundreds of years, written in three **languages**: Hebrew, Aramaic, and Greek. The Bible also includes many different kinds of writings: narratives, letters, psalms, poetry, and an "apocalypse," to name a few. Some of its books have multiple authors—for example, the Gospel of John. Near the end of John, this statement appears: "This is the disciple who is testifying to these things and has written them, and we know that his testimony is true" (John 21:24).

Notice the "we" in this verse. This sentence shows clearly that a group of people beyond the original "disciple whom Jesus loved" (whom this verse names as the source of the material in the book) had a hand in composing this Gospel. "*We* know" that what this disciple said is true. So even some books that we often think of as written by a single person had a more complex origin than just a solitary author composing at his or her desk.

BOX 1.1

LOCATING MATERIAL IN THE BIBLE

Books of the Bible are divided into chapters and verses. These divisions are used to locate particular passages within the books. The regular way the divisions are written is chapter number, colon, verse number. For example, chapter 21, verse 24 is written 21:24.

▶ The Emergence of the Canon

The process of collecting the various writings into a single book took several centuries, and the decisions about which books would constitute the Bible involved a great deal of thought and discussion. In the end, the thirty-nine books of the **Protestant Old Testament** (the **Hebrew Bible** counts the same writings as twenty-four books by combining pairs of books like 1 and 2 Samuel into one and the Twelve Minor Prophets into one; see also the discussion of the Apocrypha below) and the twenty-seven books of the **New Testament** were the writings in which the faith communities heard the voice of God in a distinctive way, a way that led them to designate these books as authoritative guides for their lives and beliefs.

The term **canon** designates a collection of writings that carries authority in a given religious community. The English word *canon* comes from the Greek *kanon*, which means a measuring stick. The canon is the standard by which a religious community evaluates beliefs, practices, and ethical behavior. We may wonder why anyone would want such a standard. Why not let each person determine what is right? Even if you decide that you want a standard, how do you decide what it is? Who decides?

Why Standards?

While it seems to run counter to our desire for freedom of thought and action, every group must have standards; without them there can be no *group*. They may be an aggregation of people in a single location, but without things that bind the people together, they are not a group.

Every group must have a purpose and agree upon means of working toward that purpose. Bridge clubs, poker groups, and political movements all have agreed-upon purposes and rules by which they conduct themselves. Sometimes those rules are explicit and sometimes they are implicit, but they are always there. Just try hiding a card up your sleeve if you think your poker group doesn't have rules! Likewise, all religious groups must have some guide for their beliefs and practices. Without those, you have no reason to come together as a religious group.

Boundaries. Not only do all religious groups need a guide for their beliefs and practices, they also need means of determining their boundaries. Every group must have ways to determine who is in and who is out. Again, without boundaries, you do not have a group, because being all-inclusive renders membership meaningless. The early church and **Second Temple Judaism** needed boundaries that set them off from the **polytheistic** world, and even from each other. They needed ways to determine what their identity was to be.

Determining what your identity is includes clarifying who you are not. So groups need some means of rejecting beliefs and practices that violate their core beliefs. This does not mean that people within the group must be narrow-minded, only that they need ways to be clear about who they are. If you belong to a group that has openness or inclusiveness as a central value, you cannot allow a person who successfully works at excluding as many people as possible to be part of your group. Everyone must draw boundaries. This task is particularly urgent when the group faces opposition or persecution, because people want to be clear about what they are willing to suffer for.

BOX 1.2

SECOND TEMPLE JUDAISM

Second Temple Judaism refers to the forms of Judaism that existed from approximately 515 B.C.E. to 70 C.E. This period begins when the temple in Jerusalem was rebuilt after it had been destroyed by the Babylonians in about 587 B.C.E. and ends with its destruction in 70 C.E. by the Romans.

The Canon of the Hebrew Bible

Like all groups, Second Temple–period Jews and early Christians needed authorities to which they could appeal when there were disputes about their identity, about what they should believe, and about how they should live. Both groups turned to books as their guides. So both the Jewish community and those who believed in Christ developed a canon, a set of authoritative writings. I will first sketch how the canon of the Hebrew Bible developed, and then turn to the New Testament.

A Complicated Process

The process of collecting the books of the Hebrew Bible was complicated. First, many of the books show evidence of having been written by more than one person and of drawing on other written sources for some of their content. Indeed, some of the books seem to have incorporated material written hundreds of years before the texts we now have came together (we will discuss this in more detail in subsequent chapters). Many of the books of the Hebrew Bible are

FIGURE 1.1 **THE WESTERN WALL OF THE TEMPLE**

This wall is the most intact part of Herod's Temple that remains. The sanctuary of the temple and the area for sacrifices stood above this wall. The Romans destroyed the other parts of the temple complex in 70 C.E. when they sacked Jerusalem to end a revolt. Getty

open about drawing on other sources for material. They tell you to read those other books if you want to know more about the subject they have been discussing. Here are a few examples of the many places where the text sends the reader to consult such works and gives their names:

Numbers 21:14:
 the Book of the Wars of the LORD
Joshua 10:13:
 "the Book of Jashar"
1 Kings 11:41:
 "the Book of the Acts of Solomon"
1 Chronicles 9:1:
 "the Book of the Kings"
1 Chronicles 29:29:
 "the Book of Samuel"
Deuteronomy 17:18-19:
 "the king is to keep a copy of this law"

These notations suggest that the writers of the biblical texts take what they find in other books and give them a religious or theological interpretation. The biblical writers interpret the events of the nation's past so that those events reveal something about the people's relationship

BOX 1.3

DESIGNATIONS OF YEARS

The common scholarly conventions for the designations of the eras have changed so that it is more inclusive. The designation B.C. (Before Christ) has been replaced by B.C.E. (Before the Common Era) and A.D. (Anno Domini; in the year of our Lord) has been replaced by C.E. (Common Era), the time when both Judaism and Christianity exist.

with God. In addition to the texts that retell Israel's national story, the books attributed to prophets were often completed only after the prophet's death. One clear indication of this process of writing is that they often refer to the prophet in the third person rather than in the first person; that is, the prophetic books often say the word of the Lord came to *him*, rather than saying it came to *me*.

"The book of the law." Since many of these books were composed by multiple writers and sometimes rewritten over centuries, we should expect that gathering them into a single volume was also complex. The process did not get started as early as we might think. There was no large collection of authoritative books that Israelites could consult until about the sixth century B.C.E. The story of King Josiah (640–609) shows how late the process of gathering these books started. In 2 Kings 22:8-13 we hear that Josiah commissioned a refurbishing of the neglected temple of God in Jerusalem. During the renovations, workers found "the book of the law" in a back room of the temple. When some officials read this newly discovered book, they became aware that they had not been living by its commands at all. Worried about this state of affairs, they called on a prophet, Huldah, to verify that the book really was the word of God. After she confirmed that it was, Josiah began a sweeping reform based on what this text commands. Though it might seem unbelievable to us, this story says that during Josiah's reform the people kept the Passover for the first time in three hundred years (2 Kgs. 23:21-23).

This story shows that the Israelites did not possess an extensive collection of writings by Moses or anyone else that gave instructions on how they should live and worship. They found this one book and were surprised by its instructions. So the process of developing a canon, a group of authoritative writings, did not begin until some time after this point. It is important to note that this story took place in about 620 B.C.E., only about thirty-five years before the kingdom of **Judah** fell. This means that the work of assembling the canon began in earnest during the **exile**.

Developments after the Exile

When Judah (the second of the two Israelite nations) fell in 587 B.C.E., a large part of the population was forced to migrate to **Babylon** (located in today's Iraq). While Judah was in exile, the Babylonian Empire fell to the Persians

BOX 1.4

Read 2 Kings 22:8-10. What does this passage suggest about the authority of prophets in ancient Israel? What does it suggest about the status of women who possess this gift?

(located roughly in today's Iran). The Persians' policy concerning regions in the more distant parts of the empire differed from that of the Babylonians, so they allowed the people of Judah to return to Jerusalem around the year 539. The Persians granted the Judahites and other distant regions permission to govern themselves by their ancestral laws.

BOX 1.5

Read Nehemiah 8:1-8, 13-18. Notice the mention of the leaders and how they functioned on this occasion. How do you think the writer wants readers to understand the place of the Law in ordering society?

Ezra and the "book of the law of Moses." The first evidence for a collection of authoritative books within Judaism appears as the people of Judah returned from exile and began the process of semiautonomous governance. The book of Nehemiah tells about the return of some exiles and the establishment of the law of the land. It says that the priest Ezra gathered the people in Jerusalem and read to them the "book of the law of Moses" (Neh. 8:1-3). While Nehemiah describes the book as what God gave Moses, there is no evidence that it existed in written form, particularly in the form that Ezra read, until sometime during the exile. After all, before they found it in a back room of the temple, neither the king nor the temple's priests knew of its existence at the time of Josiah, the king who reigned just a few years before the first wave of the exile. Yet when the exiles return just about eighty years later, they possess a collection of writings by which they can govern their religious and civic lives.

FIGURE 1.2 **TORAH SCROLL**
Early eighteenth century. Art Resource

The three parts of the Hebrew Bible. We do not know what was in the collection from which Ezra read, but it probably included much of what is now in the **Pentateuch**, the first five books of the Bible. These books are called the **Torah** in the Hebrew Bible. Other books were collected and began to be revered over the next two hundred fifty years. By the mid-second century B.C.E. the book called Ecclesiasticus or Sirach (part of the Apocrypha) could refer to a collection of writings divided into three groups: "the Law, the Prophets, and the other books," very close to the divisions of books of the Hebrew Bible still used today. While some discussion continued about which books should be included, and some included books were still being reedited, the basic contours of the collection were in place at this point.

The Dead Sea Scrolls. Until the discovery of the **Dead Sea Scrolls** in 1947, our earliest extensive Hebrew manuscripts of the Bible came from about 1000 C.E. Among the Dead Sea Scrolls are copies of at least part of the Hebrew text of every book in the Hebrew Bible except Esther. These copies were made just before and during the time of Jesus. For the most part, the scrolls demonstrate the care with which the copyists preserved the ancient text. But in some cases, we can see the ways that some books of the Hebrew Bible were still under construction. For example, some of copies of Jeremiah found among the scrolls are like the longer text in the Greek translation, others like the later accepted

FIGURE 1.3 **QUMRAN**

One of the caves in which the Dead Sea Scrolls were discovered, near Qumran. Among the Scrolls are copies of portions of every book in the Hebrew Bible except Esther.

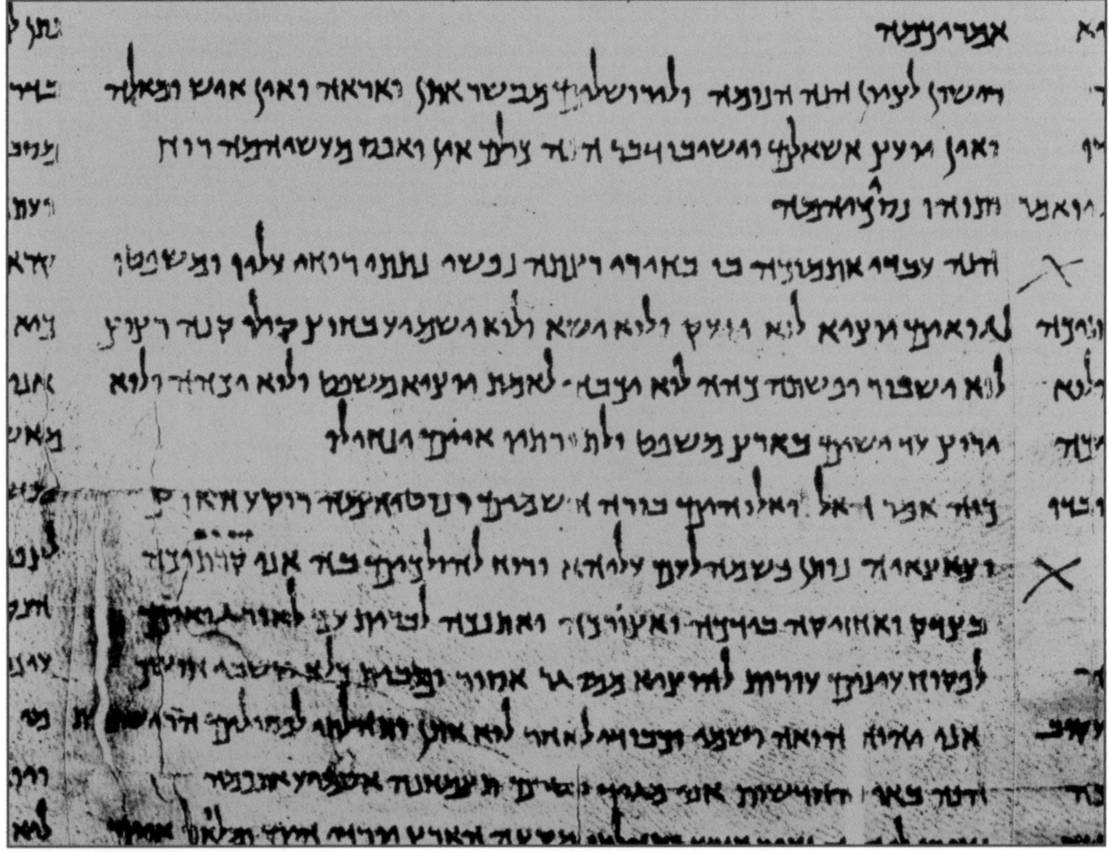

FIGURE 1.4 **SECTION OF A SCROLL FROM QUMRAN**

The Dead Sea Scrolls give us some of our best evidence for the form of the Hebrew Bible's text in the first century. This is a section from the Isaiah Scroll. Art Resource

biblical text, and another has different expansions so that it is significantly longer than that found in the Bible today.

The Completion of the Canon of the Hebrew Bible

Our other most important evidence for understanding what Jews were reading as guides for their religious life is the **Septuagint**. The Septuagint is a translation of the Hebrew Bible into Greek that was completed near the end of the second century B.C.E. That translation included all the books now found in the Hebrew Bible (Old Testament) and the books often called the Apocrypha. Many Jews viewed these books as authoritative, at least in some way.* While the list was not completely decided upon, there

*There were disagreements among different groups about which books were authoritative. For example, Sadducees accepted only the Torah as authoritative, while Pharisees accepted all thirty-nine books as authoritative.

was wide enough agreement about its content that first-century Jews could refer to the Torah, Prophets, and Writings, confident that other Jews knew what they meant. The first-century Jewish historian **Josephus** could refer to *the* books of Scripture. His accounting seems to amount to the thirty-nine books now in the Hebrew Bible. While there was a wide and broadening consensus about which books to include in the canon, there was no definitive delimiting of the canon until the end of the first century C.E. Before its destruction in 70 C.E., the temple had been a vitally important element in defining what it meant to be Jewish. Once it was destroyed, these texts (and their interpretation) became the central guide for determining what it meant to be a faithful Jew. Thus the canon of the Hebrew Bible was the result of ten centuries of work and thought.

▶ The Christian Canon

The Protestant Old Testament contains the same books as the Hebrew Bible, though they appear in a different order and are numbered differently. The Roman Catholic Bible includes as **deuterocanonical** the books called the **Apocrypha**. These seven books plus additions to Daniel and Esther were part of the Septuagint.[2] Later Judaism did not include these books in its canon, in part because most were not originally written in Hebrew. They remained within the canon in some parts of the Christian tradition because they were in the Septuagint, the translation of the Hebrew Bible that was the primary Bible of the early church. Furthermore, the presence of these books in the Septuagint led to their inclusion in the **Vulgate**, the fifth-century translation of the Bible into Latin. The Greek Orthodox Bible includes two additional books, 3 Maccabees and 2 Esdras, books also preserved in Greek and known widely in the early church.

The earliest Christian writings. The Septuagint was not only the early church's first Bible, but also nearly its only Bible through the first century. The earliest book of the New Testament (probably 1 Thessalonians) was not written until around 50 C.E. The latest of the New Testament books (probably 2 Peter) was composed around 125. The books of the New Testament also come from many different authors, and a number of them are written anonymously. Paul wrote his letters, the earliest writings in the New Testament, between the years 50 and 65. The New Testament Gospels began to be written soon after that and were probably all written by the year 100. By then, there were already collections of Paul's letters to churches circulating among the early communities of Christ believers.

The question of authority. From the earliest time after the death and resurrection of Jesus, the **apostles** were the central authorities within the church. The church needed to know more than simply what Jesus said or did and how he had died; they needed to know what these things meant. Knowing specific facts about the life of Jesus was less important than being able to interpret those facts in a way that was appropriate to what the church confessed about him. From the earliest times, the apostles were the people that the church saw as authorized to interpret the life, teaching, death, and resurrection of Christ. Many interpretations of the life of Jesus were current in the first century: some saw him as a great reformer within Judaism, others as a political rebel, and still others as a misguided artisan. These interpretations

CHART 1.1

THE CANONS OF THE TANAKH (JEWISH BIBLE) AND THE CATHOLIC AND PROTESTANT OLD TESTAMENTS

TANAKh

Torah
- Genesis
- Exodus
- Leviticus
- Numbers
- Deuteronomy

Prophets

Former
- Joshua
- Judges
- 1 Samuel
- 2 Samuel
- 1 Kings
- 2 Kings

Latter
- Isaiah
- Jeremiah
- Ezekiel
- The Twelve:
  - Hosea
  - Joel
  - Amos
  - Obadiah
  - Jonah
  - Micah
  - Nahum
  - Habakkuk
  - Zephaniah
  - Haggai
  - Zechariah
  - Malachi

Writings
- Psalms
- Proverbs
- Job
- Song of Songs
- Ruth
- Lamentations
- Qoheleth (Ecclesiastes)
- Esther
- Daniel
- Ezra-Nehemiah
- 1 Chronicles
- 2 Chronicles

CATHOLIC OLD TESTAMENT

Pentateuch
- Genesis
- Exodus
- Leviticus
- Numbers
- Deuteronomy

Historical Books
- Joshua
- Judges
- Ruth
- 1 Samuel
- 2 Samuel
- 1 Kings
- 2 Kings
- 1 Chronicles
- 2 Chronicles
- Ezra
- Nehemiah
- Tobit
- Judith
- Esther (including Greek portions)
- 1 Maccabees
- 2 Maccabees

Poetry/Wisdom
- Job
- Psalms
- Proverbs
- Ecclesiastes
- Song of Solomon
- Wisdom of Solomon
- Sirach (Ecclesiasticus)

Prophets
- Isaiah
- Jeremiah
- Lamentations
- Baruch (including the Letter of Jeremiah)
- Ezekiel
- Daniel (including the Prayer of Azariah and the Song of the Three Young Men, Susanna, and Bel and the Dragon)
- Hosea
- Joel
- Amos
- Obadiah
- Jonah
- Micah
- Nahum
- Habakkuk
- Zephaniah
- Haggai
- Zechariah
- Malachi

PROTESTANT OLD TESTAMENT

Pentateuch
- Genesis
- Exodus
- Leviticus
- Numbers
- Deuteronomy

Historical Books
- Joshua
- Judges
- Ruth
- 1 Samuel
- 2 Samuel
- 1 Kings
- 2 Kings
- 1 Chronicles
- 2 Chronicles
- Ezra
- Nehemiah
- Esther

Poetry/Wisdom
- Job
- Psalms
- Proverbs
- Ecclesiastes
- Song of Solomon

Prophets
- Isaiah
- Jeremiah
- Lamentations
- Ezekiel
- Daniel
- Hosea
- Joel
- Amos
- Obadiah
- Jonah
- Micah
- Nahum
- Habakkuk
- Zephaniah
- Haggai
- Zechariah
- Malachi

CHART 1.2

THE DEUTERO-CANONICAL BOOKS OF THE ROMAN CATHOLIC CANON (AND THE PROTESTANT APOCRYPHA)

Tobit
Judith
Wisdom of Solomon
Ecclesiasticus (Sirach)
Baruch (including the Letter of Jeremiah)
1 Maccabees
2 Maccabees

In addition to these seven books, the Protestant Apocrypha also includes

- 1–2 Esdras
- Additions to Esther*
- Letter of Jeremiah*
- Prayer of Azariah and the Song of the Three Young Men*
- Susanna*
- Bel and the Dragon*
- the Prayer of Manasseh

*These writings are included within other canonical books in the Catholic canon, but are separate writings in the Protestant Apocrypha.

rested on the same facts the church had about the ministry and death of Jesus. The question was not what happened, but what those actions, particularly Jesus' death, meant.

Apostolic authority. Our earliest accounts agree that the church relied on the apostles for the proper interpretations of the life, ministry, death, and resurrection of Jesus. They asserted that he was genuinely God's **Messiah** (literally "annointed one"; in Greek, *Christos*) or Messiah designate. Though it was nearly impossible to believe, given how his life ended, Jesus was the one in whom God had chosen to be present among God's people and to initiate the end times. Understanding the resurrection as God's vindication of Jesus' teachings, life, and death makes this interpretation plausible. It was those closest to Jesus, the Twelve, who the church said most clearly understood the meaning of his life, death, and resurrection. To these twelve disciples the church added Paul, because he had a direct experience of the risen Christ, and James, the brother of Jesus, who became the leader of the Jerusalem church around the year 44 or 45.

The need for authoritative writings. In the earliest years of the church's existence, when someone wondered what a person who confessed Christ should do or believe, they would ask an apostle. What does Peter say this action of Jesus means? What does James say this saying of Jesus means? What does Paul say Christ believers should do in this situation? But by 65–70 many, probably most, of the apostles had died. Then the churches turned to those who knew the apostles best, but soon those associates of the apostles gave different answers when asked what an apostle would have told them to believe or do. (Of course, the apostles had themselves also given different kinds of answers to the same questions.) Since various leaders gave so many, and even contradictory, answers the church began to look to written sources for guidance. Then the question became, which writings have apostolic authority?

The church also felt the need to identify a set of authoritative writings because there were competing and mutually exclusive forms of Christianity. In the second century there were Gnostics, Marcionites, and Montanists, to mention just a few. Since these groups had contradictory teachings, the church needed an authoritative guide for its beliefs and practices.

BOX 1.6

INTERPRETATIONS OF JESUS

The range of interpretations that might have been given Jesus' ministry can be seen by a few examples from reports in the New Testament. Mark 3:19-27 reports that some who saw Jesus' miracles thought he was empowered to do them by the devil. Acts 5:33-39 tells of people who claimed to be called by God to oppose the power structure and who gathered followers and had political aspirations. They were, of course, defeated by the Romans. The Gospel of John has the people in charge in Jerusalem say the Romans will see Jesus as a political threat (11:45-51). So a wide range of interpretations of the life of Jesus appeared even during his lifetime.

They believed that some of these teachings denigrated human life and the God of Israel, so they sought a means to reject such teachings.

The first Christian canon. Not only were there teachings that the main body of the church rejected because they were dangerous, but in at least one case someone put together a canon that most found unacceptable. In the first half of the second century, **Marcion** went to Rome, where he made a bid to become a bishop. He taught that the God of the Hebrew Bible was not the Father of Jesus Christ. The God of Israel, he said, was too violent and vindictive to be the loving Father revealed by Jesus. He therefore rejected the whole Hebrew Bible and accepted only Luke as his Gospel (which he edited to suit his theology). He proposed that his edited version of Luke and ten (edited) letters of Paul serve as the body of authoritative writings—the canon—for the church. The larger body of the church rejected Marcion's theology and canon. They insisted the God of Israel *was* the Father of Jesus Christ and defended the authority of the Hebrew Bible as well as that of the Gospels of Matthew, Mark, and John.

The criterion of apostolicity. As the church began to assemble a group of authoritative texts, the most important characteristic a writing needed to be included among them was apostolicity; that is, it had to be written by, or related in some other way to, an apostle. Since the apostles had been the authorities within the church from its inception, the church looked to their writings as guides once the apostles themselves were no longer available. They saw the Pauline letters as clearly apostolic, but Matthew, Mark, and Luke were all written anonymously. Very soon after their composition, however, traditions grew up that attached each to an apostle: Matthew was said to be written by the apostle Matthew; Mark was written not by an apostle but by a disciple of Peter who wrote what Peter

BOX 1.7

APOSTOLICITY

Some connection to an apostle was one of the most important criteria for a writing to be considered authoritative as the Christian canon emerged. It was important that a book be written by one of the Twelve or Paul or James—or by someone closely associated with one of them.

preached about Jesus; similarly, Luke was written by an associate of Paul.

These traditions probably do not record actual historical connections to those apostles, but they do demonstrate the importance the church placed on relating each authoritative book to an apostle. The introductory words of the book of Jude exemplify the importance the church placed on a connection to an apostle. Jude identified himself as the brother of James. If he was the brother of James, he was also the brother of Jesus. But Jude made no claim to that immediate connection to Jesus, because that would not have established his authority the way a connection to the apostle James did. It is not simply what Jesus said or did that was authoritative, but the meaning the apostles gave to what Jesus did or said that mattered. So Jude had to attach himself to an apostle to get a hearing.

Common usage and coherence. In addition to needing an apostolic connection, a writing also had to be known and used widely across the Christian world. A text known primarily in Asia Minor (today's Turkey) or Egypt did not achieve the prominence needed to become authoritative for the whole church. Furthermore, for the wider church to begin accepting a book as genuinely apostolic, it had to agree with what later would be called the "rule of faith." That is, its content had to cohere with the range of beliefs that the early church accepted.

The Closing of the Christian Canon: A Gradual Process

There was no one moment in the early church when a council suddenly decided what books would be authoritative and then closed the debate. Such decisions took several centuries. Some accounts of the development of the canon make it sound as though the emperor **Constantine** adopted Christianity as the religion of the empire, immediately got together with his cronies in the proverbial smoke-filled back room, decided on the canon, and then imposed it on the church. Nothing could be further from the truth. While Constantine was interested in having Christians agree with one another about beliefs, he did not have a determinative role in the development of the canon. By the time he stepped on the stage, most of the decisions had already been made.

Debated books. Relatively few books were debated for very long. By the mid-second century, most churches (and there was no central governing body at this early date) accepted ten letters of Paul and the four Gospels as authoritative. By 200 nearly everyone accepted those fourteen books along with Acts, 1 Peter, and 1 John. There were still disagreements about other books; among those that got the most debate were Hebrews, Revelation, and the *Shepherd of Hermas*. But some collections of books for Christians contained books that few people know of today, though many of them still exist. The late-second-century list from Rome known as the **Muratorian Canon** included the books mentioned above plus three more letters attributed to Paul (1 and 2 Timothy and Titus), Jude, 2 John, Wisdom of Solomon, the *Apocalypse of James*, and the *Apocalypse of Peter*. The church eventually judged that the last two were not genuinely apostolic or authoritative.

Athanasius and Jerome. Discussions about the canon continued through the fourth century, after the time of Constantine. The fourth-century church historian Eusebius says that nearly everyone accepts twenty-two books: the four Gospels, Acts, thirteen letters of Paul, Hebrews (which he also attributes to Paul), 1 John, 1 Peter, and Revelation (though elsewhere he says Revelation is disputed). He then lists some writings that are disputed, all of which eventually became part of the canon. Finally he lists several books that are not accepted as authoritative but that may be good reading, though they do not bear authoritative status. **Athanasius**, bishop of Alexandria, is the first person to list as a group the books now found in the New Testament. In his Festal Letter of Easter in 367, he lists these twenty-seven as the books that contain true Christian teaching. But this declaration did not end the discussion. When **Jerome** (342–420) discusses which books the church accepts as authoritative, he lists the same twenty-seven as Athanasius, but comments that the "Latins" (the Western church) do not accept Hebrews and the "Greeks" (the Eastern church) do not accept Revelation. Jerome was to be one of the most influential people in this discussion because he included the twenty-seven current books of the New Testament in his Latin translation of the Bible. That translation, the Vulgate, became the Bible of the church for centuries to come, and so almost by default the books included in it became those the church recognized as authoritative.

The Reformation and the Council of Trent. Still, the discussion was not over. No official declaration of the church fixed the canon until the sixteenth century, when that declaration came as a reaction to Martin Luther's questioning the value and teachings of four New Testament books: Hebrews, James, Jude, and Revelation. The Counter-Reformation **Council of Trent** responded by declaring it an article of faith that one accept the current twenty-seven books as canonical. Most people within the church, both Catholic and Protestant, have accepted this definition of the New Testament since that time. The Catholic Church retained the Apocrypha in their canon of the whole Bible at this time, while the Protestants did not include them. In this decision, the Catholic Church was following the lead of the Vulgate, which had included those books.

▶ Conclusion

The present-day church received the collection we call the Bible from its ancestors in the faith. The faith community discussed and debated which writings should be authoritative until they reached a broad consensus. There was not a simple hierarchical imposition from Constantine or anyone else. In the end, the believing communities (postexilic and pre-rabbinic Jews for the Hebrew Bible and the early church for the New Testament) gathered these writings, claiming them as the texts by which they would lead their lives and derive their understandings of God, the world, and one another. They bequeathed them to those who followed them (the Jewish community and the church) as books that give life and engender relationship with God, as books in which later believers could also hear the voice of God.

▶ LET'S REVIEW ◀

In this chapter we learned about:

- The Bible as a collection of books
  - Written in three languages
  - Written over many centuries
- The need for a canon
  - Boundaries
  - Identity
- The formation of the canon of the Hebrew Bible
  - Multiple sources and editions of individual books
  - Collection in exile and postexilic period
- The formation of the Christian canon
  - Need for expansion of the canon
  - Criteria for granting a work authority
  - The closing of the canon

▶ KEY TERMS ◀

Apocrypha
Apostles
Athanasius
Babylon
Biblical languages
Canon
Constantine
Council of Trent
Dead Sea Scrolls
Deuterocanonical
Exile
Gnostics
Hebrew Bible
Huldah
Jerome
Josephus
Judah
Marcion
Messiah
Muratorian Canon
New Testament
Old Testament
Pentateuch
Polytheism
Second Temple Judaism
Septuagint
Torah
Vulgate

▶ QUESTIONS FOR REVIEW ◀

1.1 What does it mean to call the Bible the "canon"?
1.2 Why do groups need a canon?
1.3 When did the Hebrew Bible begin to take a relatively firm shape? Why then?
1.4 What is the Apocrypha? Why is it not part of the Hebrew Bible?
1.5 How did Marcion influence the church to develop a canon?
1.6 Looking back, what criteria did the church (sometimes unconsciously) use to identify the books that should be authoritative, that is, should be part of the canon?
1.7 How did Jerome influence the stabilization of the canon?
1.8 How did Martin Luther influence the formation of the canon?

▶ FOR FURTHER READING ◀

F. F. Bruce, *The Canon of Scripture*. Downers Grove, Ill.: InterVarsity, 1988.

William R. Farmer and Denis M. Farkasfalvy, *The Formation of the New Testament Canon: An Ecumenical Approach*, ed. Harold Attridge. New York: Paulist, 1983.

Robert M. Grant, *The Formation of the New Testament*. New York: Harper & Row, 1965.

Lee Martin McDonald, *The Biblical Canon: Its Origin, Transmission, and Authority*. Peabody, Mass.: Hendrickson, 2007.

2 From Then to Now
The Transmission of the Bible

IN THIS CHAPTER, YOU WILL LEARN ABOUT

- Textual criticism—how scholars determine what the ancient authors actually wrote
- Types of translations
  - Formal correspondence
  - Dynamic equivalence

If the church designated the books in the Bible as those through which God speaks most clearly and authoritatively, how do we know we are reading the same books they selected? That is, what sort of assurance do we have that they have not been changed over the centuries? How did these texts get from the first century to the present day? Before the invention of the printing press, the only way to distribute or preserve a text was to copy it by hand. Sometimes a **copyist** had a manuscript on his desk and copied it. When a document was slated for wider distribution, a room full of copyists would listen to someone read the text and each would make a copy—with the result that both of these methods of copying created problems with accuracy.

The academic field of biblical studies includes the discipline of **textual criticism**, whose primary purpose is to establish the most accurate form of the biblical text. In this chapter we will look at some of this discipline's techniques and results as a way of examining how closely today's biblical texts match those that the early church selected or that the authors first composed.

Textual Criticism

The Transmission of the Text of the Hebrew Bible

We do not know much about the earliest transmission of the sources that eventually came together to make up the Hebrew Bible. We can see that various stories and texts were written, edited, and reedited over the course of centuries. At some point, some of these texts came to be preserved as the word of God. They include some very early material, as early as 1000 B.C.E. It is even possible that some of the psalms were written by David (at least they are attributed to him). The story in 2 Kings 22 of Josiah's workers finding the book in the temple points to some written texts (however much they were ignored) being preserved as early as the sixth century B.C.E. Once the Israelites began to select and preserve certain texts as the word of God in a special sense, and so began to view them as authoritative, it became important to maintain the precise wording of those texts. Some texts continued to be edited into the first century B.C.E. (as noted in chapter 1, one version of the text of Jeremiah is significantly longer in the Dead Sea Scrolls than in other manuscripts). But other texts took a stable form at an earlier time. After the canon of the Hebrew Bible was selected, Judaism granted a great deal of sanctity to these texts and developed significant means to preserve their exact form. The success of this effort is clear from the congruence of the **Masoretic text** (c. 1000 C.E.) and the Dead Sea Scrolls for most books.

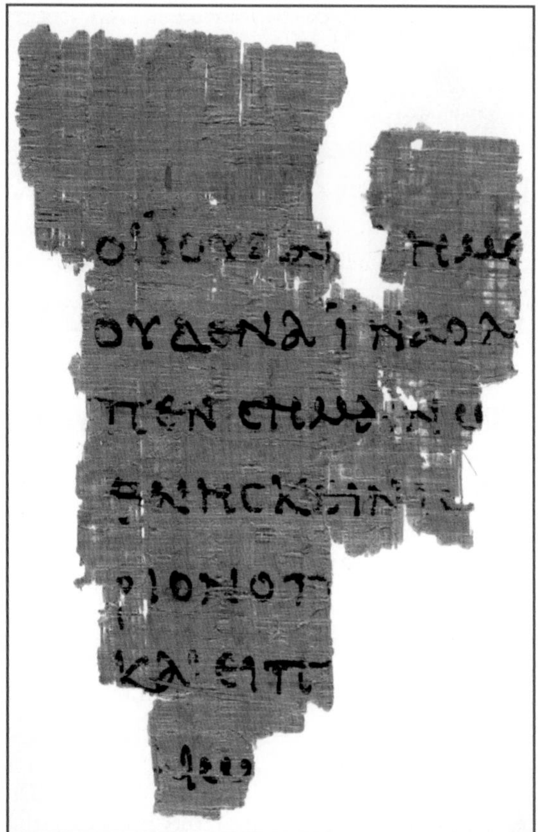

FIGURE 2.1 **GOSPEL OF JOHN FRAGMENT**

P[52], a fragment of the Gospel of John dated about 125. About the size of a credit card, this fragment has John 18:31-33 on the front and 18:37-38 on the back. John Rylands University

The Transmission of the Text of the Christian Bible

Papyrus manuscripts. We know more about the transmission and preservation of the Bible in Greek than we know about the way the Hebrew Bible was passed on. The books of the New Testament were often joined with a Greek translation of the Hebrew Bible. Our earliest copies of parts of the New Testament are written on **papyrus**, a type of paper made of reeds. The earliest copy of part of the New Testament is on a credit-card-size piece of papyrus that was written in about 125. It contains part of the Gospel of John on each side, and so is probably what remains of an early copy of that book.* The twelve volumes of the **Chester Beatty Papyri** come from about the year 200

*The technical designation of this fragment is P[52]. All the papyri are designated with an uppercase P followed by a superscripted number.

and contain most of the New Testament. These papyrus sheets are among the most important as scholars try to determine what the authors of the New Testament books actually wrote.

Uncials. The other extremely important early evidence for the text of the New Testament comes from **uncials**. Uncials are copies of the New Testament that are written all in uppercase letters and on vellum (writing material made of leather). The two most important witnesses (manuscripts that give the best evidence for the text) in this category come from the fourth century. These two **codexes** (manuscripts in the form of books rather than scrolls or loose leaves) are **Codex Vaticanus** and **Codex Sinaiticus**. Both belong to a family of manuscripts that seem to have remained fairly close to the originals. Other groups of manuscripts clearly added material for clarification or even (in their view) correction. We will look at that issue below.

FIGURE 2.2 **CODEX VATICANUS**

Page from the fourth-century Codex Vaticanus. This codex (early form of book that replaced scrolls) is one of the earliest and most complete copies of the biblical books. Vatican Library

BOX 2.1

THE CODEX

The transition from unwieldy scrolls to the codex—manuscripts in book form—took place in the early Christian period.

Quotations. Other important but more limited evidence for what the New Testament authors originally wrote includes those places where first-, second-, and third-century writers quote books that would eventually become part of the New Testament. Sometimes these authors simply allude to biblical texts, but at other times they directly quote them, even noting that they are quoting the words of a particular apostle or book. These brief quotations give us important information about the text of the earliest copies of the New Testament books that were circulating among churches. But some of these quotations also contain errors because the writers would often quote them from memory.

Copyists' errors. From the relative wealth of manuscripts of the New Testament that we have from the first few centuries, we can detect the kinds of changes that crept into the text as it was repeatedly copied. We know many of these kinds of mistakes from personal experience. When we copy from a book, we are not always accurate. Students often have quotations

FIGURE 2.3 **ANCIENT EGYPTIAN SCRIBES AT WORK**

From the tomb of Ti (c. 2465–2325 B.C.E.). Art Resource

in papers that are just a word or even a letter off. You can tell the copied material does not quite read as it should, or the change may even significantly alter the quotation's meaning (e.g., if the word *not* were left out). Sometimes copyists of the New Testament would accidentally leave out a word or whole line when the previous word or line had the same ending—their eye just skipped from one line (or word) to the next. Sometimes the opposite happened: they wrote a word once that should have been written twice. Think of the sentence: "I saw that tabby cat cross the road." This sentence also makes good sense if it reads: "I saw that that tabby cat crossed the road." If the second "that" is inserted, the other change ("ed" added to "cross") is likely to follow. The meaning of the sentence may change little, but the change does allow different nuances. Of course, if the sentence originally contained the word twice, it still reads relatively well if the copyist leaves out the second "that" (providing he also changes the verb). Copyists might also mistake one letter for another—remember that they are each reading another person's handwriting.

In addition to these and similar errors that occur when copying from a written text, other mistakes arise from situations where the text was being read to a group of copyists. Think of the word "there." If you are listening to someone reading a text and you are transcribing their words, you must be very careful with such words. If your attention wanes just a bit and the reader comes to the word "there," you may end up writing "their" or "they're" instead of "there." The only way to know which of these words you should write is to be aware of the context.

Intentional changes. All of the changes we have talked about so far are mistakes, but there were also intentional changes to the text. Sometimes scribes inserted their own spellings of words. There were no completely standardized dictionaries, so regional or even personal differences appear in the spelling of some words. Sometimes copyists changed the grammar of a passage so that a sentence read more smoothly. Other times they changed the text to eliminate historical problems or to harmonize the Gospels. They also changed the text to support their own theological positions. When doctrinal disputes raged about **Christology** or the Spirit or some other issue, copyists sometimes changed the biblical text to be sure it could be read only one way—their way. This happened more often where a text was ambiguous enough that readers could find support for various positions in a controversy. But in other places, a word (or more) was simply changed to support a particular theological position. John 1:18 suffered such a change. When third- and fourth-century Christians were engaged in the controversy over whether Christians should confess that Jesus is divine, a scribe changed John 1:18 so that it read: "the only begotten god," rather than the original "the only begotten son."*

Weighing and Sifting the Variant Readings

In addition to comparing the dates of manuscripts and grouping them into families that seem to come from the same or similar earlier manuscripts, textual critics have guidelines that help them determine which reading was earlier and so closer to the wording of the original author. Among these rules are the following:

1. The more difficult reading is probably earlier. Copyists are less likely to change a text so that it is harder to read. On the other hand, they often change the wording so it is easier to read, perhaps by accident or perhaps assuming they are correcting an earlier mistake.
2. The shorter reading is usually preferred. Copyists are more likely to add explanatory remarks than they are to delete parts of the text.
3. The reading that is more different from similar texts is preferred. Copyists are more likely to harmonize (sometimes accidentally) than to make texts contradict or stand in tension with one another.

*This example is cited by Bart Ehrman in *The Orthodox Corruption of Scripture: The Effect of Early Christological Controversies on the Text of the New Testament* (New York: Oxford University Press, 1993), 78–82. See that book for an accounting of many such changes.

4. An unusual use of a word or phrase is preferred over the common or proper use. Scribes are less likely to introduce a peculiar use of a word or phrase than they are to change or delete one.

None of these or any other rules textual critics use is always correct. The rules are often balanced against one another, and all in conjunction with the dates of manuscripts in which a reading is found and the families (or groupings) to which the manuscripts belong. But a careful use of these rules and procedures has led to the recovery of most of the original text of the New Testament. Most textual critics would say that the text of the New Testament is at least 90 percent secure; that is, 90 percent of the wording in the Greek New Testament is what the earliest church was reading. Much of what remains uncertain is of little importance. Sometimes it is a question of whether "the" or "a" was originally in the text. But there are also places where the difference is important. Fortunately, those places are not as numerous as they might be if it were not for the enormous amount of evidence that we have about the text from early centuries.

A Striking Variant

There are some surprising results of textual criticism. A quick look at the end of the Gospel of Mark in the New Revised Standard Version (NRSV) or other recent translations that include notes about variations in the Greek texts provides an example. Earlier translations (including the King James Version) end Mark at chapter 16 verse 16 (16:16). But the NRSV and other recent translations give multiple endings. While it is still being discussed, most textual critics think Mark originally ended at verse 8. The best fourth-century manuscripts end Mark at verse 8 (though the longer ending was known before then). So all of verses 9-16 were probably a later addition to the original. The existence of several different endings of Mark supports this conclusion. Some ancient manuscripts add an ending of only a few lines, others an ending about a fourth the length of the conclusion that extends through verse 16. Scholars think that copyists added all of these endings because if Mark concludes at the end of verse 8, its conclusion reads: "and they [the three women who find the empty tomb] said nothing to anyone, for they were afraid." Many have found this a difficult, even unacceptable, ending for Mark. So some scribes composed endings that have the women tell others and some have Jesus appear to them and the disciples. The copyists thought they had good reason to supplement the original ending, but Mark's ending can be meaningful if read in the context of the whole book and in the context of what its original audience faced.*

Only a few other well-known passages have so little claim to be part of the original text of the New Testament. (See chapter 12 and textbox

BOX 2.2

THE MEANING OF AN ENDING

Read Mark 16:1-8. Scholars think this was the original ending of the Gospel. What do you think an author might intend to convey by ending a story in this way?

---

*See Morna Hooker, *Endings: Invitations to Discipleship* (Peabody, Mass.: Hendrickson, 2003).

12.8 for another well-known example: the story of the woman caught in adultery in John 7:53—8:11.) While such additions to the biblical text may be surprising, even shocking, Christians may take comfort in the fact that we know about them. Textual critics have succeeded in finding the major alterations and developing a more reliable text. It may have been more comfortable for believers in earlier centuries not to know about these textual problems, but we now possess a biblical text closer to the original writings than those more comfortable readers had. So if we want to understand what the biblical writers hoped to convey to their readers, we have the good fortune of possessing a text very close to what they actually wrote. This provides a more secure place from which to begin our work of interpreting their words, and thus for Christians to find the texts' message about God, Christ, and humanity.

▶ Translations

Once text critics establish a fairly secure text of the Bible in Hebrew (the Hebrew Bible; Christianity's Old Testament) and Greek (the New Testament), that content is still not available for most people until it is translated into their native language. The many translations available in English vary according to their translators' philosophy of translation and views about the results of textual criticism.

Formal Correspondence and Dynamic Equivalence

Translators must adopt a way to approach their work of bringing a text out of one language and into another. We may track approaches to translations on a spectrum that has formal correspondence on one end and dynamic equivalence on the other. A purely **formal correspondence** translation would be as much a word-for-word rendering as possible. Those with experience of another language know that one cannot simply give a direct word-for-word translation of a paragraph or even a sentence because languages are structured differently. For example, languages differ in word order. Some languages, like English, usually have the subject come before the verb in a sentence that states a fact. Other languages, like Greek, depend on changes of the words' endings and beginnings to signal what function they have rather than relying primarily on their order in the sentence. So if a translation of the New Testament into English were to follow Greek word order, it would make no sense in English.

Languages also have very different idioms and figurative expressions that do not transfer from one language to another. For example, translating "hit the hay" literally into any language would probably not convey the idea that the person was going to bed. In such cases, translators must try to find equivalent expressions or give the meaning without using an idiom.

The American Standard Version. The English translation that adheres most closely to the formal correspondence ideal is the American Standard Version of 1901. Its translators worked hard to maintain even the sentence structure and word order in Greek, a strategy that produces a translation that closely adheres to the individual words of the text. It is, however, very difficult to read and sometimes distorts the meanings of sentences by retaining elements of

Greek style and syntax. Few other translations have adopted such a rigorous attempt at formal correspondence because of the inherent difficulty in reading and failing to provide a clear guide to the text's meaning.

Paraphrastic translations. At the other end of the spectrum of translations, **dynamic equivalence**, we find works such as *The Message*, the Living Bible, and the Good News Bible. These are really paraphrases rather than straightforward translations. That is, they take the ideas the translators think the biblical texts convey and put them into their own words. These can be much easier to read than other sorts of translations because they employ more modern metaphors and ways of speaking. They can be valuable as introductions to reading the Bible and to devotional reading, but are not the translations one should use when doing more detailed reading and study of the Bible.

These translations do not serve well for more in-depth study because they incorporate so much of their translator's interpretations that they deny the reader the opportunity to see the multiple meanings a text might have. That is, paraphrases and other dominantly dynamic equivalence translations give the reader more the translator's interpretation of the text and less what the text actually says.

Balance. Most translations fall somewhere between these two extremes. Some lean more toward dynamic equivalence, others toward formal correspondence. You can decide which kind of translation is most helpful by identifying the purpose of your reading. If you want easy reading for devotion and encouragement, dynamic equivalence translations may be more helpful. If you want to study a passage in depth to understand its meaning in its own context or to determine what it would tell Christians to believe or how to live, you need a translation that leans more toward formal correspondence.

King James Version, New King James Version, Revised Standard Version. Various translations adopt similar balances in translation strategies. The **King James Version** (KJV), New King James Version (NKJV), and Revised Standard Version (RSV) have similar translation strategies. All three try to express the meaning of the text in ways that remain fairly close to the original wording and structure, while also producing fairly good English prose. These translations generally allow the ambiguity of texts to remain, and so permit the reader to wrestle with the meaning(s) of such texts. These translations provide clear English, but often include complicated sentences and even unusual syntax, if

BOX 2.3

THE DANGER OF MORE INTERPRETIVE TRANSLATING

The NRSV does a good job of choosing to render *adelphoi* (literally "brothers") as "brothers and sisters" because it captures the meaning, as a good dynamic equivalence translation does. Some of the NRSV's other translations of this term are much less successful. When the NRSV translates it with the word "friends" (or similar alternatives), it sacrifices too much of the term's familial connotation and so provides a less adequate translation.

that best reflects the range of meanings possible for the text.

New Revised Standard Version, New International Version, New International Version Inclusive Language Edition. One step closer to the dynamic equivalence model are the New Revised Standard Version (NRSV), the New International Version (NIV), and the NIV Inclusive Language Edition (NIVI). These all strive to produce a more easily readable text that remains faithful to some of the language and structure of the original. But they are more interpretive than the translations in the previous group. The interpretive renderings make the text clearer, but sometimes thereby close off possible understandings. The NRSV and NIVI clarify the meanings of some texts by translating terms that are male in the original with more inclusive language. For example, both translations often translate the plural Greek term *adelphoi* (brothers) with "brothers and sisters." This correctly captures the meaning of the expression in the greetings of Paul's letters, even as it changes the wording found in the Greek text. This example shows how these translations lean toward expressing the text's meaning in the vernacular rather than adhering as closely to the original wording as translations such as the RSV. Again, this aids some readings, but hinders others. The more detailed your study of a biblical text, the more you need to work from a translation on the formal correspondence side of the spectrum. If you were studying the importance of the term *brother* or the idea of familial language in the New Testament, the NRSV and NIVI would not be the most helpful translations. But if you want to understand the flow of thought in Romans, those translations might be more helpful than many others.

BOX 2.4

A TRANSLATION FOR THE JEWISH COMMUNITY

The *Tanakh* (an acronym for *Torah, Nebi'im* [Prophets], and *Ketubim* [Writings]) is the Jewish Publication Society's translation of the Hebrew Bible. Jews have used "Tanakh" as the name for their Bible since ancient times.

Other translations. The translation strategy of the New English Bible (NEB) stands between the NRSV, NIV, and NIVI, on the one side, and the New American Standard Bible (NASB), New Jerusalem Bible (NJB), and Tanakh (NJPS), on the other. The latter translations introduce more interpretation into their renderings of the biblical texts; that is, they do more to direct (and limit) one's interpretation of the texts than the translations in the previous groups. Such translations can enhance our reading of the text, but when reading them we must remember that many of the interpretations they assume are disputed. If you read only one of these translations, however, you will not know that its interpretation of a passage is open to question.

Individuals and committees. We should also note that some translations are done by committees of scholars, while others are produced by a single individual. Translations by single individuals include *The Message* and the J. B. Phillips translation. This kind of translation has the virtue of being expressive and possibly more

CHART 2.1

SCALE OF TRANSLATION THEORY USED IN VARIOUS TRANSLATIONS

FORMAL CORRESPONDENCE Translators try to retain as much of the originating text's sentence structure and word order as possible.					DYNAMIC EQUIVALENCE Translators put the ideas of the originating text into the equivalent images and language of the receiving culture.
American Standard (ASV; 1901)	King James Version (KJV) New King James Version (NKJV) Revised Standard Version (RSV) New American Standard Bible (NASB)	New Revised Standard Version (NRSV) New International Version (NIV) Inclusive Language NIV (NIVI)	New English Bible (NEB)	New Jerusalem Bible (NJB) Tanakh (NJPS)	Good News Bible Contemporary English Version *The Message*

The Rheims Version, Douai-Rheims Version, the Challoner-Rheims Version, and Confraternity Version were translated into English from the Vulgate (the Latin translation of Jerome) rather than from Greek texts, though the translators gave some attention to Greek manuscripts.

consistent in its presentation of particular concepts. The reader gets, however, a single person's understanding of the text's message. The advantage of a translation produced by a committee is that the various members of the translation team can balance one another's idiosyncrasies and theological inclinations. Committees also, however, often have theological or ideological inclinations. For example, the team that translated the NIV has more scholars with conservative leanings, while the translators of the NRSV include more scholars with liberal leanings. Still, there was enough breadth on both committees that some balance was maintained. The more limited the spectrum of translators on a team, the more likely that their theological and ideological perspectives will color the translation.

One can often determine much about the strategy used in a translation by reading its preface, which frequently includes not only how the translation was done but also the range of people involved in the work. So reading the preface can help you select the Bible that fits best the purpose you have in mind.

A classic that needs translation. Before leaving discussion of translations, a word about the King James Version may be helpful. This translation was a wonderful accomplishment in the seventeenth century. It remains a beautiful translation, perhaps the most beautiful translation of much of the Bible. But it has significant drawbacks. First, it translates the Bible into seventeenth-century English. The English language has developed in significant ways over the last four hundred years, and some of those developments mean that words have changed meanings. Therefore, the older wording sometimes fails to convey what the text means or what the translators intended. The word *conversation* in 1 Peter 1:15 is a good example. The KJV reads: "But as he which hath called you is holy, so be ye holy in all manner of conversation." It sounds here as if Peter is calling the readers to reflect holiness in the way they talk. But in the seventeenth century "conversation" meant the conduct of one's whole life.

This broader meaning is what 1 Peter has in mind, because the Greek word behind the English "conversation" is *anastrophē*, a term that means "manner of life." The NRSV translates the term "conduct" to capture the meaning in twenty-first-century English the way "conversation" did in the seventeenth.

The same Greek word and translation in the KJV render another passage in 1 Peter almost nonsensical. In 3:15 the writer gives this instruction to women married to nonbelievers: "ye wives, *be* in subjection to your own husbands; that, if any obey not the word, they also may without the word be won by the conversation of the wives." How can it be that the husband is won over by a conversation that has no words? Of course, when we know that "conversation" means conduct of life, not dialogue, the passage makes perfect sense. This is just a single example of many such changes in the meanings of words. The New King James Version (NKJV) updated the translation's language so that these problems appear less frequently. That also means, however, that the new translation loses some of the familiarity and beauty of the original.

Unfortunately, there is an important problem with the NKJV: it disregards much of the work of textual critics. Textual criticism, trying to discern the most ancient reading of the biblical texts, had not really been used in conjunction with biblical texts when the KJV was produced. So the KJV relied on the *Textus Receptus** or the received text as the basis for its translation. The *Textus Receptus* was produced by Erasmus of Rotterdam in 1561 and was the Greek text on which many translations since the Reformation had been based. This text is based on what is known as the Byzantine family of texts. There are many manuscripts in this family of Greek manuscripts and it served as the basis for the Latin Vulgate. But this family of manuscripts does not include our oldest witnesses for the text of the New Testament. Most text critics think other groups of manuscripts represent readings that are closer to the original compositions of the biblical writers. But the NKJV continues to rely on the *Textus Receptus*, so this translation does not represent what most scholars think is the closest we can get to the original text of the Bible. Sometimes the differences in the texts have little effect on the meaning, but at other times, there is a great deal of difference—particularly when large sections are involved. For example, the KJV and NKJV include Mark 16:9-16. But as we saw above, the best and most ancient copies of Mark indicate that those verses were not part of that Gospel when it was written or first began circulating to churches along with the other three canonical Gospels. Some segments of Christianity have based rather radical practices (e.g., these are the verses that mention believers handling snakes) on this passage, which was probably not part of Mark originally but was added over two hundred years later. Such differences in the text can be important when believers use the Bible to help them make decisions about how to live and what to believe.

▶ Conclusion

The work of text critics provides a text of the Bible that is very close to what the original collectors of those materials were reading. A good study Bible will have notes that indicate where there are some questions about what word appears in a text. When we exercise care in our use of translations, we can begin to see the richness of the biblical texts and begin to understand more clearly what they want to convey to believers about themselves, the world, and God.

▶ LET'S REVIEW ◀

In this chapter we learned about:

- Early transmission of the biblical texts
- Textual Criticism
  - —Definition
  - —Need for it
- Transmission of text of the Hebrew Bible
- Transmission of the text of the Christian Bible
  - —Types of materials and manuscripts
- Criteria for evaluating variant readings
- Translations
  - —Types of translations
  - —Identifying specific translations by their type
  - —The *Textus Receptus*

▶ KEY TERMS ◀

Chester Beatty Papyri
Christology
Codex
Codex Sinaiticus
Codex Vaticanus
Copyist
Dynamic equivalence
Formal correspondence
King James Version
Masoretic text
Papyrus
Textual criticism
Textus Receptus
Uncials

▶ QUESTIONS FOR REVIEW ◀

2.1 How do we know that the text of the Hebrew Bible we have today is much like the text the Jewish community was reading in the first century?

2.2 What ancient manuscripts do scholars see as the most important evidence for what New Testament authors actually wrote? Why do they think these are so important?

2.3 What are some unintentional changes that came to be part of some copies of biblical texts? What are some intentional changes? Explain how each got into the text.

2.4 What are some criteria textual critics use to decide what the original text was?
2.5 Tell about translation strategies and give examples of translations that use various strategies.
2.6 Why is it important to know that the King James Version relies on the *Textus Receptus*?

▶ FOR FURTHER READING ◀

D. R. Ap-Thomas, *A Primer of Old Testament Text Criticism*. Philadelphia: Fortress Press, 1966.

J. Harold Greenlee, *The Text of the New Testament: From Manuscript to Modern Edition*. Peabody, Mass.: Hendrickson, 2008.

Bruce M. Metzger and Bart D. Ehrman, *The Text of the New Testament: Its Transmission, Corruption, and Restoration*, 4th ed. New York: Oxford University Press, 2005.

James D. Tabor, "Older Is Not Always Better: Remembering Westcott and Hort," Bible and Interpretation Website 2009 http://www.bibleinterp.com/opeds/tabor_357913.shtml

Ernst Würthwein, *The Text of the Old Testament,* trans. Erroll F. Rhodes, 2nd ed. Grand Rapids: Eerdmans, 1995.

Images of and links to more exploration of Codex Sinaiticus:
http://www.bl.uk/onlinegallery/sacredtexts/codexsinai.html

3 Inspiration
The Claim That God Speaks in a Text

IN THIS CHAPTER, YOU WILL LEARN ABOUT

- The history and range of understandings of what it means when believers say the Bible is inspired by God
- Ideas about inspiration in exilic and postexilic Judaism
- The early church
- Plenary inspiration in the third to fifteenth centuries
- Reformation ideas
- Twentieth- and twenty-first-century views
  - Fundamentalism
  - Noninerrant content
  - The functional view

The subject of the **inspiration** of Scripture nearly always produces controversy. The moment the question comes up, people choose sides and begin to recite well-worn phrases. People make all sorts of claims for and charges against the Bible when inspiration is the topic. Talking about the inspiration of the Bible engenders such emotion in part because it relates to questions about the truth found in the Bible and what authority the Bible should have for the church and for Christians. So we need to think carefully. I begin by briefly tracing the development of the idea of inspiration and the way it has been understood throughout Christian history. We will see that some ideas about inspiration do not accord well with the kinds of writings we find in the Bible, and I will suggest a way for believers to understand inspiration that both fits what we find in Scripture and provides the church with guidance for its life.

▶ Two Translations of 2 Timothy 3:16-17

Many discussions of inspiration begin with a quotation from the New Testament, 2 Timothy 3:16-17. The NRSV reads: "[16]All scripture is inspired by God and is useful for teaching, for reproof, for correction, and for training in righteousness, [17]so that everyone who belongs to God may be proficient, equipped for every good work." This is the usual translation and a proper one, but it is not the only way to understand this passage. The translators of the NRSV give this as an alternative translation for the beginning of verse 16 in the note at the bottom of the page: "Every scripture inspired by God is also . . ." The difference between these translation alternatives is significant. The first claims that all Scripture is inspired, while the second says that *when* a scripture is inspired, then it is useful for teaching, and so on. So the alternative translation allows that some scripture may not be inspired.

Both of these translations are possible because the word *is* does not appear in the Greek text. Greek grammar and sentence structure allow "is" to be omitted in many sentences, leaving the reader to insert that verb into the right place. But sometimes it is not clear where the "is" should be inserted. The alternative translations above are equally possible. So this commonly cited passage requires more interpretive effort than many who use it seem to notice.

FIGURE 3.1 **MATTHEW AND THE ANGEL**

This painting by Caravaggio (1573–1610) envisions inspiration as a process in which the words in the Bible come directly from God (through the angel). Thus, in this representation, the words of the Bible are the words of God.

Wikimedia Commons

For the sake of this discussion, we will assume that the usual translation of verse 16 is correct.

Even when we allow this, the passage does not support many of the claims about inspiration some people use it to buttress. Notice carefully what this passage says that being inspired does for Scripture. According to these verses, inspiration by God assures us that the writing will be "useful for teaching, for reproof, for correction, and for training in righteousness." That is, inspiration assures the reader that the Bible helps a person live a devout life; it brings the reader teaching and instruction, encouragement and correction. This passage says nothing about the things so many want to argue about when they talk about inspiration: nothing about historical accuracy or scientific facts.

The purpose of inspiration. Verse 17 gives the ultimate purpose for the inspiration of Scripture: to equip God's people to do good works. According to this passage, God speaks through Scripture so God's people can be prepared to do God's will in the world. Again, this text makes no claim about accuracy or infallibility in history, science, or geography. The real purpose of inspiration is to direct the lives of God's people so that they please God and do the work God wants done in the world. These verses claim nothing else about Scripture!

"Scriptures": The referent. Finally, we should note that when 2 Timothy was written there was no New Testament. Since most New Testament scholars think 2 Timothy was written quite late in the first century, it is possible there were some small collections of Christian writings (the four Gospels, some letters of Paul), but nothing like the complete New Testament (see chapter 1 above for discussion of the collection of the books of the New Testament). Indeed, some of the New Testament books were not yet written. So when 2 Timothy mentions Scripture, it is referring to the Hebrew Bible (or the Greek translation of it), the only Bible the early church had.

▶ The History of the Concept

If 2 Timothy does not make the claims about science and history we often hear when people talk about inspiration, then how did those views develop? To understand that, we need to trace the ways inspiration has been understood in the past.

Developments within Judaism

The idea that some books contained a deposit of revelation about God and about how to live one's life began its rise to prominence at the time of the exile of Judah (sixth century B.C.E.). In exile Judah lost the temple and the promised land; the priesthood was set adrift without the temple and there seemed to be few prophets speaking God's word. When the Judahites (the only remaining Israelites) could not find the word of God in these familiar places, they had to look elsewhere for guidance. In response to the loss of these sources of knowledge of God's will, the people began to gather for worship in synagogues and to look to writings, particularly the Torah (which was compiled during the Exile), for God's word. The written word became the locus of divine revelation. Before it had been in people (e.g., priests and prophets) and places (e.g., the temple and Sinai); now they found this needed word in written texts. As late as fifty years before the exile, the people of Judah had no collection of books that guided their walk with God. But when they returned to Jerusalem after sixty to eighty years in exile, they possessed a collection of writings on which they would base their government and religious lives. Now these writings served as guides for priests, prophets, and all the people of God.

BOX 3.1

PHILO USING ALLEGORY

One of the main ways the Jewish scholar and philosopher Philo interpreted the biblical texts was by using allegory. He and his contemporaries saw allegory as a valid way to find meaning in a text. Some examples of his discussion of and use of allegory are: *On Abraham* 15.68: "The migrations as set forth by the literal text of the scriptures are made by a man of wisdom, but according to the laws of allegory by a virtue-loving soul in its search for the true God" (F. H. Colson translation in Loeb Classical Library [Cambridge, Mass.: Harvard University Press, 1935], vol. 6).

On Abraham 11.52: "These words do indeed appear to apply to men of holy life, but they are also statements about an order of things which is not so apparent but is far superior to the order which is perceived by the senses" (Colson translation, ibid.).

Interpreting the command to Abraham to leave his homeland, Philo gives it this meaning: "Depart, therefore, out of the earthly matter that encompasses thee: escape, man, from the foul prison-house, thy body" (*On the Migration of Abraham* 2.9; Colson translation in Loeb Classical Library [Cambridge, Mass.: Harvard University Press, 1932], vol. 4).

Developments in the Church

Following this development within Judaism, the earliest church assumed that God spoke through Scripture, but they did not limit revelation to Scripture. The early Christians also believed that God spoke through members of their community who had been granted the gift of prophecy. Prophecy was not predicting the future so much as it was proclaiming the message God had at a particular moment for the prophet's church. Since the early Christians believed that all members of the church possessed God's Spirit, the church would examine the message of the prophet to discern whether the words were truly those of the Spirit. They may not have drawn a sharp distinction between the word of God in books and its presence in the community through the prophets. After all, God spoke to them through both.

Paul. Still, believers accorded some books special authority; they used them to guide their faith and form the way they lived. Such books, they judged, provided the reliable word of God. The first books to have this status in the church were the books of the Hebrew Bible, which many Christians read in a Greek translation. But having these books as authorities created severe difficulties for the non-Jews of the church because there were many commands in them that they never observed. In fact, Paul had argued that if Gentiles did keep certain commands in the Mosaic covenant (those that signaled conversion to Judaism), they would cut themselves off from Christ, and so from salvation. So they had to make some sense of how these books could guide their lives, even while they did not literally keep all the commandments found in them.

Paul is among the interpreters of the Bible who did not read it for its literal sense. One of the alternative reading methods he used was **allegory** (see particularly Gal. 4:21-31). This way of reading was picked up by many Christian interpreters. Other readers of the first century also used allegory to read authoritative texts. **Philo** of Alexandria, a first-century Jew, also used it extensively to interpret the texts of the Hebrew Bible, though his interpretations were very different from those of the early church.

FIGURE 3.2 **ORIGEN (185–250 C.E.)**

Origen was an important leader of the church, teacher, and biblical scholar in the early third century. Many of his writings are still extant, including works of biblical interpretation, refutations of accusations against Christians, sermons, and an explanation of Christian theology. Among the many things he was known for is his belief that biblical texts have multiple meanings. Wikimedia Commons

Allegory: Origen and Chrysostom. Christian interpreters from at least the third century used allegory not only to make sense of commands they did not keep, but also to explain factual or historical mistakes they found in the text. Writers such as **Origen** (185–250) and **John Chrysostom** (347–407) talked about the Spirit making accommodations to the authors of biblical books when they found contradictory texts or historically inaccurate statements. Note that these writers (and many others) knew that the facts were wrong. But by using allegorical readings they said that God spoke through these inaccuracies to reveal a spiritual message that was true. This view could be called "plenary inspiration" because these writers held that the text was full of meaning, full of the word of God, even when it was not factually correct. For several centuries, Christian interpreters continued to use allegory to interpret the Bible and to deal with those places where they found inconsistencies and inaccuracies.

The Reformation. This movement brought a new approach to Scripture. Both Martin Luther and John Calvin rejected allegorical interpretations of the Bible because they believed this method had been abused to impose harmful meanings on texts. (Luther and some others did, however, allow a "spiritual" interpretation [another type of nonliteral interpretation] of some texts.) The Reformers did recognize the historical and factual problems that exist in the text, but argued, much like Origen and Chrysostom, that the Spirit's accommodation to the writers of biblical texts allowed those errors. They also asserted that the Spirit continues to work through these texts so that it influences the readers as well as the writers. But if the

BOX 3.2

ORIGEN ON READING THE BIBLE

Origen believed that biblical texts have levels of meaning:

> The individual ought, then, to portray the ideas of holy Scripture in a threefold manner upon his own soul; in order that the simple man may be edified by the "flesh," as it were, of the Scripture, for so we name the obvious sense; while he who has ascended a certain way (may be edified) by the "soul," as it were. The perfect man, again, and he who resembles those spoken of by the apostle, when he says, "We speak wisdom among them that are perfect, but not the wisdom of the world, nor of the rulers of this world, who come to nought; but we speak the wisdom of God in a mystery, the hidden wisdom, which God hath ordained before the ages, unto our glory," (may receive edification) from the spiritual law, which has a shadow of good things to come.
>
> (*On First Principles* 4.1.11, trans. Frederick Crombie, *Ante-Nicene Fathers,* ed. Alexander Roberts and James Donaldson, vol. 4 [reprint Grand Rapids: Eerdmans, 1956], 359)

At times he even denies that readers should accept a literal meaning:

> But as there are certain passages of Scripture which do not at all contain the "corporeal" sense, as we shall show in the following [paragraphs], there are also places where we must seek only for the "soul," as it were, and "spirit" of Scripture.
>
> (*On First Principles* 4.1.12, ibid., 360)

sole authority for the church is Scripture, as Luther claimed, then Scripture must be wholly reliable—with no errors in what it tells readers about God, Christ, the world, who Christians are as the people of God, and how they should live. Calvin's more stringent rejection of allegory amplified the problem of claiming Scripture as the sole authority for the church, while still recognizing inaccuracies in it. The problem was: How can one claim that Scripture is infallible and demand a literal reading, when there are historical and factual errors? Particularly among those influenced by Calvin, belief in Scripture's infallibility as a guide for faith broadened over time to encompass historical and factual information. While others had employed allegory to deal with historical problems, this avenue was closed to these interpreters as they developed their doctrine about the nature of Scripture.

The Enlightenment. Questions about what it means to say that Scripture is inspired increased as the ideas of the **Enlightenment** caught hold. It was in this period that interpreters began to pay more attention to the different readings found in various manuscripts. The existence of variant readings made people ask which reading should be seen as part of the infallible text. Furthermore, literary critics showed that there

FIGURE 3.3 **JOHN CHRYSOSTOM (347–407 C.E.)**

John Chrysostom was the bishop of Constantinople and a theologian. His last name means "golden tongue," given to him because of his fame as a good preacher. More of his writings survive than for any other of the Greek "church fathers." Although he used these methods less than Origen, he found allegorical and mystical meanings in the biblical texts. Byzantine fresco in Chora, Turkey. Wikimedia Commons

were multiple authors for some texts and that some of our biblical books went through various stages of writing. They even argued that some of the biblical writings contained legends. At the same time, rationalists denied the possibility of miracles, and so said that the accounts of miraculous deeds in the Bible could not be historical. By the nineteenth century these and other questions made it difficult to maintain the ideas of inspiration and inerrancy that had developed since the Reformation.

The move toward Fundamentalism. Professors A. A. Hodge, Charles Hodge, and B. B. Warfield at Princeton Theological Seminary were among the leaders who reacted against these "attacks" on the Bible. These scholars stand at the beginning of what we know as **Fundamentalism**. They rejected the conclusions of much contemporary scholarship about the nature of the biblical texts and defended an understanding of Scripture based on the Reformation's affirmations of its infallibility. A. A. Hodge argued that the wording of the **autographs** (originals) of the biblical texts was without error of any kind. (Of course, this is of little help because we do not have the original text of any biblical book, only copies of copies.) Most proponents of the post-Reformation definition of inerrancy did not go as far as to say that the Spirit dictated every word to the biblical authors. They did, however, say that in some way every word came from God, yet God did not violate the author's personality. Within the Roman Catholic community, M. J. Lagrange asserted that, while God was the ultimate author of Scripture, the human authors wrote freely, even as they expressed God's word perfectly.

Plenary (verbal) inspiration. The theological justification for claiming that Scripture is without error in matters of geography, history, and even science has been that these claims are inherent in the claim that it is inspired by God. If the Bible is the word of God and God

FIGURE 3.4 **LUTHER PREACHING**

In this painting done during his lifetime (1483–1546 C.E.), Luther is gesturing toward the cross. His teaching emphasized the work of Christ as the means of human salvation. He argued that this message comes solely from Scripture and did not need the intervention of church authorities. Art Resource

is perfect, then God would not have produced anything other than a perfect Bible. In this equation, "perfect" means correct in every possible way; inspiration guarantees infallibility in all matters. This view is often called **plenary** or **verbal inspiration**.

This view came to popular and radical expression in the well-known book by Harold Lindsell, *Battle for the Bible* (1976). Lindsell thought some evangelical Christians had begun to soften their position on infallibility and so he argued for adherence to a very particular understanding of it. He asserted that the Bible is true in medicine, chemistry, astronomy, everything. This is the case because God caused the writers to choose the precise words we find in the Bible.

It is important to note that this is a new understanding of inspiration. Christian writers of the third and fourth century recognized the historical and geographical errors in the biblical texts and still understood the Bible as the authoritative text for the church.

Weaknesses of the theory of plenary inspiration. Those who follow Lindsell in his plenary view of inspiration fail to explain the numerous difficulties in the biblical texts. For example, the Bible contains some irregular spellings of words and grammatical constructions. It also has errors of geography, history, and science. If we say that only the autographs were **inerrant**, we are left without an inerrant text because we do not have those originals.

More important than whether someone can manufacture a resolution to some geographical or historical inaccuracies is what Lindsell's and subsequent Fundamentalists' understanding of inerrancy makes of the biblical writers. This view of inerrancy makes authors of biblical texts little more than simply conduits through which the word of God flowed to get onto the pages

FIGURE 3.5 **JOHN CALVIN (1509–1564 C.E.)**

In addition to his religious writings he was involved in Swiss politics, believing that the law of the city should be the law of God. His rejection of allegorical readings and insistence on a literal interpretation of the Bible have been very influential, leading Calvinists in later centuries to develop the understandings of inspiration found at the beginning of the Fundamentalist movement. Painting by Hans Holbein the Younger, 1509. Wikimedia Commons

of the Bible. The problem with this position is that it violates what the biblical texts themselves claim. Seeing the prophets who say, "Thus says the Lord," as conduits for God's word may make some sense. After all, they seem to claim that their message contains direct instructions from God. But this understanding of inspiration does not make sense for some other kinds of writings in the Bible. For example, when the text contains prayers to God, Lindsell's view seems to suggest that God is writing prayers to God's self. Or when we find psalms of praise, is this God offering praise to God's self? Is there no human response to God in the text? We render many of the psalms powerless if they are only God's words rather than a genuine reaching out to God on the part of God's people. Seeing the biblical writers as mere pipes through which God poured words is inadequate for the depth and significance of many texts of the Bible.

BOX 3.3

Paul used allegory in Galatians 4:21-31. Read this passage and look at what happens to the identity of Sarah and Hagar in this allegory. Remember that Isaac (son of Sarah) is the ancestor of Jews. What unusual thing does allegory allow Paul to do with this story from Genesis? What does this show you about how allegory can be used?

▶ Two Other Theories about Inspiration

The conclusion that a popular notion about inerrancy is inadequate for the biblical texts need not lead Jews and Christians to abandon the assertion that the Bible is inspired, because there are many other ways to think about inspiration. In recent discussions, theories about inspiration can be divided into two types: those that say inspiration has to do with the content of the texts and those that say it has to do with the ways the texts function when read among believers.

FIGURE 3.6 **THE GREENWICH OBSERVATORY**

Isaac Newton worked in this observatory. In places such as this, scientists and mathematicians began to use observation and the principles of science to begin to understand the world in a new way. This kind of study has been so successful in creating new technologies, including medicines and devices that make our lives easier, that some have thought that scientific observation and experiment hold the key to discovering all kinds of truth. Art Resource

Inspired Content

Some say that divine inspiration means that the Bible's content comes from God; they are inerrantists in the sense we have just discussed. Others say that the Bible contains truth about who God is and offers readers distinctive ideas about God that are not found as clearly in other writings, but they do not argue that every statement in the Bible is factual—only that the Bible gives readers new or clearer information and ways to think about God. Some who hold this view would say that readers see who God is through the ways the stories in the Bible reveal God to them. As the Bible's stories depict God's interaction with God's people, they reveal who God is and what God expects of God's people. In all these ways of approaching inspiration it is the religious content of the Bible that comes from God.

Inspiration as Effectiveness

Others say that the Bible is inspired only when God speaks to the church through it; that is, the texts are a vehicle through which God becomes present in the believing community. In this understanding, it is not the content of the texts or the teachings about God that are inspired. Rather, the stories and teachings found in the Bible are records of past moments of God's presence with God's people and they evoke a present experience of God among readers. In this outlook, the Bible becomes the word of God when it reveals God to the church. So inspiration occurs as the believing community reads the text, not (only) when the writer penned the words.

While some theologians plant themselves firmly in one or another of these camps (inspiration delivers content or refers to function), readers do not have to choose between these alternatives as if they were mutually exclusive. To say that the Bible is inspired may simply make the broad claim that God's Spirit works through those who wrote, canonized, and now read and apply these texts. Christians claim that the Bible is inspired because it is through these texts that God has chosen to be with them, and it is through these texts that they learn how to enter the relationship with God that their forebears had.

A Mediating Position

Those who maintain that the Bible is inspired and are looking for a way to understand it that takes into account what we know about the text and what kinds of ideas have been suggested, may find the definition of John Goldingay helpful. He defines inspiration in this way: "Scripture mediates divine revelation apprehended in human experience. It does so by means of theological reflection on the part of its writers, whose theological reflection provides models as well as resources for our own."* This understanding of inspiration includes elements of both the content and functional definitions of inspiration. Goldingay's statement affirms that Scripture contains a revelation from God. But note that the writers did not just copy words received from God onto a page. This revelation comes in the midst of human experience; Scripture contains an account of the writers' experience of God. But this is not raw experience; rather, it is experience that the writers (and their communities) have reflected upon. Scripture records their

*John Goldingay, *Models for Scripture* (Grand Rapids: Eerdmans, 1994), 360.

theological reflections on experiences of God. Thus it provides content about who God is and what God wants for the world, even though the message is not in words received directly from God.

Biblical models of faith and life. Goldingay's description of Scripture also finds something else for the believing community. The Bible not only provides content, it also gives models of theological reflection that can help Christians think about how to interpret *their* experiences of God and God's word. The Bible provides its readers with examples of people who use their knowledge of God to discern what they should believe and do in their situation. Their examples can help the church today think about what it means to live faithfully in this moment. The Letters of Paul show especially clearly this process of theological reflection. In these writings Paul responds to specific problems or questions with instructions that draw on his understanding of who God is and what God has done for God's people through the life, ministry, and teachings of Jesus. Paul does not just quote Jesus or passages from the Hebrew Bible; he thinks about how those resources should be used to figure out what his churches should do at that moment. That is, Paul is not a literalist when it comes to applying Scripture or sayings of Jesus.

▶ Conclusion

So as we think about the claim that the Bible is inspired, we may say that the Bible can serve believers as a reliable guide for faith in two ways: what it tells the church about God and what it models for the ways the church can use that knowledge to think about its own questions and problems. Allowing that the Bible contains reliable content about God and our world does not entail adopting a literalist or inerrantist stance. The Roman Catholic community provides a helpful model to other Christians as well for thinking about Scripture. Many within this tradition see inspiration as a promise that the Bible is inerrant in matters of faith and morals, but not in other areas (e.g., history, science, and geography). In many ways this understanding returns us to something like what we saw in 2 Timothy at the beginning of this chapter. It recognizes the Bible as profitable for teaching and moral exhortation, so that the people of God may be prepared to do good works.

▶ LET'S REVIEW ◀

In this chapter we learned about:

- The development of the idea of inspiration
  - In Israel
  - In the early church
  - The meaning of plenary inspiration in the early centuries
  - From the Reformation to the mid-twentieth century
  - The new meaning of plenary inspiration
  - The development of Fundamentalism
- Proposals for the meaning of inspiration in the late twentieth and early twenty-first centuries
  - Inspiration provides content
  - Scripture is inspired when it functions to evoke the word of God
  - A combination?

▶ KEY TERMS ◀

Allegory
Autographs
John Calvin
John Chrysostom
The Enlightenment
Fundamentalism
Inerrancy (understood in different ways)
Inspiration
Martin Luther
Origen
Philo
Plenary inspiration
The Reformation

▶ QUESTIONS FOR REVIEW ◀

3.1 When did Israelites begin looking to texts as a prominent place to hear God's word?
3.2 How did Christians in the first four centuries deal with the problem of finding historical, geographical, or factual mistakes in the Bible?
3.3 What led those who came after Luther and Calvin to begin to redefine inspiration?
3.4 Describe the beginnings of the Fundamentalist movement. What moved them to define inspiration as they did?
3.5 What is the rationale for defining inspiration in the ways Fundamentalists did in the twentieth century?
3.6 What are two basic ways to think about what it means to say the Bible is inspired?

▸ FOR FURTHER READING ◂

James W. Aageson, "Reading Biblical Texts: Truth, Fact, and Myth," Bible and Interpretation Website (No date, but is a condensation of the author's book published in 2000) http://www.bibleinterp.com/articles/aageson_biblicaltext.shtml

Paul J. Achtemeier, *Inspiration and Authority: Nature and Function of Christian Scripture.* Peabody, Mass.: Hendrickson, 1999.

John Goldingay, *Models for Scripture.* Grand Rapids: Eerdmans, 1994.

Peter C. Hodgson and Robert H. King, eds., *Christian Theology: An Introduction to Its Traditions and Tasks.* Philadelphia: Fortress Press, 1985.

Wilfred C. Smith, *What Is Scripture? A Comparative Approach.* Minneapolis: Fortress Press, 1993.

PART 2

What Is the Story of the Hebrew Bible?

4 The Pentateuch, Part 1
Genesis

THIS CHAPTER DISCUSSES THE COMPOSITION, HISTORY, AND FIRST BOOK OF THE PENTATEUCH:

- Incorporation of four earlier sources
- Genre of the first eleven chapters of Genesis
  - Comparison with other writings of the time
  - Purpose of such writings
- Genre of the rest of Genesis
- Purpose of similar writings

The first five books of the Bible are often called the Pentateuch (Greek for "five books"), while the Jewish community commonly calls them the Torah, which means *instruction (from God)*. These books begin with the creation of the world and tell the story of God's dealings with the world through Israel's ancestors up to the moment of Moses' death just before the Israelites begin their movement into Canaan.

Authorship

Moses?

Following Jewish (and later Christian) tradition, the headings of these books in many translations of the Bible identify Moses as their author. However, nothing in the text of these books indicates who wrote them. The tradition that assigns them to Moses, the main figure in Exodus–Deuteronomy, arose as the Jewish community came to see them as authoritative. People who now think Moses wrote these books modify that claim to account for the end of Deuteronomy, the last of the five books. The final chapters of Deuteronomy tell of Moses' farewell address to the people of Israel and of his death and burial. Obviously, it is a bit difficult for Moses to tell the story of his own death and burial. The last three verses of Deuteronomy (34:10-12) also have the perspective of a later writer who claims that there has not been a prophet like Moses since the time of Moses. So it seems that many years passed between the death of Moses and the time when Deuteronomy was completed.

In addition, there are times that the text mentions places that did not exist in the time of Moses. In Genesis 14:14 speaks of the city of Dan, but according to Judges 18:28-29 the city named Dan was not called that until the Israelites had taken over the land following the death of Moses. Then Genesis 36:31 speaks of the time before the Israelites had a king. This seems to assume knowledge of an Israelite king, a development that did not take place until long after Moses' death. Texts such as Genesis 13:7b use terms used only in later times to describe inhabitants of Canaan in the time of Abraham. An outstanding example of the problems that arise if you assume that Moses wrote these texts is the account of the revelation of God's name to Moses. The story of the burning bush suggests that the name of God had not been known to the Israelite ancestors (Exod. 3:13-15) and a few pages later the text says explicitly that God was not known by name to them (6:2-3). But the account of the covenant ceremony in Genesis 15 has both God and Abraham call God by that name (vv. 7-8). This is best explained if these two stories come from different sources that tell the story differently rather than from the pen of a single author. These and other examples of things that reflect a time after the death of Moses indicate that these books were written later than the time of Moses. So we need to think about how they were composed.

BOX 4.1

Read Deuteronomy 34:10-12 and Acts 3:17-26. This segment of Acts has Peter and John identify Jesus as the "prophet like Moses." When the author of Acts identifies Jesus in this way, what does he want readers to understand about Jesus and the connection of the church to the historic faith of Judaism?

Four Sources: J, E, D, P

Most scholars of the Pentateuch think that these five books contain material written by a number of people over a long period of time. In the 1870s the German scholar **Julius Wellhausen** proposed that these books are a compilation of four distinct earlier writings that were artfully woven together.* While scholars have modified and clarified his proposal, most accept the broad contours of Wellhausen's theory, the **Documentary Hypothesis**. Scholars identify these four different sources by how they speak of God and by the kinds of things they are interested in and concerned about.

*The series of articles in which he originally proposed this idea were published together in *Die Komposition des Hexateuchs und der historischen Bücher des Alten Testaments* (Berlin: G. Reimer, 1899).

BOX 4.2

A CRITICAL INTRODUCTION

We need to know certain things about a biblical book to be able to understand it more clearly. The basic collection of this knowledge often appears in a critical introduction. This sort of introduction includes discussions of:

Authorship—who wrote it
Date—when it was written
Literary integrity—whether the book was originally written as it appears or whether some parts were added later
Occasion—what prompted the author to write
Purpose—what the author intends to accomplish with the writing
Theological themes—the main religious ideas on which the work focuses

J, the Yahwist. The earliest of these sources was composed sometime around the tenth century B.C.E., about the time of King David. This writing often uses **Yahweh**, God's name as revealed to Moses, to refer to God. That name appears in the King James Version as "**Jehovah**" (sixteenth-century English, like German, rendered the first Hebrew letter of God's name with a J), though most scholars today render it "Yahweh." Because of its use of the personal name of God, this source is called "**J**." Other parts of the Pentateuch use God's name, but they have other characteristics that set them apart from the J source (as we will see).

The Jerusalem Bible and the New Jerusalem Bible do use "Yahweh." In place of the name itself, many English translations substitute "the LORD" (with the last three letters written in small capital letters). These translations refrain from using the name of God out of respect. One of the Ten Commandments is: "You shall not take the name of the LORD your God in vain" (Exod. 20:7 NKJV). Many, particularly those in the ancient Jewish community, came to believe that people should nearly always avoid using the name of God, so they could be certain not to use it in vain. One way to avoid using God's name in vain is to replace it with "the LORD" whenever it appears in the text. This practice follows the ancient tradition that began in the Jewish community, which reads *Adonai* (Lord) wherever the divine name YHWH occurs.

The J source appears initially in Genesis 2:4, where for the first time the text speaks of "the LORD God." At this point, Genesis starts over in its telling of the creation story (more on this below).

E, the Elohist. The second source that became part of the books of the Pentateuch is called "**E**" because it uses the word *Elohim* to speak of God. When you see the term "God" in an English translation of the Hebrew Bible, it usually represents this Hebrew word for God. (This way of referring to God also appears in the other sources of the Pentateuch.) The E source appears for the first time in the stories about **Abraham** in Genesis 20. It shows considerable interest in the Israelites' life as a confederation of tribes, and less interest in the monarchy that developed in Israel's history. It was written around the eighth century.

D, the Deuteronomist. The name of the third source derives from its theological perspective.

BOX 4.3

THE NAME OF GOD

The King James Version uses "Jehovah" to bring the name of God into English because its rendering was influenced by the way Germans had brought the name into their language. The Hebrew letter that begins the name of God comes into German as a J but into English as a Y. Similarly, the sound of the Hebrew letter in the middle of "Jehovah," which came into German as V, sounds more like the English W. So "Jehovah" and "Yahweh" are two ways to bring the same Hebrew name into English; the latter is closer to the sound of the Hebrew.

It is called "**D**" because it is found mostly in the book of Deuteronomy. This book proclaims that if the nation obeys God it will be blessed, but if it disobeys it will be punished. This perspective on Israelite national history dominates much of the Bible. This outlook assures the Israelites that God remains in the covenant with them even when they face national disasters, because such calamities are the result of God working within the parameters of the covenant. Much of this material was written in the sixth century B.C.E., when the nation of Judah had fallen to the Babylonians, though some of it was composed in the aftermath of the earlier fall of the nation of Israel. (The Israelites had split into two kingdoms by the end of the tenth century B.C.E.) Thus the D material helps explain why the nation fell and how the people can regain favor with God and so see the reestablishment of their nation.

P, the Priestly source. The final major source that went into the books we now have as the Pentateuch is called "**P**," for its interest in priestly matters. This source shows concern for matters that involve ritual and other things related to proper worship. It includes regulations about temple worship and narratives that mention things such as clean and unclean animals. This source was finished sometime in the late sixth or fifth century.

The combination: JEDP. The two earliest sources (J and E) were probably combined by sometime in the seventh century. Later someone added the material of D to the growing collection of writings. Finally, in the sixth century the Priestly writers began to add their material to the narratives. The final versions of these books were probably completed in the late sixth to mid-fifth centuries. The books that are the culmination of the combination of these sources is probably what Ezra read to the people when he gave them the laws they were to live by when they returned from exile (Nehemiah 8; see above in chapter 1).

The Wellhausen version of the Documentary hypothesis relies on an evolutionary model of a single line of development of ideas about God that many scholars now question. Many now see independent oral and written sources that represent different viewpoints and political interests. For example, the traditions that formed J represent the interests of the nation of Judah, while those that formed E represent the nation of Israel. Some doubt that there was a coherent written E source, but rather a collection of traditions, perhaps much of it oral, that provides narratives about some ancestors. Some independent blocks of material that have been proposed include the exodus story (Exodus 1–15), the description of the Tabernacle (Exodus 25–31), the Holiness Code (Leviticus 17–26), and the Balaam story (Numbers 22–24). Some scholars also date the writing of all of the sources, including J, to the sixth or fifth centuries. Such sources were combined at various times. They are finally brought together to create what we find in the Pentateuch.

Whatever dates we assign to the various parts, two things seem clear. First, the texts that we now have are composed of multiple sources that have been brought together to provide their readers with specific ways to understand their national history, religious obligations, and God. Second, a fairly extensive form of these texts took shape during the exile. They reflect the concerns of that period, and those who returned to Judah began to shape their laws and identity around them.

So no single author wrote the books of the Pentateuch. Rather, these books include people's thoughts and experiences of God over hundreds of years. As their stories about God and the origins of their nation emerged, they saw various ways that God had been with them, and different ways that God had acted. Eventually, they brought these materials together and shaped them into the five books of the Pentateuch to provide an understanding of God, the world, and God's people. The writers and editors of these texts relate their views about God's care for the world and humanity, and about God's covenantal relationship with the people of Israel. So these books contain accounts of their experiences of God and their reflections on those experiences through which the people came to recognize God's word and will.

▶ Varieties of Genres

Whenever we read, we have to take account of the type of material we are reading. This is true of things written today, as well as of biblical writings. We will never understand what we are reading if we do not recognize the text's literary type, its genre. For example, we cannot read a novel as we read the newspaper. We do not criticize a novel for not being factual, because we know it is fiction and so not intended to be factual. Were someone to tell us not to read a novel because he had looked up all the records available and the lead character of the novel never existed, we would know that the person had seriously misunderstood what a novel is. We must always make sure we know what kind of literature we are reading.

We seldom need a lesson in genre. From the time we could read, we have been taught how to distinguish one kind of writing from another. We all know it is fine for a character in the comics to fly or leap over a tall building. But if the front page of a newspaper had a story about a man running faster than a bullet or leaping over a building, we would know something was wrong. When we make these distinctions, we are using a keenly developed literary sense. The front page and the comics are delivered together, often have much the same print, and appear on the same type of paper. Yet we easily know the difference. Beyond the newspaper, we learn other important differences, such as those between prose and poetry and between fiction and history. We know immediately when we pick up a math textbook and have no trouble

CHART 4.1

THE DOCUMENTARY HYPOTHESIS

Source	Century B.C.E.	Characteristics
J (Yahwist)	10th century	• Uses the name Yahweh for God • Uses anthropomorphic imagery for God • Gives attention to God's promises and their fulfillment • First appears at Genesis 2:4
E (Elohist)	8th century	• Uses Elohim to refer to God • Angels and dreams represent the presence of God (rather than anthropomorphism) • Begins with the Abraham narrative
D (Deuteronomist)	7th century	• Emphasizes the importance of obeying God's law: obedience brings blessing, disobedience brings troubles • Makes Jerusalem the only proper place for temple worship • Found most extensively in Deuteronomy
P (Priestly writer)	6th century	• Has first story of creation in Genesis • Emphasizes legal and priestly matters (cult, ritual, identity of authorized priests [and other genealogies]) • Emphasizes that the covenant with God is eternal • Gave the Pentateuch its basic shape

distinguishing it from a program at a sporting event. Yet both contain a lot of mathematical formulations. We do not expect to learn how to compute averages or percentages from an event program, but we do expect those calculations to appear there. And we do not expect information about our favorite team in a math text. We know something is wrong with the person's expectations, rather than with the sporting event program, if the person throws down the program exclaiming that it had no explanations about how to calculate percentages. Or think of a person who criticizes a poem for not providing scientific proof that what it says about love is true. That person has misunderstood what a poem is, and what truth it wants to convey. We must always recognize what genre we are reading if we hope to understand it.

It seems rather easy to make distinctions about literary genre when talking about contemporary writings. It is harder, however, when we turn to ancient literary types, including those in the Bible. The Bible contains many literary types, and if we do not want to be like the person who expects to learn how to do statistics from an event program, we must understand them on their own terms. Many arguments about the Bible arise because we misunderstand what kind of material we are reading. Sometimes we recognize important differences. We know we cannot read the psalms as narratives; they must be read as poetry. We also know that parables are not historically factual. That Jesus' parable of the Good Samaritan is not historical takes nothing away from the power of the story of a stranger who stops to help someone who has been left for dead.* Parables make their points without being historical or factual.

▶ The Narratives of Genesis 1–11

To properly understand the earliest parts of Genesis, we must understand what their literary type is, what such writings intend to provide the reader, and what they do not. The beginning of Genesis is a type of poetic or symbolic narrative. Its stories intend to give the reader an understanding of the world and how to live in it. We must not evaluate such narratives by whether they are scientifically correct or historically accurate. These stories care nothing about those matters. They do, however, intend to be true. Just like parables, the truth of these narratives is not determined by whether things happened just as the text describes them or by whether they relate historical or scientific facts.

Stories like those told in Genesis 1–11 give their readers a way to understand the world; they want to help readers cope with the world as they experience it as a place of both goodness and difficulty, both beauty and injustice. We evaluate this type of writing by whether it tells us the truth about the meaning of the world and humanity's place in it, not by whether it is scientifically or historically correct. In this way the stories of Genesis are like parables; they may be true in a real sense even when they are scientifically and historically inaccurate. Such distinctions are difficult for us because we have been brought up in a culture where everything must be proven correct empirically or scientifically to be seen as valuable.

But we do not really live within the bounds of judging all things according to whether they are scientifically demonstrable. Consider the assertion that human beings are valuable. That is not an empirically provable assertion. Neither is the claim that murder is bad or that love makes life better. But these truths are much more important to the quality of our lives than many facts are. Many historical facts have no significance to the meaning of our lives. I may know the color of George Washington's eyes, but knowing it does not make my life more meaningful. The same may be said for many facts of history, or even of science.

The function of the narratives. The stories in the early part of Genesis intend to tell readers some very important truths. They tell readers who they are in relation to God, and why

*This parable is found in Luke 10:25-37.

BOX 4.4

THE TERM *MYTH*

In the field of religious studies, to call a story a myth is a great compliment. It does not mean that a story is false; rather a myth is a narrative that gives expression to a fundamental belief about the world or life in the world. Myths are not factual in the sense that they tell of historical events, but they are true if they express something true about the meaning of human life.

humans act as we do, as individuals and as communities. They offer insight into ourselves and our world; that is, they set out a worldview. Providing us with a way to understand ourselves and find meaning in our lives is much more important than any historical fact they might tell us. We must not impose twenty-first-century scientific expectations on these ancient texts, because they never intended to convey historical or scientific fact. As we will see shortly, the stories told in these chapters provide good evidence that we must not look for such factual details as we read them. The writers of these stories were always interested in something much more important than correct historical or scientific data; they sought to show why life has meaning.

▶ Two Creation Stories

When we read the first two chapters of Genesis carefully, it becomes obvious that they contain two different stories about the creation of the world. In chapter 1 God creates the world in six days and rests on the seventh. But 2:4 says, "In the day that the LORD God made the earth and the heavens." Here, it seems, God creates the world in a single day. Not only that, but in chapter 1 male and female humans are made at the same time, while in chapter 2 God makes Adam and then hunts for a mate for him, finally creating Eve from his rib. If we are looking for historical accuracy, these stories are irreconcilable. Further, these accounts are contrary to scientific evidence. If, however, we are seeking to understand God's relationship with the world and the place of humanity within it, both stories afford readers important insights.

The Priestly Account

The account of creation in chapter 1 comes from the P source, from that circle of priests who wrote in the sixth century, a time when the people were hearing a different account of creation. An earlier Babylonian work, known as the *Enuma Elish*, says that many gods together made the world. Genesis 1 deliberately follows the pattern of the *Enuma Elish*, having things happen in parallel ways and having similar functions, but asserts that the world and all things in it were made by the one God of Israel.

BOX 4.5

EVERYONE WAS A POLYTHEIST

Polytheism is the belief in and worship of many gods. All people in the ancient world worshiped multiple gods. This is why it was so difficult for the Israelites to comply with the demand that they worship only the LORD.

Genesis 1 presents an alternative to the *Enuma Elish*'s polytheistic account of how the world came into being by arguing that it all came from the one God. Genesis 1, then, does not provide a scientific account of how the earth came into existence; it has no interest in such matters. Its question is, *who* made it, not how long did it take. Genesis 1 accepts the time scheme of an earlier, non-Israelite account of creation to make its more important point about who created the world. It is easy to see that Genesis 1 does not give a scientific account of creation if we just notice that it has day and night before there is a sun. As we know, day and night are the result of the world turning on its axis so that the sun shines on one part and then on the other. There cannot be a day or night, as we understand them, without a sun.

Science and truth. To say that Genesis does not give a scientific account of creation does not lessen its value or importance. It just recognizes the text for what it is, rather than trying to make it something else by imposing expectations that its author did not intend to fulfill. This reading honors the text rather than diminishing its value. Science can never prove wrong what Genesis proclaims as true. Science may identify the physical forces operative in the material construction of the world, but it cannot tell one whether those forces have God as their origin. It is simply outside the realm of scientific competence to make or deny an assertion about the presence of God in creation or in any other event. The tools of science are wonderful, but they are effective only for a certain kind of investigation.

Some philosophers speak of "**universes of discourse**" or "domains of thought" when discussing this point. These philosophers point out that different fields of thought have different ways of evaluating claims. Ethicists operate in particular ways, historians in others, and scientists in yet other ways. Scientists have amazing tools to observe, record, and manipulate the material world. Their methods for analyzing those observations have led to life-saving drugs and computers and all kinds of things that make our lives easier. Scientists have refined their tools and methods so that they can understand and create amazing things. Indeed, scientists have been so successful that we tend to think their methods work for everything. But those methods only work for some kinds of questions: how far is it to a planet, what stops the growth of cancer cells, and so on. The methods of science, however, cannot answer (for example) ethical questions.

FIGURE 4.1 **EARTH**

The Earth as seen from space. Wikimedia Commons

Similarly, science cannot tell us whether the accounts of creation in Genesis are true or false. Science simply does not have the tools to make that judgment because Genesis does not intend to make assertions that can be measured empirically. Genesis tells readers something much more important than how long it took for the earth to take its present form. Genesis asserts that the earth and we as its inhabitants have significance and meaning. The accounts of creation in Genesis proclaim that the world is related to God and that God cares for it. This gives the earth and human beings inestimable value and significance—God cares about them! Science that stays within its proper bounds of competence cannot affirm or deny this assertion. Statements about God's relationship with the world and scientific facts belong in different domains of thought that have different ways of proving their claims and different kinds of evidence for their claims.

The Creation Narrative in J

Genesis 1–11 is not a scientific or historical account. Its second story of creation begins at 2:4b. Notice that the editors of Genesis did not meld the two stories (one from the tenth century and one from the sixth) into one account. Rather, in this place Genesis has two tellings of the same event, the creation of the world. Chapter 1 gives details about what was created on each of six days to oppose alternative accounts of creation that attribute creation to many gods in the same number of days, while chapter 2 (the earlier account) focuses its attention on humanity. Chapter 2 has God create only Adam, rather than both male and female at the same time (as in chapter 1). The story in chapter 2 of the search for a mate for Adam clearly indicates that we are not reading history or science. In this story, God has Adam name all the animals while looking for a mate. Imagine God and Adam sitting on a hill with the animals parading by. As the various animals come before Adam, God says, "Do you think that one would be a good mate?" Adam keeps demurring. Maybe God is disappointed a few times. "I really thought the wombat would be the one!" Such a scene is ludicrous. Do we really think God did not know that the appropriate mate for a human is a human?

> *BOX 4.6*
>
> Read Genesis 1:31. Why does the description of the creation as "very good" require Genesis to tell a story like that of the fall?

Implications of the Two Accounts

If we look for the meaning of this story, we see God's intimate care for humans, and perhaps a conception of the ways men and women are related to one another and to the rest of creation. These affirmations about God and God's world are more important than how many days it took to create the world. These assertions invest believers' lives with meaning and value, and give believers a place in the world. According to believers, recognizing those values and relationships and conducting their lives in accord with them can make their lives good in ways that correct information about the physical construction of the world cannot.

The goodness of creation. One of the most important truths both creation accounts tell

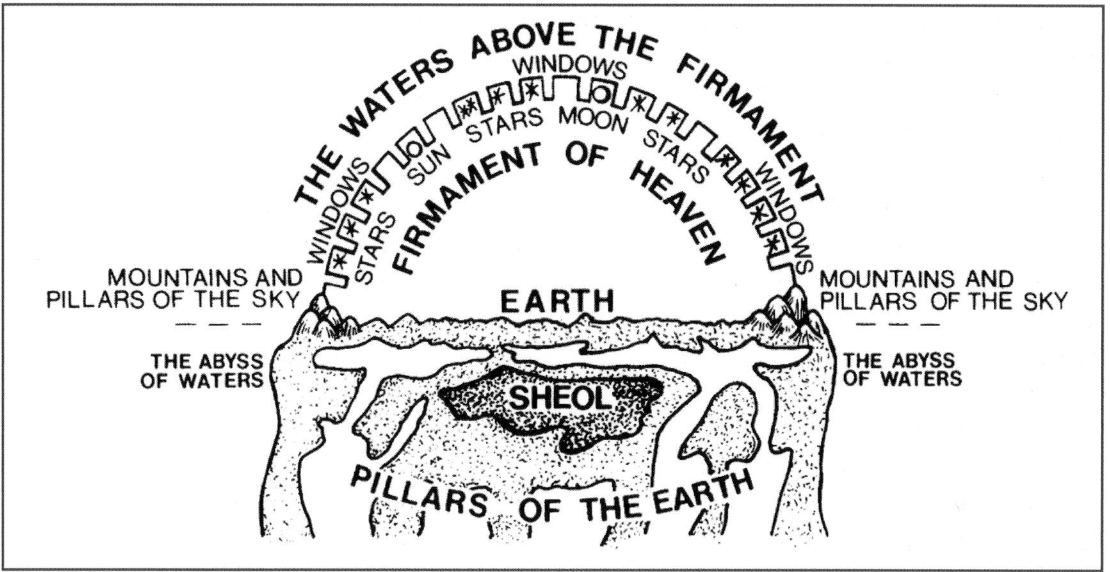

FIGURE 4.2 **GENESIS COSMOS**

The cosmos as people imagined it at the time Genesis was written.

readers is that the world God made is good. Things work as they should. So the world originally reflected the goodness of God. But this is not how we experience the world. We know the world is a more ambiguous place, perhaps even a hostile place. It is not the "very good" place Genesis 1 describes. Fortunately, the story of Genesis does not leave its readers with an idealized vision. It goes on to tell us why the world is not the way God wants it by relating the story of what Christians later came to call "**the fall**."

The authors of Genesis use narrative, that is, story, to relate their understanding of God and God's relationship with the world because narrative is a more powerful medium than simply stating propositions. The comparison with parables is again apt. Why would Jesus bother telling stories rather than just speaking shorter and clearer propositions about what God wants or about the nature of the kingdom of God? There is always more to a narrative than what one can express by stating a factual proposition. Hearing a story involves elements of our humanity beyond those engaged when analyzing a factual statement. The effectiveness of a story depends on it touching our hearts as well as our minds, our emotions as well as our thought processes.

Genesis engages the reader's whole person when telling these stories. Narratives of God being with people on intimate and friendly terms bear more and richer meanings than the proposition that God cares deeply for us. The story relates something deeper and wider than that mere proposition. So Genesis graces its readers with a story that can form their lives and their understanding of the world.

▶ The Fall

Like the accounts of the creation, the story of what Christians call the fall (Genesis 3), which continues the second creation narrative, is not literal history. Again, elements of the story demonstrate that we cannot read it as a scientific or factual account. First, the story has a tree with fruit that can give one ethical or spiritual knowledge like God's. Physiologically, we know there is nothing we could eat that can transmit specific ethical information to our minds. That is not the way the digestive tract, or the brain, works. Similarly, we know there is no food that can make us live forever. Yet Genesis has God put Adam and Eve out of the garden of Eden for fear that they will eat of a particular tree and live forever. Or consider the scene where God is taking a stroll in the garden (maybe an afternoon constitutional) and cannot find Adam. Do we really envision God taking a walk or not knowing where Adam is? These and other elements of the story demonstrate that we are not reading history.

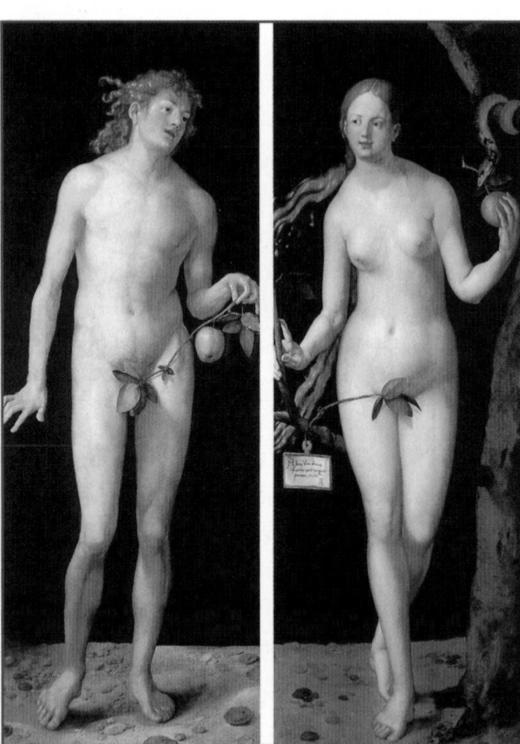

FIGURE 4.3 **ADAM, EVE**
Albrecht Dürer, 1507. Wikimedia Commons

Rather than giving us history, the writer is trying to explain why we experience the world as we do. Why isn't it the ideal place described in chapters 1–2? The answer Genesis gives is that humans have violated what God wants in the world, and that violation has brought terrible consequences. The story of the fall tells us that the world we live in now is not what God intended.

Primordial Sin

Genesis 3 relates the story of Adam and Eve being expelled from the garden of Eden, that ideal place God had made for them. This story admits multiple readings and allows some ambiguity as it relates the fall. Some interpreters think it points to disobedience as the central sin of Adam and Eve (and so of humanity). Others say the story has Adam and Eve undertake an illegitimate attempt to be like God, to take for themselves divine prerogatives. Still others argue that this episode brings a blessing because human beings must possess the "knowledge of good and evil" to be fully human. There is an important aspect of truth to this last interpretation, but it is not sufficient by itself. Our conscience is necessary for us to be fully human, but that conscience also means that we live with guilt. The problem is not that we have guilt, but that we have good reason for it! In addition, the text has the serpent tempt Adam and Eve (and here they represent all people) by telling them that the fruit will make them like the gods. So however much attaining a conscience is a necessary part of being fully human, something more is going on here.

Violation of God's will. This text contends that human beings violated God's will in a way that shows they were untrustworthy. As a result, they were expelled from paradise and the ground was put under a curse. It is important to notice that living under this curse is not what this writer saw as God's will for the world, although many people have read the curse in Genesis 3:14-19 as though it expressed God's will for the structure of human relationships, especially that between husbands and wives. But this is a misreading of the passage. The writer included this curse to tell readers that the world is not what God intended it to be. This curse explains what the writer thought happens to the world and human relationships when people violate the will of God.

Curses. When the writer of this passage looked at the world, he knew there was something wrong. The way the world works does not fully reflect the goodness of God; it is not that "very good" place God said it was. After all, it was clear that people had to work so hard ("by the sweat of your brow," 3:19 KJV) that it made their lives miserable and even shortened their lives. Too many women suffered too much and too many died in childbirth for the world to be such a good place. As Genesis tells it, this story explains how the world got into the miserable condition it is in. Crops are too hard to grow, and society and family are structured in ways that do not reflect God's character or will. Rather than being a prescription for the way things should be, this curse is a description of the way things are.

Overcoming the curses. We work to overcome the conditions this curse describes in many ways. Farmers use pesticides, fertilizers, and new strains of plants to make farming easier. They even ride in air-conditioned tractors, so they do not have work "by the sweat of [their] brow." Other people work in air-conditioned buildings because we do not think sweating at work is a good thing. When we make such efforts at making life easier, and so surmount the difficulties of life that the curse acknowledges, we are trying to make the world a little more like that "very good" place Genesis says God intended. Yet, while trying to escape the effects of the curse in some ways, in other ways many have said that the curse reflects God's will. Less than a hundred years ago, some people argued that women should not receive anesthetics when giving birth because God said they should suffer in childbirth. Of course, those who made that argument were later in favor of tractors and air-conditioning!

If believers recognize that this curse does not reflect God's will for life (as they do when they make work less difficult), then it cannot serve as the basis for how they organize their families. When the author of this section of Genesis looked at the subjection of women to their husbands, he saw it as part of what had gone wrong with the world. This curse is not a pattern for how to structure the world or families (as our use of tractors and air-conditioning recognizes), it is a description of the way things are when people violate God's will. So unless believers are ready to reject all the things that make the work of their livelihoods easier, they cannot use this passage to assert that wives should be submissive to husbands. Remember, this family structure is part of what Genesis says is wrong with the world.

Another part of this passage shows clearly that most believers do not read it consistently as a command from God about how to organize their lives. It says that because the serpent deceived Eve, humans will hate snakes and hit them on the head (3:14-15). Few would argue that because Genesis says people will hate snakes that stomping on them is a command of God. Yet this statement of the way things are with snakes (and with much of the animal world) is the same kind of statement as that about the subjection of wives.

If readers of Genesis want to see the world as God wants it to be, they must look at what happens before the curse. According to Genesis, God intends work to be fulfilling, but not oppressive. God intends family relations to be other than hierarchical. And God does not intend snakes to be so scary. Working for what God wants in the world will not include perpetuating the conditions described in this curse.

▶ After the Fall

With the story of the fall, Genesis has brought the world closer to the way the writers actually experienced it. But things get worse—and quickly. Almost immediately there is murder, even worse, it is fratricide in the world's first family (Genesis 4). Cain, Adam and Eve's first son, kills his brother Abel because God accepted Abel's sacrifice but not Cain's. The text does not say why God accepted one sacrifice and not the other; it does tell of Cain's anger and his refusal to accept any responsibility for his brother. As punishment for committing the first murder, God sends Cain away from his family.

Elements of this story again indicate that we are not reading a historical account. Cain fears that people will kill him when he wanders the earth; thus God puts a mark on him to protect him. If we follow the story of Genesis closely, the only other people in the world are Adam and Eve. If this is history, Cain's question makes no sense because there is no one to kill him. Furthermore, we hear that he gets a wife. Where his wife came from is a problem only if we mistake this text for history. Read as a narrative that provides an interpretation of the world, such details are unimportant. Indeed, the writers seem to care nothing about such apparent difficulties.

As if murder within the family were not bad enough, things get still worse as the story progresses. Otherworldly beings ("sons of God," Genesis 6:1-4) violate the order of things and have children with human women. These children, called the **Nephilim**, are very powerful and violent. They contribute to making the world the sort of place that God regrets having made.

▶ The Flood

Parallels

The story of the flood immediately follows the story of the Nephilim. The flood story in Genesis 6–9 draws on earlier, non-Israelite stories, just as the creation account in chapter 1 did. Centuries before the flood story in Genesis was written, various cultures of the ancient Near

East had stories of a worldwide flood. The Genesis flood narrative has several parallels with the Epic of Gilgamesh, a story with several versions (one written around 1700 B.C.E. and based on earlier Sumerian versions): the gods tell a person to build a boat so that he survives the flood; the hero gathers and saves the animals; and he offers the gods a sacrifice after a safe landing. So in many respects the story in Genesis sounds much like the other flood stories being told in the surrounding cultures, but it also has some important differences.

Differences. The first important difference between the Genesis flood story and the other flood stories is that it is about the one God rather than about many gods working to send the flood. The reason for the flood is also very different. In the Epic of Gilgamesh the gods flood the earth on a whim; they are capricious and humans seem of little importance to them. But in Genesis God floods the world because of its wickedness. Things are not just bad, but "every inclination of the thoughts of their hearts was only evil continually" (Genesis 6:5). Things had gotten about as bad as they could, so there is a just reason for the flood. Noah is the *only* righteous person in the world, and God saves him. Therefore, God acts with what the writer sees as justice rather than capriciousness.

This picture of God is very different from the image many in the ancient world had about the gods. In that world, people saw the gods as capricious, but the God of Israel acts with justice.

Another important difference between the Genesis account of the flood and others is the way it envisions the relationship between God and humans. In the Gilgamesh Epic the gods

FIGURE 4.4 **GILGAMESH**

Gilgamesh, relief from the palace of Sargon II (eighth century B.C.E.), now in the Louvre. Wikimedia Commons

seem to have forgotten that they receive nourishment from the burned sacrifices humans offered them. When they send a flood, no one remains to offer sacrifices and so to sustain them. When Utnapishtim (the person who built the ark and saved the animals) comes out of his ark, he offers a sacrifice that the gods gather around like flies because they are so hungry. The God of Genesis is not dependent in any way on humans or their sacrifices. Instead of needing a meal, God takes the opportunity of Noah's sacrifice to make a promise: God promises never again to destroy the whole world with a flood, giving the rainbow as the reminder of that promise. So the flood becomes an occasion for blessing.

FIGURE 4.5 **UTNAPISHTIM**

The account of Utnapishtim and the flood from the Epic of Gilgamesh; cuneiform tablet from Nineveh, now in the British Museum. Wikimedia Commons

Interwoven Sources

As we have seen with other stories in Genesis, the flood narrative is not a historical account. Again, the genre of the story and its ancient, and earlier, parallels make that clear. So too do the inconsistencies within the story. The Genesis account combines two different tellings of the great flood, as the report of the number of animals Noah takes onto the ark suggests. In chapter 6 (vv. 19-21) Noah gets two of each kind of animal, but in chapter 7 (vv. 2-3) he gets seven pairs of some animals. These latter animals are the kinds that the Mosaic law will declare as clean, that is, acceptable for the faithful to eat. Most scholars think that the sixth-century priestly writers, who were concerned about matters such as clean and unclean foods, added the note about how many clean animals Noah took. After all, the righteous person who saves all of humanity ought to keep the proper commandments about food!

Poetic Narrative

The distribution of animals across the globe also makes a literalistic reading of the flood narrative impossible. If all the species of animals in the world were somewhere in the Middle East six thousand years ago, there was no way for them to get to Australia or the Americas. It does more justice to Genesis to simply acknowledge that the type of story it tells is neither a scientific nor a modern historical account. Its genre is of a different sort.

Acknowledging that the flood story is a poetic and symbolic narrative does not raise any question about the story's truth, because it was not written as a historical account. It was written to help readers understand God and the world in which they live. This narrative demonstrates how important holy living is to God. Living a life given over to evil is an offense to God, yet after the flood God promises to care for humanity no matter how wicked the world becomes. Conveying this understanding of God is more important for Genesis than whether a person named Noah literally built a big boat a few thousand years ago, and this promise does not depend on the story being a factual account. Recognizing that this story is not history does not suggest that God cannot act in extraordinary ways in the world; it only acknowledges the nature of the literary form through which the message is delivered.

Canaan and Ham

The final story about Noah (Genesis 9) is a disturbing episode that played a role in ancient Israel's justification of its dominance of the native peoples of Canaan. In later times, Europeans and Americans used this narrative to justify the enslavement of Africans. After the flood, Genesis says that Noah planted a vineyard and eventually made wine. One day he became so drunk that he passed out naked in his tent. Ham, Noah's youngest son, saw his father naked and, it seems, went to make fun of him with his older brothers. Instead of further shaming their father, the two older sons walked into Noah's tent backward and covered him with some clothing. When Noah woke up and found out how Ham had treated him, he put a curse on Ham's son, Canaan. The curse was that Canaan and his descendants would be his uncles' slaves.

The effects of the story. Israel used this narrative to support their exercise of dominance over the other inhabitants of Canaan. Notably, Canaan had done nothing to Noah—he was simply the son of the one who presumably acted disrespectfully. Yet Canaan was the one cursed to be a slave to his uncles. The genealogy that follows makes Canaan's descendants the nations that Israel must defeat in the land of Canaan to establish its national territory. Since those nations fell under the curse from Noah, they could be treated as slaves. The curse of Noah, then, permitted the Israelites to mistreat the Canaanites without thinking it unjust; the oppression of Canaan's descendants was simply the consequence of the sin of the ancestor. So this story had a political function.

In more recent times, some used this episode in the American debate about slavery. Advocates of slavery said that the "curse of Ham" was a darkening of his skin. His descendants, then, were Africans, whom lighter-skinned descendants of Noah's other two sons were allowed to enslave. Thus the biblical text was said to show that God favored slavery of Africans. This use of the story misreads it in multiple ways. First, the story says nothing about the curse darkening the skin of its recipient. Indeed, the people listed as descendants of Canaan in the next chapter are groups that inhabited the Middle East, not Africa. Next, it was not a curse on Ham, but on his son. While this seems unjust, it shows how the passage functioned for the Israelites; that is, it was a justification for exercising dominance over Canaanites. Finally, perhaps the one bright note about this episode is that the curse is not from God; this curse comes from Noah. The implication of including it in the text may be that God concurs, but the text does not say so explicitly, and it may be that the author of the text thought the curse could be effective without God enforcing it.

▶ Origins and Babel

After the stories associated with Noah's family, the authors of Genesis account for the origins of various nations, professions, and languages through genealogies. Genesis then provides an **etiology**, a narrative that describes the origin of something, as a second explanation for the existence of so many languages in the world. This etiology is the story of the **tower of Babel** (Genesis 11). This story also contains elements that demonstrate why we cannot read it as a scientific or historical account. The people decide to build a city with a tower that will reach into heaven. As we saw in the fall, human pride leads them to fail to distinguish themselves from God; they want to intrude into God's domain. God's reaction suggests that God thinks the people really can build a tower that will reach to heaven. Such a project makes no sense within our view of the universe with its planets, stars, and galaxies. We do not think that heaven is a place that is a particular and reachable height above the world. We think of

FIGURE 4.6 **THE GREAT ZIGGURAT OF UR**

A ziggurat is a mudbrick temple and tower. This ziggurat, at the ancient city of Ur (in today's Iraq), was built for the moon god Nanna before 2000 B.C.E. This ziggurat is in the region where Abraham lived when God called him. Corbis

heaven as, perhaps, another plane of existence, not a place just a bit higher than where we are. After all, we have sent people to the moon, so we know that no one can build a tower so high that it will reach God's dwelling place. Yet this narrative proceeds as though it were possible to complete such a structure.

The Babel story deals with issues that involve human pride, not with measurements telling how high one has to build a tower to reach heaven. The metaphorical nature of the story is unmistakable, and its lessons are very important. This story emphasizes the distinction between God and humans, and demonstrates that humanity must respect that distinction by not usurping divine prerogatives. The story also tells of the proliferation of languages, a fact of life that at times makes things more difficult.

The Babel story brings us to the end of the first section of Genesis. After this story, the world becomes a place we can recognize, where things work in ways that are familiar to us. Heaven is not so near that you can build a tower to reach it, snakes do not talk (although there is a story in the book of Numbers where a donkey talks, but that is seen as incredible), and the rainbow is already in place. With the ordering of the world completed, Genesis introduces a new kind of story.

▶ Israel's Ancestors

Near the end of chapter 11, Genesis narrows its focus to a single family, that of **Abraham and Sarah**. The stories of this family and their descendants take up the rest of Genesis. The narratives that make up this part of Genesis belong to the genre of **legend**, the kinds of stories ancient peoples told about their ancestors. Such stories may contain very ancient remembrances of ancestral tradition, but they are not what we call history. These kinds of narratives help define and explain a people's character. They give narrative accounts to clarify what makes them distinctive and who they understand themselves to be by tracing their characteristics back to their ancestors. While these self-definitions are being shaped, the authors of Genesis also use this legendary material to clarify the people's understanding of this God with whom the descendants of Abraham, as a people, have a special relationship.

Abraham

The story of the ancestors of the Jewish people begins with Abraham; he responds to God's call (Genesis 12) and thus becomes the father of all who claim this heritage. The text gives no explanation for why God chooses Abraham (whose name at this point is Abram); it says only that God calls him. God tells Abraham to leave his homeland with the promise that God will make him a blessing to the whole world. So as the call comes to Abraham, and through him to his descendants, election (that is, being chosen) involves the task of being a blessing to the world, even as it is a privilege.

Weakness and faith. As the story of Abraham unfolds, it becomes obvious that he is not always a giant of faith. He and others in these narratives often serve as examples of what God's people are really like—good and bad, strong and weak, rather than just paragons of virtue to imitate. These ancestors of Israel demonstrate both great faith and great weakness. When these characters are not exemplars, their stories intend to demonstrate that God remains with God's people even when they are unfaithful. Abraham's journey to Egypt provides a prime example (12:10-20). Afraid that the Egyptians will kill him to take his beautiful wife Sarah, Abraham lies and says that she is his sister. (It does not help to note that she was his half-sister, because concealing that she was also his wife remains an intentional deception and so a lie.) Despite his dishonesty that causes the degradation of Sarah, whom Pharaoh takes into his harem, God blesses Abraham so that he leaves Egypt wealthier. Thus God blesses Abraham even as he sins. This story sets a pattern for the patience God shows to Abraham's descendants: God remains faithful, even when God's people do not.

Abraham and Lot. Abraham is no wandering loner; he is a wealthy sheik. As Genesis 13 tells the story, Abraham takes along his nephew Lot when God calls him. Both Abraham and Lot have wealth that includes herds and servants to tend them. Genesis says the combined herds of the two become too large for their employees to work together peacefully, as each tries to provide for their master's possessions. When Abraham and Lot decide to split up, Abraham gives Lot the choice of where to settle. Lot

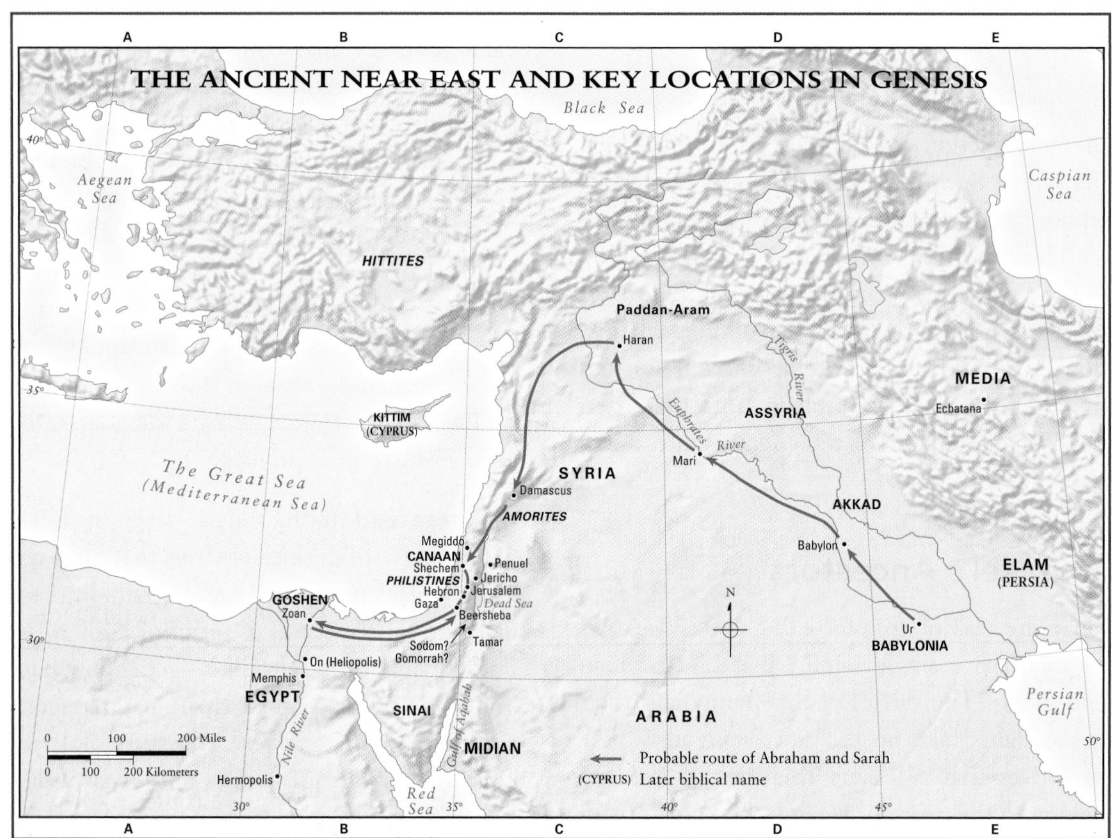

MAP 4.1

chooses to live in a fertile area near an urban center, while Abraham agrees to inhabit a more arid region.

Soon after they split up, Lot gets caught up in a war and the enemy takes him and his belongings captive. When Abraham hears of Lot's capture, he puts together an army of his own. Genesis 14 says that he musters a band of over three hundred men trained in combat, all of whom had been born in his household. That is, all of these men's parents (at least their mothers) were in the company that traveled with and were owned by Abraham. This suggests that he had over a thousand people in his employ. Some of these were slaves, some free.

While this number of employees clearly establishes Abraham's wealth and status, his army remains very small to put up against the armies of the three kings who had joined forces and successfully raided neighboring cities. Yet, because God is with him, Abraham defeats them and brings home Lot with all his possessions, as well as everything else the three kings had taken in their attacks.

The promise. After this episode, God repeats the promise that Abraham would have many descendants, but he and Sarah still have no children (Genesis 15–16). Since both Abraham and Sarah are getting old and remain unable to have children, they take things into their own hands. Sarah gives him a slave woman named Hagar with whom to have a child, and so acquire an heir. Hagar has a son named Ishmael, but God tells Abraham that this will not be the child through whom the promise is fulfilled. Still, Ishmael will be the ancestor of many. In the genealogies that follow in Genesis, Ishmael becomes the ancestor of Arabs.

God renews the promise of a son to Sarah and Abraham after Sarah has reached menopause and Abraham is 100 years old (Genesis 17). Sarah laughs at the heavenly messengers who bring this news, but the messengers assure them that it will happen. Genesis draws out the birth of the child of promise to suggest that everything that happens to fulfill God's promises is God's doing. This story also introduces the theme of barren wives that will continue throughout Genesis and will reappear in other biblical books, including 1 Samuel, 2 Kings, and the Gospel of Luke.

Sodom and Gomorrah. The same messengers who renew the promise of a child for Sarah have other, and disturbing, news for Abraham (Genesis 18). They tell him that they have come to destroy the cities of **Sodom and Gomorrah** because those cities are so wicked. We must read this narrative carefully because so many people use it in discussions about homosexuality. We should begin by noticing the subject that the text announces as its topic. God tells Abraham that what is about to happen is a lesson in doing righteousness and justice (18:19). Similarly, when the heavenly messengers explain to Lot why they are destroying the cities, they say that an outcry against them has gone up before the LORD (19:13). These explicit statements about its meaning should play an important role in our understanding of the story.

Read in its context, the story of Sodom is about the injustice the city perpetrates against the powerless. The prophets of Israel use the language of "outcry" to talk about the pleas of the oppressed. Israel had important laws against abusing the stranger in their midst, but many societies did not. In the ancient world,

FIGURE 4.7 **ABRAHAM**

Abraham, depicted in a fresco from the third-century C.E. synagogue at Dura-Europos. Wikimedia Commons

nonresidents of a region had few legal protections. People with no clan connections were often seen as less than human, as people who could be abused with impunity unless a powerful person or group protected them. The heavenly messengers who had appeared to Abraham go to Sodom with no such protections. Lot takes them in and tries to protect them, but the more established residents threaten him, as one new in town and having a tenuous position in the society.

When the men of the city surround Lot's house, they are there to humiliate and rape the strangers, who have no clan protection. The men of Sodom refuse Lot's daughters because they have some protection (remember that Abraham and his warriors are not far away). This act of the men of Sodom is not about which sex they rape, but about perpetrating violence against people without protection. The sin of Sodom is violence and injustice against the weak and powerless, just as God's decision to tell Abraham about the city's destruction suggests (18:19).

A similar story in Judges confirms this understanding of the Sodom story. Judges 19–20 tells of a man and his concubine who get to the city of Gibeah at evening. As they prepare to sleep in the town square (just as the messengers did in Sodom), a man who was not a native of the city takes them in for the night. That night the men of the city surround the house where the travelers are staying and demand that the owner send out the stranger so they can rape him. The resident who took the travelers in refuses, but then the traveling man throws his concubine to the mob. They rape her all night and she dies from her injuries. When the husband sends word to all the other tribes of Israel that this has happened, they unite and destroy the offending city.

The obvious parallels with the Sodom story make plain that the problem was not who the people wanted to rape, but that they abused a person who had lower status because she lacked clan protection. The drastic punishment in both stories is judgment on these acts of social injustice.

This understanding of the Sodom story differs significantly from the one usually given. But this reading fits both the times in which the story is set and the way the text tells the story better than an interpretation that understands it to be about homosexuality. Even if the Sodom story is about sexual relations, it is not about consensual sex, but about rape. The Bible certainly opposes rape, no matter who the victim is.

Abraham bargains with God. The Sodom story also gives other important information about God and Abraham. After the messengers tell Abraham of their plan to destroy the cities of Sodom and Gomorrah, Abraham tries to dissuade God by appealing to God's justice (18:23-33). He asks God to spare the city if there are as few as fifty righteous people, and God agrees. Abraham continues to bargain until God agrees to spare the city if God can find as few as ten righteous people. Of course, in the end, the messengers do not find even that many. Still, this conversation demonstrates the intimacy and influence that Abraham has with God. More importantly, it shows that God is both just and merciful. God is not willing to punish the innocent and is willing to spare the guilty for the sake of a few good people.

The promise fulfilled. A year after the messengers' visit to Abraham and Sarah, Sarah bears a son (Genesis 21). Finally, Abraham has an heir. They name him Isaac, which means "laughter," because Sarah laughed when the heavenly messengers said she would have a son. The birth of this child demonstrates the faithfulness of God to God's promises. Even when it is no longer humanly possible, God fulfills the promise. The story shows God's people that God's promises are trustworthy, even when the situation seems hopeless.

Dissension. Some troubling episodes follow this birth. First, Abraham (at Sarah's bidding) throws out Hagar and her son Ishmael to secure the full inheritance for Isaac (21:10-21). Then Abraham hears God command him to offer Isaac as a sacrifice, and he starts to carry out the command, only to be stopped at the last minute (22:1-18). These stories appear in the middle of a collection of texts that command justice for strangers and prohibit child sacrifice! Such stories may suggest that Abraham was weak and unable to understand God clearly or that he sometimes showed great faith (as the later author of the New Testament book of Hebrews [11:17-19] will interpret the story of the near sacrifice of Isaac). However we understand these stories, the birth of Isaac begins the next phase of the story.

When Isaac is old enough to marry, Abraham sends a servant back to Aram-naharaim, Abraham's homeland, to secure a wife for his son (Genesis 24). With divine intervention, the servant finds **Rebekah**, who agrees to marry Isaac. Sometime after the marriage of Isaac, Abraham dies (25:7-8). Sarah had died apparently long before the marriage of Isaac (23:1-2).

Faithfulness and grace. The story of Abraham highlights the faithfulness and trustworthiness of God. Despite all of Abraham's failings and misunderstandings, God remains in covenant with him and blesses him because of their relationship with one another. So God's grace and patience are an underlying theme in this account of the origins of the people of Israel.

The covenant does not depend on the people being perfect, but on God's grace. Indeed, the story of their revered ancestor demonstrates God's faithfulness to God's people, even in the face of their faults and unfaithfulness. So Abraham's descendants are the people with whom God has a special relationship and covenant. This identity should definitively shape their behavior and self-understanding.

Isaac

By securing Isaac's wife from Aram, the author of Genesis keeps Abraham's descendants distinct from the other inhabitants of Canaan. In fact, in the stories of these earliest male descendants of Abraham, those who do not marry women from Aram are written out of the ancestry of Israel. Maintaining this distinction from the peoples around them allows Israelites to take the land of Canaan from the Canaanites. If they had admitted closer family ties, taking the land would have been a violation of the rights of those to whom they were related.

Jacob

The story of Isaac and Rebekah continues with the birth of twins (Genesis 25). Even though these brothers are twins, the firstborn holds the position of primary heir. But as in prior stories, such patterns do not hold true. When **Esau** is born, his brother **Jacob** is holding onto his heel. This symbolizes the way Jacob will trip up Esau for the rest of their lives, and will be a trickster in his dealings with nearly everyone. First, Jacob gets Esau to sell him the birthright of the firstborn for a simple meal. Still, Esau was in line to be the next leader of the clan. But when Isaac is about to die, Rebekah helps Jacob trick the old, nearly blind Isaac into giving the blessing of being the leader to Jacob rather than to Esau (Genesis 27). Esau is so angry that he plans to kill Jacob when his father dies, so Rebekah schemes to send Jacob away with Isaac's blessing. Importantly, he leaves not only in fear, but also to get a wife from the people of Abraham. Meanwhile, Esau marries a Canaanite and so seals his exclusion from the promises to Abraham.

Jacob's dream. On his way to Paddan-aram, Jacob stops at Bethel, where he has a dream in which a ladder to heaven appears with angels going back and forth between earth and heaven (28:10-22). God here gives Jacob the promise of Abraham that he would have many descendants and that through him the world would be blessed. It is important to note that, again, the unexpected person gets the blessing from God; Jacob is neither the oldest son nor the better person. God's choice is not bound by social and cultural expectations.

Jacob's wives. In Paddan-aram Jacob finds his way to the house of **Laban**, a relative of Abraham (Genesis 29–30). There he falls in love with **Rachel**, Laban's younger daughter, and agrees to work for Laban for seven years to earn the right to marry her. Laban agrees, but at the end of the seven years Laban tricks Jacob into marrying his older daughter **Leah**, explaining that it is the custom for the older daughter to marry first. It seems that Jacob has met his match in trickery with Laban. Jacob agrees to work seven more years if Laban also gives him Rachel as his second wife. Again, Laban agrees. When Rachel bears no children, she gives Jacob a slave to have children for her. Then, when Leah

FIGURE 4.8 **JACOB'S LADDER**

Jacob's dream of a ladder going into heaven. Fresco in the catacomb of the Via Latina. Wikimedia Commons

stops bearing children, she gives Jacob another slave with whom he has more children. Finally, Rachel herself has one child, **Joseph**. When Joseph is born, Jacob has eleven sons and at least one daughter. These eleven sons and the twelfth born later are the ancestors of the tribes of Israel.

Jacob's return. When, after over twenty years, Jacob decides to return to Canaan with his large family, he asks Laban for severance pay for the years he had worked for his father-in-law (Genesis 31). They agree that Jacob is to take all the spotted animals born to Laban's flocks that year. But then Laban removes all the spotted animals and gives them to his sons so that no spotted animals will be born. Jacob retaliates by placing striped sticks within sight of the stronger animals when they breed. Following the logic of magic (still heard today when people tell a pregnant woman not to look at something because it will mark her baby), the animals who see the stripes have spotted babies. It works so well that Laban and his sons become angry enough that Jacob decides to sneak away with his family and his possessions.

Household gods. As they are running away, Rachel steals her father's household gods (31:19). Laban is incensed by both the flight (with the flocks) and the taking of his gods. When Laban catches up with them, Jacob insists that he has not stolen anything and allows Laban to search his possessions. Laban does not find the gods because they are hidden under Rachel's saddle, and when the people with Laban come to search, she asks them not to make her stand because of her period. They accede and so never find the gods. Laban and Jacob do, however, make peace and Jacob continues to Palestine to face his brother.

This last tale shows that the ancestors of Israel worshiped many gods, because the religious reason Rachel has to steal Laban's gods is to worship them. To this point, God has not told the people not to worship other gods. In fact, this commandment does not appear until the giving of the Ten Commandments, ostensibly hundreds of years later. Before that time, the ancestors of the Israelites worshiped multiple gods, with the God of Abraham as one (perhaps the chief) among them. The story may also intend to denigrate those other gods as powerless and unworthy because they allow a menstruating woman to sit on them, if the teller intends readers to think Rachel is telling the truth.

Jacob remains a tricky and unlikable person. When his company gets close to the place Esau lives, Jacob sends ahead messengers, then his flocks and servants, then his wives and children (Genesis 32). He waits behind to see if Esau kills them before he ventures into range of the brother he so egregiously injured. But Esau is forgiving and graciously receives Jacob and his family. This again highlights the strangeness of God choosing Jacob over Esau, making evident that God's grace accounts for the blessings bestowed on God's people.

Nocturnal wrestling. While Jacob remains behind, he has another extraordinary experience. He wrestles with a heavenly being until morning, when the "angel" injures Jacob and changes his name to Israel. This name may mean "God strives" or "one who strives with God." Israel, of course, becomes the name by which the nation will be known. Thus, even though Jacob remains cowardly and unworthy, God remains faithful to him and in communication with him. Human faults do not annul God's

BOX 4.7

GOD AT WORK BEHIND THE SCENES

Joseph asserts that what has happened to him contributed to the fulfillment of God's plan. When he reveals himself to his brothers, he tells them not to be distressed by their bad intention in selling him into slavery, because "God sent me before you to preserve life" (45:5). The passage repeats this sentiment in the following verses.

CHART 4.2

THE TWELVE SONS OF JACOB

Birth Order	Name	Meaning of Name	Mother	
1	Reuben	See, a son	Leah	
2	Simeon	Hearing	Leah	
3	Levi	Joined; attached	Leah	
4	Judah	God be praised	Leah	
5	Dan	He has judged	Bilhah	Rachel's servant or slave
6	Naphtali	My wrestling	Bilhah	
7	Gad	Good fortune	Zilpah	Leah's servant or slave
8	Asher	Fortunate one	Zilpah	
9	Issachar	Man of hire	Leah	
10	Zebulun	Dwelling	Leah	
11	Joseph	He will increase	Rachel	
12	Benjamin	Son of the right hand	Rachel	

faithfulness, and human failings do not prohibit God from accomplishing God's purposes for the future people of Israel and, through that people, for the world.

Joseph

While in Canaan (Palestine), Rachel has a second son, Benjamin (Genesis 35). The two sons of Rachel are Jacob's favorites, in part because their mother is his favorite wife. Joseph, the older of the two, is arrogant and boastful toward his brothers, even claiming that they and his parents would one day bow to him. When the brothers can stand his arrogance no longer, they kidnap him and sell him into slavery, telling their father he was killed by a wild animal (Genesis 37). Meanwhile, the traders who bought Joseph sell him to a man in Egypt.

Joseph in Egypt. After suffering false accusations and being sent to prison, Joseph eventually becomes the second most powerful person in Egypt because he interprets the pharaoh's dreams correctly (Genesis 39–41). He predicts the coming of a famine and outlines what provisions the nation needs to make. Everything happens just as he predicts. The famine covers such a wide area that it also affects Canaan, so that Joseph's brothers must come to Egypt for food. There, just as he predicted, they bow before Joseph, who is now in charge of the distribution of grain. After inflicting some mental anguish on them, Joseph reveals his identity and invites the whole family to come to Egypt. They accept his invitation and the whole family of Jacob moves to the region of Goshen in Egypt (Genesis 42–47). Thus, through this strange chain of events, God rescues God's chosen people from the ravages of a severe famine. So God remains powerfully at work, directing events to accomplish God's own (sometimes hidden) purposes.

▶ Conclusion

Genesis ends here. Its stories have told the readers of God's creation of the world and the choosing of Abraham and his descendants. They have shown God's faithfulness despite the behavior of some of these ancestors. These narratives show that God is loving, gracious, and committed to the covenant with Abraham and his descendants. God's covenant relationship with Israel clearly rests not on the people's faithfulness but on God's word. These stories also explain how the Israelites' ancestors ended up in Egypt. We are now ready for the exodus story, the story that carries as much theological weight as any in the Hebrew Bible; perhaps only the creation story is as important.

▶ LET'S REVIEW ◀

In this chapter we learned about the Pentateuch:

- Its Compositional History
  - —Not authored by Moses
  - —Documentary Hypothesis
  - —Revisions to the Documentary Hypothesis
- The various genres within the Pentateuch
- Content and Meanings of the poetic narratives of Genesis 1-11
  - —Creation (in the context of other creation narratives)
  - —Fall
  - —Flood (in the context of other flood narratives)
  - —Babel
- Beginning of the legendary material in Genesis 12 and the particular history of Abraham and his descendants
  - —Isaac
  - —Jacob
  - —Joseph and the clan moving to Egypt

▶ KEY TERMS ◀

Abram/Abraham
Babel
D source
Documentary Hypothesis
E source
Elohim
Enuma Elish
Epic of Gilgamesh
Esau
Etiology
Fall
Garden of Eden
Genre
Isaac
J source
Jacob
Jehovah
Joseph
Laban
Leah
Legend
Nephilim
P source
Rachel
Rebekah
Sarah
Sodom and Gomorrah
Universes of discourse
Wellhausen
Yahweh

▶ QUESTIONS FOR REVIEW ◀

4.1 What are the distinctive characteristics of each major source that makes up the Pentateuch?

4.2 Why is it important to identify the genre of a document correctly?

4.3 Explain how parables can be true and yet not factual. How might this help you read other parts of the Bible (for example, the first chapters of Genesis)?

4.4 How are the creation accounts in Genesis and Enuma Elish alike? How are they different?
4.5 Why does Genesis include the story of the fall?
4.7 Compare the flood story in Genesis with the flood story in the Epic of Gilgamesh. What does this comparison show about what Genesis wants to say about God?
4.8 What is the point of the story in which Noah curses his grandson Canaan?
4.9 What in the story of the destruction of Sodom and Gomorrah suggests that it is about violence and injustice against the defenseless?
4.10 Why do the ancestors of the Israelites always get their wives from some place other than Canaan?

▶ FOR FURTHER READING ◀

Althalya Brenner, ed., *A Feminist Companion to Genesis*, Feminist Companion to the Bible 1/2. Sheffield: Sheffield Academic, 1993.

Walter Brueggemann, *Genesis*, Interpretation. Atlanta: John Knox, 1982.

Robert R. Cargill, "Forget about Noah's Ark; There Was No Worldwide Flood," Bible and Interpretation Website 2010: http://www.bibleinterp.com/articles/flood357903.shtml

John J. Collins, *A Short Introduction to the Hebrew Bible*. Minneapolis: Fortress Press, 2007, 15–54.

Mark Elliott, "Biblical Archaeology and Its Interpretation: The Sayce-Driver Controversy," Bible and Interpretation Website 2003 http://www.bibleinterp.com/articles/The_Sayce_Driver_Controversy.shtml

Terence E. Fretheim, *The Pentateuch*, Interpreting Biblical Texts. Nashville: Abingdon, 1996.

Ronald Hendel, ed., *Reading Genesis: Ten Methods*. Cambridge: Cambridge University Press, 2010.

R. W. L. Moberly, *The Theology of the Book of Genesis*. Old Testament Theology. Cambridge: Cambridge University Press, 2009.

W. Sibley Towner, *Genesis*, Westminster Bible Companion. Louisville: Westminster John Knox, 2001.

Gordon Wenham, "Pentateuchal Studies Today." *Themelios* 22, no. 1 (1996): 3–13. http://www.biblicalstudies.org.uk/article_pentateuch_wenham.html

5 The Pentateuch, Part 2
Exodus through Deuteronomy

IN THIS CHAPTER YOU WILL LEARN ABOUT THE FOLLOWING BOOKS:

- Exodus
  - Israel's Rescue from Egypt
  - The establishment of God's covenant with Israel
  - The beginning of a pattern of the people's unfaithfulness
- Leviticus
  - Regulations—for priests, and to separate Israelites from their neighbors
- Numbers
  - A census of the Israelites
  - More stories of Israel's time in the wilderness
- Deuteronomy
  - A repetition of the law and encouraging obedience
  - The Death of Moses

The remaining four books of the Pentateuch (Exodus, Leviticus, Numbers, and Deuteronomy) build on the stories of Genesis. They assume that God has a special relationship with the Israelites because of the promises God made to Abraham and the ancestors. The idea that God chose them as a special people and maintains a unique relationship with them rests on those promises, just as the important idea of a promised land does.

The stories in these books continue to use the genre of legend. Like the stories in Genesis, these are more than stories of one's people; they are theological narratives. They communicate the writers' understandings of the God to whom Israel is related. They also set out how the people must live within that relationship. Conveying these religious and ethical points constitutes the most important aspects of these stories. No story in the Hebrew Bible has more importance than the exodus. It is the cornerstone of Israel's understanding of God and their own existence in covenant with God. This story explains how God rescued the Israelites from slavery, formed them into a people, and made them God's own. At the same time, the exodus makes God's care for the oppressed a central element of the way God relates to the world. Overall, the stories demonstrate that God remains faithful to the people, despite their unfaithfulness to God.

▶ Exodus: Deliverance and the Beginning of the Nation

Moses: Preparation for Leadership

When the book of Exodus opens, the family of Jacob that moved to Egypt at the end of Genesis has become so large (hundreds of thousands) that the new Egyptian dynasty thinks they represent a threat. The reigning pharaoh responds to this perceived threat by enslaving the whole population of the Israelites and imposing infanticide for male children. Jochebed gives birth to Moses in this setting. She hides him until he becomes too large, and then sends his sister Miriam to float him down the river in a basket. The pharaoh's daughter happens to find Moses and, pitying him, takes him to raise as her own. Miriam, watching all this from a distance, asks the princess if she would like a wet nurse for the baby. When she says yes, Miriam brings Jochebed, who then nurses her son and so participates in his early life.

Although raised in the palace, Moses is aware of his heritage. One day, when he is about forty, he sees an Egyptian abusing a Hebrew (Exodus 2). In the process of intervening, Moses kills the Egyptian and so must flee Egypt. He spends the next forty years as a shepherd in Midian (an area on the western edge of today's Saudi Arabia), where he marries a Midianite woman named Zipporah, with whom he has two sons. One day while tending the sheep, he sees a strange sight on Mount Horeb: a bush is on fire, but the fire does not burn up the bush (Exodus 3). When Moses investigates this peculiar phenomenon, God speaks to him from the flame and commissions him to return to Egypt to free the Israelites. Moses is more than reticent, but after God shows him some powerful signs, he reluctantly agrees to the task.

The name of God. When speaking to Moses from the bush, God introduces God's self as the God of Abraham, Isaac, and Jacob. Moses knows of this God, but does not know God's name. According to this text, it is here that God's name (Hebrew: *YHWH*, Yahweh) is revealed for the first time (3:14). That name, which the King James Version translates as "Jehovah" and the New Revised Standard Version renders as "the LORD," means something such as "I am the one who exists" or "I am who I am." This is a momentous occasion because knowing the name of a god signals an intimacy with that god. Here God reaches out to Israel by revealing this vital information, and this new

FIGURE 5.1 **FINDING OF MOSES**

The finding of Moses is depicted in this fresco from the third-century C.E. synagogue in Dura-Europos, on the Parthian border. Wikimedia Commons

self-revelation signals the initiation of a new relationship between God and the people of Israel.

The Exodus

Aaron, Moses' older brother, meets Moses in the wilderness, and they return to Egypt together. Moses and Aaron tell their oppressed and enslaved people that God has seen their misery and is ready to deliver them from it (4:27-31). Moses and Aaron then gain an audience with the pharaoh and ask him to allow these thousands of slaves to go on a week's trip to worship their God. Of course, Pharaoh refuses to give his slaves a week's head start at what he must see as an escape attempt (5:1-9). He reasonably asks why he should listen to the God of his slaves. In response, Pharaoh increases the slaves' workload. Eventually Moses shows Pharaoh miraculous signs as evidence that God is with him and warns of dire consequences if Pharaoh refuses (7:1-13).

The ten plagues . . . the Passover. A series of ten plagues follows (7:14—12:32). Before each plague, Moses warns Pharaoh of what is to come, only to have Pharaoh dismiss him.

FIGURE 5.2 **MOSES REMOVES HIS SANDALS**

A twelfth-century Christian icon shows Moses removing his sandals to be addressed by God.
Wikimedia Commons

Once the disaster comes, Pharaoh calls Moses and asks him to remove it, promising that the people may go to worship their God. But each time Pharaoh recants when the plague abates. The first plague turns the Nile River to blood so that there is no water in the country, except among the Israelites. The plagues that follow are that the land is infested with frogs, then gnats, then flies, then the livestock die, then everyone breaks out in boils, then thunder with hail that covers everything, then locusts, and then constant darkness. Each time the plague affects only the Egyptians, not the Israelites. But a final plague threatens everyone: the firstborn child in every family in Egypt will die, except for those who perform the correct ritual. God says this final plague will cause Pharaoh to let the Israelites go. This story is the origin of the **Passover** celebration, the feast that celebrates God's deliverance of Israel from slavery, at the high cost of the death of many innocent first-born Egyptian children (Exod. 11:5).

Moses tells the Israelites to slaughter a lamb and smear its blood on their doorframes, so that the angel of death will pass by without taking their firstborn (Exodus 12). Moses also instructs them to cook the lamb and eat it with bread that has no yeast, because there will be no time for it to rise. They must eat and be ready to leave.

Deliverance at the sea. When every firstborn child of all the Egyptians (including their animals) dies, Pharaoh calls Moses and tells him to take the people and go. As the Israelites leave, their neighbors give them "parting gifts" to get rid of them. After all, their presence has now inflicted severe pain on all Egyptians. The Israelites start to leave Egypt, but get only as far as the Red Sea before Pharaoh's grief turns to anger and he sets out to catch and kill them (Exodus 14). As the Egyptian army approaches, the Israelites' escape is impeded by the Red Sea. But God rescues them by dividing the sea, so that the people walk through on dry land. When the army follows them into the sea, it closes in on them and decimates the army. Thus God frees the Israelites from their slavery in Egypt.

"A mixed multitude." Several aspects of this story deserve notice. First, the text gives an interesting description of those who follow

FIGURE 5.3 **MIRIAM DANCES**

The Hebrews cross the sea on dry land as Miriam dances in an illustration from the ninth-century Chludov Psalter. Wikimedia Commons

Moses out of Egypt. Besides there being a million people (600,000 men plus women and children), the text calls the group "a mixed multitude" (12:37-38). That is, this is not an ethnically homogeneous group. While their basic identity is Israelite, other oppressed peoples leave Egypt with them and so are included in the rescue. When we find passages that seem to report ethnic cleansing in the biblical texts,* this note about the people who leave Egypt together should temper our reading of them. Texts such as this one in Exodus (and there are others) suggest that the writers had something other than ethnicity in view when they speak of (and for) the mass killing of other peoples. (See chapter 6 for a discussion of the meaning of such stories.)

Pharaoh's heart is hardened. One of the disturbing aspects of the exodus story is how the text speaks of the way Pharaoh changes his mind after each plague abates. Rather than saying that Pharaoh changed his mind, Exodus sometimes says that "Pharaoh's heart was hardened" (e.g., 8:19; 10:20), implying that God caused Pharaoh to refuse to let Israel go. Since the exodus story is not objective history, but a theological narrative, it is designed to reveal who God is and how God acts among God's people and throughout the world. The exodus story, and particularly the story of the plagues, wants to demonstrate that God is more powerful than the Egyptians and their gods in every way (10:1-2). Furthermore, the multiple plagues constitute part of God's

BOX 5.1

THE NAME OF THE SEA

The traditional name given to the place the Israelites crossed into the desert is the Red Sea. This name comes from the Septuagint, but the original Hebrew word with "sea" does not mean "red." Many think a better translation of the Hebrew for this place is "Reed Sea," so that the name derives from the reeds that grew along the bank. Still others supply a different vowel (the original Hebrew did not have all the vowels in the text, just as Modern Hebrew does not) so that the name is the "Uttermost Sea," which would symbolize chaos. Whichever name is preferred, the basic point is that God has power over both Pharaoh and the sea (a symbol of chaos and danger, no matter what its name is).

*The book of Joshua has several examples of the Israelites being commanded to exterminate the population of a city that they conquer (see Joshua 10:40).

judgment on the injustice perpetrated against the Israelite slaves. The tellers of the story seem to think that justice will not be done until the Egyptians have suffered multiple plagues, so God causes Pharaoh to bring multiple plagues upon the nation.

Victory over chaos. It is somewhat strange that the sea plays any part in this story. There are many ways to leave Egypt that do not involve crossing water, and few that do when going toward the Sinai Peninsula. But by involving the sea in the story, the author of Exodus suggests that God is more powerful than the forces of chaos. In various myths of creation in the ancient Near East, the gods wrestle with the sea, the symbol of chaos, in order to form the world. Exodus echoes those stories by having God divide the sea and then use it to defeat Israel's enemies. Telling the story as the author of Exodus does, then, emphasizes God's might and power, not only over the Egyptians but also over cosmic powers (evident especially in the ancient poem in Exodus 15).

Complaints in the wilderness. Readers might expect that after this mighty deliverance the Israelites would trust God (and Moses) to take care of them. Not so. Almost immediately, they begin to grumble. In Exodus the people never trust God. When they suffer their first water shortage, God helps them find some but it is undrinkable. Of course, God tells Moses how to make it drinkable (15:23-25). When the food begins to run out, they not only complain about Moses' leadership but also opine about the good times in Egypt, where at least they had enough to eat. God responds by sending food from the sky every morning (except the Sabbath). They called this food "manna" (16:2-35). When they run short of water again, rather than remembering how God supplied them with water before and asking God for help, they complain against God and Moses (17:1-7). Yet God provides them with water. All of these episodes take place before the people get to **Mount Sinai** to receive the **Ten Commandments**. These stories intend to show God's great patience with the Israelites, so that when punishments do come it is obvious that they are more than deserved. These narratives also demonstrate the way God continually supplies the people's needs. God can be trusted to take care of God's people; God never abandons them, even when they are ungrateful. Thus God's grace stands out as the dominant theme of God's dealings with the people when we read these stories as a group.

The Law of Moses

The giving of the law at Mount Sinai is another signal event of the story (Exodus 19). When the presence of God descends on the mountain, the same mountain on which Moses saw the burning bush, the people are not allowed to touch it because God's presence makes it so holy. God allows only Moses and Aaron to come onto the mountain. Although the people cannot touch the mountain, they must purify themselves because they are so close to the presence of God. After the Israelites commit themselves to being God's people, Moses goes up the mountain to receive the law, part of which is the Ten Commandments (20:1-17).

The law of retaliation. At this point, Exodus suspends the narrative to introduce laws about social, economic, and religious life. Perhaps the most famous of these commands prescribes the

FIGURE 5.4 **ST. CATHERINE'S MONASTERY, MOUNT SINAI**

This is the Eastern Orthodox monastery at which Constantine von Tischendorf found Codex Sinaiticus, also known as Codex א [Aleph], the first letter of the Hebrew alphabet. Tischendorf called it Aleph rather than using the usual way that such manuscripts are designated because he was convinced it was the most important manuscript of the Bible ever discovered. He was correct that this fourth-century copy of the Bible is among the most important still in existence. Art Resource

proper response when someone harms another; it says one is to exact "life for life, eye for eye, tooth for tooth," and so on (21:23-25). This seems like an extremely harsh system to us, but the reaction of the original readers would have been very different. If we remember the absence of a centralized government and the extreme ways that people often responded to harm inflicted by people outside the clan on those within the clan, this was a drastic *limitation*. If someone caused a person in your group to lose an eye, your group might well try to inflict that same damage on many people related to the offender. This command limits that sort of clan (we might say mob) retaliation, so that the response is more proportional. Thus, while we hear this command as one that authorizes drastic violence, they saw it as very restrictive. Such commands functioned to limit violent responses, not to encourage them.

CHART 5.1

DIFFERENT LISTS OF THE TEN COMMANDMENTS

Based on long-standing traditions, the Catholic and Protestant and Jewish listings of the Ten Commandments differ. They contain the same commands, but number them differently. (These are adapted from various translations.)

Jewish Version	Catholic Version	Protestant Version
1. I am the LORD your God who brought you out of Egypt.	1. I am the Lord your God who brought you out of the land of Egypt. You shall have no other gods before me and shall not worship other gods.	1. You shall have no other gods before me.
2. You shall have no other gods before me.	2. You shall not take the name of the Lord in vain.	2. You shall not make any idols (graven images).
3. You shall not take the name of the LORD your GOD in vain.	3. Remember the Sabbath day, to keep it holy.	3. You shall not take the name of the LORD in vain.
4. Remember the Sabbath day, to keep it holy.	4. Honor your father and mother.	4. Remember the Sabbath day, to keep it holy.
5. Honor your father and mother.	5. You shall not kill.	5. Honor your father and mother.
6. You shall not murder.	6. You shall not commit adultery.	6. You shall not kill.
7. You shall not commit adultery.	7. You shall not steal.	7. You shall not commit adultery.
8. You shall not steal.	8. You shall not bear false witness.	8. You shall not steal.
9. You shall not bear false witness.	9. You shall not covet your neighbor's wife.	9. You shall not bear false witness.
10. You shall not covet.	10. You shall not covet your neighbor's house or goods.	10. You shall not covet.

The golden calf. After more than ten chapters of instructions and laws, Exodus returns to the narrative. We hear that Moses stays on the mountain for over a month, and the people have begun to think he is not coming back. After all, he is an eighty-year-old man who has been gone alone for forty days (24:18)! The people persuade Aaron to create an image of a god they are familiar with, so they have a god to worship and to credit with rescuing them from Egypt. Aaron has them bring their gold, which he molds into the image of a calf. When God notices what they are doing, God tells Moses he is going to destroy them all and make a nation

BOX 5.2

THE *LEX TALIONIS*

This is the Latin name of the command that restricts response to a wrong to exacting precisely what was done to the injured person. The command reads: "If any harm follows, then you shall give life for life, eye for eye, tooth for tooth, hand for hand, foot for foot, burn for burn, wound for wound, stripe for stripe" (Exod. 21:23-25). This command prohibits a response that goes beyond what an offense warrants or extending the retaliation to inflict punishment on the perpetrator's extended family or clan. Even so, we never see such commandments put into practice. Later rabbinic commentators would even say this command is impossible to practice.

from Moses, but Moses persuades God not to annihilate the people (32:1-14).

These conversations between God and Moses—and there are a number of them throughout the story—always appear for the benefit of the book's readers. They provide explicit commentary about why God deals with Israel as God does. In this story, the Israelites are ungrateful and falsely attribute their deliverance to another god. Why, then, does God remain in relationship with them? The answer appears, in part, in what Moses says in his dialogue with God. Moses first notes that if God destroys the people, the Egyptians will say that God brought them out to kill them. God does not want to be known as a God who acts in such ways, because that is not in accord with God's generous and loving nature; God is the God who rescues the powerless. God's reputation matters because God wants it to match God's true character. Moses also reminds God of the promises made to Abraham and the ancestors, so that God's faithfulness is also at stake. Since Moses makes a persuasive case, based on God's own character, God relents.

Punishment. When Moses descends the mountain and sees what the people are doing, however, he reacts drastically (32:15-35). He grinds the image of the calf into dust and puts it into the drinking water. In addition, he gathers to himself everyone willing to worship only God and reject the gods of Egypt, and then tells them to kill everyone who continues to worship the calf Aaron made. In addition to all of this, God sends a plague. God then sends the people away from Sinai because they are so unfit for God's presence to live among them. Eventually, and at Moses' pleading, God agrees to reveal God's will to the Israelites so they can learn to live as God's people.

The tabernacle. After they leave Mount Horeb, God meets Moses regularly in a specially designated tent outside the camp (33:6-11). God renews the covenant with Israel and gives more commandments about how they must live within the covenant. These instructions include directions about how to build the **tabernacle**, a portable worship structure, so that the people can worship God appropriately (35:4—39:43). The commandments in Exodus (and Leviticus) make Israel's manner of life distinctive, and interpret this distinctiveness as a sign of their relationship with God. Exodus ends with the presence of God descending to live among the

FIGURE 5.5 **OASIS AT KADESH BARNEA, SINAI PENINSULA**
This oasis is near the place where Moses sent spies into Canaan (Numbers 13:26). Art Resource

people. The signs of this presence are a pillar of cloud that rests over the tabernacle by day and a pillar of fire at night.

"You shall have no other gods." The episode with the golden calf at Sinai shows that the Israelites, like all people in the ancient world, believe in many gods. Israel commits itself to worshiping only one God, but they continue to believe that the other gods exist. Even the form of the commandment makes this clear: "You shall have no other gods before me" (20:3). This way of stating the command assumes that there are other gods. So while the people of Israel continue to believe that other gods exist, they promise not to worship them. This is a new commandment; before this, the Israelites had worshiped multiple gods. But at Sinai, and in the wake of the mighty acts of God that saved them from slavery, God demands singular allegiance. The Israelites' commitment to worship only God constitutes an important stipulation of the covenant God makes with them, and it becomes a key responsibility in their relationship with God.

Covenant and grace. Before leaving the story of the giving of the law and the establishment of the covenant, we need to identify clearly the covenant's foundation. Too often people characterize Judaism or the **Mosaic covenant** as legalistic, with God waiting eagerly to punish any misstep. This is a serious misunderstanding of Judaism and the covenant. Before God utters a single commandment to the people, the preamble to the Ten Commandments contains the words: "I am the LORD your God, who brought you out of the land of Egypt, out of the house of slavery" (20:2). This introduction asserts that the whole covenant is based on the gracious act of God that brought Israel to Mount Sinai; all relationship with God is based on God's grace and goodness. At Sinai the people accept the offer to enter the covenant, and thus become God's special people. So the people as a whole accept the identity given their ancestors. This covenant entails both blessings and responsibilities. Failure to meet those responsibilities results in punishment, but does not cause God to annul the covenant. God remains in covenant with Israel throughout all of the Bible. Even when there are drastic punishments, God enacts them within the scope of the covenant, not because the covenant has been revoked or because God has put the people out of it. As strange as it sounds, the punishments are part of being in the covenant. When people violate their agreement with God, the covenant stipulates that they are to receive punishment as a way to turn them back to proper behavior in their relationship with God. Deuteronomy will devote significant attention to this understanding of the covenant.

FIGURE 5.6 **BABYLONIAN CODE OF HAMMURABI**

There were other law codes in Israel's environment, most notably the Babylonian Code of Hammurabi. In this copy, the most extensive to survive, the king Hammurabi (left) receives the laws from the god Shamash (seated). This stele is on display at the Louvre Museum.

Wikimedia Commons

Leviticus: Ritual Purity and the Holiness Code

The Priests

The book of Leviticus interrupts the narrative of the Israelites' journey to Canaan. It is a manual of instruction that contains material passed down in oral form long before it was committed to writing. The first sixteen chapters of Leviticus deal with various sacrifices and the holiness and ritual purity that priests must possess to enter the tabernacle or temple. According to Numbers 25 (and this view is assumed throughout Leviticus), all priests must come from a particular family within the tribe of Levi (the descendants of one of Jacob's sons). The text assumes that priests are married and spend only part of their time at the sanctuary; they serve there on a rotating basis and have duties out among the people when they are not engaged with liturgical duties at the sanctuary.

Ritual Purity

After these instructions, chapters 17–26 address all the people of Israel. Leviticus views **ritual purity** as a requirement for everyone who wants to enter the presence of God. Many ancient peoples concerned themselves about ritual purity, that is, being properly prepared to approach a god or holy space. Various acts could make a person ritually impure, including giving birth and sexual relations. Ritual purity often concerns giving or taking life, acts that many believed infringed on the prerogatives of the gods, who alone had the right to give or take life. Since humans take these things upon themselves constantly, they are ill prepared to come before gods because they have done things that are only appropriate for gods to do. Therefore, human beings must prepare themselves before they can approach the gods. Whether it was because of this concern or some other, ancient people universally thought that people needed ritual preparation to enter the focused presence of a god. Leviticus has already given direction about how priests must live and prepare to enter that presence and lead worship; now it instructs others on how they must prepare to come into God's presence at worship.

BOX 5.3

Read Leviticus 18:2-5 and 19:1-2, where God requires that Israel be "holy." Note the contrasts made with other peoples. Remembering that "holy" means both a moral characteristic and being separate, how do you think these commands led its readers to live in relation to non-Israelites?

We must not equate ritual impurity with sinfulness. In fact, a person might become unclean by following one of God's commandments. For example, one of the ways people showed proper respect for their parents (as the Ten Commandments required) was to give them a proper burial, but being in the room with a corpse rendered a person unclean (Numbers 19:11). So by doing the right thing the person became unclean and so unable to enter the immediate presence of God at the temple. Or consider the command to "be fruitful and multiply." Israelites saw children as a great blessing, yet both the act that leads to their production and the act of giving them birth render the people involved unclean. So we must draw a clear distinction between "unclean" and "sinful." Of course, sins can also make a person unclean, but this should not lead us to equate sin and uncleanness.

FIGURE 5.7 **TABERNACLE**

An artist's conception of the Tabernacle. Wikimedia Commons

The Holiness Code

Scholars often call Leviticus 17–26 the **Holiness Code** because these chapters give instructions for all Israelites on how to live a holy life, particularly a life that is distinct from the nations around them. Holiness has at least two aspects in Leviticus: it refers to living a moral life and to being distinctive or different. Indeed, God's holiness includes both of these facets because God is morally holy and God is unlike all other things or beings. The commands in Leviticus 17–26 call God's people to be different from those around them, just as God is different from all other gods. Furthermore, the people must imitate God's moral character in their lives, a point the book makes explicitly in several places, where it says that God's people must be holy because God is holy (e.g., 19:2; 20:7, 26; 21:6, 8). The writer makes the same connection with the character of God when he gives a command and then says, "I am the LORD your God" (e.g., 18:4, 30; 19:3, 4, 10, 25, 31, 24; 20:7). The whole of chapters 17–26, then, delineates how the people should reflect God's holiness by living lives that are distinct from their neighbors. Furthermore, God's holiness provides the best pattern for human life because, as Genesis has already told us, God created humans in God's own image. So to reflect who God is also reflects who we truly are.

Marriage laws. Within the Holiness Code, chapters 18–20 constitute a separate section with its own introduction and conclusion. This section sets out instructions about social morality and identifies marriage as the cornerstone of a good society. The code's introduction states explicitly that these instructions intend to make Israelites very different from the peoples around them: it says the Israelites must not live as people do in Egypt or in Canaan; rather they must follow the directives in this book for forming their society and living their lives. The first group of commands rejects Egyptian (and Canaanite) practices of marrying close relatives. (The pharaohs often married their sisters.) In response to such practices, Leviticus sets firm limits about how close a relative a person could marry, excluding all members of the nuclear family, as well as aunts and uncles.

BOX 5.4

THE INTERMARRIAGE OF THE ANCESTORS

While some of the ancestors of Israel violated the standards given in Leviticus about who a person could marry, we should remember that they were not yet subject to the regulations of the Mosaic covenant. While some later Jewish interpreters found some of the behavior of some of their ancestors troubling, on matters such as this they did not think the ancestors had sinned because the law had not yet been given.

Sex. Instructions that specifically counter Canaanite practices begin in 18:19. This section contains Leviticus's instructions about homoerotic relations. Male with male relations are prohibited just after the Israelites are forbidden to sacrifice their children to Molech. We do not know much about Molech worship, but it likely involved child sacrifice (a known practice in that region in ancient times, particularly common in Carthage until as late as the first century B.C.E.). The most probable reason for prohibiting homoeroticism is that the writers see it as a Canaanite practice: Israelites must not engage in homoeroticism because that is what Canaanites and other foreigners do. This is one of the ways Israelites must be different from the nations around them, a point the verses immediately following make explicitly and at length. Leviticus prohibits these particular sexual practices because the peoples that surround Israel engage in them. Therefore, one of the ways Israelites must be distinct appears in the form of their marriages and their sexual practices. These differences purposefully make it difficult for Israelites to mingle with non-Israelites. Later Jewish discussions of homoeroticism indicate that a basic problem with such relations was that they are characteristic of non-Israelites, that is, they see homoerotic relations as a distinctly Gentile phenomenon, and so Jews should reject it.

Other laws. After these commands about sexual relations, the same section of Leviticus gives instructions about how to worship, harvest fields, breed animals, deal with one another fairly, and about what foods are acceptable. In all these areas Israel must be different from the nations around them. The prohibition about homoerotic relations is one of the commands designed to make Israelites different from their neighbors. Eating unclean food is an abomination (20:23-26), just as prohibited sexual relations are. The prescribed consequences for violating various regulations range from death to ostracizing the perpetrator(s). If the people as a whole fail to keep the commands, their behavior will require God to reprimand them so they will live as they should.

The Function of the Laws

When thinking about these commandments concerning how to live and construct a society, we usually do not emphasize enough their function of setting Israel apart from those around them. These directives intend to make Israel so distinct that the differences will keep them separate from other peoples. Israel's most difficult task, perhaps, was becoming a people who worshiped only God. Nearly everyone in their cultural setting thought that idea was crazy. Gods had particular functions and regions. There was a god for shepherds and another for farmers. There was a god of the hills, one of the valleys, one of storms, one of war, one of fertility, and so on. Gods were everywhere, and success in any endeavor required currying the favor of the proper gods. To suggest that a person should worship only one god was nearly unthinkable for most people of that day, but this was what God commanded Israel to do. The stories in Judges, 1 and 2 Samuel, and 1 and 2 Kings show that Israel did not become a people that worshiped only God before the exile (sixth century B.C.E.); they always worshiped and sought the help of other gods.

A people set apart. When its writers and editors completed the final draft of the Pentateuch in the exile (or soon afterward), the cultural situation remained the same: everyone worshiped multiple gods. In this cultural environment, these biblical writers were trying to create a society in which it was possible to worship only God. The only way to do that, they thought, was to isolate Israel by demanding practices that would make them so distinctive, indeed so odd, that they would have to be separate from the peoples around them. This was the only way they saw to turn Israel in the direction of worshiping only God. This is a primary reason for the food regulations, the rules about marriage and society, ritual practices, and many other commands in Leviticus and throughout the Pentateuch.

No medical explanations account for these practices (as has sometimes been said); rather, the goal is to isolate Israel from the practices of their neighbors. The authors of these books believe that the only way Israelites will begin to worship only God is to separate themselves from their neighbors. So these instructions have a sociological function that has a theological goal.

Leviticus also pays a great deal of attention to Israel's worship, especially the proper way to offer various sacrifices. People today sometimes understand these sacrifices as offerings given to establish a relationship with God. Particularly, we think Israel needed to offer sacrifices because committing a sin put a person out of the covenant, or out of relationship with God.

But this way of thinking misconstrues the basic meaning of sacrifices. First, only a few of the different kinds of Israel's sacrifices served to atone for sin. Many others were ways to offer thanks and praise to God for the blessings of crops or children or any other blessing. Even sacrifices offered to atone for sin were not offered because God had cut off relations with the one who sinned; rather, Israel offered sacrifices within the structure of the covenant. The covenant, as we saw in Exodus, was established through the gracious acts of God: God had already brought the Israelites out of Egypt, and had already offered to be in relationship with them. Indeed, God had promised Abraham and the ancestors that God would have a special relationship with their descendants. When Israelites sinned, God did not eject them from the covenant. Instead, sacrifices for sin were the covenant's provisions for these expected failures. Sacrifices help maintain the covenant by rendering what was expected after a failure to live by its laws, but they never functioned to establish the covenant or to bring anyone into it. Sacrifices were not an attempt to get on God's good side; Israelites assumed they were God's chosen people. So the sacrifices simply constitute part of the people's share in maintaining their covenant with God. The entire book of

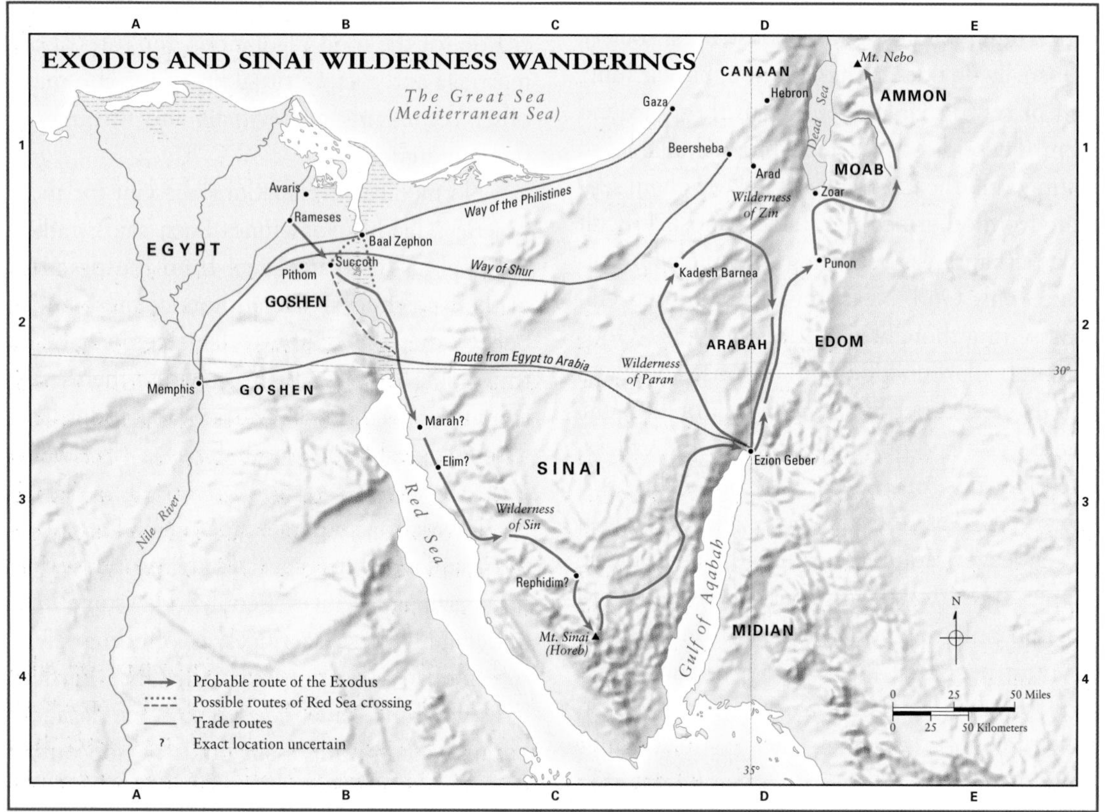

MAP 5.1

Leviticus is really about maintaining this relationship with God.

Conclusion

The most basic message of the many and detailed commandments in Leviticus is that God's people must reflect who God is by being holy, that is, by adopting the prescribed practices that make them morally and culturally distinct. They adopt this life of holiness because God is holy. Leviticus 11:44, a passage quoted in the New Testament as a reason to live the way God commands, summarizes the basic intent of the whole book: "Be holy, for I am holy."

▶ Numbers: In the Wilderness

Distinctive Contents

The book of Numbers is not as much about a census as its name makes it sound. Instead, it relates Israel's exploits during its wanderings in the wilderness between the escape from slavery and the beginning of the conquest of Canaan. In fact, the title of the book in Hebrew is "In the Wilderness." While Numbers contains more instruction about how to live and worship (particularly in the tabernacle, the mobile sanctuary), it also has many of the better-known stories about Israel's travels in the wilderness. What stands out about the people is how they constantly whine! They complain about nearly every aspect of their existence; even when God gives them what they need, they complain about the solution.

Interpretive narratives. These stories continue to be interpretive narratives, not what we today call history. The writers tell prototypical stories about their ancestors to show who God is, how God has been with them, and how they as a people regularly responded to God. These stories of their ancestors' recalcitrance demonstrate God's graciousness and show just how long God has been patient with "us." Such stories explain how the nation of God's people could fall and, at the same time, exhort readers to be faithful.

FIGURE 5.8 **JOSHUA AND CALEB**

Joshua and Caleb return from spying out Canaan; painting by James Tissot. Wikimedia Commons

Reconnoitering Canaan. Numbers begins with detailed instructions about ritual life, worship, and other matters (including a census), but then shifts to recounting stories of the wilderness wandering. From the beginning of this journey, it tells of the people complaining because they are tired of the manna God sends them every morning for food (11:4-9). In response, God sends quail to satisfy them, but also a plague to punish them. When they get to the border of Canaan, Moses sends in twelve spies to do reconnaissance (Numbers 13). Ten of the twelve return saying that the cities are too well fortified and the peoples too strong for the Israelites to carve out a place to live. The people believe the ten rather than **Joshua and Caleb** (the other two spies), and so refuse to launch an invasion of the land—a decision that reflects a lack of faith in God's power to bring them victory. As a compromise that rejects worse punishments, God sentences the people to wander in the desert for forty years, that is, until all the people who were adults when they left Egypt die. The only exceptions are Joshua and Caleb, the two spies who said the Israelites could take the land. When the people hear this fate, they mount an invasion that does not have God's blessing and are soundly rebuffed (Numbers 14).

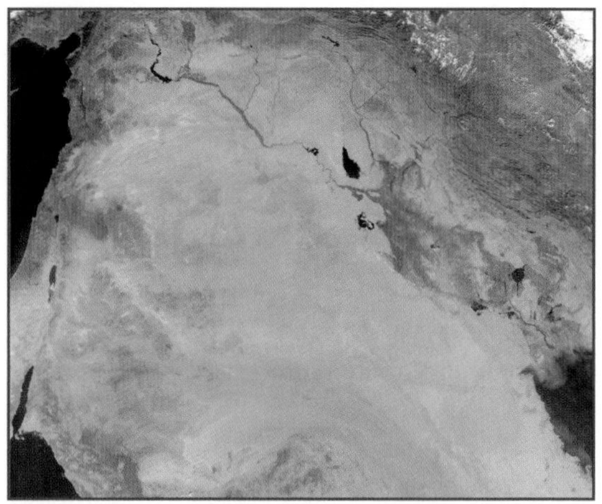

FIGURE 5.9 **THE FERTILE CRESCENT**
The Fertile Crescent is the area of fertile land that extends from the Persian Gulf to the Nile valley and lies between the Arabian desert and the mountains of Armenia. The Tigris and Euphrates rivers flow through this region and the empires of the Assyrians and Babylonians arose in this region. The Egyptian empire also developed on its rim. NASA

Conversations with God. The story of Israel refusing to invade Canaan is one of the many places that Numbers inserts conversations between God and Moses in which God is ready to destroy the people but Moses talks God out of it. As we saw before, these conversations are for the benefit of the readers. They remind the readers of why God has been patient: God acts graciously and exercises patience with the people because such goodness is the behavior that is consistent with God's character. It is only because of God's grace that God remains in relationship with God's people. Although they are unfaithful, God continues to bless them and remain with them because God is gracious and forgiving. Again, this helps readers in and after the exile interpret their situation; they are no longer an independent nation because they as a people have continually been unfaithful. Therefore, the exile and subordination to other nations is what they should expect. In this interpretive paradigm, these hardships do not indicate that God has forsaken them, only that they are receiving just punishment for their violations of the covenant. They can, then, remain hopeful that God will reverse their fortunes if they become and remain faithful.

Korah's rebellion. Numbers includes many engaging, and some disturbing, stories. One episode recounts the attempt of a group following a man named Korah to have their families included among the priests (Numbers 16–17). God rejects their request, affirming the selection of Aaron's family by causing his walking stick to produce buds and by having the earth split open and consume the leaders of the opposition movement. Perhaps this story seeks to remind readers of the holiness of God by showing how important it was to approach God in the ways God commands. While confirming the authority of Moses in selecting who the priests of Israel should be, the story suggests that honoring God's will as it is known through Moses must play a part in the way one approaches God in worship.

Water in the wilderness. In another story, the people again complain about water. God tells Moses to command a rock to give water and a fountain would spring from it (Numbers 20). But in his anger at the people's murmuring Moses hits the rock with his walking stick rather than speaking to it. God brings forth the water, but Moses' failure to follow God's specific instruction results in God barring him from Canaan; God permits him only to glimpse it from afar.

Scholars remain uncertain about why Numbers invests this strange, and seemingly minor, episode with such significance. Among the various interpretations offered, some think Moses' sin was disobedience, while others think Moses was taking credit for what God was doing. However we understand Moses' actions or God's reaction, having Moses die before the people enter Canaan prepares the way for a new era in Israel's story—Moses' death means they must have a new leader.

Balak and Balaam. One of the most entertaining stories of Numbers has non-Israelites for its main characters. When Balak, king of Moab, sees the huge company of Israel near his border, he gets worried and sends for **Balaam**, a person known to be in touch with gods (perhaps a priest), to curse the Israelites (Numbers 22–24). After Balak's servants relay the request to Balaam, the God of Israel speaks to him in a dream, telling him not to go with them. Later, in another dream, God instructs him to go, but only to do what God tells him. As Balaam goes, the donkey he is riding keeps veering off the road, even running him into a wall, and finally just lying down. Exasperated, Balaam beats the donkey; now God gives the beast the power to speak. It tells Balaam that he has saved his life because an angel with a sword was poised to kill him each time he ran off the road. God then lets Balaam see the angel, so he will be certain to do as God commands. When he gets to King Balak, Balaam warns Balak that he can only do what God commands. Balaam goes out to curse Israel, as Balak had brought him to do, but only blessings on Israel come out of his mouth. After this happens four times, Balaam goes home without cursing Israel.

This story makes a number of important points. First, it reinforces God's commitment to Israel. We are near the end of Numbers, a book that tells of how the people have been whiny, ungrateful, and unfaithful throughout, and yet God will not allow them to be cursed. Second, it is notable that God speaks with the non-Israelite Balaam. Even though Balaam is a person who worships other gods and has a reputation for being influential with them—that is the only reason King Balak would have sent for him—he also knows and communicates with the God of Israel. So God's presence and word are known beyond the borders of Israel.

FIGURE 5.10 **MOSES AND THE ROCK**

Moses strikes the rock to bring forth water in this fresco from a Christian catacomb near Rome.
Wikimedia Commons

Phinehas and violence. The next major episode in Numbers is a story of unfaithfulness (Numbers 25). Israelites marry non-Israelites and, of course, the non-Israelites bring their gods with them. Predictably, these marriages lead Israelites to worship the gods their spouses worship. In response, Moses orders the execution of everyone in the camp who worships Baal, a god the Israelites will worship for the next five hundred years. When one couple comes to beg for mercy, a priest named **Phinehas** rushes forward and kills them. This radical act stops a plague that had killed twenty-four thousand people.

Some have taken the act of Phinehas as a pattern for the way they should live their faith, arguing that the faithful should use violence to enforce their beliefs. But in our time of weapons of mass destruction and different understandings of the ways societies function, this is not an appropriate model to imitate directly when discerning how to live for God.

This story does, however, exemplify an important lesson for Jews and Christians; it demonstrates the importance of faithfulness to God. This story teaches that nothing is as important as faithfulness, not even one's own life or that of others. While Jews and Christians see such depth of commitment to God as a proper perspective from which to live their lives, each generation must undertake the task of determining how to embody that commitment in ways that honor God in their time and setting. Killing those of other faiths is not one of those ways today.

Cities of refuge. As it began, Numbers concludes with instructions about how to live. It includes directions about how to organize life in Canaan, including the beginnings of a justice system. It calls for the establishment of **cities of refuge**, places to which those who commit a homicide may go to receive a fair trial, rather than simply be killed in retaliation (Numbers 35). Numbers also recounts Moses' appointment of Joshua, one of those faithful spies from the early part of the book, to lead the people into Canaan to secure a homeland (27:12-23).

Conclusion

The stories in Numbers constantly describe the Israelites as unfaithful and ungrateful to God. As noted above, this kind of account of their ancestors helps those who are turning to God explain the fall of their nation and their own exile. The stories as a whole suggest that the Israelites failed to live according to the covenant from the beginning. Thus their national disgrace is what they should expect. Christians cannot read these stories as an indictment against Jews. Rather, as Paul sees things in the New Testament, Christians have been brought into the heritage of God's people, Israel. These wanderers, then, become the ancestors of Christians as well as of Jews. These stories tell Christians and Jews alike what their spiritual ancestors were like and, most likely, what they are like as well. They provide comfort as believers see how patient God is, and they warn against unfaithfulness as they see what it warrants.

▶ Deuteronomy: Restating the Law

The Form of the Book

The book of Deuteronomy consists of Moses' farewell speeches to the Israelites. Knowing that his death is imminent and that the people are about to enter the promised land, Moses tells them how they must live. The name of the book means "second law." The book uses the farewell addresses to restate the law, with narratives added to illustrate its points. Moses retells brief versions of many stories found in other books of the Torah and regives the Ten Commandments, along with other commands found throughout the preceding four books. So Deuteronomy recapitulates much of the instruction already given about how to live, while supplying illustrative commentary.

The book does not contain actual speeches given by Moses, and Moses did not write the book. Not only does it open by talking about Moses in the third person ("he," rather than "I"), it also ends with an account of his burial. Obviously, Moses was not around to write that section. As with the other books of the Pentateuch, Deuteronomy was written hundreds of years after the death of Moses. Deuteronomy probably contains some early traditions, and an early version of it may well have been the basis for the reforms King Josiah enacted in the seventh century.

BOX 5.5

THINKING FURTHER: A "PROPHET LIKE MOSES"

Read Deuteronomy 34:10-12 and Acts 3:17-26. This segment of Acts has Peter and John identify Jesus as the "prophet like Moses." When the author of Acts identifies Jesus in this way, what does he want readers to understand about Jesus and the connection of the church to the historic faith of Judaism?

The Deuteronomistic History

Deuteronomy's restatement of the law sets the pattern for the interpretation of Israel's history that appears in the books that follow. In fact, the books that come after Deuteronomy in the Hebrew Bible (Joshua, Judges, 1–2 Samuel, 1–2 Kings) are called the **Deuteronomistic History** because they narrate stories of Israel's life according to the pattern Deuteronomy sets out. The speeches in Deuteronomy assert that the covenant requires certain behavior from the people, and if they adhere to those requirements, God will bless them. However, if they do not fulfill the conditions of the covenant (primarily by keeping the law), God will punish them. Through both obedience and disobedience, the people remain in the covenant with God. Indeed, the punishments form part of the covenant's stipulations, functioning somewhat like the penalty clauses built into some contracts. If a contractor fails to complete the work in the time allotted or in the way specified, contracts often contain penalties the contractor must pay. So here, if the people fail to comply with their part of the covenant, the covenant has built-in penalties, just as it has prescribed ways to make amends. Thus even the punishments are evidence that God continues to be in relationship with Israel.

A good summary of this pattern appears in 11:26-28: "See, I am setting before you today a blessing and a curse: the blessing, if you obey the commandments of the LORD your God that I am commanding you today; and the curse, if you do not obey the commandments of the LORD your God."

Law as Response to Grace

These words about obedience do not indicate that the relationship between God and Israel was legalistic. The authors of these texts always see God's grace as the basis for the covenant's establishment and as the reason it remains in place. God had demonstrated that grace in the exodus and in caring for the people in the desert; now God is about to exercise it again by giving them the land. But the people must actively participate in their relationship with God. They must behave as people who have a relationship with a God who is holy. Therefore, keeping the law is their response to the acts of God's grace. When the people fail to live with and respond to God appropriately, God provides means for them to make amends—and all of this is for the people's own good.

When we think of keeping the Torah, the Law, we often think of it as a terrible burden, because we have misunderstood its function and its place in God's relationship with Israel. The Torah did not function as a way Israel could earn a relationship with God; rather, God acted with grace to claim Israel as God's own.

FIGURE 5.11 **MOSES VIEWING THE PROMISED LAND**
Painting by Frederic Edwin Church (1826–1900). Wikimedia Commons

The people, then, respond in gratitude by committing themselves to keeping the Law.

The Shema. Deuteronomy also contains the Shema, the single-sentence summary of Israel's faith that many Jews still repeat today. Moses says the people should recite this affirmation daily and teach it to their children. They are to post it where they will see it constantly and keep it continually on their hearts: "Hear, O Israel:

BOX 5.6

RECITING THE TORAH

Read Deuteronomy 6:4-9. Notice the place that this passage gives the Law in a person's life. Why do you think Deuteronomy gives that place to the Law?

FIGURE 5.12 **SHEMA**

Shema—the single word, in Hebrew, is painted above the entrance to the New Synagogue in Třebíč (in the Czech Republic); built in 1707.
Wikimedia Commons

The Lord is our God, the Lord alone" (6:4). This foundational confession, with its implicit command to worship only God, precedes the command to love God with all of one's being and thus keep God's commandments.

▶ Conclusion

Deuteronomy closes the Pentateuch, recapitulating both the law and the stories of God's dealings with God's people from Abraham forward. The Pentateuch brings its readers from the claim that it is the God of Israel (not other gods) who created the world to the brink of the conquest of Canaan, the act that will fulfill the promise God made to Abraham so long ago. God has rescued the people from slavery in Egypt, entered into a covenant with them, and given them the law as a guide to their lives with God and with one another. Although God has continually had to work with flawed people (Abraham, Jacob, Joseph, even Moses, and others), God has refused to abandon them.

Yet the stories in these books—particularly those that tell of the wilderness wanderings—also demonstrate that God expects faithfulness. These books, then, offer encouragement because they show that God remains committed to those who have faults, while at the same time they exhort readers to be faithful, as they chronicle God's judgment on continual unfaithfulness.

▶ LET'S REVIEW ◀

In this chapter you learned more about the Pentateuch:

- Exodus
  - The rescue from slavery and care for the people in the desert
  - Mount Sinai
- Leviticus
  - Instructions for priests
  - the Holiness Code
  - Importance of distinctiveness from neighboring peoples
- Numbers
  - Tales of the unfaithfulness of the Israelites and God's continuing commitment to them
- Deuteronomy
  - Farewell addresses from Moses
  - Explicit statement of the Deuteronomistic pattern

▶ KEY TERMS ◀

Balaam
Cities of refuge
Deuteronomistic History
Exodus
Holiness Code
Joshua and Caleb
Mosaic covenant
Mount Sinai
Passover
Phinehas
Ritual purity
Shema
Tabernacle
Ten Commandments

▶ QUESTIONS FOR REVIEW ◀

5.1 Why might the "eye for an eye" command be seen as an advance in justice?
5.2 What is the narrative function of the conversations between God and Moses?
5.3 Why was the golden calf story included in the narrative of Exodus?
5.4 What do the punishments God brings on Israel say about the covenant relationship between God and Israel?
5.5 What do commands in Leviticus imply about coming into the presence of God?
5.6 Why do the books of the Torah give commands that make Israelites so different from those around them?
5.7 How does Deuteronomy say that the fortunes of the nation of Israel are tied to obedience to the law?
5.8 How could the people view the Law as a gift from God?

▶ FOR FURTHER READING ◀

Joseph Blenkinsopp, *The Pentateuch: An Introduction to the First Five Books of the Bible*. New York: Doubleday, 1992.

Joseph Blenkinsopp, *Treasures Old and New: Essays in the Theology of the Pentateuch*. Grand Rapids: Eerdmans, 2004.

Althalya Brenner, ed., *Exodus to Deuteronomy*, Feminist Companion to the Bible 2/5. Sheffield: Sheffield Academic, 2000.

John J. Collins, *A Short Introduction to the Hebrew Bible*. Minneapolis: Fortress Press, 2007, 55–93.

Terence E. Fretheim, *The Pentateuch,* Interpreting Biblical Texts. Nashville: Abingdon, 1996.

Frank H. Gorman, "Leviticus, Book of," in *New Interpreter's Dictionary of the Bible*, ed. Katharine D. Sakenfeld, 3:645–51. Nashville: Abingdon, 2007.

William Johnstone, "Exodus, Book of," in *New Interpreter's Dictionary of the Bible*, ed. Katharine D. Sakenfeld, 2:371–80. Nashville: Abingdon, 2007.

Baruch A. Levine, "Numbers, Book of," in *New Interpreter's Dictionary of the Bible*, ed. Katharine D. Sakenfeld, 4:283–94. Nashville: Abingdon, 2007.

S. Dean McBride, "Deuteronomy, Book of," in *New Interpreter's Dictionary of the Bible*, ed. Katharine D. Sakenfeld, 2:108–17. Nashville: Abingdon, 2007.

John McDermott, "Historical Issues in the Pentateuch," Bible and Interpretation Website: http://www.bibleinterp.com/articles/Pentateuch.shtml

Marvin A. Sweeney, *TANAK: A Theology and Critical Introduction to the Jewish Bible*. Minneapolis: Fortress Press, 2011.

6 The Israelites Tell Their Story
Interpretations of National Disasters

THIS CHAPTER DISCUSSES THE DEUTERONOMISTIC AND CHRONICLER'S HISTORIES, RUTH, AND JUDAH'S RETURN FROM EXILE:

- Joshua and the conquest
- Judges and non-Israelite inhabitants of Canaan
- Ruth
- 1 and 2 Samuel: stories of the first two kings, Saul and David
- 1 and 2 Kings: the remaining kings of the Israelites
- 1 and 2 Chronicles: same stories as 1 and 2 Kings, but a different perspective
- Ezra and Nehemiah: returning from exile

The books called the Deuteronomistic History tell Israel's story from the conquest of Canaan through their monarchies and finally through the fall of the Israelite kingdoms. These books—Joshua, Judges, 1 and 2 Samuel, 1 and 2 Kings—are called the Deuteronomistic History because they tell the story of the national life of Israel in a way that illustrates what Deuteronomy says about the consequences of being faithful or unfaithful to God. Just as we saw with the narratives in the Pentateuch, these books are not as interested in relating facts about what happened in the past as they are about interpreting the life of the people and the nation(s) in a way that shows who God is and why the Israelites as a people could end up in the national predicament in which they find themselves during the exile.

▶ The Scope and Purpose of the Deuteronomistic History

The version of these narratives that appears in our Bibles took shape in the time of the exile. These books try to explain the great national disaster that has befallen God's people in the sixth century B.C.E.; the overwhelming disaster is that there is no Israelite nation and that they are in exile. The people of Judah have been defeated by the Babylonians and forced to live outside their homeland. How can they believe in the God of Abraham, who promised them a land and swore to be in covenant with them, when they are in exile? Has God been unfaithful? What has happened to the promises of God? What has happened to God's covenant with them? Is God the God the prophets have preached or much smaller and weaker? How could the Babylonians defeat them if God is on Israel's side?

These narratives of the people's lives and their interaction with God offer an explanation for the current devastation and, in answering these questions, offer a word of hope to the exiles. The book of Deuteronomy asserts that if the people are unfaithful, God will give them over to their enemies; if they turn to God, however, God will rescue them. This is how the covenant works; these are the stipulations of the relationship Israel has with God. The people remain in covenant with God as long as they respond with repentance. If they persist in unfaithfulness forever, they can put themselves out of the covenant. Indeed, the story these books tell will recount how a large segment of the people do just that. But those now in exile can read these stories and know that God can respond to their cries for help and their repentance by acting mightily on their behalf.

These stories tie together the cult (that is, proper worship), military conquest, and the presence of God and God's word in the prophets. They recount the beginnings of Israel's ideas about prophets in the leadership of Joshua and the "judges." God's will and word are made known to these figures and God works through them to accomplish God's will. These books emphasize God's faithfulness to the covenant, and so God's grace and trustworthiness.

▶ Joshua: The Invasion

The book of Joshua tells of the Israelites' conquest of the land of Canaan. While questions about the historical accuracy of the stories found in this book abound, the narratives themselves are concerned about making theological points. Among those points is that the Israelites' possession of the land fulfills promises made to Abraham. By the end of the book, Abraham's descendants possess the land that God promised. Thus the book as a whole demonstrates God's faithfulness to God's promises. God does not abandon the people, even though they have been unfaithful, because God always keeps God's promises. This message is particularly important when heard by people who have lost the land and are questioning God's trustworthiness.

Preparing for Conquest

The book of Joshua begins with Israel's preparation to invade the lands on the western side of the Jordan River. In chapter 5 Joshua must tell the people that the men are to be circumcised

FIGURE 6.1 **MERNEPTAH STELE**
The earliest mention of "Israel" outside of the Bible comes from an engraved pillar (or stele) set up by the Egyptian pharaoh Merneptah in which he claims to have plundered Canaan and "laid waste" the people Israel and "destroyed" their offspring. Wikimedia Commons

and all are to celebrate the Passover. These are two signal elements of keeping the covenant. Circumcision is the sign of the covenant that Genesis says God gave to Abraham and to his descendants. The book of Joshua says that during Israel's time in the wilderness (forty years), no one had been circumcised. Joshua interprets circumcision in this context as an act that cleanses the people of their previous experiences. It is the moment when the disgrace of slavery in Egypt is removed from them (5:9).

We also hear that no one had observed the Passover during the wandering in the wilderness. This comment gives us some hint about the ways the biblical narratives idealize their ancestors and read practices of the times of the authors back into earlier days. In the story of the exodus, Moses commands the people to keep the Passover feast every year, and the book seems to assume they did. After all, since the one who gave the command, Moses, was the people's leader, we would assume that he along with the people kept that command. But Joshua tells us that the wilderness ancestors did not keep the Passover, that celebration of the mighty act of deliverance from Egypt. Renewing its celebration at the beginning of the conquest reminds both the readers and the characters in the narrative of God's earlier powerful acts on Israel's behalf. Thus it prepares us for the acts of God to come.

Jericho

Just as the abortive effort at an invasion of Canaan in Exodus started with an expedition of spies, so now Joshua sends in spies. The first city they investigate is Jericho (Joshua 2). Its leaders have seen the hordes across the river and are on the lookout. Once the leaders of Jericho think spies have been sent in, they start a search for them. The Israelite spies ask a prostitute named Rahab to hide them. She obliges them, but makes them promise to spare her and her family when they take the city.

Part of this story's point is that God is about to give this land to the Israelites, and

FIGURE 6.2 **A WALL OF ANCIENT JERICHO**

Archaeologists have unearthed the walls of ancient Jericho seen here. Their height and width possessed a significant challenge to any enemies, though it may have been constructed originally as a retaining wall. Jerry Sumney

even Rahab can see it. At the same time, this narrative also shows that those who cooperate with God's plan can be taken into the people of God. So the destruction that comes upon the inhabitants of the land is not motivated by ethnic purity considerations.

Joshua employs an unusual military strategy for conquering Jericho (Joshua 6). He has seven priests carrying the ark of the covenant lead the army in marching around the city once a day for six days. On the seventh day, after they all march around the city seven times, the priests blow their horns, and the walls of the city miraculously fall. This story vividly demonstrates that God is giving Israel the land; they do not possess it because they are stronger or have a better army, but because God gives it to them to fulfill the promises made to the ancestors.

Achan and the spoils of battle. Since the battle is won entirely by God, all the spoils of this first victory are to be God's alone. But one soldier, Achan, cannot resist taking a few things

(Joshua 7). No one finds him out until Israel squares off against the next city. This time, they attack in the more traditional way, but there is an enormous change of fortunes. Rather than having the walls crumble before them with no effort, the enemy defeats them in battle. When Joshua asks God why they lost, God tells him that someone violated the ban against taking spoils from Jericho. When the guilty person is found, Joshua executes him and his family. Only after this act can Israel move ahead with the conquest.

This episode demonstrates at least two things. First, it shows that these texts work with ideas of corporate guilt. When a family member does something, it implicates the whole family. So it is not just Achan, but also his wife and children, who suffer. Second, it clearly establishes the link between the necessity of obedience to God and national success. If Israel hopes to survive as a nation, it must obey God's statutes. These connections between military and national success, on the one hand, and the faithfulness of God, on the other, are dangerous, as today's terrorist attacks in the name of God demonstrate. But they are part of the fabric of all the writings within this section of the Bible. Still, for believers they convey the message that faithfulness to God is linked to communal well-being.

Slaughter

The book of Joshua moves from these initial stories into a series of accounts of the ways Israel defeated various cities of Canaan and often engaged in wholesale killing of the inhabitants, and even of their livestock. Israel must be separate from the peoples around them! We will discover at the beginning of the next book (Judges) that there was less killing of the prior inhabitants than Joshua suggests. Still, this book envisions mass killing as the will of God at that moment in time. This killing is seen as good not because it keeps Israel ethnically pure, but because the writers of these stories think that the only way the people will be faithful to God and avoid the harmful behavior associated with worshiping other gods is if the temptation to worship other gods is removed. As they see it, that can be accomplished only by ridding the land of the people who worship those other gods.

We must remember that these writers are in exile. They believe they are there because they have been unfaithful to God. Given that nearly everyone in the world worships multiple gods, they think the sole way they as a people will worship only God is if they are separate from those who worship other gods. As they look at their past, the only means they can imagine to achieve this separation includes the extermination of the people who worship those other gods.

The basic point these writers want to make is that nothing is as important as faithfulness to God. Their way of illustrating this point, however, seems to violate what we know about God from the larger story the Bible tells. It is hard for readers today to understand how those ancients could have envisioned killing so many people as an expression of God's will. On the one hand, however, we should remember that believers in God in the twentieth and twenty-first centuries have often claimed that God's will involves killing thousands. Whether we think of death camps, the armies fighting to defeat Hitler, or those who fly planes into buildings, some people

FIGURE 6.3 **REGION OF JERICHO TODAY**

The natural water supply helps make this a fertile region still today. Jerry Sumney

have thought, at one time or another, that killing others was doing God's will. On the other hand, we are correct to reject the notion that the extermination of populations is an acceptable means of expressing faithfulness. Believers must examine both the fullness of biblical resources and their own environment to find those better ways to emphasize faithfulness to God.

The Distribution of Land

As the book of Joshua draws to a close, the writer envisions the Israelites possessing most of Canaan, and the book devotes considerable attention to distributing the land among the twelve tribes (Joshua 15–22). Ten of these clans settle on the west side of the Jordan and two on the east. The book provides such detail about these arrangements because its authors are in Babylon, looking toward the time when they return to settle the land and distribute it among those who go back. In addition, it claims all that land for its people (even if ten of the twelve tribes have already been lost for nearly two hundred years). As they distribute the land, they reserve some areas as "cities of refuge," those places people may go when they have killed someone accidentally (Joshua 20). In most cases, since there was no strong national government, families or clans sought their own justice by killing the person who caused the death of their kin.

These cities enable an advance in the administration of justice because a judge determines whether the death is murder or an accident. If it is an accident, the killer can remain in the city under its protection. If it is murder, the person is released to the clan of the person killed. Again, while this may seem cruel, it institutes a new layer of protection for the accused and makes a significant stride toward a more humane justice system.

Covenant Renewal

In the final scenes of the book Joshua calls the people together to renew their covenant with God (Joshua 23–24). He recounts all God has done for them and then gives them the choice to serve God or the gods of the peoples around them. Having given them this choice, he utters his well-known commitment: "but as for me and my household, we will serve the LORD." The people follow Joshua and renew their commitment to God. The book then ends with the death of Joshua.

Conclusion

This book not only has exciting stories of warfare and conquest, it also tells of mass exterminations of the indigenous populations. Even more disturbing to many today, it interprets these gruesome acts as following God's commands. Still, through these troubling stories, the writers of Joshua try to make some important theological points. First, they dramatize the dependence of God's people upon God for all blessings. It is God, not the Israelites themselves, who establishes a homeland for the people. God does this as an expression of God's faithfulness to Israel's ancestors and to the covenant with the Israelites. These stories also highlight the importance of obedience to God—the running theme of this whole section of the Bible.

▶ Judges: The Quest for Continuing Dominance

Context, Scope, and Recurring Pattern

The book of Judges tells Israel's story from the death of Joshua to within a few decades of the establishment of a monarchy. This book relates stories about the way the Israelites continue to fight the earlier inhabitants of Canaan for dominance in the region. The Israelites had no national government in this period, but in times of crisis leaders emerged who brought the tribes together to fight off common enemies. We know these leaders as "**judges**."

The book contains the stories of twelve judges, the same number as the traditional number of the tribes of Israel. These judges are charismatic leaders who gain their authority through their contact with the Spirit of God. Some ecstatic experience probably served as the evidence of this communication and authorization from God. These early leaders led the people to war under the banner of the LORD. This connection between God and success in war continued throughout ancient Israel's history.

According to the opening chapter of Judges, the problems with their neighbors arose because the Israelites had failed to exterminate them during the conquest. Rather, they lived among these earlier inhabitants and so came

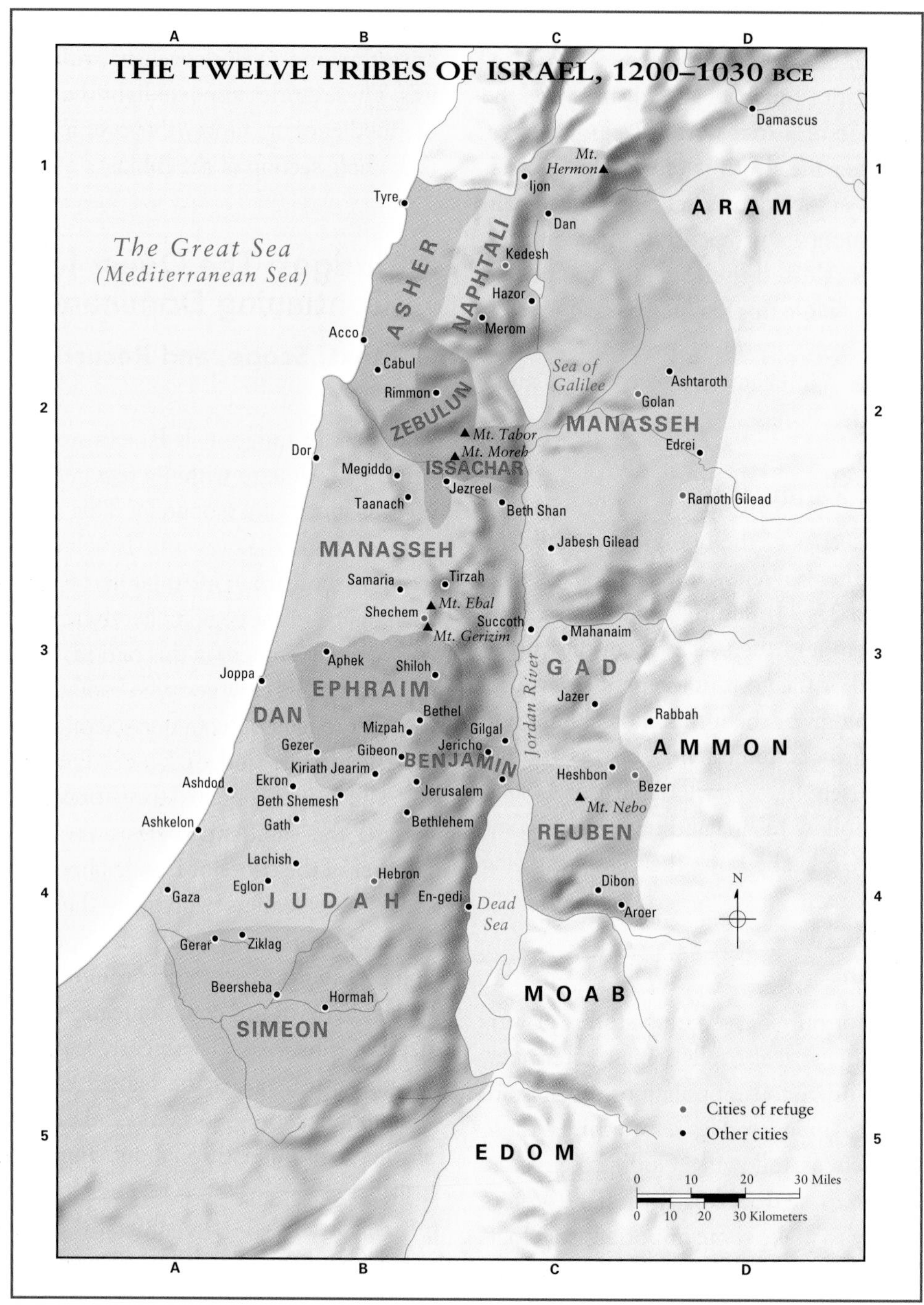
THE TWELVE TRIBES OF ISRAEL, 1200–1030 BCE
A
B
C
D
1
2
3
4
5
Damascus
Mt. Hermon
Ijon
Dan
ARAM
Tyre
The Great Sea
(Mediterranean Sea)
ASHER
NAPHTALI
Kedesh
Hazor
Merom
Acco
Cabul
Rimmon
Sea of Galilee
Ashtaroth
Golan
ZEBULUN
Mt. Tabor
Mt. Moreh
MANASSEH
Edrei
Dor
Megiddo
ISSACHAR
Jezreel
Taanach
Beth Shan
Ramoth Gilead
Jabesh Gilead
MANASSEH
Samaria
Tirzah
Mt. Ebal
Shechem
Succoth
Mt. Gerizim
Mahanaim
Aphek
Shiloh
Joppa
GAD
EPHRAIM
Jordan River
Jazer
DAN
Bethel
Rabbah
Mizpah
Gilgal
Gezer
Gibeon
Jericho
AMMON
BENJAMIN
Kiriath Jearim
Heshbon
Bezer
Ashdod
Ekron
Jerusalem
Beth Shemesh
Mt. Nebo
Bethlehem
Ashkelon
Gath
REUBEN
Lachish
Hebron
Dibon
Eglon
Gaza
JUDAH
En-gedi
Dead Sea
Aroer
N
Gerar
Ziklag
Beersheba
Hormah
MOAB
SIMEON
Cities of refuge
Other cities
EDOM
0 10 20 30 Miles
0 10 20 30 Kilometers

MAP 6.1

under their influence. As a result, the Israelites did not keep the covenant with God; particularly, they worshiped the gods of those neighboring peoples. Therefore, God allowed those other peoples to attain political and military dominance.

A cycle of unfaithfulness, oppression, and restoration. Israelites worship these other gods from the beginning. After chapter 1 explains that the various tribes allow the former inhabitants to remain among them, chapter 2 says that the Israelites worship the gods of those people. The writer sets out the pattern for the whole book in 2:11-19. The Israelites do "what is evil in the sight of the LORD" by worshiping other gods, and so God allows their neighbors to defeat them. When the people cry out to God, God sends a leader to rescue them from oppression. But they immediately turn back to the other gods once God saves them. This happens twelve times in this one book! And at the end of the book, there is no end of this cycle in sight.

Deborah

A few of these judges stand out either because of who they are and how they achieve victory for Israel or because of what they show us about the Israelites in this period. The first of these is Deborah, the only woman among the judges (Judges 4–5). She lives in a time when a Canaanite king has subjected the tribes of Israel. She is recognized as a prophet and as a person who could adjudicate among litigants before her call to lead the fight to reestablish the independence of the tribes. She receives a call from God and proceeds to recruit Barak, a general, though she tells him that he will not receive credit for this battle because the victory belongs to God. Barak follows Deborah's battle plan and routs the Canaanites. But the opposing general, Sisera, escapes and flees to a territory that is not involved in the conflict. There a woman named Jael offers him food and a place to hide and rest. Thinking he is safe, he accepts. But while he is asleep, Jael drives a tent peg through his temple. For a warrior this death is humiliating because a woman kills him. This story both gives God the credit for the victory and shows that women held some important positions in Israelite culture. Women are among the people to whom God speaks and through whom God acts.

Gideon

The story of **Gideon** also reveals some important facets of Israelite life. When we first see Gideon, he is threshing wheat (6:11). But instead of doing this on a threshing floor (as it was usually done), he is doing it in a winepress. That is, he is hiding, perhaps below ground, so that the Midianites will not see him and destroy his wheat. Gideon is not the picture of bravery! While he is hiding in the winepress, an angel comes and says, "The LORD is with you, you are a mighty warrior" (6:12). Gideon responds by saying that if God were with him and the people, they would not be suffering as they do. Without responding to this, the angel commissions Gideon to defeat the Midianites. Gideon tries to excuse himself by saying that his family is not powerful and he is its weakest member. But God says he is the one to deliver the people. Gideon asks for a sign that this messenger is really from God, so the angel uses his walking stick to burn up some food Gideon had placed on a rock. This convinces Gideon that his visitor is truly an angel.

Gideon and Baal. That night God tells Gideon to destroy his father's altar to **Baal** and "the sacred pole" (or **Asherah**), a representation of Baal's consort. Furthermore, he is also to sacrifice to God a bull intended for Baal. Gideon does this under the cover of night, so no one will see him. When the people find out that Gideon is responsible for this act, they want to kill him. But his father intervenes, saying that Baal can kill Gideon if that is what Baal wants. This story shows us the way that worship of other gods was part of the fabric of life for Israelites in this era: the household of one of the judges was responsible for the community's altar to Baal. In this story everyone—even the families of those who call Israel to faithfulness—worships multiple gods. This is the portrait of Israelite society that the book of Judges wants readers to get from its stories. By painting their ancestors in this way, the authors are showing how they as a people have always violated the covenant. Thus they should expect the punishment from God that they now experience in Babylon.

Battle strategy. After Gideon destroys the altar of Baal, he asks for another sign (6:36-40). He places a wool fleece on a threshing floor and asks God to make dew collect on the fleece, but to leave the floor dry. When that happens as he had asked, he then wants God to do the opposite the following night. So the next morning the floor is wet and the fleece is dry. Now Gideon acquiesces and gathers an army (7:1-7). God tells Gideon that the army is too large, so he sends home 122,000 men because they are afraid. He has only 10,000 soldiers left. God says this is still too many. So he sends them to get a drink of water from the river. Then he sends home everyone who scoops up water in his hand to drink and keeps only those who lap the water like a dog. Now he has only 300 soldiers left. With this small number, it will be clear that the victory comes from God, not the military prowess of Gideon or the army.

When night falls, Gideon divides his army into three groups. Each soldier has a trumpet and a torch, lit but hidden inside a jar. At the signal, all blow their trumpets, break their jars, and shout, "For the LORD and for Gideon." The Midianites think they are surrounded by thousands of warriors and in the confusion either kill one another or run away. Again, this victory clearly belongs to the LORD.

As the army divides the spoils of their victory Gideon asks for a gold earring from each soldier, which he uses to construct an image that the people worship (8:24-27). So the victory over the Midianites did not convince the people, or even Gideon, to worship only God as God had commanded. Still, God gave them forty years of peace. So this story ends with an amazing demonstration of God's patience and mercy.

Samson

Romantic entanglements. One of the most disturbing stories in Judges is that of Samson (Judges 13–16). In this story God uses an immoral, murderous bully to deliver the people. The Philistines had dominated the Israelites for forty years when this story begins. Samson was a nazirite, one who took a vow not to cut his hair or drink alcoholic beverages. But he decided to marry a Philistine woman against his parents' wishes. As Judges tells the story, his parents opposed the marriage because they "did not know that that this was from the LORD;

for he was seeking a pretext to act against the Philistines" (14:4). Thus, God was about to use Samson's violation of usual custom (while Philistines were not technically Canaanites, marriage to whom would violate the covenant, this story makes them undesirable outsiders; 14:3) to accomplish God's purposes.

At the engagement party, Samson makes up a riddle and bets thirty people a suit of clothes each that they cannot solve it. When they cannot, they threaten the bride-to-be so she will coax the answer from Samson. She does as they ask and the thirty men win the bet. Samson is furious. Judges says that "the spirit of the LORD rushed on him" so that he went to a neighboring town, killed thirty people, took their clothes, and paid the bet. Then he went back to his father's house.

When Samson finally returns to visit his wife, he finds that she has married another man. For revenge, he catches three hundred foxes and pairs them up by tying their tails together. He then ties torches to each of the hundred and fifty pairs and sends them running through the grain fields at harvest time. This destroys the Philistines' crop for the year. Once the Israelites find out what he had done, they are afraid of retribution and so tie him up and deliver him to the Philistines. When they get to the Philistines, again "the spirit of the LORD rushed on him." Now he breaks the ropes and finds the jawbone of an ass and kills a thousand people.

Delilah and the end of Samson. The final sequence in the Samson story begins with Samson falling in love with Delilah. Philistine officials bribe her to learn the secret of his strength. She eventually discovers that he will lose his strength if his hair is cut. So one night as he sleeps they cut his hair. Without his superhuman strength, the Philistines subdue, blind, and imprison him. Later, the Philistine clan leaders have a party at which they decide to bring in Samson to mock and to celebrate their victory over him. Enough time has passed that his hair has grown out. While at the party, Samson finds the pillars of the building, asks God for his old strength, and then uses it to pull down the columns and collapse the building. Thus he kills all the leaders of the Philistines and himself, an act that frees Israel from domination by the Philistines.

The Samson story has God work through a person who is by no means virtuous or an example for the people of God. Still, God frees the people. The story underscores God's will to accomplish good things for Israel. God uses a person with enormous character flaws who lives in almost constant violation of the covenant to rescue the people. This story demonstrates that God continues to act graciously toward the Israelites in the very face of their unfaithfulness. God goes far beyond the demands of the covenant in showing them grace. This story exemplifies the lengths to which God is willing to go to express graciousness and mercy to Israel.

Atrocity and Gibeah

The final story in Judges is also disturbing (Judges 19–21). An unhappy concubine of a Levite leaves him and returns to her father's house, which was more than a day's travel away. After a few months, the man goes to seek reconciliation and succeeds. On their trip home, they stop to spend the night in Gibeah, a place inhabited by the tribe of Benjamin. At this point, the story is a parallel to that about

Sodom in Genesis 19. An old man takes them into his house because they are strangers there and so have no clan to protect them. Notably, this story sets the stage for lawlessness by saying that there was no king in Israel. After dark, the men of the city surround the house where the couple had taken refuge and call for the owner to send out the man so they can rape him. The owner refuses, but the Levite pushes the concubine out into the mob. The men rape her all night and finally kill her. The Levite takes her body home, cuts it into pieces, and sends a piece to each tribe of Israel, explaining what the Gibeonites had done. The tribes come together and attack Gibeah and the rest of the tribe of Benjamin. They kill so many Benjaminites that special arrangements have to be made to secure a future for that clan.

The commonalities between this gruesome story and that of the city of Sodom demonstrate that the story of Sodom is about rape and abuse of the powerless, not about homosexuality. The Gibeah story indicates that the rape (and in the case of Sodom, attempted rape) is about asserting power, not about which sex the people rape. The more direct point this story wants to make in Judges is that the people's unfaithfulness expresses itself in egregious ways. Furthermore, the loose confederation of clans with no central government could not succeed in bringing them to live in justice and faithfulness to God. So this story, and the whole book of Judges, ends by saying: "In those days there was no king in Israel; all the people did what was right in their own eyes" (21:25). This interpretation prepares us for the next stage of the story.

BOX 6.1

CONCUBINE

A concubine is a second-class wife, bound to a husband who has other wives. She has fewer rights and a lower position within the household than a full-fledged wife.

Conclusion

Throughout its pages, Judges emphasizes the Deuteronomistic pattern: unfaithfulness to God brings defeat by enemies, but God responds to repentance by saving the people from those enemies. Its support of this interpretation of Israel's history is the most important point the book wants to make. This emphasizes the importance of faithfulness for God's people, on the one hand, and the way they can rely on God's graciousness when they fail, on the other.

▶ Ruth: A Tale of Loyalty and Love

The Jewish arrangement of the biblical books groups Ruth near the end, with Song of Solomon (Song of Songs), Ecclesiastes, Lamentations, and Esther, all books read during religious festivals. The Christian Bible places Ruth immediately after Judges and before 1 Samuel. It is an interlude of sorts, because it interrupts the story of the life of the nation that 1 Samuel will resume. The story happens during the time of the judges, but it is not structured to exemplify the pattern of Deuteronomy the way the surrounding writings are. The story of Ruth does not move us directly toward the establishment of the monarchy. It does, however, establish the lineage of **David**, Israel's idealized king.

The book tells of two sons of an Israelite woman named **Naomi**, both of whom marry non-Israelite women and then die without having children. Naomi decides it is best to return to her kinspeople in the region of Judah (the area around Jerusalem). The daughters-in-law volunteer to go to live in Judah with her, but Naomi tells them to return to their own people to find husbands. One agrees to this, but the other, **Ruth**, insists that she will go with Naomi. In her effort to convince Naomi, Ruth utters the immortal words: "Where you go, I will go; where you lodge, I will lodge; your people shall be my people, and your God my God" (1:16). Naomi finally acquiesces and allows Ruth to come with her.

Boaz. This sets in motion a system known as **levirate marriage**. In this system, the closest relative of a man who dies with no children must marry the widow and have children in the name of the man who died. In this way the extended family's wealth and property stay intact. A man named Boaz is second in line to marry Ruth, and Ruth happens to glean in his fields (Ruth 2). Boaz follows the humane custom of not harvesting the corners of his fields so that the poor can gather that grain for themselves. When Boaz sees Ruth, he takes an interest in her and makes special provision for her by telling his harvesters to leave her extra grain; he even feeds her lunch. Boaz tells Ruth not to go to any other fields to glean, but only to come to his and she will be treated well. Near the end of the harvest season, at Naomi's urging, Ruth goes to him at night and asks him to marry her through the levirate system (Ruth 3). Boaz agrees to marry her if the closer kinsman will give up his claim. The closer kinsman does surrender his right, and so Boaz marries Ruth (Ruth 4).

A Moabite ancestress. This endearing story illustrates the way the levirate system worked, and why on occasion it did not (the closer kinsman would not marry her because her children might lessen his children's inheritance). But more importantly, it establishes the genealogy of King David. The end of the book identifies Ruth as the great-grandmother of David. This lineage demonstrates that Israel's rules about not mixing with others were not about ethnic purity, because this story makes Israel's ideal king one-eighth Moabite. Further, Naomi and other Israelites accept Ruth in part because she agrees to worship only God. This again shows that the problem with non-Israelites is not their ethnicity, but their worship of other gods. Ruth presents no danger to the community because she does not worship the gods the Moabites worship and so does not tempt Israelites to worship those gods.

▶ 1–2 Samuel: The Monarchy Begins

The Last of the Judges

First and Second Samuel are a single book in the Hebrew text. They pick up the story of God's dealings with the Israelites where Judges left off and follow the rise and prophetic ministry of **Samuel**. First Samuel opens with **Eli** in charge of a major sanctuary to God in Shiloh, a town in south-central Palestine. Eli serves there as priest, prophet, and judge. Thus the stories that begin this saga assume a close connection between prophecy and the formal worship of God at the sanctuary. Eli holds this position in

FIGURE 6.4 **IMAGE OF BAAL, RAS SHAMRA, SYRIA**

Dated fifteenth century B.C.E. Baal was one of the most important gods in Canaanite religion. Since he is the storm god, this image shows him wielding a lightning bolt. Wikimedia Commons

part because of his experiences of God and in part through heredity. This last point is important because the story presupposes that, if things work as they should, Eli's sons will assume his position when he dies. But their corruption leads God to reject them.

One day Eli sees a woman praying at the sanctuary; her lips moved but she made no sound, so he assumes she is drunk (1:9-16). He soon discovers that she is begging God for a child because she is barren. To apologize for his mistake, Eli promises her a son. In turn, she promises to devote the son to God. She does have a son, and after he is weaned (usually around three years old) she brings him to live in the sanctuary compound with Eli and his sons. Her son is Samuel (1:19-28).

One night while he was still young, Samuel hears someone calling him (3:3-9). He assumes it is Eli and goes to ask what he wants. Eli says he did not call Samuel. The third time Samuel hears the voice and goes to Eli, Eli tells Samuel that God is the one calling him. When Samuel responds to God, God tells him that Eli's sons are corrupt and will not succeed Eli. The next day Eli forces Samuel to reveal the message from God. This sad message is not news to Eli, because he had already heard it from others and from "a man of God."

The Philistine Menace and the Ark Narrative

Eli's sons die leading the Israelite army against the Philistines (ch. 4). They lead the army by carrying the **ark of the covenant** into battle. The ark of the covenant was a specially designed box that contained various religious artifacts (notably the tablets of the law, and Aaron's rod that flowered to show he was God's choice for priest) and represented the presence of God. In some ways this representation served in the way statues did for other cults, because it was the sign of the focused presence of God in a place.

The military significance of the ark. Carrying this religious symbol into battle (a common practice according to these texts) exemplifies the connection the Israelites make between success in war and their relationship with the Lord. But this time the Israelites lose; even though the ark is with them, God is not. Eli himself falls and dies when he hears the news of his sons' death and that the Philistines have captured the ark of the covenant (4:12-18).

The ensuing tale about the ark, which was purportedly overlaid with gold, demonstrates that the peoples of ancient Palestine saw war as a battle between gods, as well as between armies (chs. 5–6). As part of the spoils of war, the Philistines put the ark in the temple of their god **Dagon**. But the first night that the ark is in his temple the image of Dagon falls over; after the Philistines put him back up, the second night he falls again and his head and hands fall off. When they move the ark from Dagon's temple, a plague breaks out wherever they take it. Eventually, they send it back to the Israelites.

The ark and the presence of God. The story clearly assumes that the ark somehow conveys the presence of God. It also teaches that Israel's defeats are the result of the people's unfaithfulness, not God's lack of power, because it shows that God has power over Dagon—even in Dagon's temple. Furthermore, all the Philistine attempts to control the power of God that is present through the ark fail. So this story also returns us to the lesson about national defeat that the Deuteronomistic History continually emphasizes.

BOX 6.2

WHAT ARE READERS TO THINK ABOUT HAVING A KING?

Read Judges 21:25. Remember that Judges ends this way to explain why a terrible massacre had taken place and as a comment on the whole story of the people's recurrent unfaithfulness to God that has unfolded in the book. Compare that comment with 1 Samuel 8:10-18 and 12:19.

Samuel Anoints Saul, the First King

Back in Israel, Samuel is now in charge, and has become both the religious and military leader of the tribes (ch. 7). When the Philistines again attack the Israelites, Samuel calls the people to repent of worshiping other gods and then leads them to victory, just as the former judges had done. When the war is over, the people say that they need a king (ch. 8). Samuel feels rejected when they make this request, but God tells him that the people have rejected not Samuel but rather they had rejected God from being king. Samuel warns the people of the abuses they will suffer if they have a king, but they insist. So Samuel anoints **Saul** as the first king of the tribes of Israel. Now for the first time they have a standing single government that binds all the tribes together.

Samuel's warnings about having a king stand in tension with the statements in Judges that lament the absence of a king who could impose order. So there are two traditions about kingship among the Israelites. One sees it as necessary for safety from enemies and the maintenance of a stable society, and another fears the abuses that follow from one person's assumption of such great power among a people. Both strands of tradition have a significant element of truth. A national government helps establish order, but power inclines kings to abuse their subjects.

Saul Is Rejected

Saul begins his reign as God's choice for a king (chs. 9–11). But after some initial military victories over Israel's enemies, he presumes the privileges of a priest by offering a sacrifice instead of waiting for Samuel (ch. 13). God grants Israel victory but tells Saul, through Samuel, that his descendants will not rule after him. Perhaps this story opposes the consolidation of priestly and royal power into a single person, and protects

FIGURE 6.5 **THE ARK OF THE COVENANT**

Lorenzo Ghiberti (1425–1452) depicted Israelites carrying the ark of the covenant on the doors of a baptistery in Florence, Italy. The ark, which contained the tablets of the Ten Commandments (and a few other items), was the symbol of the center of God's presence among the Israelites. Because it was such a holy object, no one was to touch it. So it was carried on poles, as shown in this relief. Art Resource

the role of the priest from being usurped by people outside the line of Aaron.

Shortly after this, Saul makes a mistake that is similar to the one Achan made at Jericho (Joshua 7). Rather than destroying the spoils of war as God had commanded, Saul brings some home (1 Samuel 14). Because of this failure to obey God, Samuel says that God rejects Saul from being king (chs. 15–16). Saul continues to reign, but without God's authorization. This story illustrates that kings are disobedient to God from the inception of the monarchy. Thus its demise, along with the nation's, is what the people should expect within the framework of the covenant.

David and Saul: Rivalry for Power

Once God rejects Saul, we begin to hear about David (16:13). First, Samuel goes to Bethlehem and anoints David, who is the youngest and seems least likely among his father's eight sons to be a candidate for the next ruler of the nation—he is just a shepherd boy. As happened in so many stories in Genesis, God chooses against cultural expectations. The story then shifts and we hear that David plays the lyre to soothe a troubled Saul (16:23). In the next story (ch. 17), David is back to being a shepherd boy and the person assigned to deliver food to his brothers, who are warriors. In this story Saul does not know David. During his visit to his brothers, the young David, who has no military training or equipment, kills the Philistine giant Goliath and so wins the war for Israel. This episode illustrates the power of faith over military might and, when those in exile hear it, it intimates that faithfulness can lead to the restoration of the nation.

Traditions about David. This collection of stories brings together at least two traditions about David. One has him serve as a court musician; the other identifies him as a shepherd unknown to the king. Both traditions portray David as a mighty warrior. Even as he continues to play the lyre for Saul, the people know him as a powerful military leader. As history, these traditions are difficult to reconcile. But as windows into the makings of an ideal king, they fit together much better. David can lead in battle and play soothing music; he can herd sheep and kill giants. Thus he has both power and compassion, along with a deep commitment to God.

The end of Saul. Once Saul comes to see David as a rival and competitor for the throne, he repeatedly tries to kill him (18:11, 25; 19:10, 15). So David becomes a fugitive, but still refuses to kill God's king—even when he has the opportunity (24:3-7). Finally, David leaves the country to serve as a general in the army of a neighboring king. The book of 1 Samuel ends with the defeat and death of Saul and most of his sons, including David's close friend Jonathan.

The Reign of David

Stories about the reign of David fill 2 Samuel. David is a person of great faith and enormous faults. He sometimes trusts and praises God in beautiful ways; then he takes the wife of another man, whom he later has murdered. So he is yet another example of God working with and through flawed individuals to bless God's people.

After Saul's death, David returns to Hebron in Judah, where he is anointed king (2 Samuel 1). But Ishbaal, a son of Saul, reigns over the remainder of the country seven and a half years.

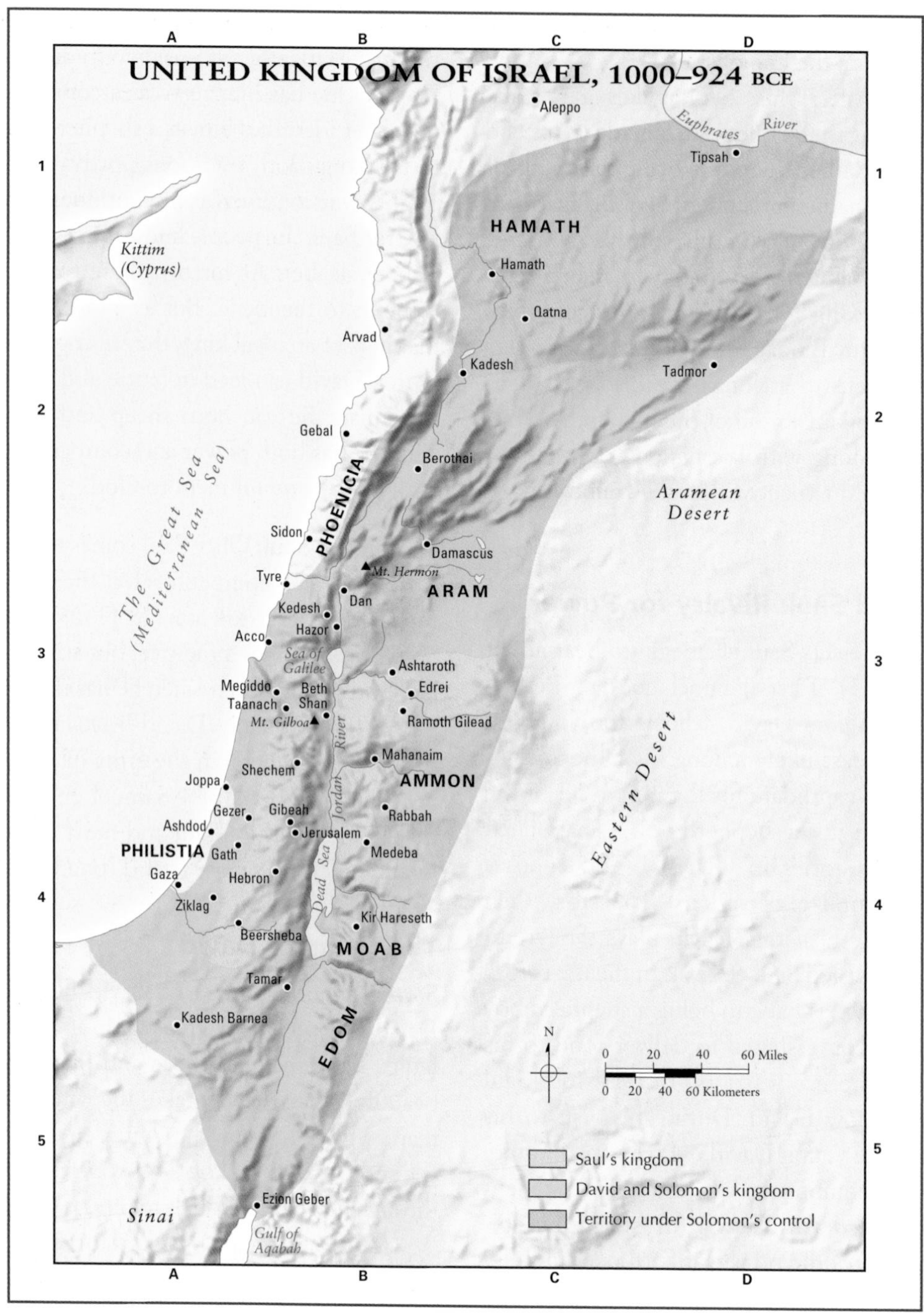
UNITED KINGDOM OF ISRAEL, 1000–924 BCE
A
B
C
D
1
2
3
4
5
Aleppo
Euphrates River
Tipsah
Kittim (Cyprus)
HAMATH
Hamath
Qatna
Arvad
Kadesh
Tadmor
Gebal
Berothai
PHOENICIA
The Great Sea (Mediterranean Sea)
Aramean Desert
Sidon
Damascus
Mt. Hermon
Tyre
ARAM
Dan
Kedesh
Hazor
Acco
Sea of Galilee
Ashtaroth
Megiddo
Beth Shan
Edrei
Taanach
Mt. Gilboa
Ramoth Gilead
Jordan River
Mahanaim
Shechem
Eastern Desert
Joppa
AMMON
Gezer
Gibeah
Rabbah
Ashdod
Jerusalem
PHILISTIA
Gath
Medeba
Hebron
Gaza
Dead Sea
Ziklag
Kir Hareseth
Beersheba
MOAB
Tamar
Kadesh Barnea
EDOM
N
0 20 40 60 Miles
0 20 40 60 Kilometers
Saul's kingdom
David and Solomon's kingdom
Territory under Solomon's control
Ezion Geber
Sinai
Gulf of Aqabah

MAP 6.2

When Ishbaal is assassinated, David takes control over all of the tribes. During his war-filled reign, David subdues central Palestine and moves the capital from Hebron to **Jerusalem** (chs. 2–5). But when he initiates plans to build a temple to God, the prophet Nathan tells him not to build it because he is a man of war, but to leave that task to his descendants whom God would establish (7:4-13). This explanation for God's refusal to let David build the temple stands in tension with seeing God as the one who gives Israel victory in battle. This distancing of God from warfare suggests that such activity is not at the center of God's nature.

God promises David that his descendants will reign after him, but David's own reign remains difficult. Besides wars with the peoples on Israel's borders, one of his own sons, Absalom, stages a coup (chs. 15–17). David eventually regains the crown, but must continue to fight to maintain the borders of his kingdom. David's reign spans forty years (1 Kgs. 2:11). The length of his reign becomes the standard for judging faithfulness to God; faithful kings rule forty years, others have shorter reigns.

▶ 1–2 Kings: The Story of Two Kingdoms

Like 1 and 2 Samuel, 1 and 2 Kings are a single book in the Hebrew Bible. The books of Kings tell the story of Israel's rulers from the death of David through the fall of the nation of Judah.

The editorial perspective. The Deuteronomistic editors of these books report that most Israelite kings act in ways that make them unacceptable to God. The most common description of a king is that he "did what was evil in the sight of the LORD." The most prominent evil they commit is to worship other gods. These books make such unfaithfulness the reason for the downfall of the nations and the exile of Judah to Babylon. They want to demonstrate how patient God has been with the people, in spite of the people's repeated turning from God; the kings lead the way in this worship of other gods and the people willingly follow.

The Reign of Solomon

First Kings opens with the death of David and the ensuing struggle for succession. **Solomon** eventually wins and asks God for the wisdom to rule well (1 Kgs. 3). God grants Solomon not only wisdom but also wealth and long life. The nation of Israel reaches its peak under Solomon (at least, as these books tell the story). Solomon builds the temple to God that his warrior father, David, had been forbidden to construct (ch. 6), but he also builds temples to many other gods. One of the ways nations formed alliances in the ancient world was for their ruling families to intermarry. Thus Solomon marries hundreds of women from surrounding kingdoms and powerful clans to solidify his place in the region and gain powerful allies. These marriages also mean, however, that he needs to provide for the religious practices of these wives. So he builds temples to their gods and supports the worship of those gods with government funds. So even the wise Solomon fails to maintain faithfulness to God. God responds to this infidelity by telling Solomon that the kingdom would be taken from his descendants (ch. 11).

The Divided Kingdom

When Solomon dies, ten of the twelve tribes secede (ch. 12). They accept as their king Jeroboam, a general whom the prophet Ahijah had anointed while Solomon was still alive. This begins the period of the "divided kingdom," an era that lasts much longer than the seventy-five years when the twelve tribes were a single nation (thirty-three years under David and forty under Solomon). The two nations existed for over two hundred years. The larger nation, which kept the name **Israel**, possessed the territory north of the region around Jerusalem. It survived until about 722 B.C.E., when the Assyrians conquered it and dispersed its population throughout its empire. The smaller nation occupied Jerusalem and some territory to the south. Its name became **Judah**, the name of the region around Jerusalem. It fell to the Babylonians in 587/586 B.C.E., and its leading citizens were sent into exile.

Jeroboam I. One of the first acts of Jeroboam, the first king of the new nation of Israel, was to set up a golden calf to worship at the northern and southern borders of his territory (12:28-31). The sanctuary at the southern border was designed to keep the people in that area from returning to Jerusalem to worship and so beginning to desire reconciliation with their estranged kinsfolk. This act of idolatry sets the pattern for the account of the kings throughout 1 and 2 Kings; they constantly lead the people to worship various gods in addition to the God of Abraham and Moses.

Ahab and Elijah. Among the kings that the text identifies as evil, 1 Kings gives special attention to Ahab (869–850), who reigns in the northern kingdom, Israel. He and his queen Jezebel exemplify all that is wrong in Israel, particularly because they vigorously support the cults of Baal and Asherah (16:29-33). The prophet **Elijah** represents the most outstanding opponent of Ahab's administration. Elijah announces that God is sending a drought, presumably in response to the predominance of Baal worship (17:1). During this three-year drought, Elijah miraculously supplies a widow and her son with oil and flour from which they and he eat. And when the widow's son dies, Elijah raises him from the dead (17:8-24).

The contest at Mount Carmel. The drought finally ends with a showdown at Mount Carmel (18:20-40). Elijah challenges 450 priests of Baal and 400 prophets of Asherah to a contest to determine which god is real. The priests of Baal build an altar to their god and Elijah builds one to God. Each places a sacrifice on their respective altar, agreeing that the true god would send fire on the altar dedicated to him. Elijah gives the 450 priests hours to pray and chides them along the way; he suggests that perhaps Baal is on vacation or taking a nap when no fire is forthcoming. Then Elijah has barrels of water

BOX 6.3

THE GOD BAAL

Baal was a Canaanite god whom the writers of the Hebrew Bible saw as God's main rival for the worship of the Israelites. Baal was a storm god who was also ruler of the Canaanite pantheon. As storm god, Baal could do damage or bring needed rain.

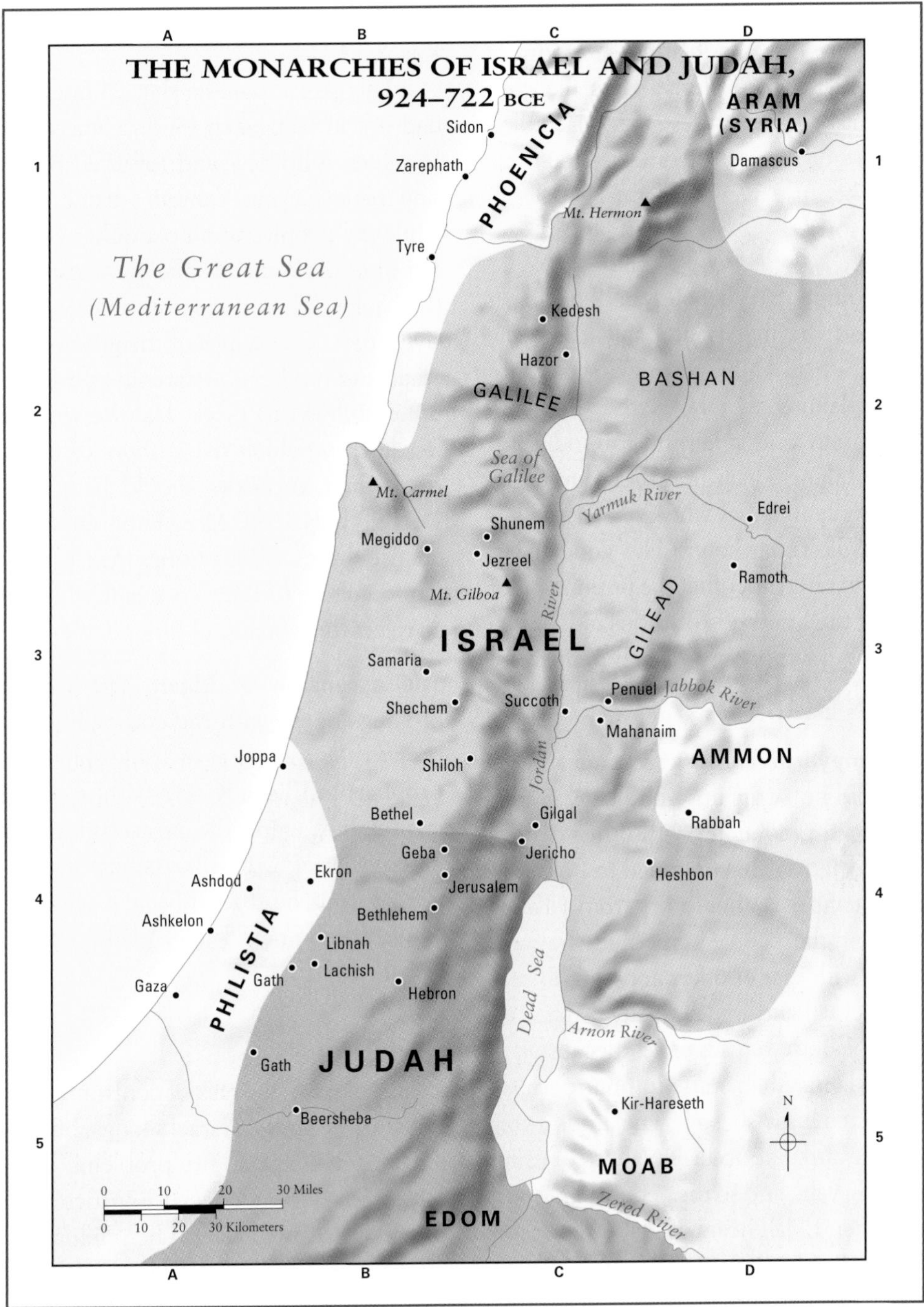

THE MONARCHIES OF ISRAEL AND JUDAH, 924–722 BCE
A
B
C
D
1
2
3
4
5
ARAM (SYRIA)
Damascus
Sidon
Zarephath
PHOENICIA
Mt. Hermon
Tyre
The Great Sea (Mediterranean Sea)
Kedesh
Hazor
BASHAN
GALILEE
Sea of Galilee
Mt. Carmel
Yarmuk River
Edrei
Shunem
Megiddo
Jezreel
Ramoth
Mt. Gilboa
Jordan River
GILEAD
ISRAEL
Samaria
Penuel
Jabbok River
Shechem
Succoth
Mahanaim
AMMON
Joppa
Shiloh
Bethel
Gilgal
Rabbah
Geba
Jericho
Heshbon
Ashdod
Ekron
Jerusalem
Bethlehem
Ashkelon
PHILISTIA
Libnah
Gath
Lachish
Gaza
Hebron
Dead Sea
Arnon River
Gath
JUDAH
Kir-Hareseth
N
Beersheba
MOAB
0 10 20 30 Miles
0 10 20 30 Kilometers
EDOM
Zered River

MAP 6.3

poured on his altar and prays once. Fire immediately consumes the sacrifice and evaporates all the water. The Lord clearly wins the contest. Elijah has the 450 priests of Baal killed (but not those of Asherah—some speculate he spares them because many thought of Asherah as God's consort).

A faithful remnant. When Jezebel hears that Elijah has had the priests of Baal killed, she orders his death (19:1-2). So Elijah goes into hiding, complaining that he is the only person in the nation who is faithful to God. God responds by telling Elijah that there are seven thousand people in Israel who do not worship Baal (19:18). This may sound like good news, but we need to remember that the population of Israel was in the hundreds of thousands. Even painting a rosy picture, just a small percentage of people in Israel worshiped only God.

Naboth's vineyard. This does not mean that the people did not worship God. They apparently worshiped God along with other deities. The temple in Jerusalem continued to function, as did other temples. A final story from 1 Kings illustrates how the people combined the worship of God with that of other gods. Ahab sees a nearby vineyard and wants to buy it (ch. 21). The owner, Naboth, refuses to sell because it is his ancestral land. Ahab starts to pout because Naboth rejected his wish, so Jezebel finds a way to get the vineyard. She accuses Naboth of using God's name in vain, and so the people stone him to death. When Elijah hears of Naboth's death, he tells Ahab and Jezebel that their punishment for this deed of extreme injustice will be that dogs will lick Ahab's blood and eat Jezebel's body. Three years later this happens to Ahab (22:37-38), and several years later to Jezebel (2 Kgs. 9:30-37).

This story suggests that, although Naboth had not in fact taken God's name in vain, the Israelites still knew and followed the prohibition against using Yahweh's name in vain, all while the people worshiped other gods. So the Israelites did not abandon the worship of God; they just did not commit themselves exclusively to it. The stories of the gruesome ends of Ahab and Jezebel illustrate the consequences of unfaithfulness to God. They serve as another lesson from which the authors of these books think their ancestors should have learned to worship only God. Most importantly, the writers use these stories to urge their present readers to adhere to their covenant with God, and so reject the worship of other deities.

The ascension of Elijah. The second book of Kings opens with the end of Elijah's ministry and the transition of leadership among the prophets to **Elisha**. God's faithful prophet Elijah does not simply die; he ascends to heaven in a fiery chariot (2:11-12). As he is swept up, his cloak falls behind for Elisha, a symbol that he would be the next leader of the school of the prophets.

Elisha

Elisha takes up the task of confronting the polytheistic practices of Israel's kings, but also gives significant attention to problems the people face. He confronts social injustice by providing relief to a widow and her children who are about to be sold into slavery to pay their debts (4:1-7). When he hears of her plight, he tells her to gather all the empty vessels any of her neighbors have and then miraculously fills them with oil for her to sell. As a result, she has enough money to pay her debts and to live on thereafter. On other occasions, Elisha purifies poisonous water for people and feeds a hundred people from just a bit of food (4:38-44).

Elisha and Naaman. One of the best-known stories about Elisha involves Naaman, a general in the army of Aram (one of Israel's often unfriendly neighbors; ch. 5). This general has leprosy. When an Israelite servant girl tells him that Elisha has the power to cure this dreaded disease, he decides to ask for Elisha's help. But when Naaman arrives at the prophet's residence, Elisha refuses to greet him formally, only sending his servant to tell Naaman to wash in the Jordan River seven times to be healed. This important official is incensed at this apparent slight and the means of the cure, but the people in his company finally convince Naaman to do as instructed, and he is healed. When he returns to thank Elisha, the prophet refuses any gifts. Naaman commits himself to worshiping only the Lord, but this creates a problem. He serves in the court of a king who worships another god and expects his subjects to do likewise. So Naaman asks that he be allowed to pretend to worship the other god when in the presence of his king. In what seems a rather odd turn of events, Elisha grants him permission to act in this deceptive manner. This concession may speak to how some Israelites thought about their conduct while among those who worship many gods, particularly as they live in Babylon. Could they pretend to worship other gods to make their lives easier (or perhaps avoid persecution) in Babylon (or later in other places)? Elisha's response to Naaman may permit that way of practicing their faith in difficult circumstances.

BOX 6.4

THE GODDESS ASHERAH

Asherah was one of the three highest goddesses of the Canaanite pantheon. She was commonly represented by a wooden pole or a tree. She was a mother goddess and often the consort of the father god, El. In other settings, she was seen as the consort of Baal. At some points in the history of the Israelites, she was probably viewed as the consort of the God of Abraham. We see this from the presence of an Asherah pole in the Jerusalem temple (see Josiah removing it in 2 Kgs. 23:4) and from a few inscriptions that suggest it.

Elisha and Jehu. When the focus returns to the political situation in Israel, we see Elisha anoint Jehu, an army commander, to be king in Israel (ch. 9). This occurs while Joram, a son of Ahab and Jezebel, is on the throne. Jehu deposes and kills not only Joram and his mother Jezebel (who is then eaten by dogs), but also all Ahab's descendants (ch. 10). This terrible fate of Ahab and Jezebel's children again demonstrates the far-reaching consequences of unfaithfulness—it even affects one's children. In his campaign to secure power by eradicating the descendants and bases of the previous king's power, Jehu also kills priests and worshipers of Baal. Still, the writers of Kings say that he leaves in place the golden calves on his border (10:29), so the fortunes of Israel continue to decline because the nation continues to venerate other gods. The authors of these stories would not want

CHART 6.1

KINGS OF THE UNITED AND DIVIDED MONARCHIES

Date	Israel	Judah
		Rehoboam (922–915)
	Jeroboam I (922–901)	Abijah (915–913)
		Asa (913–873)
900	Nadab (901–900)	
	Baasha (900–877)	
	Elah (877–876)	
	Zimri (876)	
	Omri (876–869)	Jehoshaphat (873–849)
	Ahab (869–850)	
850	Ahaziah (850–849)	Jehoram (849–842)
	Jehoram (849–842)	Ahaziah (842)
	Jehu's Revolt (842)	Athaliah (842–837)
	Jehu (842–815)	Joash (837–800)
	Jehoahaz (815–801)	Amaziah (800–783)
	Jehoash (801–786)	
	Jeroboam II (876–746)	Uzziah (Azariah) (783–742)
750	Zechariah (746–745)	
	Shallum (745)	Jotham (742–735)
	Menahem (745–738)	
	Pekahiah (738–737)	Ahaz (735–715)
	Pekah (737–732)	
	Hoshea (732–724)	
725	*Fall of Israel* (722/721)	Hezekiah (715–687)
700		
		Manasseh (687–642)
650		
		Amon (642–640)
		Josiah (640–609)
		Deuteronomic reforms (621–)
		Jehoahaz (609)
		Jehoiakim (609–598/597)
600		Jehoiachin (598/597)
		First Babylonian sack of Jerusalem (598/597)
		Zedekiah (597–587)
		Fall of Jerusalem (587)
		Babylonian captivity (587–538)

FIGURE 6.6 **MOABITE STONE**

The Moabite Stone, a stele erected by Mesha, king of Moab, to commemorate his victory over King Omri of Israel. Wikimedia Commons

their readers to miss the contrast between God being the one who enabled Jehu's victory and the new king's continuing to promote the worship of another god.

Deuteronomistic evaluations. The writers of 1 and 2 Kings do recognize a few good kings. Jehoash (or Joash; 837–800) of Judah numbers among them (chs. 12–13). He repaired the temple of God in Jerusalem and God rewards him with success, including the expansion of his territory. But Jehoash is assassinated before he completes his forty-year reign. This disrupts the pattern of the relationship between God and the nation that the book promotes, because the king is faithful but still dies violently.

The books of 1 and 2 Chronicles repeat much that we find in 1 and 2 Kings, though from a bit different perspective. But all four books agree that God rewards a king's faithfulness, usually with success and a forty-year reign. So when 2 Chronicles recounts the reign of Jehoash, its writers assert that idol worship gained ground late in his reign (24:17-18). Thus they imply that his early and violent death comes as a result of this movement toward unfaithfulness. So they adjust the story to fit the Deuteronomistic pattern.

The End of the Northern Kingdom

The prophet Elisha dies around the year 800, some fifty years before the emergence of those prophets from whom we begin to have writings. Amos, Hosea, Micah, and Isaiah (among others) all prophesy in the approximately eighty years between the death of Elisha and the fall of Israel. Those eighth-century prophets stand in the tradition of Elisha and his predecessor Elijah. They all call the people, and particularly their leaders, to worship only God and to express their faith in God through lives that enact social justice.

BOX 6.5

THE DEUTERONOMISTIC PATTERN

Read Deuteronomy 30:15-18. How have the stories in the Deuteronomistic histories related to what we read in this passage?

The nation of Israel (the northern kingdom) falls to the **Assyrian Empire** in 722 B.C.E. The writers of 2 Kings, not surprisingly, attribute this defeat to unfaithfulness to the covenant (17:5-18). Since Israel refused to worship only God, God allows the Assyrians to defeat their armies and take their land. When the Assyrians send the inhabitants of Israel into exile, the story of a large segment of Israelites comes to a close. The ten tribes who were part of that kingdom are assimilated into other populations and never return as an identifiable people. They are now sometimes called the ten lost tribes.

Josiah's Reform

While the nation of Judah remains after the fall of Israel, its future does not look bright. Second Kings charges that Judah is guilty of the same unfaithfulness that brought the downfall of the northern kingdom. But there is a glimmer of hope. **Josiah** (640–609) comes to the throne as a boy of eight (ch. 22). After a few years he undertakes a thorough renovation of the temple of God in Jerusalem. In a back room some workers find the "book of the law" that demands exclusive allegiance to God, along with moral regulations and instructions about proper ritual. Once the prophetess Huldah authenticates the book, Josiah introduces sweeping reforms (ch. 23). He destroys images of Baal and Asherah (one of which was actually in the temple of God) and reinstitutes the Passover.

The writers comment that the Passover had not been celebrated since the time of the judges (23:21-23). This aside reveals something about the worship practices of ancient Israelites. They did not even observe the central feasts that celebrate the acts of God's deliverance of the people from Egypt. This remark may suggest that God was not always even chief among the gods worshiped in Israel and Judah. It more clearly indicates that the celebrations that come to be so meaningful in later times were either unknown or not observed in the time before the fall of Judah.

The death of Josiah. As a result of his reforms, things go well for Judah through most of Josiah's reign. But like Jehoash he dies violently, short of the ideal forty-year reign (23:28-30). This again violates the expectation that faithfulness will bring the reward of peace and comfort. Once more, 2 Chronicles provides an explanation. It asserts that Josiah did not listen to the word of the LORD that came through Neco, pharaoh of Egypt, and so died in battle against Neco (35:22). At our distance it is hard to imagine how Josiah could be expected to recognize the voice of God coming through a king of Egypt. Still, this explanation makes the story conform to the pattern Deuteronomy sets out in which faithfulness brings blessing and disobedience brings punishment.

The End of Judah

As many reforms as Josiah instituted, they are not enough. The people immediately return to the worship of other gods and Judah becomes a vassal state within the **Babylonian Empire** in 604, only five years after Josiah's death (2 Kgs. 24–25). The Babylonians take into exile (which they would perhaps call "protective custody") an initial group of leading citizens, mostly relatives of the royal family, as insurance against rebellion. These exiles serve basically as hostages. Dissatisfied with this state of affairs, the people in Jerusalem revolt several

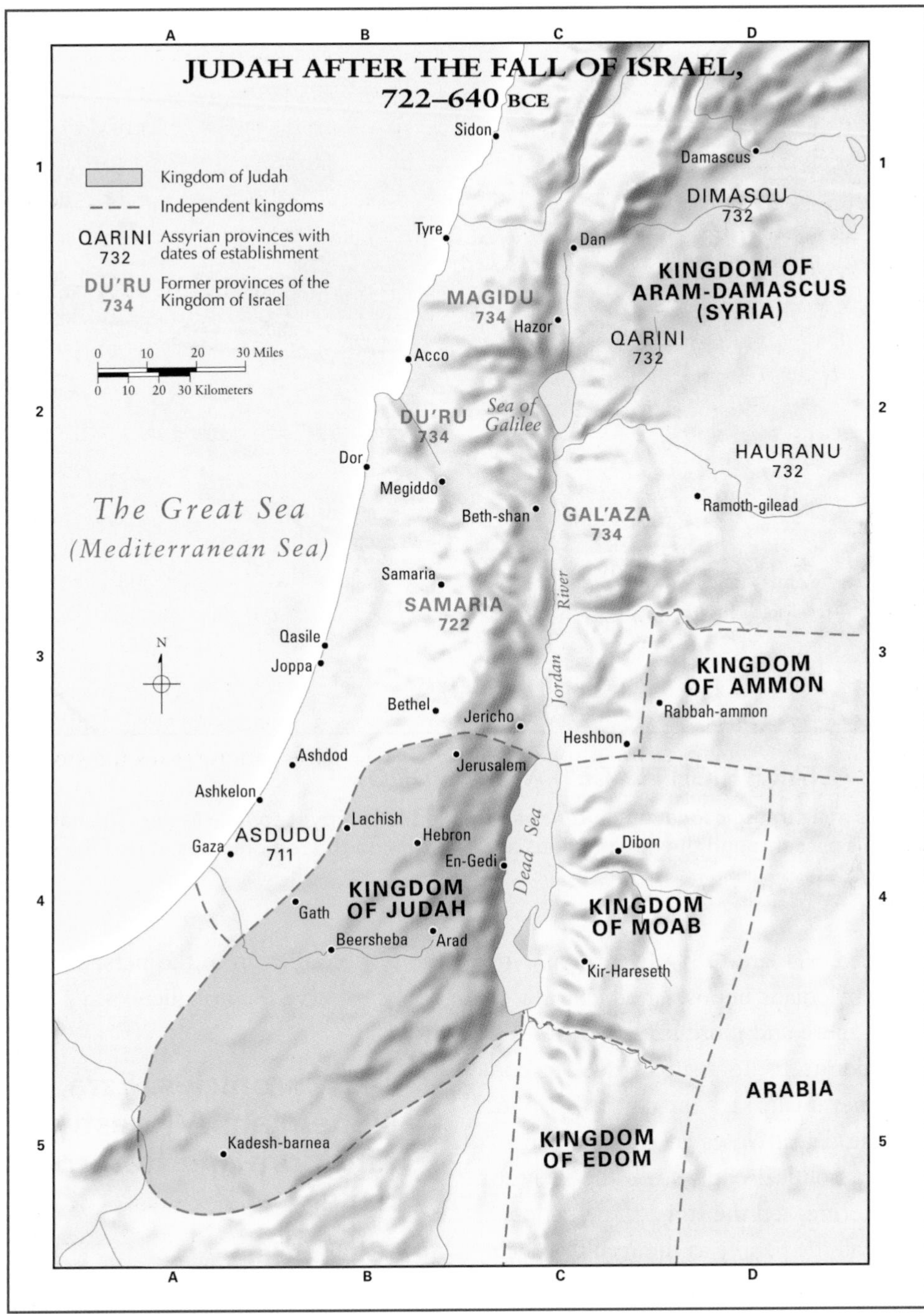
JUDAH AFTER THE FALL OF ISRAEL, 722–640 BCE
A
B
C
D
1
2
3
4
5
Kingdom of Judah
Independent kingdoms
QARINI 732 Assyrian provinces with dates of establishment
DU'RU 734 Former provinces of the Kingdom of Israel
0 10 20 30 Miles
0 10 20 30 Kilometers
N
Sidon
Damascus
DIMASQU 732
Tyre
Dan
KINGDOM OF ARAM-DAMASCUS (SYRIA)
MAGIDU 734
Hazor
QARINI 732
Acco
Sea of Galilee
DU'RU 734
HAURANU 732
Dor
Megiddo
The Great Sea (Mediterranean Sea)
Beth-shan
GAL'AZA 734
Ramoth-gilead
Samaria
SAMARIA 722
Jordan River
Qasile
Joppa
KINGDOM OF AMMON
Rabbah-ammon
Bethel
Jericho
Heshbon
Ashdod
Jerusalem
Ashkelon
Lachish
Hebron
Dead Sea
Dibon
Gaza
ASDUDU 711
En-Gedi
KINGDOM OF JUDAH
Gath
KINGDOM OF MOAB
Beersheba
Arad
Kir-Hareseth
ARABIA
Kadesh-barnea
KINGDOM OF EDOM

MAP 6.4

FIGURE 6.7 **ALTAR ("HIGH PLACE") AT MEGIDDO**

Megiddo was at a strategic location on the road that led from Egypt to Asia Minor. The nation that controlled this pass through the mountainous area, controlled the region. Thus, it was the site of numerous battles. Marshall Johnson

times between 604 and 587. In response to each, the Babylonians impose another wave of exile, taking more and more leaders of Jerusalem to Babylon to try to assure peace. To end the unrest, they finally sack the city in 587/586. This crushing defeat closes an era of independent Israelite political entities. As the Deuteronomistic writings tell the story, these national disasters befall the people as the result of their unwillingness to keep their covenant with God. Though God had been patient for hundreds of years, they had not repented and so now face the terrible (but from the perspective of these books, deserved) consequences.

▶ 1–2 Chronicles, Ezra, and Nehemiah: A Priestly Kingdom and Return from Exile

1–2 Chronicles

Though they are not a part of the Deuteronomistic writings, this is a fitting place to discuss 1 and 2 Chronicles and the books of Ezra and

FIGURE 6.8 **KING JEHU**

King Jehu of Judah is shown prostrating himself before Shalmaneser of Assyria, c. 827 B.C.E. Detail from the "Black Obelisk" of Shalmaneser.

Wikimedia Commons

Nehemiah. These four books manifest a more priestly point of view than those of the Deuteronomistic writings. These four books give special attention to Levites, priests, and the Temple. Still, they remain firmly committed to the pattern set out in Deuteronomy.

In its present form, Chronicles clearly comes from the postexilic period. This is particularly evident from its last chapter, where the writer tells of the proclamation of the Persian king Cyrus (539–530) that allows the people of Judah to return to their homeland and build a temple to their god. So Chronicles extends the story past the fall of Judah, it ends on the hopeful note of the beginning of the return to the land.

Much has happened on the world stage since the fall of Jerusalem. Cyrus has defeated the Babylonians and begun to reorganize the structure of the way the provinces were governed. The **Persian** empire has instituted a policy of repatriation for many peoples, including those of Judah. The new empire allows outlying states to live by their own laws, so long as they maintain their relatedness to the empire by supporting various requests and paying their taxes. This new policy led some people of Judah to support Persian rule. On the island of Elephantine in the Nile River there is a Persian military outpost that stationed Jewish soldiers. According to the papyri found there, they worshiped God, kept the Passover, spoke Aramaic (the language of Palestine), and had a temple to God (even though other Jews said the Jerusalem temple was to be the only temple for God). As the power of the Persian Empire was waning, somewhere around 410, other inhabitants of the region destroyed the Jewish temple at Elephantine, perhaps a move to reduce or overthrow Persian power in the region.

The first nine chapters of Chronicles set out an exhaustive genealogy that begins with Adam and traces the ancestry of all the tribes of the Israelites, but gives special attention to the tribes of Judah, Levi, and Benjamin. These tribes made up the nation of Judah: Judah was the dominant remaining tribe, Benjamin was the tribe of David, and the Levites were the priests. These three tribes are traced to the time of king Saul, with some even being traced through the time of the exile. These genealogies were important because the people's identity was tied to what land they belonged to. In addition, they helped to legitimate the positions of the priests and governing authorities.

Chronicles only recounts the monarchy of Judah; it leaves out the northern kingdom of Israel. This work sees the united kingdom of David and Solomon as the ideal time. If we start counting after the genealogies that begin the work, Chronicles devotes over half of its space to the united kingdom. After the split, the northern kingdom is mentioned only when telling of its contacts with Judah. For this book, Judah is the legitimate nation.

While 1 and 2 Chronicles retell some stories so that they adhere to the deuteronomistic pattern even more closely (as we noticed with their accounts of Jehoash and Josiah), they also give more emphasis to the individual's response to God. When a person experiences difficulties it is less because of the sins of the ancestors and more his or her own responsibility. The importance of observance of the law is present from the beginning of its narrative, as king Saul dies because he did not keep it (1 Chron. 10:14). Chronicles has many more prophets in Judah than what we see in Kings. They often call kings to repent. It is the people's failure to listen to these prophetic calls to faithfulness that finally leads to the fall of the nation (2 Chron. 36:15-16). With its emphases on Torah observance and personal responsibility, the book can call its readers to faithfulness as they return from exile and face hardship in the land.

Chronicles is also concerned to identify proper worship as a part of faithfulness to God. This emphasis begins with having David be concerned about proper worship throughout his reign. This emphasis is not surprising if we remember that rebuilding the temple was one of the biggest religious issues of the first decades of the return from exile. The leaders saw that rebuilding as a necessary element of faithfulness to God. The narrative of Chronicles supports the drive to rebuild the temple.

BOX 6.6

THE CHRONICLER

The author (or authors) of 1 and 2 Chronicles probably lived in the fourth century and was related to the author of Ezra and Nehemiah (some scholars think it is the same person). Chronicles repeats many stories that are in 1 and 2 Kings, but makes them cohere more closely to the Deuteronomistic outlook and pays more attention to priestly concerns.

Read the accounts of the end of king Joash in 2 Kings 12:17-21 and 2 Chronicles 24:17-25. What principle of these texts does Chronicles make explicit that remains unsaid in 2 Kings?

Ezra and Nehemiah

The first group of the exiles returned soon after 539. Many, but not most, Israelites return to Jerusalem and the surrounding region. Work on restoring the temple did not begin until about 520 under the governor Zerubbabel. It was finished in about 515. Ezra does not return until 458, when the Persian king Artaxerxes I (465-424) sends him. Nehemiah arrives as governor in 445.

The books of Ezra and Nehemiah tell of the returnees' continuing struggles to establish themselves politically and economically. These books recount the establishment of a society based on the books of the Law (i.e., the Torah). Most of these books came together during the 50 to 70 years of the Exile. Now, the people returning to Jerusalem begin to commit themselves to a structure of society that will reflect what they find in those books as the will of God. They now see this as the way to please God and so to maintain their place in the land God had promised.

It is during this period of return from exile and commitment to God and the Torah that a number of significant common beliefs become more pronounced. The belief that the people of Judah should worship only one God becomes more widely accepted. Accompanying this belief was the idea that Jerusalem was the only place God was to have a temple. This bound the people to a national and religious past that helped them maintain their identity as the people who have been chosen to be in relationship with God.

But the people did not all agree about what faithfulness to God should include. Some of the disagreements are evident in the marriage practices of the people of Judah. Ezra and Nehemiah call the faithful to agree not to marry outsiders (Ezra 9:1-10:44; Neh. 10:28-39). Others saw nothing wrong with marrying outsiders. This is evident from the lists of people in Ezra 10 who had foreign wives. Ezra thought this matter was so important that he had the men divorce non-Jewish women and send their children away with them. Ezra and Nehemiah saw this regulation as a way to help the people remain faithful to God because it removed the temptation to worship the gods of their spouse.

In addition to prohibiting marriage to outsiders, Nehemiah also argued that faithfulness included keeping the Sabbath and other religious holy days and supporting the temple. He saw these practices as a part of the religious core for those seeking to be faithful. These relate closely to the determination to connect their identity and observance to the ancestral faith as it was formulated in the Torah and the other materials that came into being and prominence in the exile and the early days of the people's return to Jerusalem.

The beliefs and practices that develop during this period and the immediately following time are formative for what Judaism becomes. Our evidence for the specifics of what transpires after the year 400 comes only from archaeological finds. But when evidence begins to reemerge in the second century B.C.E., the commitments of the people of Judah (now starting to be called Judea) to worship the one God and to maintain distinctive observances (including the Sabbath) set them apart from their neighbors in obvious ways. The religious commitments that

BOX 6.7

WAS THERE AN EZRA?

The books of Ezra and Nehemiah give the priest Ezra a leading role in studying and teaching people to observe the Law in Jerusalem. Some interpreters have thought that Ezra may be a construct of these texts because he does not appear in two other texts that speak of the collection of sacred writings in the temple after the return from exile. Sirach 49:11-13 and 2 Maccabees 2:13-14 both tell of this collection and name those who led in the process (including Nehemiah), but neither mentions Ezra. On the other hand, there is a strong Ezra tradition in some groups. There are multiple writings within the apocalyptic tradition that claim Ezra as their author. This suggests at least that there is a strong tradition of a leader named Ezra who was influential in the decades following the rebuilding of the temple.

rose to prominence in the Persian Period (539-334/330) led many to resist Hellenization even to the point of enduring martyrdom. These commitments and beliefs shaped what Judaism would be from that point forward.

▶ Conclusion

The fall of Judah signaled the end of Jewish self-rule for four hundred years. Not until the late second century B.C.E. would an independent Jewish state again exist—and it would have a very short lifespan. This loss of self-rule was a national disaster that created a crisis of faith. Those who had worshiped God knew that the covenant promised a land and a kingdom—both were now gone. So what are they to make of this situation and of what they had believed about God's relationship with them?

When people today read various stories in the Deuteronomistic books, they often see God as cruel or impatient. When read as a whole, however, these texts give a very different impression. The writers of the Deuteronomistic History and the Chronicler's History were giants of faith. The exile posed an enormous challenge to their belief in God, but they remained confident in God and in God's faithfulness. Their faith led them to interpret their national disaster in light of their faith rather than allowing it to destroy their faith. If God is faithful, and yet the people have not enjoyed the fulfillment of God's promises for a kingdom and a land, then the explanation for their fate must rest in their own unfaithfulness to God and the covenant they had entered with God. After all, it was clear that most Israelites had not worshiped only God; they constantly worshiped multiple deities—as did everyone else in the world. So these writers tell the story of their own people in ways that emphasize this failure to keep the covenant.

Thus the account of Israel's life that we read in the Deuteronomistic writings is thoroughly theological and completely an act of faith. It is an act of faith because it assumes that God remains committed to God's people and will respond to their repentance by remaining in covenant with them.

All of these writings assume that God remains loving and committed to the descendants of Abraham. So the faith of these writers tells them that God is fulfilling the stipulations of the covenant. That is, the covenant calls for God to allow the Israelites to suffer defeat if they do not live up to their end of the covenant. Their side of the covenant is: worship only God and keep the commandments. They had done neither. Few other than the prophets and those close to them had at any time worshiped only God, so the exile is what they should expect.

As noted in connection with the stories in Numbers, these accounts of the Israelites' unfaithfulness must not be read by present-day Christians as indictments against Jews of the first or the twenty-first century. These interpretations of their own history are the biblical writers' explanations for their national disasters and calls to repentance for all who would be faithful to God. It is unlikely that most Israelites thought they were living in constant rejection of the God of their ancestors, yet the Deuteronomistic writers interpret their behavior in that way. As Christians look at previous generations, they see places where their predecessors were unfaithful to God and what God wants in the world. No doubt, subsequent generations will see our blind spots. The spiritual ancestors of both Jews and Christians often exemplify our inability to perceive God's will clearly. The biblical accounts of their lives call believers to strive to live more faithfully and to trust in the patience and mercy of God, especially because they know that God did not leave the people in exile. Instead, God responded to their repentance with blessing and grace.

The Deuteronomistic History is not secular or political history—but this should not be surprising. While the kind of history we usually think of would look to military strategy or the dynamics of the political movements of empires as reasons for the fortunes of a nation, these books have a different perspective. Writing out of their faith, these authors give their readers something more important than a simple recounting of facts. They provide the people what they need to sustain faith in God and to make the world understandable in the exile and beyond. These writers move the nation toward the worship of one God because they not only explain how they could have lost their land, but also declare that God is with the people in Babylon. Joseph Blenkinsopp describes the work of these writers in this way:

"In an age of disorientation and discontinuity, of endings and beginnings, the exilic Deuteronomists summoned the remnant of Israel to return to its origins in the belief that the God of the Exodus, the God of Moses, though hidden, would again reveal his face: 'From there you will seek Yahweh your God, and you will find him if you search after him . . . for Yahweh your God is a merciful God; he will not fail you or destroy you or forget the covenant with your fathers which he swore to them'" (Deut. 4:29, 31).*

The existence of this belief in the one merciful and faithful God of the universe owes an enormous debt to these exilic writers.

---

* *A History of Prophecy in Israel,* rev. ed. (Louisville: Westminster, 1995), 165.

▶ LET'S REVIEW ◀

In this chapter, we have learned about the Deuteronomistic History and the Chronicler's history and their theological interpretations of the life of the Israelites from the conquest to the Babylonian exile:

- Joshua
  - —Conquest of the land through the power of God
- Judges
  - —Repeated unfaithfulness brings repeated defeats
  - —God repeatedly rescues the people despite their unfaithfulness
- Ruth
  - —Not really part of this literature
  - —Has a non-Israelite as the great-grandmother of David
- 1 and 2 Samuel
  - —Continuing unfaithfulness, even among the leaders
  - —Saul
  - —David
- 1 and 2 Kings
  - —Continuing unfaithfulness
  - —Solomon
  - —Divided kingdom (Israel and Judah)

- — Fall of Israel because of worship of other gods
- — Fall of Judah because of worship of other gods
- 1 and 2 Chronicles
  - — More priestly perspective, not part of the Deuteronomistic school
- Ezra and Nehemiah
  - — Story of Judahites returning from exile
  - — New commitment to living for God

▶ KEY TERMS ◀

Ark of the Covenant	Deuteronomistic History	Judges
Asherah	Eli	Levirate marriage
Assyrian Empire	Elijah	Naomi
Baal	Elisha	Persian Empire
Babylonian Empire	Gideon	Rahab
Chronicler's History	Israel	Ruth
City of Refuge	Jericho	Samson
Dagon	Joshua	Samuel
David	Josiah	Saul
Deborah	Judah	Solomon

▶ QUESTIONS FOR REVIEW ◀

6.1 Why does the book of Joshua tell the stories of Israel's conquest of Canaan the way it does?

6.2 How do stories in the book of Judges reflect the Deuteronomistic pattern? How important is this pattern to the central point of the book?

6.3 What is the function of the book of Ruth? What does it say about the Israelites' attitude toward non-Jews?

6.4 According to the interpretation of the authors of 1 and 2 Samuel and 1 and 2 Kings, why do the nations of Israel and Judah fall? What does this interpretation tell readers about the purpose of these books?

6.5 Why do 1 and 2 Chronicles sometimes change parts of the stories found in 1 and 2 Kings?

6.6 How do the Deuteronomistic writings interpret the destruction of the northern kingdom and the defeat and exile of Judah?

▸ FOR FURTHER READING ◂

Klaus-Peter Adam and Mark Leuchter, *Soundings in Kings: Perspectives and Methods in Contemporary Scholarship*. Minneapolis: Fortress Press, 2010.

Joseph Blenkinsopp, *Judaism, the First Phase: The Place of Ezra and Nehemiah in the Origins of Judaism*. Grand Rapids: Eerdmans, 2009.

Antony F. Campbell and Mark A. O'Brien, *Unfolding the Deuteronomistic History*. Minneapolis: Fortress Press, 2000.

John J. Collins, *Does the Bible Justify Violence?* Minneapolis: Fortress Press, 2004.

Philip Davies, "Minimalism, 'Ancient Israel,' and Anti-Semitism," Bible and Interpretation Website (No date, but cites a 2002 article) http://www.bibleinterp.com/articles/Minimalism.shtml

William G. Dever, *The Lives of Ordinary People in Ancient Israel: Where Archaeology and the Bible Intersect*. Grand Rapids: Eerdmans, 2012.

Terence E. Fretheim, *The Deuteronomic History*, Interpreting Biblical Texts. Nashville: Abingdon, 1983.

Mark Hamilton, "Who Was a Jew? Jewish Ethnicity During the Achaemenid Period," *Restoration Quarterly* 37 (1995): 102–17. http://www.acu.edu/sponsored/restoration_quarterly/archives/1990s/vol_37_no_2_contents/hamilton.html

Charles David Isbell, "From Yahwism to Judahism," Bible and Interpretation Website 2008 http://www.bibleinterp.com/Isbell_YtoJ_1.shtml

Steven L. McKenzie, "Deuteronomistic History," in *New Interpreter's Dictionary of the Bible*, ed. Katharine D. Sakenfeld, 2:106–8. Nashville: Abingdon, 2007.

———. *Introduction to the Historical Books: Strategies for Reading*. Grand Rapids: Eerdmans, 2010.

Richard D. Nelson, *The Historical Books*, Interpreting Biblical Texts. Nashville: Abingdon, 1998.

Marvin A. Sweeney, *TANAK: A Theology and Critical Introduction to the Jewish Bible*. Minneapolis: Fortress Press, 2011.

Efraín Velázquez II, "The Persian Period and the Origins of Israel: Beyond the 'Myths,'" Bible and Interpretation Website 2009 http://www.bibleinterp.com/articles/persian.shtml

The Center for Online Judaic Studies. http://cojs.org/cojswiki/Main_Page.

7 "Thus Says the LORD"
Israel's Prophetic Tradition

THIS CHAPTER EXAMINES THE MESSAGES OF THE HEBREW PROPHETS:

- Their focus of attention on the injustices of social, economic, and cultural systems
- Their call to Israel and Judah to worship only God
- The classical prophets of the eighth century
- The preexilic prophets' warning of consequences of unfaithfulness
- The exilic prophets' call for faithfulness and offer of hope
- The postexilic prophets' reinterpretation of earlier prophets and call for faithfulness in new times

The prophets of Israel contributed much to the ways Judaism and Christianity understand God and how God's people should live. These prophets gave voice to the beliefs that God demands justice and that God is willing to forgive when the people repent. The prophets had experiences of God that led them to develop the theology that we saw in a developed form in the Deuteronomistic History. Like the Deuteronomistic historians who came after them, these prophets offered a religious interpretation of the political and international events that influenced their nations and region. Unlike the Deuteronomistic historians, these prophets spoke of current events rather than the past. In this process, they came to envision a God to whom the whole world owed its existence and who remained faithful in the covenant with Israel. Israelite prophecy traced its origins to Moses, the one who experienced God's presence most powerfully. This tradition developed through the judges and then through leaders such as Eli, Samuel, Elijah, and Elisha.

The eighth century B.C.E. begins the period of **classical prophecy**. Interpreters have often made the prophets that belong to this era the standard by which they evaluate other prophets. These prophets were not, however, dramatically different from their immediate predecessors, Elijah and Elisha. Among the biggest distinctions between previous prophets and those of the eighth century are that the latter preserved their messages in writing and spent more time delivering their messages to a broader segment of the people, not just to the king and political leaders.

▶ The Classical Prophets

The Prophetic Books

The writings in our Bibles do not come directly from the prophets whose names appear in their titles. These books are the result of combining what the prophets said with various additions (including narratives about the prophets) and interpretations. Even the way these books speak of the prophets indicates that they come from a hand other than that of the prophet himself. Instead of being written in the first person ("I"), they are commonly written in the third person ("he"). So the prophets' message and activity are part of the subject of a narrative that is not written from the perspective of a participant in the action. At least some of these books that record and interpret the life and message of the prophets continued to be edited over the course of a few hundred years. As noted in chapter 2, the book of Jeremiah (a prophet who lived in the seventh century) continued to be edited and reworked as late as the second century B.C.E. So various writers shaped its content for nearly five hundred years. These reworkings helped the community use and understand the prophets' messages in later decades and centuries.

The Ethics of the Prophets

The main sphere of morality for these prophets is the sociopolitical. They oppose the oppressive and exploitive sociopolitical and economic systems that structured all of the ancient world, including Israel, because these systems favored the rich, giving them even greater advantages over the poor. These systems allowed the rich to sell the poor into slavery or to take their land to pay even small debts. The Israelite prophets call for reforms to such systems and insist that God wants justice and mercy for the poor. These prophets also express concern about matters that reach beyond social justice; their messages include requirements in the arena of personal morality and the demand that the people worship only God. Various prophets emphasize one of these things or the other, but they all proclaim God's demands in all aspects of life.

▶ Amos: Justice and Judgment

The Setting

The earliest of the writing prophets is **Amos**. He receives his call to be a prophet after the time of Ahab and Jezebel, but before the fall of the nation of Israel. He is active as a prophet sometime around 750 B.C.E. Many of Amos's prophecies address both Judah and Israel, but some focus solely on Israel (the northern kingdom) and its rulers in Samaria. Amos is well informed about international affairs, as well as being a good poet. He knows which nations pose a threat to his country and the ways such nations are likely to behave. Thus his prophecies sound plausible when he announces the defeat of nations in the surrounding region because everyone knows that the armies of the powerful Assyrian Empire are headed in their direction.

Not a Professional Prophet

Elijah and Elisha had each been the head of a "school of the prophets." Students in these schools were sometimes called "the sons of the prophets." We might call this institution the seminary of its time. In this school, students learned about God and what God expected of the covenant people. They also cultivated techniques for receiving experiences of God and for attaining messages from God in those experiences. Many who went through this school (and there were probably others) eventually earned their living by serving as advisors for officials of the temple and the king's court. Given this way of making their living, they were open to the temptation to condition their message to suit what their employers wanted to hear. This is certainly the charge some of the biblical prophets bring against them. Amos makes a point to distinguish himself from these prophets on the king's payroll. He says he did not receive the training available at the school of the prophets and that he did not really want to be a prophet (7:14-15). Furthermore, since he did not depend on government officials or other wealthy people for his income, Amos was free to speak the truth.

The Day of the LORD

Amos takes a traditional theme that offered hope and turns it against the people of Israel and Judah. When the people had been oppressed, they had prayed for the "**Day of the Lord**," the time when God would deliver them from their oppressors. Amos proclaims that the Day of the Lord is near, but now Israel's warrior God has declared war on the Israelite nation. So the coming of the Day of the Lord is bad news rather than good news (e.g., 5:18-20).

BOX 7.1

Just as God is sometimes presented as a warrior in texts of the Hebrew Bible, God also appears in the New Testament as a warrior who takes vengeance on the wicked. Images of divine destruction of God's enemies with Jesus as the one wielding the weapon appear in 2 Thessalonians 1:6-10; Jude 14–15; Revelation 17:13-14; 19:11-16. In all the Bible, these acts of God defend the righteous and impose justice on those who do evil.

Amos and the Nations

Amos also uses a literary form that he (or the prophetic tradition) borrowed from the proceedings between an overlord and a vassal, when the vassal has acted in ways that violate

BOX 7.2

THE DAY OF THE LORD

Read Amos 5:18-20. Consider how radically different this is from what others have meant when they describe the Day of the Lord.

the arranged terms. The opening chapters of Amos have an "**indictment-verdict**" **pattern** as a central element with the verdict introduced by "So" or "Therefore." The form reads: "For three transgressions and for four, I will not revoke the punishment." Then Amos lists the wrongs the accused has committed before issuing the verdict. He starts with the neighbors and enemies of the Israelites. God is about to bring judgment against these nations because of their excessive violence in wars against their neighbors. Amos's hearers must have been pleased to hear that God was about to punish their enemies in Damascus, Gaza, Tyre, and others places. But the audience's joy quickly turns to shock and horror when Amos includes Judah and Israel among those God will punish (2:4—9:10). God's own people have committed grievous sins, and so should expect judgment like that meted out to their neighbors.

Amos and the Sacrificial System

Amos's accusations against the nations of Israel and Judah mainly concern social injustice (but also sexual immorality and other personal sins, along with worship of many gods; see 2:6-8). In his condemnation of the social and economic structures, Amos engages in a radical critique of temple worship, asserting that God refuses the worship, sacrifices, and thanksgiving the people offer at religious festivals (e.g., 5:21-23). Amos insists that God wants justice and righteousness rather than worship. In these places Amos speaks in exaggerated oppositions. The problem does not lie in the form of the temple worship itself. Rather, the worship is unacceptable because the wealthy and elite classes in Israelite society use the religious institutions to legitimate the political and economic status quo, a system that abuses the poor and gives privileges to the wealthy. Amos sees Israel's worship as radically sinful because those in authority use it to support a sinful political system. Amos asserts that God accepts worship only when the worshiper lives a proper life; his message defines that life primarily in relation to whether a person treats the poor fairly.

The indictment-verdict pattern Amos uses reinforces a paradigm of divine activity that later prophets adopt and that the Deuteronomistic Historians accept. Amos makes national peace a result of faithfulness and national tragedy, whether through natural phenomena (e.g., earthquakes or floods) or political foes, the consequence of unfaithfulness. This pattern makes us uncomfortable because we can all cite exceptions to the rule. But Amos declares that God's response to the people's faithfulness or unfaithfulness comes to expression in such events.

Amos's Distinctive Message

It is important to notice two things about this form of Amos's message. First, he does not have personal troubles and tragedies in view as he sets out this paradigm, but rather the fate of the people as a whole. He does not assert that every difficulty in an individual's life is the result of a sin; rather, he is speaking about the direction of the life of the whole community. While he might well have thought that some tragedy comes into the lives of wicked people as a result of their sin, that is not the subject he is addressing.

Second, Amos assumes that God remains in the covenant with the Israelites through times of national disaster. These disasters are evidence not that God deserts them but that

God continues to operate within the bounds of the covenant. God uses these disasters to call the people back to faithfulness (just as we saw in Judges). Since this is the case, Amos also prophesies a restoration after judgment and repentance.

The prophet Amos clearly teaches that God cares about all aspects of the ways people live. He emphasizes God's concern for the poor and God's condemnation of people who support and profit from unjust social systems. For Amos there is also no impermeable separation between social and personal morality. God's people must live holy lives that reflect God's character in their behavior both in matters of social justice and in matters of personal ethics.

▶ Hosea: The Faithfulness of God

Hosea begins his careers as a prophet at about the same time as Amos (c. 750), but continues a bit longer, until about 720. Hosea preaches only in the northern kingdom of Israel. While he is concerned about social justice, he gives more attention to proper worship and the need to end the worship of gods other than the LORD.

Hosea's Message

Gomer. Much of Hosea's prophecy comes in the form of an allegory. God tells Hosea to marry a "wife of whoredom" (1:2) because the people of the land prostitute themselves to various gods. Whether Gomer, the woman he marries, is a prostitute or a promiscuous woman is not altogether clear. Whichever she is, she is unfaithful to Hosea throughout their marriage. In the allegory, her unfaithfulness symbolizes the nation's unfaithfulness to God. The people's unfaithfulness does not consist in abandoning the worship of God, but in worshiping other gods along with the Lord.

BOX 7.3

THE NAMES OF HOSEA'S CHILDREN

In Hosea 1:4-11, Hosea gives his children symbolic names to announce the coming judgment on Israel: Jezreel (named after the site of a bloody coup), Lo-Ruhamah (means not pitied), Lo-Ammi (not my people). To announce that reconciliation will come after judgment, Hosea reinterprets or changes these names. He says Jezreel means "to plant" (the meaning of the word); changes Lo-Ruhamah to Ruhamah, "pitied"; and changes Lo-Ammi to Ammi, "My people."

Notice how quickly Hosea mentions the restoration of the people after they are punished.

Symbolic names. Gomer bears three children during her marriage to Hosea. Hosea gives each a symbolic name, names that are increasingly dismal. He names the first Jezreel (1:4), the site of the bloody coup in which Jehu killed Jezebel and all Ahab's descendants. This child's name represents the decimation of Israel by its foes. Hosea calls the second child Lo-Ruhamah, which means "not pitied" (1:6). This name signifies that the time of God's mercy and of prophetic intervention with God for the people has past. Hosea gives his third child the name Lo-Ammi, "not my people" (1:8) (put more colloquially, "Not-my-kid"). This name indicates that the special relationship between God and Israel has come to an end; God no longer considers Israel God's child. Thus Hosea predicts a dark future for the nation.

In the end, hope. These devastating predictions about Israel's future do not, however, give the whole picture. Hosea also envisions a time of repentance and restoration. After the curse, there will be blessing if the people turn to the Lord. Hosea gives his children's names new meanings to signify this hope (2:1, 22-23). No longer will Jezreel point to death; it will revert to the meaning of the word, "God sows." Thus God promises to plant the people in the land again. Lo-Ruhamah will become Ruhamah, and so mean that God does have pity and mercy for them. And Lo-Ammi will become Ammi, "My people," so that God reclaims Israel as God's child. Thus, like Amos, Hosea proclaims that unfaithfulness brings national disaster, but he also insists that God responds to repentance and rewards faithfulness.

Hosea's message reminds believers of the importance of putting God first in life. Hosea's original readers worshiped other gods to gain economic and social advantages. While readers today often do not face the temptation to worship other gods (though some manifestations of New Age spirituality seem to present that possibility), most of us struggle to keep things in proper perspective. The New Testament writer of Colossians identifies greed as idolatry (3:5), and thus would apply Hosea's message to people who let attaining economic success be more important than serving God. That understanding of worshiping other gods makes Hosea's warnings about idolatry a challenge to many, perhaps most, believers today.

▶ Micah: What the LORD Requires

Micah's Context

Micah also appears on the scene in the last half of the eighth century. He predicts the fall of both Israel and Judah, but prophesies mostly in Judah, the southern kingdom whose capital is Jerusalem. Some scholars think he was a disciple of Amos and Hosea because his teaching seems to build on theirs. Micah focuses his criticisms on the way some had separated ethics from worship. Like Amos, he asserts that God does not accept the worship of those who engage in unjust social and economic practices. He is particularly critical of the rich who take the land of the independent small farmers.

In this area of the ancient world, the wealthy amassed and retained their wealth through acquiring large farms on which they employed tenant farmers who received only subsistence wages, while all the profit accrued to the owner. Taking the land of a small farmer often meant that the wealthy person then employed that same farmer at a degrading wage that allowed the farm to support the owner's opulent lifestyle. Micah argued that God found such economic systems unacceptable and that those who profited from them deserved God's condemnation.

Micah's Message

Micah's prophecies criticize the monarchy less than Amos's. Still, he distinguishes himself from institutional prophets, who serve at the pleasure of the political and religious leaders. He, like Amos, claims a personal mission from God rather than following the usual course of training to be a prophet. Thus, also like Amos, he could speak the truth to the powerful without fearing the loss of his livelihood.

A classic text. Many readers find Micah 6:6-8 a good summary of the message of the eighth-century prophets:

> With what shall I come before the LORD, and bow myself before God on high? Shall I come before him with burnt offerings, with calves a year old? Will the LORD be pleased with thousands of rams, with ten thousands of rivers of oil? Shall I give my firstborn for my transgression, the fruit of my body for the sin of my soul? He has told you, O mortal, what is good; and what does the LORD require of you but to do justice, and to love kindness, and to walk humbly with your God?

This wonderful flourish summarizes the social concerns of the prophet, but does not indicate that worship is unimportant. Read in the context of the whole book the passage means that worship is acceptable to God only when accompanied by practices of justice, kindness, and humility. Micah rejects the idea that forgiveness comes only through official rituals,

FIGURE 7.1 **RUINS OF SAMARIA**

Samaria was the capital of the nation of Israel after its separation from Judah. Marshall Johnson

but does not reject those rituals as a meaningful way to worship God. He only points out that the worshiper's life should conform to God's will.

For all his emphasis on social justice, Micah does not lose sight of the importance of combining it with appropriate worship. For this prophet, faith expresses itself in working for social justice and proper worship of God. Neglect of either practice is less than what God expects.

▶ Isaiah: Justice, Judgment, and Restoration

A Tripartite Book

The book of Isaiah has a complicated literary history. It contains material from no less than three prophets who write in the name of Isaiah. Chapters 1–39 (except for ch. 35) come from the eighth-century **Isaiah**, who prophesied in Judah and Jerusalem; chapters 40–55 derive from a prophet who wrote while in exile during the sixth century; and chapters 56–66 were composed after Judah's return from the exile.

Isaiah of Jerusalem

The original Isaiah began his ministry in 742, the year King Uzziah died. Isaiah says that in that year he experienced a **theophany** (a vision of God) that commissioned him to begin his work as a prophet (ch. 6). So he also relies on a direct commission from God, rather than the training that other prophets received. Isaiah advises the new king not to make an alliance with Assyria, the empire that would defeat the northern kingdom only twenty years after Isaiah's call. King Ahaz, though, eventually rejects this advice and no longer receives Isaiah or listens to his messages.

Christian Interpretation?

Some of the better-known passages by the prophets come from Isaiah. As early as the Gospel of Matthew, the church began using parts of Isaiah to understand the life and ministry of Jesus. Many subsequent church members have viewed texts from Isaiah and other books of the Hebrew Bible as predictions about Jesus. This would certainly surprise Isaiah. The things Isaiah talks about have their fulfillment in or close to his own time. Matthew and other early Christians thought texts had multiple meanings, even multiple levels of meanings. So when they said that a text spoke of Jesus, they did not necessarily mean that the prophet intended to speak about Jesus. These texts referred to Jesus only in the minds of readers who already believed in him. These believers in Christ used these passages to clarify and give more specific content to their beliefs about Jesus. They believed that the God who acted in Jesus was the same God who had acted in Israel's past. Thus, they thought, one should expect parallels that help believers understand what God has done in Christ.

The sign of Immanuel. These Christian readers gave the prophetic texts new meanings. Writers like Matthew must have known they were inserting meanings that were not in the minds of the prophets. We will discuss this more fully in connection with the Gospel of Matthew, but here we must look at one text in Isaiah that many Christians hear as a prediction about Jesus. Isaiah 7 recounts a time when the situation in Jerusalem looks desperate. The armies of Aram and Israel have laid siege to Jerusalem, the capital of Judah,* and it appears that Judah might succumb to the attack. In this setting, Isaiah comes to King Ahaz with good news: God says Jerusalem will not fall. Moreover, the king can ask for any sign he wants from God and it will happen. Since this message comes from Isaiah, who constantly prophesies doom on Jerusalem, King Ahaz is suspicious when he hears this reassuring prophecy. He seems to think that Isaiah's ploy will be that when Ahaz names a sign, it would not come to pass and so indicate that the real prophecy is that Jerusalem *will* fall. So Ahaz refuses to ask for a sign. Isaiah responds by saying that it is bad enough that the king tests Isaiah's patience, now he is testing God's. So Isaiah comes up with a sign of his own. Seeing a young pregnant woman, he says, look at her, she will name her son Immanuel, which means "God with us." This name is a great act of faith in difficult circumstances. Isaiah says that before this child is two or three years old, he will be eating honey and cottage cheese. (The child can only eat these things if the siege has been lifted so that those foods are available.) And, by that time, the land of the kings that trouble Jerusalem will be in distress.

This sign can be useful to King Ahaz only if it comes true immediately. The sign could not show that Isaiah's prophecy was true unless the child is born in the very near future. It would not help convince Ahaz that Isaiah was right to tell him that in about 750 years a child will be born, and before that child is three years old, the kings that trouble Ahaz will be dead. *Of course* those kings would be dead 700 years later! Such a distant prediction offers the desperate people in Jerusalem nothing. Even if that child were to be the savior of the world, all the people Isaiah addressed would be long dead—perhaps after being tortured by the armies that had already surrounded Jerusalem.

Matthew's reading. But when Matthew reads about a child whose name is "God with us," he automatically applies it to Jesus because, for him, that is who Jesus is: God's presence with us. Matthew does not need to think that Isaiah had such a distant birth in mind to use this passage in his proclamation about Jesus. Since Matthew knows Jesus as the very presence of God in the world, he uses this passage in Isaiah to express that belief. When he does that, he gives the Isaiah text a new meaning. When Isaiah spoke it, this passage was not about Jesus—in fact, no Israelite prophet made direct predictions about Jesus. Early Christians, however, begin applying texts of the Hebrew Bible to Jesus because they give such clear voice to their experience of the way God had acted through Jesus. This is one way the church secured the link between how God had acted among the Israelites and how God had acted in Christ. We will have occasion to discuss the way New Testament writers use prior Scripture in our treatment of Matthew, but now we must return to the earlier message of Isaiah.

Isaiah's Message

The original Isaiah lives in a time of looming disaster. He sees the might of the Assyrian Empire being brought to bear on the small nation of Judah. The outcome is obvious. Isaiah does not, however, attribute the success of the Assyrians to their size or military skills; rather,

*Note that Israel and Judah, the two nations composed of the Israelite tribes, were sometimes at war with one another.

for him they succeed because God gives them the victory. He is convinced that the injustice of the nation's social and economic systems and their worship of other gods have been so rampant that the holy God he experienced in his theophany will bring disaster upon the nation of Judah, the people who should have known and responded to God's presence. But the point of this disaster is neither to completely destroy the people nor to annul the covenant; rather, it is to produce a people who will live as God calls them to live. Even this devastation is evidence that God will not completely abandon them. God remains in covenant with them and so will raise them up from the rubble as a people who live as the covenant demands. Isaiah draws on the messages of Amos and Hosea, so he is working within a tradition. Isaiah's message does not include a hope that the nation can avoid disaster. The hope he offers is for a time after the nation falls. Still he calls on the people to begin to live in the presence of God with a faith that includes both ethics and proper worship. Thus Isaiah calls for a faith that encompasses all of life, from the way one acts in personal and business life to giving proper attention to God. His own profound experience leads him to call others to recognize the presence of God in their midst and to conform their behavior to what having that presence with them requires.

BOX 7.4

CYRUS THE PERSIAN

Read Isaiah 45:1-2. Note how differently Isaiah talks about the foreign king Cyrus than what we saw prophets say about foreign kings in preexilic texts. Why would Second Isaiah see Cyrus in such positive terms?

Second Isaiah

Second Isaiah, whose message appears in chapters 40–55, writes when Judah has been in exile for about fifty years (c. 535 B.C.E.). The context of his message is clearly Babylon rather than Jerusalem at the time when the Assyrian Empire is a threatening presence. This Isaiah mentions Babylonian deities (e.g., Bel and Nebo in 46:1), rather than Assyrian or Canaanite gods, and he seems familiar with some of the myths associated with those Babylonian divinities.

A joyful message of hope. Second Isaiah sees the Persians' growing power and so the approaching end of the Babylonian Empire. He gives God the credit for the Persians' success against the Babylonians and even calls the Persian king **Cyrus** God's anointed one, that is, God's messiah (45:1). Isaiah is confident that God has selected Cyrus to bring benefits to God's people in exile. Since the Persian Empire's policy is to repatriate exiled peoples, their victory likely means that the Judeans will be allowed to return to their homeland. As he looks to this future return, Second Isaiah reminds the people that their former unfaithfulness was the cause of the exile. He devotes much of his message to showing how foolish it is to worship idols. The people must, he argues, reject those gods and respond to God's new act of grace by committing themselves to God so that God will continue to bless them.

Third Isaiah

Third Isaiah, whose message is preserved in chapters 56–66, speaks from a time after the return from the exile (500–450 B.C.E.). He is probably part of a prophetic group that calls its members "servants of the LORD." Few of the returnees seem to listen to them, and some even abuse them. Third Isaiah understands the suffering of his group as beneficial for others, and believes it can even lead God to forgive them. This prophet, then, engages the question of why God's prophets and the faithful suffer, even though they are the ones who obey God. This Isaiah also calls the people to stop worshiping other gods while there is still time; he envisions a future of great blessing, if only the people will repent and worship God alone. This Isaiah has a wider vision of the blessings God will bring on the world than some of his predecessors. Israel's faithfulness will bring blessing not only on them but on the whole world, because God will spread God's kingdom throughout the world.

A broad vision. This wider vision would influence the early church to see Jesus' mission as one that includes Gentiles and stretches to the ends of the earth. Furthermore, the interpretation this prophet gives his (and the group's) suffering for God's truth would significantly influence the early church's understanding of Jesus and their own experience of persecution. Thus this

BOX 7.5

THE SERVANT SONGS

Second Isaiah contains four sections known as the Suffering Servant Songs or just the Servant Songs (42:1-9; 46:1-6; 50:4-11; 52:13—53:12). These "songs" or poems develop the idea that a prophet who is part of the group that maintains faithfulness to God will endure suffering for the good of the nation. Like the presentations of Moses, Jeremiah, and Ezekiel, this "servant" of God serves as an example of the obedience God wants from God's people. Further, his suffering leads to exaltation by God, so those who follow his example in faithfulness can expect God to respond in a similar fashion. Beyond this exemplary function, some within Judaism had come to see the suffering of martyrs and prophets as acts that bring closer the day of restoration, but only if the people begin to follow the example of faithfulness the prophets set.

Instead of seeing the Servant as a person, a number of scholars understand him to be the nation of Israel through whom God will bless the world.

In later times, Christians read the Servant Songs to interpret what Jesus had done for them. These poems are clearly not about Jesus or anyone who lived hundreds of years after the time of Isaiah. But the church believed that what these poems expressed about Israel's return from exile now described what Jesus had done for the whole world. As Christians did this, they were reading new meanings into these texts, as we saw Origen and Philo do in chapter 3.

writer begins to articulate a view that the martyrdom traditions of both Judaism and Christianity will develop, and that the early church will use to interpret the suffering and death of Jesus. This prophet can still help people of faith think about how their experience of opposition may advance the cause of God's will.

Our look at the messages of Second and Third Isaiah has led us through the trauma of the Babylonian exile and to the time of their return to Judea. But we must now go back to the seventh century, the time before the exile, to hear the message of other prophets in the time that leads up to the fall of Judah.

▶ Jeremiah: Looming Judgment and Future Restoration

The Man and the Book

By his own account (1:2), **Jeremiah** begins prophesying in about 627, just over a hundred years after the original Isaiah. Jeremiah also calls the people to stop worshiping other gods and to act justly, warning repeatedly that failing to repent will bring disaster. His predictions of doom form so much of his message that the king and leading priests ban him from the temple precinct (36:5), even though he is probably a priest (see 1:1). But this does not stop Jeremiah from propagating his message. Jeremiah works with a secretary named Baruch, who transcribes his messages. So when Jeremiah can no longer go to the temple himself, he sends Baruch there to read the compilation of the first twenty years of his preaching (ch. 36). When the temple and government officials hear the message, they take Baruch to King Jehoiakim. As Baruch reads the scroll, the king cuts off each piece he has read and throws it in the fireplace. When Baruch returns to Jeremiah, the prophet has him rewrite the whole scroll and even expands its message. Many scholars think that the scroll Baruch transcribed became the nucleus of chapters 1–25 of the book of Jeremiah we have now.

Jeremiah's Message

Despite the gloom and doom that Jeremiah prophesies, his message contains important words of hope. Though he predicts the fall of Judah, God tells Jeremiah to buy a plot of farmland (ch. 32). This investment makes no sense if the nation is about to fall, because he would lose the land. But Jeremiah's purchase of the field signifies that God's punishment of Judah will not permanently remove them from their land. After the fall of the nation, God will restore them.

Experiencing the End

Jeremiah actually lives through the initial siege of Jerusalem and gives advice about the policies the nation should adopt in its aftermath. In 597

BOX 7.6

A CONFLICT BETWEEN WORDS AND DEEDS?

What do you make of the tension between the prophecy of the fall of Jerusalem and the prophetic action of buying a field that you see in Jeremiah 32:1-15? What do you think the reaction of the people around Jeremiah would be?

the Babylonians successfully invade Jerusalem, but do not destroy the city. They do, however, take many of the nation's nobles and leaders into exile. (The priest and later prophet Ezekiel is among those they take.) These nobles serve primarily as (mostly well-treated) hostages to guarantee the cooperation of those left in charge in Jerusalem.

At this point, Jeremiah calls for cooperation with the Babylonians. Many other prophets, however, say that God wants the nation to revolt. The leaders choose revolt and so the Babylonians return for a second siege. During this siege, the rulers in Jerusalem imprison Jeremiah because he continues to call for cooperation rather than revolt (chs. 37–39). He is released from jail only after the Babylonians again subdue Jerusalem. Jeremiah then goes to Egypt (ch. 43), where according to tradition he dies.

The book of Jeremiah seems to have been put together by a group with the same views we see in the Deuteronomistic History. It was mostly complete just a couple of decades into the exile (c. 550), but as we noted in connection with the formation of the canon (chapter 2), different versions of Jeremiah existed into the second century.

This book presents Jeremiah's life as exemplifying faithfulness in the face of adversity. In the middle part of his ministry he is persecuted because he proclaims that temple worship is not enough to secure the nation's future. He says God demands obedience to the commandments of the covenant, rather than just continuing worship. Once the siege of Jerusalem begins, Jeremiah's situation worsens. During a temporary lifting of the siege, Jeremiah is arrested falsely for deserting to the enemy (ch. 37). Afterward, the king summons him, and Jeremiah still says the nation will fall. When he is returned to prison, though under more tolerable conditions, he continues to tell people that the city is doomed. As a result, he is thrown into an empty cistern (an underground water reservoir; ch. 38). Even though the king makes sure he is rescued before he dies, Jeremiah continues to warn the king that the city would fall (38:1-28). Jeremiah lives through the destruction of Jerusalem by the Babylonians and continues to tell people to turn to God before even worse things happen (see chapters 42–44). In the midst of these troubles, Jeremiah also tells the people that there is a future for the nation if they repent, though only after the disaster. This presentation of Jeremiah's refusal to falsify his message, even in the face of great suffering, set him out as a paradigm of the unheeded prophet who remains faithful. This image of the prophet was probably shaped by the servant poems in Isaiah (especially see Isa. 49:1-6; 50:4-9), which see the servant of God suffering for the people.

In many ways, the writer of the book of Jeremiah uses these narratives to shape the prophet's life so that it follows the pattern set by Moses. Both have a ministry of forty years, proclaim God's law, intercede for the people, accept rejection because of their faithfulness, and face challenges to their authority. These parallels suggest that the author of the book of Jeremiah sees the prophet Jeremiah as the prophet like Moses that Deuteronomy mentions (18:15); perhaps this writer sees Jeremiah as the last in the line of prophets of this sort. The fall of the nation suggests to this writer that a new kind of prophet may be needed in the time to come.

FIGURE 7.2 **RUINS OF JERUSALEM**

Ancient Jerusalem from the time of David. Corbis

The Book of Lamentations

Tradition says that Jeremiah also wrote the book of Lamentations. While this is doubtful, it was probably written by someone who endured the fall of Jerusalem. This book consists of mourning poetry that grieves over the fall of Judah and Jerusalem. It gives us a glimpse of the devastation those in Jerusalem felt when their nation fell.

BOX 7.7

A MATTER OF THE HEART

Read Jeremiah 31:31-34. Why does Jeremiah think that the people have failed to keep the Law? What does he think God must do to make it possible to keep the Law?

▶ Zephaniah, Nahum, Habakkuk, Obadiah

These four prophets arise in the years just before and after the fall of Jerusalem. They witness the fall of Assyria, the empire that had

BOX 7.8

THE POETRY OF LAMENTATIONS

The first four poems (chapters) in the book of Lamentations are in acrostic form: one stanza (though with varying numbers of lines per stanza) for each of the twenty-two letters of the Hebrew alphabet. The final poem has twenty-two verses.

destroyed the northern kingdom of Israel, and the rise of the Babylonian Empire. So they offer their messages of warning and hope in turbulent times.

Zephaniah: The Day of the Lord

Zephaniah proclaims his message in the years that precede Josiah's reforms. He began preaching about 630. Like Amos, Zephaniah warns that the Day of the LORD will bring judgment on Judah because they continue to worship multiple gods (1:4-6, 14-18). Zephaniah identifies with "the humble of the land" (2:3) who live righteously and obey God. So he also expresses concern about the unjust economic system that persisted in Judah.

In addition to his warnings and calls to repentance, Zephaniah also envisions a restoration of God's people after their devastation (3:14-20). He envisions a glorious renewal that involves more of the world than just Judah. In these prophecies, foreigners also gather in Jerusalem to worship God (3:8-10). Thus the restoration of Judah includes an expansion of their influence on the world and so a blessing to many peoples as they gather to honor God.

Nahum: The Downfall of Nineveh

Nahum prophesies most likely in the early decades of Josiah's reign (640–609). His book is an oracle against Nineveh, the capital of Assyria, that predicts the city's downfall because of its unjust treatment of the nations it conquers. The fall of Assyria is good news for Judah because it signals the defeat of the greatest threat to its security. Nahum declares that God has delayed this action against the Assyrians, but is now ready to act. Unlike Zephaniah, Nahum does not call the people of Judah to repent; his focus remains on God's judgment against the Assyrians.

For Nahum, the defeat of Assyria should lead the people of Judah to celebrate joyfully the religious festivals of the LORD (1:15). The reforms of King Josiah may have been, in part, a response to Nahum's message. When Josiah institutes the celebration of these festivals, it has a political as well as a religious meaning. Such celebrations of the acts of Judah's God begin to distance the nation from Assyrian domination, because they honor the God who is about to defeat that empire. Thus, in Nahum, the religious revival is also a nationalistic revival.

Habakkuk: "Yet I Will Rejoice"

Habakkuk likely appears soon after the death of Josiah. He faces the question of why bad things happen to good people; the good king who led the people to worship God has just been killed in battle against the Egyptian army. How can this be? The Deuteronomistic pattern (i.e., God rewards the righteous and punishes the wicked) has broken down. So Habakkuk questions God about the victory of the wicked over the

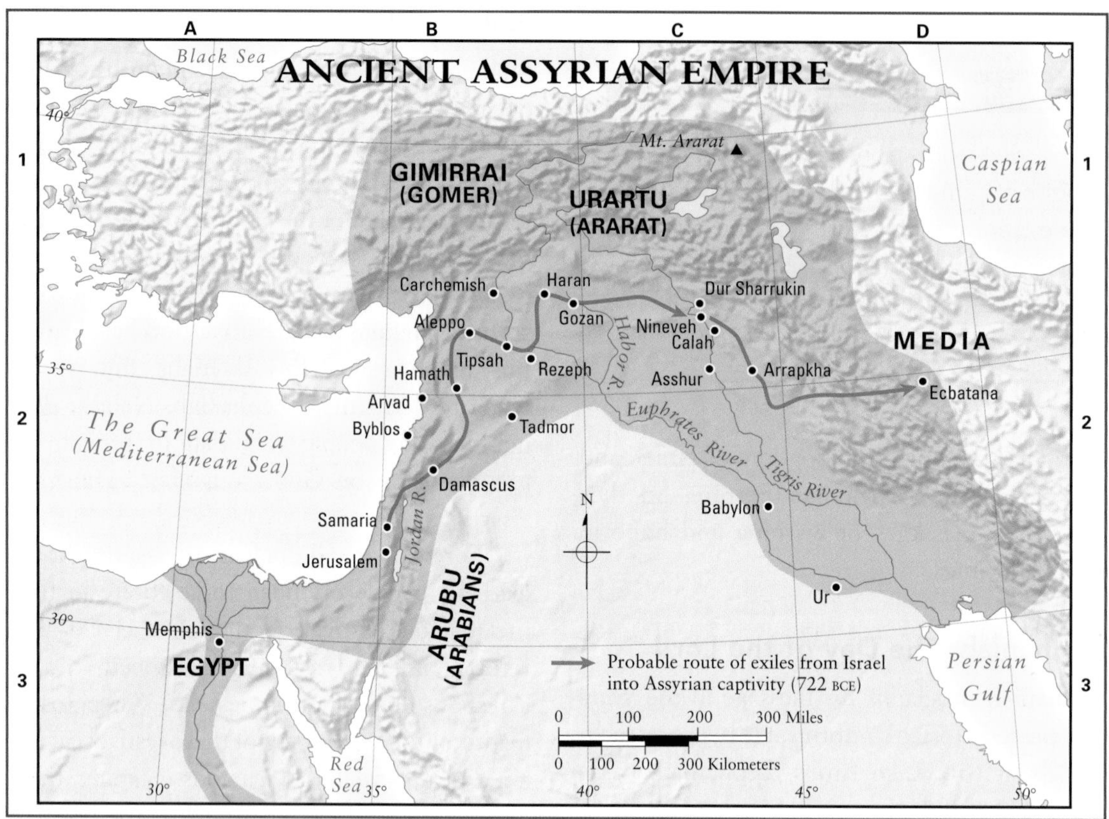

MAP 7.1

righteous (1:2-17). God responds by saying that the conquerors have come to punish the wicked (2:1-19). But this answer is not sufficient because the righteous (including a righteous king) are suffering along with the wicked. Habakkuk receives no good resolution of this matter. Still he concludes that the righteous must stay faithful because there is no place to turn but to God. The book of Habakkuk closes with a beautiful expression of enormous faith in God:

> Though the fig tree does not blossom,
> and no fruit is on the vines;
> though the produce of the olive fails,
> and the fields yield no food;
> though the flock is cut off from the fold,
> and there is no herd in the stalls,
> yet I will rejoice in the LORD;
> I will exult in the God of my salvation.
> God, the LORD, is my strength;
> he makes my feet like the feet of a deer
> and makes me tread upon the heights.

Habakkuk continues to look to God because however bad things get, God is the only source of salvation.

Obadiah: Woe to Edom

Obadiah, the shortest book in the Hebrew Bible, consists of three oracles against the

Edomites, and one against all Judah's enemies. Although the date of the prophet is uncertain, he perhaps composes these pieces soon after the fall of Jerusalem. The Edomites had tried to take advantage of the disaster in Jerusalem by annexing territory that had been part of Judah. Obadiah responds by proclaiming that God would punish Edom, and all Judah's enemies, because of their violent and unjust behavior. Though they do it in a manner that seems vengeful, these oracles express the prophet's confidence in God to work justice in the world.

▶ Ezekiel: God Is Present

Ezekiel stands out as one of the most important prophets for the development of the faith of both Judaism and Christianity. He is deported and experiences the subsequent fall of Jerusalem while he is in exile in Babylon (located in modern Iraq). He interprets the fall of Judah and finds God present among the exiles in ways that enable people to maintain, and even strengthen, their faith in God.

The Context

Ezekiel is among the first Judeans the Babylonians take into exile. This indicates that he was from an aristocratic family (1:3). He begins having visions in Babylon in about 593, not long after arriving there, and remains active as a prophet for at least twenty years. As a priest, Ezekiel expresses concerns about ritual and worship practices, as well as about fidelity to God. Many of his ideas intersect with the group of priests that helped finalize the books of the Pentateuch (see above, chapter 4).

Ezekiel's First Visions

God's presence in the exile. The first twenty-four chapters of Ezekiel chronicle his experiences in Babylon and the events in Jerusalem that lead up to its fall. In his visions, he sees priests in Jerusalem continuing to worship multiple gods, even in the temple of God (ch. 8). (No doubt he would have witnessed these activities firsthand when he served in the temple before his exile.) Through his visions he also watches each misstep in Jerusalem that makes its destruction inevitable. Simultaneously, he has experiences of the presence of God in Babylon. This is a surprising development on two counts. First, many people thought of gods as linked to regions and particular functions. Ezekiel's experience of God's presence in Babylon means that God can be anywhere, even in the faraway center of the enemy's capital. Second, it means that despite Judah's crushing defeat, a consequence of their unfaithfulness, God has not abandoned them. God has determined to be present among them even as they are suffering. These are astonishing and wonderful revelations about God.

The chariot-throne. Ezekiel is known best for his extravagant visions at the beginning of the book. (These visions are so strange that some twentieth-century readers have claimed that Ezekiel saw a UFO.) In his first vision, Ezekiel sees creatures with all kinds of wheels and eyes moving with amazing speed across the landscape (ch. 1). This vision is intentionally breathtaking because of the nearly unbelievable news it reveals: these images represent the chariot-throne of God (and so the special presence of God) that is coming to reside with the people in exile. The Lord moves from Jerusalem to

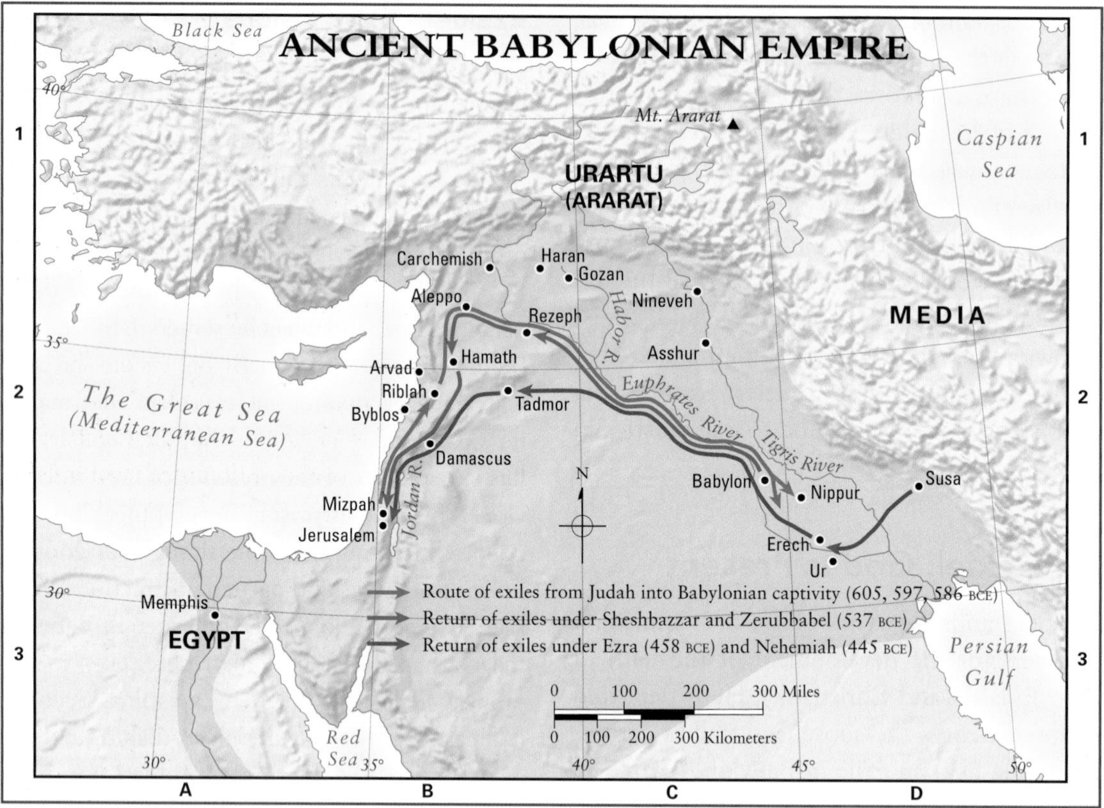

MAP 7.2

Babylon because that is where God's people are. This news brings comfort to those required to live in the strange land of Babylon, because it proclaims that God has not abandoned them. But there is more.

BOX 7.9

EZEKIEL'S ASTONISHING VISIONS

The report of the visions that appear in the first chapters of Ezekiel are part of the escalation of dramatic language that helped launch the imagery of apocalyptic, the literary form we see fully developed in the book of Revelation. His imagery is so powerful that it continued to be used and reinterpreted for hundreds of years within apocalyptic literature.

God's departure from Jerusalem. Ezekiel's initial series of visions also offers an explanation for how Jerusalem, God's holy city, could fall. Commonly, ancient peoples interpreted the rise of an empire to the power of the leading god or gods of the successful nation. Ezekiel, however, continues to see the Lord as the strongest of all gods, even as the capital of God's people falls and God's temple is destroyed. Through this first series of visions, Ezekiel watches the presence of God progressively leaving Jerusalem so that when the Babylonians sack the city and destroy the temple, God's presence no longer resides in those places (ch. 10). Thus the city and temple do not fall because God is weak, but because God has left those places and allowed the Babylonians to seize them. God's departure from Jerusalem does not, however, mean that God has abandoned the people, because God's presence now resides with them in exile. So through these visions Ezekiel defends the power of God, expands the people's understanding of who God is, and assures them that God remains in relationship with them.

Since God has not abandoned the people in exile, Ezekiel argues that the people must now turn to serve God more faithfully than ever before, because all their hope for return lies with God (11:14-21; see chs. 36, 39). They must not, then, worship the gods of the Babylonians, even though they seem powerful. The prophet contends that only by repenting and finally turning to worship God exclusively can the exiles hope to return to their homeland and the life God wants for them.

Oracles against the Nations

In chapters 25–32, the second part of Ezekiel, we find oracles against the foreign nations that

FIGURE 7.3 **ISHTAR GATE**

This main gate of the city of Babylon was built during the reign of Nebuchadnezzar II (605–562 B.C.E.). The exiles of Judah were in Babylon when this impressive entrance was built. Wikimedia Commons

occupy Jerusalem and the neighboring nations who aided the Babylonians. The violence of their actions, says the prophet, goes beyond the punishment God sanctions for Judah. Thus God will also punish those nations.

BOX 7.10

OTHER GODS IN THE TEMPLE?

Does what Ezekiel sees in Ezekiel 8:5-13 surprise you? What does this worship of other gods in the temple suggest about the worship of other gods in Judah and throughout the history of the Israelite nations?

Hope for Restoration

The third section of Ezekiel, chapters 33–39, offers hope for restoration and responds to questions about whether God cares about the plight of the people. The prophet explains that God takes no pleasure in the suffering of God's people, not even in the suffering of the wicked; rather, God wants these experiences to lead people to repent. Some of the exiles think they are suffering unjustly because they were not the cause of Judah's defeat. They were children or perhaps not even born when the sins were committed that led to the exile, so they ask why they should suffer for the sins of their parents. When these people question the justice and ethical

FIGURE 7.4 **CYRUS CYLINDER**

Written in Babylonian (around 539–530 B.C.E.), the cylinder tells of how King Cyrus the Persian defeated the Babylonians. Wikimedia Commons

character of God, Ezekiel responds by saying that God's punishment is not predetermined. If the people turn to God and worship only God, God will reward them.

New Temple and New Nation

The final part of Ezekiel, chapters 40–48, contains a vision of the new temple and commonwealth of God's people. The prophet goes into great detail describing this new temple and how God will dwell in it. Ezekiel predicts a greater grandeur than Judah had ever known, and in this magnificence God will be in closer relationship with God's people than in any previous era. So the book ends with a great declaration of hope.

Themes from the prophet Ezekiel have been influential in the development of Judaism. His message about the presence of God and his connection of worship and morality help mold what Judaism would become. He is among the first to proclaim that God could be and indeed is with the people in their exile. Thus the exile does not mean that God rejected Judah, because God continues to be with them. His vision of God also seems to have contributed to the ways the final editors of the Pentateuch understood God. So while his extravagant visions seem rather strange to us, they provide what the people in exile need to come to a clearer and renewed faith in God in the midst of their suffering in Babylon.

▶ Postexilic Prophets

The prophets **Haggai**, **Zechariah**, **Joel**, and **Jonah** probably all appear after the Persians allow the Judeans to return to Judah.

Haggai: Rebuild the Temple

Haggai starts his prophetic ministry about fifteen years after the first group of exiles returns to Jerusalem. Both Haggai and Zechariah urge the returnees to finish building the temple. Haggai seems to think that completion of the temple will usher in a restoration of an independent kingdom of Judah. He proclaims his message during the two years that follow the death of the Persian king Cyrus (522), a period in which there was a struggle for succession in Babylon. Haggai imagines that the weakness of the empire will enable Judah to rise. But, he asserts, this will only happen with God's help and if the returnees finish the temple. By 520, however, Darius takes firm control of the empire and it does not crumble. Thus Haggai's hope cannot be fully realized.

Zechariah: Proper Worship Requires the Temple

The prophecies of Zechariah begin at about the time Darius secures the throne, and so a few months after those of Haggai end. He adjusts the expectations of Haggai so that completion of the temple will mean that God returns, but the full restoration of the nation will be delayed until a later time. Zechariah also calls the people to take responsibility for the poor, arguing that bad treatment of the poor was an important reason for the exile (7:8-14). Thus he links proper worship and proper social responsibility. This prophet also looks forward to a time when God reverses the fortunes of the rich and the poor. Furthermore, he envisions a future in which Jerusalem will overflow with the faithful, and those faithful will include proselytes (12:1-9;

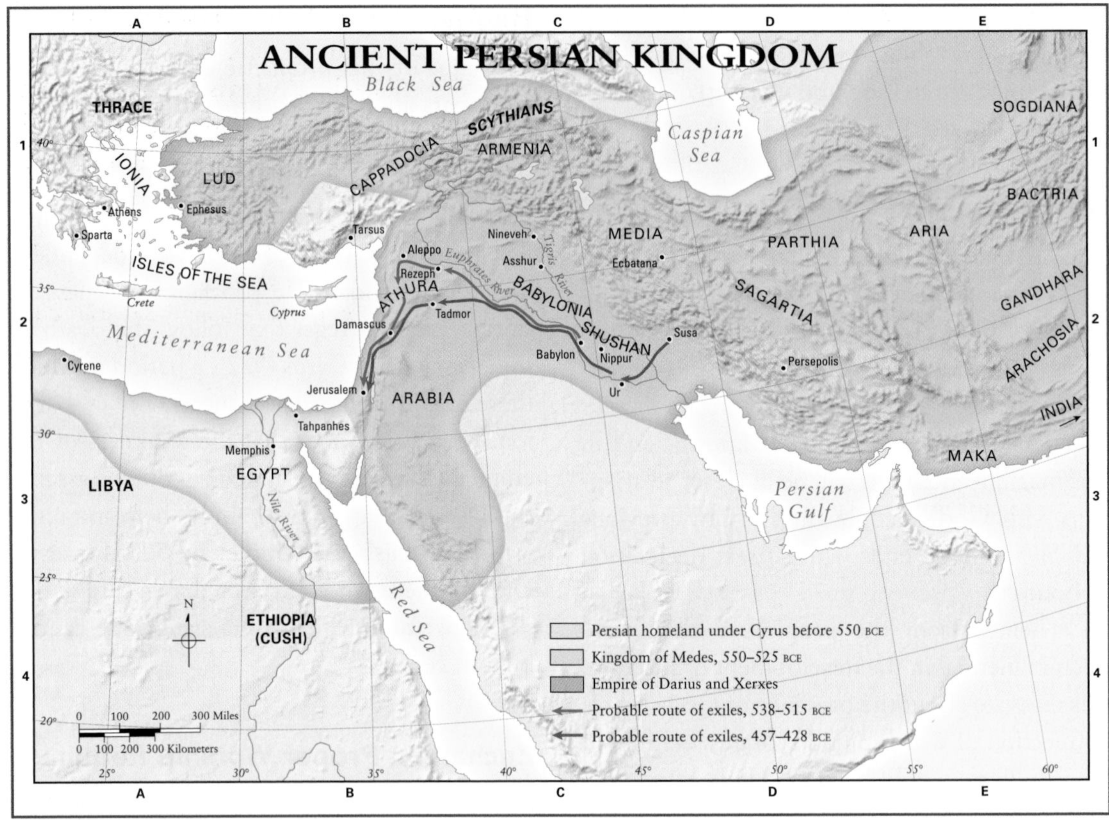

MAP 7.3

14:16). The initial stage of all of this glory, however, awaits the completion of the temple.

Clearly Haggai and Zechariah think that proper worship is a necessary part of the lives of God's people. They encourage completion of the temple so that the worship of God may take its rightful place at the center of the community's life. These prophets also make clear that emphasizing the importance of worship does not indicate a lack of concern for social justice. Indeed, worship and concerns about justice go hand-in-hand, with each reinforcing the importance of the other in the life of faith.

Malachi: Messenger of Repentance and Renewal

The book of **Malachi** is a short collection of prophetic oracles that come from the time between the reestablishment of worship in the new temple (515) and the mission of Nehemiah to help rebuild Jerusalem and the surrounding area (445). These oracles condemn the priests for failing to tithe and for offering sick or damaged animals as sacrifices to God. It seems that economic bad times have led many to think that faithfulness to God and proper worship are unimportant. After all, completion of the temple had not ushered in the reestablishment of a new monarchy or an independent Jewish state. As a result many of the returnees have begun marrying non-Israelites and worshiping their gods.

The prophet Malachi calls on the people to repent or face judgment from God. He also looks forward to a messenger from God who will lead the people to repent and serve God. He identifies this messenger as Elijah, the prophet who was taken up in a fiery chariot in 2 Kings 2. Since Elijah did not die before this ascension, Malachi can envision him returning as God's messenger. This proclamation of Elijah's coming is part of the tradition that leads people in the first century to ask whether John the Baptist or Jesus might be Elijah (John 1:21; Matt. 16:14).

Malachi, then, recognizes the difficulty people face when they try to live for God in an

FIGURE 7.5 **BAS RELIEF OF KING DARIUS I (550–486 B.C.E.)**

Darius came to the throne soon after the exiles of Judah began to return home. The prophet Haggai was active during the beginning of this king's reign. Art Resource

environment that lures them to engage in acts of unfaithfulness. So while he makes no fewer demands on the people than previous prophets, this prophet envisions a time when God would send a leader who could help them live as God's people.

Joel: Locusts as Judgment

The book of Joel is probably also written soon after the reestablishment of worship in the temple, though some think it was written before the exile. It tells of a locust plague that decimates the crops of the whole region. Those who have seen a swarm of locusts descend on a field know the way they can destroy all that is there with unbelievable speed. Joel proclaims that the way to overcome such disasters is through worship at the temple, worship in which prophets take a leading role. In his vision, these locusts become more than common locusts. His descriptions make them frightening, armor-bearing beasts that destroy everything in their path. So as the book comes together, the locusts become symbols of the coming judgment of God on the whole world. Joel is among those books that begin to look to a final and worldwide act of God's judgment. He also looks forward to God coming to live with God's people in new and intimate ways. In later centuries, the church will use some of these prophecies to interpret its experience of the coming of God's Spirit on its members (Acts 2:17-21 quotes Joel 2:28-32).

Jonah: God's Mercy on the Ninevites

Context and genre. The little book of Jonah is extremely powerful. Its story moves readers to think in wider terms than what we see in many of the prophets, and it provides a way to think about earlier (particularly, not completely fulfilled) prophecies. Jonah was written sometime after the fall of the Assyrian Empire because it uses the city of **Nineveh**, the capital of Assyria, as its central setting. It would have been too difficult to use this example while the Assyrians posed an immediate threat to the nation. Jonah is not a historical figure; rather this book is something like a folktale. The many things that happen in the book show that it uses ironic contrasts and exaggerations to make its message entertaining. (Even how it has Jonah get to Nineveh is impossible—there is no sea route to this inland capital.) But this is not (just) a children's story. This narrative, which the original author would expect everyone to recognize as a nonfactual tale, conveys very weighty messages.

The perspective. One's of Jonah's main points is that God's actions and mercy are not limited to Israelites. God acts on the sea and in Nineveh, both places beyond the boundaries of Judah. Thus this book proclaims that God is the god of the whole world and of all the world's people. And more than this, God loves all the peoples of the world—even Judah's enemies.

Jonah preaches. In the story, God calls Jonah to preach to Nineveh, to tell them that God is about to destroy them because they are wicked (1:2). Interestingly, this message does not tell them to repent; it only announces judgment. But Jonah does not want to deliver this message to the capital of the "evil empire," so he boards a ship heading in the other direction. When God brings a storm to stop Jonah's flight, it is so powerful that it nearly sinks the ship. The sailors determine that Jonah is the problem, but are reluctant to do anything about it. Finally, though, they throw him overboard. A large fish then swallows Jonah, but he does not die. Instead he sits praying in the belly of the fish for three days, then God has the fish vomit him onto shore (ch. 2). Jonah travels to Nineveh, reluctantly proclaims his message of condemnation, and sits back to watch God destroy this huge city (ch. 3). But the people of Nineveh repent (even their animals participate in the repentance), so God revokes the decree of destruction. Jonah is angry because he wanted God to destroy these evil people who had wreaked

CHART 7.1

ISRAELITE PROPHETS*

Pre-Monarchic and United Kingdom Eras

Samuel 11th–10th century
Nathan 10th century

Divided Kingdom

ISRAEL	JUDAH
Elijah early 9th century	
Elisha late 9th century	
Amos 750–740 (730)	Micah latter half of 8th century
Hosea 750–720	Isaiah of Jerusalem 742–700
	Zephaniah 650–630
	Nahum 640–620
	Jeremiah 627–587/6
	Habakkuk 609–605
	Ezekiel 595–570
	Obadiah 586–580
	Second Isaiah 540–530

After the Return from Exile

Haggai 522–520
Zechariah 520–518
Malachi between 515–445
Joel after 515
Jonah 7th–5th centuries
Third Isaiah 500–450
Daniel (the character Daniel lived in the 6th century); book composed 170–160

*Many of the dates given here are approximations.

havoc on the nation of Israel; he wants them to suffer for their wrong deeds (ch. 4). Jonah tells God that he did not want to warn these people of their impending doom because he knew that God would relent if they repented.

The universal God. This prophetic book serves, in part, as a critique of Israelite prophecy. First, it questions whether God's attention is focused narrowly on Israelites. Yes, they are God's chosen people, but God remains concerned about the rest of the world as well. Jonah demonstrates that God both extends compassion to all peoples and expects justice from them, even from the inhabitants of the evil empire of Assyria. Throughout the book, God shows mercy to everyone: Jonah, the sailors, the Ninevites; the book emphasizes God's goodness and willingness to forgive. By having God respond, even reach out, to non-Israelites, the author raises the question of whether they can become the people of God. What must non-Israelites do to receive God's mercy? Notably, the author does not expect the Ninevites to abandon their worship of other gods, only to repent of their evil deeds. So this story shows that God accepts the worship of people who are not Israelites, if they repent of their social and personal sins and begin to conduct their lives in an ethical manner.

Repentance and forgiveness. A second critique of prophecy that Jonah offers concerns unfulfilled prophecy. Earlier prophets had predicted events of both condemnation of and restoration for Judah that had not come true, at least not fully. While lack of fulfillment casts doubt on the validity of those prophets' messages, Jonah offers the exercise of God's mercy as a reason for the failure of some prophecies. He insists that there is no irrevocable link between sin and punishment. In God's mercy, God can exercise a will to save that means some prophecies of destruction will not be fulfilled. Remember, Jonah does not even call on Nineveh to repent (even though their king does), he just pronounces judgment. Still, God responds when they do repent. This was just what Jonah was afraid of! Jonah knows of, but does not understand, God's will to save. Because of God's mercy and grace Jonah's prophecy does not come true, yet he had a genuine revelation from God and his mission was a success from God's perspective—even if not from Jonah's. Thus lack of fulfillment is not a clear sign that a prophet's message is invalid; indeed, it may be a sign that the prophet was successful in moving the people to repent. This also allows that the more glorious restoration of Judah awaits further faithfulness or even is a sign of the exercise of God's mercy to its neighbors.

This short book, then, entertains while making important contributions to the outlook of what is developing into the Judaism of later periods. It helps expand readers' vision of God and God's working in the world by showing God's care for all peoples. It also emphasizes God's grace by having God spare even the most wicked when they repent. So Jonah is another example of how central grace and mercy are in the understanding of God that we find in the Hebrew Bible and Judaism.

▶ Daniel: Persecution and Radical Newness

Date and Structure

The book of **Daniel** was probably the last book of the Hebrew Bible to be written. It tells stories about a person who lived in the sixth century, but the book was likely composed in the second century during the **Maccabean Revolt**, a time of great upheaval in Judea. Daniel is one of a very few books in the Hebrew Bible that have parts written fully in the genre of **apocalyptic**, the style of writing that developed into what we find in the New Testament book of Revelation. Daniel was also written in two languages: most of the stories about people who are faithful to God and the Law (2:4b—7:28) were written in Aramaic, a language related to Hebrew, while the introduction of the book and the visions of the last chapters (1:1—2:4a; 8:1—12:13) were composed in Hebrew. The Hebrew and Aramaic parts of the book were probably written at different times, with the stories about Daniel probably circulating before the visions were written.

Alexander the Great

By the time Daniel was written, the Persian Empire had fallen. Alexander the Great had conquered most of what we know as the Middle East, along with Greece, Turkey, and parts of North Africa. Upon Alexander's premature death, his generals divided the empire into several parts. Palestine, and so the area around Jerusalem (which was then known as Judea), first came under the control of Ptolemy. This general established his own kingdom with its capital in Alexandria, Egypt. In 198 B.C.E. the Seleucids, the heirs of another of Alexander's generals, took control of the region of Judah. The capital of this kingdom was in Damascus, so these people are often referred to as Syrians.

Hellenization

Alexander had urged all the regions he conquered to adopt major aspects of Greek culture, a policy called **hellenization**. Alexander's successors adopted this policy and pressed it successfully enough that within a hundred years Greek became the language of commerce and politics throughout the region. Hellenization also involved identifying the gods of various regions with the gods of the Greeks. In this way the Greek representations of gods spread throughout the world. This addition of a few gods or identification of their gods with others created few problems in most areas because people already worshiped many gods. In Judea, however, this element of hellenization met stiff resistance.

The Maccabean Revolt

Jews refused to identify God with Zeus or any other god. The more they resisted, the more tension grew between them and the governing

BOX 7.11

THE *DIADOCHOI* (SUCCESSORS) OF ALEXANDER THE GREAT

When Alexander the Great died at a young age and without a son, twenty years of war among his generals ensued. At the end of that time, four rulers emerged who controlled most of the territory Alexander had conquered. Those four were Lysimachus, Seleucus, Cassander, and Ptolemy. A fifth survivor, Cassander's brother Pleistarchus, ruled a smaller area (Cilicia).

authorities. The ruling Seleucids tried various means to coerce those around Jerusalem to compromise, but met with little success. After the Seleucid king Antiochus IV deposed two high priests, riots broke out in Jerusalem, and a few months later full-scale revolt. Antiochus crushed the rebellion ruthlessly, but still got little cooperation from the faithful. So in 167 he outlawed the practice of Judaism in Judea: prohibiting circumcision, burning copies of the Torah, forbidding observance of the Sabbath, and putting a statue of Zeus in the temple. He went so far as sacrificing a pig to Zeus on the temple altar. To enforce the ban on Judaism, he sent soldiers into towns and villages to force people to eat pork (or be killed on the spot) and so violate their religion. When they came to the village of Modein, an old priest named Mattathias killed the first person who was about to comply with the demand (1 Maccabees 2). In the ensuing commotion, he slipped away and became the leader of a guerrilla movement. Though he died within a few months, his sons took over leadership of the movement and in three years retook the temple and gained control over parts of Jerusalem and Judea. The new Seleucid king (Antiochus IV was now dead) recognized the leaders of this movement, known as the Maccabeans, as governors in Judea. The Jewish festival of **Hanukkah** celebrates the Maccabeans' victory and their retaking and cleansing of the temple.

The Purpose of the Book

The book of Daniel was put together in the midst of this rebellion to encourage the people suffering persecution and death to remain faithful to God and God's law. It tells stories of people who lived in Babylon during the exile, that is, people who lived under foreign domination and faced demands that they abandon God laws. In these stories God blesses people who observe the food laws and saves those who refuse to worship other gods. For example, God preserves the lives of three men who are put in a furnace to be burned alive for refusing to worship another god (Daniel 3), and God keeps Daniel from being killed when he is forced to spend a night in a lions' den because he had continued to pray to God despite a royal prohibition against it (ch. 6). Such stories show that God has the power to save those who maintain faithfulness, even if God's people are suffering now. The visions in Daniel predict the imminent establishment of God's kingdom, a kingdom in which people live by God's law. Through these visions Daniel asserts that God has a plan to save God's people and that the plan is moving forward. However bad things look at the moment, God will act to make things right; God will defeat the evil and bless the righteous.

The Afterlife

Furthermore, those who suffer for their faithfulness will receive a reward from God in an afterlife (12:1-4). The overwhelming violence of the persecution under Antiochus moved the faithful to belief in an afterlife. Before this time, few Jews had believed in an afterlife. Most thought that one continued to exist only partially and temporarily in **Sheol**, a place where there was no fellowship with God and no joy. But their belief in the justice of God moves the authors of Daniel and many after them to believe in an afterlife for martyrs and the very wicked. As they see it, God must respond to the overwhelming injustice inflicted when a martyr is killed for being faithful. Since that reward cannot come in this life (because the person is dead), God must reward that faithfulness in a realm beyond this world. Correspondingly, God's justice cannot permit the apparent success of the wicked to be the last word, so they must suffer retribution in an afterlife. Again, this belief flows out of a profound faith in the justice of God. The authors of Daniel seem to believe that this afterlife comes only to the very righteous (martyrs) and the very wicked, but over the next two hundred years many (but not all) Jews came to believe in an afterlife for all people.

Daniel, then, expresses a deep faith in God in the midst of the worst of times: when faithfulness leads to terrible suffering and unfaithfulness brings respite, even success. This book teaches that faithfulness to God is always the right path, even when it leads to suffering, because God does not abandon the faithful, even those who suffer death. God's justice and love always triumph in the end, even if that end must be somewhere beyond this world.

▶ Conclusion

The Israelite prophets keep alive faith in the God of Abraham and the exodus through times when the majority of Israelites worship multiple gods. These prophets proclaim that God is faithful to the covenants with the ancestors and Moses in ways that express mercy as God remains open to and loving toward those who have violated the covenant. Even the punishment that comes on the nation of Judah is an expression of God's faithfulness to the covenant because it means that God is fulfilling the covenant's stipulations.

While any talk of punishment makes many of us today a bit squeamish, this interpretation of their national life enabled the prophets to offer hope to their hearers and to avoid diminishing the importance of grace and mercy in their understanding of God. This grace appears in the long-suffering patience of God, who has tried to nurture faithfulness in the people for hundreds of years before the national catastrophes finally come. The prophets, though, also often speak of God's justice. This characteristic of God is as important as God's grace. If God is not just, the alternative is that God is unjust—like those capricious gods of other peoples. Believers can only trust God if God is just. Furthermore, God's justice serves as the basis for the prophets' calls to the people to act justly in their relations with one another. For the prophets, God's dealings with God's people demonstrate God's overwhelming grace and patience, even as God's justice must also be expressed. Grace and justice are not opposites; the opposite of justice is injustice. The prophets see grace and justice, two aspects of God's character, working together for the eventual good of God's people.

While these prophets see God acting within the parameters of the covenant, they also urge the people to live holy lives because they have committed themselves to this covenant relationship with a holy God. The covenant demands both social and personal morality, as well as devoting their worship solely to the one true God, because God is holy and just. This prophetic message that demands both morality and exclusive worship would shape the Israelites' interpretation of their political history and the books that would become Scripture. Thus the prophets play a pivotal role in the development of Judaism and Christianity.

▶ LET'S REVIEW ◀

In this chapter, we learned about the prophets:

- The classical prophets are concerned about social justice, but also about the worship of other gods and personal morality
- Preexilic prophets predict the destruction of the nations of Israel and Judah, but also speak of restoration
- Amos
  - —Speaks to both Judah and Israel
  - —Uses the indictment-verdict pattern
  - —Uses of "Day of the LORD"
  - —Critique of sacrificial system
- Hosea
  - —Speaks to Israel
  - —Uses allegory of unfaithfulness in marriage
  - —Uses symbolic names
  - —Gives significant attention to both punishment and restoration
- Micah
  - —Mostly speaks to Judah
  - —Emphasizes social justice; says worship is acceptable only when people act justly
- Isaiah
  - —Material from three different prophets (ranging from c. 750–500 B.C.E.) incorporated into the book
  - —Different perspectives from different prophets, depending on their historical setting
- Jeremiah
  - —Lives through the fall of Jerusalem
  - —Mixes warning of doom for Jerusalem with promises of restoration
- Lamentations
  - —Song of mourning for Jerusalem
  - —Supposedly written by Jeremiah
- Zephaniah
  - —Speaks to Judah
  - —Calls for worship of the one God
  - —Has foreigners join worship in the restoration
- Nahum
  - —Seventh-century prophet in Judah
  - —Oracle of judgment against the Assyrians
- Habakkuk
  - —Questions the untimely death of the righteous, probably Josiah
- Exilic prophets call for faithfulness and offer hope
- Ezekiel
  - —Sixth-century exilic prophet
  - —Chariot throne vision envisions presence of God in Babylon
  - —Visions provide a basis for apocalyptic imagery
  - —Asserts restoration in midst of beginning of the exile
- Second Isaiah
  - —Offers hope of return to the land
  - —Speaks in the tradition of Isaiah
- Postexilic prophets call for faithfulness and predict the coming reign of God and a prominent place for the Israelites

- Haggai
  - Urges the those who return from exile to rebuild the temple
- Zechariah
  - Calls for rebuilding the temple as a prelude to a delayed restoration of the nation
  - Calls for caring for the poor, seeing lack of proper care for the poor as a reason for the exile
- Malachi
  - Calls for proper sacrifices at the rebuilt temple
  - Calls for proper worship and faithfulness in time of economic difficulties
- Joel
  - Sees coming disaster through the image of locust plague
  - Calls for repentance through worship at the temple
- Jonah
  - Tale about God's care for non-Israelites
- Daniel
  - Tales of God's rescue of those who are faithful in persecution
  - Visions of judgment assure the persecuted that God's justice will triumph in the end

▶ KEY TERMS ◀

Amos
Classical prophecy
Cyrus
Daniel
Day of the Lord
Ezekiel
Habakkuk
Haggai
Hanukkah
Hosea
Indictment-verdict pattern
Isaiah
Jeremiah
Joel
Jonah
Maccabean Revolt
Malachi
Micah
Nahum
Nineveh
Obadiah
Persians
Postexilic prophets
Second Isaiah
Sheol
Theophany
Third Isaiah
Zechariah
Zephaniah

▶ QUESTIONS FOR REVIEW ◀

7.1 How are the eighth-century classical prophets similar to and different from their immediate predecessors (such as Elijah and Elisha)?

7.2 Why did Amos find the worship of the temple in Jerusalem unacceptable to God?

7.3 What do the names of Hosea's children symbolize? What does their renaming symbolize?

7.4 Why do many people say that Micah 6:6-8 summarizes the message of the eighth-century prophets? Is there any major theme missing from this summary?

7.5 Why do interpreters think that the book of Isaiah contains material that was written over a span of two to three hundred years?

7.6 Why does Jeremiah buy some farmland just as the nation of Judah is about to fall?

7.7 What are the central messages of Ezekiel's visions of the chariot-throne of God?

7.8 What critiques of Israelite prophecy come to expression in Jonah?

7.9 How do the stories in Daniel address the time period in which the book was written?

7.10 How does national trouble help the prophets talk about the relationship between God and the people of Judah?

▶ FOR FURTHER READING ◀

Joseph Blenkinsopp, *A History of Prophecy in Israel*, 2nd ed. Louisville: Westminster John Knox, 1996.

Walter Brueggemann, *The Prophetic Imagination*, 2nd ed. Minneapolis: Fortress Press, 2001.

James L. Crenshaw, *Prophets, Sages, and Poets*. St. Louis, Mo.: Chalice, 2006.

Wilda C. Gafney, *Daughters of Miriam: Women Prophets in Ancient Israel*. Minneapolis: Fortress Press, 2008.

Abraham Heschel, *The Prophets*. 1962, reprint. Peabody, Mass.: Hendrickson, 2007.

Rodney R. Hutton, *Fortress Introduction to the Prophets*. Minneapolis: Fortress Press, 2004.

Jack R. Lundbom, *The Hebrew Prophets: An Introduction*. Minneapolis: Fortress Press, 2010.

Victor H. Matthews, *The Hebrew Prophets and Their Social World*, 2nd ed. Grand Rapids: Baker Academic, 2012.

John W. Miller, *Meet the Prophets: A Beginner's Guide to the Books of the Biblical Prophets*. New York: Paulist, 1987.

James D. Newsome Jr., *The Hebrew Prophets*. Atlanta: John Knox, 1984.

Julia M. O'Brien, *Challenging Prophetic Metaphor: Theology and Ideology in the Prophets*. Louisville: Westminster John Knox, 2008.

Marvin A. Sweeney, *TANAK: A Theology and Critical Introduction to the Jewish Bible*. Minneapolis: Fortress Press, 2011.

James Ward, *Thus Says the Lord: The Message of the Prophets*. Nashville: Abingdon, 1991.

8 An Alternative Worldview
Israel's Wisdom Literature and Esther

IN THIS CHAPTER, WE WILL LOOK AT WISDOM LITERATURE. WE WILL LEARN THAT

- Wisdom literature analyzes the way things work in the world to gain understanding of God
- Wisdom literature recognizes more ambiguity than much prophetic literature
- The book of Job questions the validity of the Deuteronomic pattern
- Proverbs offers insights into patterns of life
- Ecclesiastes examines whether human life has meaning
- Esther reflects on God's providence

▶ The Literary Type

Distinctive Contents

The books we will consider in this chapter belong among the Writings, the Ketubim, in the Jewish arrangement of the Bible. As we saw in chapter 1, the Tanakh is divided into three parts: the Torah, the Prophets, and the Writings. The Writings include books that the Christian arrangement of the Bible places with the prophets (such as Daniel) or with material that seems to fit together chronologically. For example, Ruth is placed with books that tell of the time before the Israelite monarchy in the Christian arrangement, while in the Tanakh the books of the Deuteronomistic historians appear among the prophets and are labeled the former prophets. That means that in the Tanakh, Ruth does not appear with Judges and 1 Samuel because Ruth is classified as one of the Writings rather than one of the prophets. Our treatment of the books of the Ketubim has more similarities with the Christian arrangement, with which some readers may be more familiar. Thus, Daniel and Lamentations are discussed with the prophets, Ruth with the Deuteronomistic history and Chronicles, and the books of Psalms and Song of Solomon together in the following chapter.

Among the books of the Ketubim, a group of five books is known as the Megillot, which means the Scrolls. Each of these five books (Song of Solomon, Ruth, Lamentations, Ecclesiastes, and Esther) is now associated with a particular Jewish feast. Esther is grouped with the wisdom writings in this chapter, however, because even though the book does not strictly belong to the Wisdom literature, its view of the world and God's participation in it seem similar to that of the wisdom tradition.

BOX 8.1

EGYPTIAN WISDOM TRADITIONS

One of the traditions that influenced the development of Israelite wisdom was Egyptian wisdom. Similar to Ecclesiastes, Egyptian tradition has advice given by wise people (especially kings) about how to live and understand life. The instruction of King Amen-em-het sets out advice on a topic for his son. Part of his advice reads, "Do not fill your heart with a brother, nor have a friend. Do not make intimate friends—there is no fulfillment in them. Even when you sleep, keep your heart to yourself, because no one has allies in the day of distress" (adapted from the translation by John A. Wilson in *Ancient Near Eastern Texts Relating to the Old Testament,* ed. J. B. Pritchard, 3rd ed. [Princeton: Princeton University Press, 1969], 418).

Wisdom Literature

The Hebrew Bible contains only three books that belong within the genre of **Wisdom literature**: Job, Proverbs, and Ecclesiastes. Other books have elements that derive from this tradition, but only these three belong wholly within this literary type. The Wisdom literature takes a very different approach than the other materials we have seen. Many typical Israelite themes make no appearance in the Wisdom books: there is no mention of the promises to the ancestors (Abraham, Isaac, Jacob), or of the exodus, Moses, Sinai, or of the promise of a kingdom to David. Beyond this, Wisdom does not talk about God's actions in the fate of nations or in broad sweeps of history. Rather, it deals with daily life and gives instruction about how to have a good life. The Wisdom writers are not unhistorical, they simply look elsewhere, to different places, than do the Deuteronomistic writers and the prophets. Wisdom texts give attention to the pattern of normal life to discern the acts of God.

Provenance. We do not know who wrote this material. Its authors seem to be teachers in a position to study the traditional wisdom of various clans and the more formalized wisdom traditions of other cultures. (Many ancient cultures had traditions of this sort.) Many scholars think that Israelite wisdom drew significantly on the wisdom traditions of Egypt. At the same time, these teachers collected and organized traditions that come from various groups among the Israelites. They melded these various observations about life into a view of the world that incorporates faith in God with advice about how to have the best life. The leisure needed to engage such a task suggests that wisdom teachers were connected to a school or the temple, or perhaps that they were sponsored by the royal house. Such an arrangement would not be uncommon in the ancient world.

Learning from experience. Wisdom writers discern the word of God in a way that is rather different from the way God speaks through prophets. The prophets claim a direct revelation from God; they say: "Thus says the Lord." The wisdom writers, on the other hand, observe human experience and think about what it reveals about the world and our lives in it; they draw on a broad range of human experience to find knowledge of God. They do not claim to speak for God, but rather to impart helpful advice as they pass on their insights about life. They believe that their observations about life will help others understand the world and have a good life.

God and the world. The writers of Israelite wisdom traditions believe that God is responsible for the patterns of life they see, and so trust in those patterns becomes a form of faith in God. They discern a God-given order to reality that they want to share with their readers. God is the one who created the world and set its laws in place; now they seek to understand those laws in order to live in accord with them. These writers rely on what theologians call "general revelation," that is, knowledge of God a person can discern by observing the world. So they see God deeply involved in the way the world is structured.

One of the most important things wisdom writers recognize is that things do not always work as they should (the wicked are successful, good people suffer, and so on). The recognition of the incongruity creates the need for just the sort of analysis of life that the Wisdom literature provides. Wisdom teachers acknowledge that the world is an uncertain place, yet they insist that God loves the world and remains in contact with it. So these writers are acutely sensitive to the ambiguities of life, and in the midst of this ambiguity they offer ways to be faithful to God.

▶ Job: A Problem without Resolution

The Problem of Job

The story in the book of **Job** seems to be about non-Israelites. The book draws on no traditions that are specific to Israelites, and all of its characters use international (that is, not specifically Israelite) wisdom thought in their discussions with Job. Still, the book speaks from the perspective of belief in the one God who blesses and judges. This book's real function is to raise the question of why bad things happen to good people, what theologians call **theodicy**. The book tells the story of a righteous person named Job who has all good things taken from him: his possessions are destroyed, his children die, and his health is taken. Job is probably not a historical person, but a character designed to highlight the issue the author wants to examine. Thus this story is like the parables that Jesus tells in the Gospels—it teaches a lesson by telling a story about a fictional character.

FIGURE 8.1 **JOB**

Eugène Delacroix (1798–1863). This image depicts the agony that God allowed to be inflicted on Job, even though he was faithful to God. Art Resource

Job's Story

The tale begins in a strange way. One day **satan** surveys the world for God to report on the behavior of its inhabitants (Job 1:6-12). During the report, God draws attention to Job's righteousness, only to have satan retort that Job is faithful to God solely because of all that God gives him. God rejects such a jaded view of Job and to prove God's point allows satan to test Job's faithfulness by taking away the good things in his life. So all the pain inflicted on Job comes because he is so faithful! This contradicts all that the prophets, Deuteronomistic History, and Pentateuch say about the way things work. In those writings, God blesses the righteous and sends trouble on the wicked and unfaithful, but that is not how it works in the story of Job.

Satan. Before following the course of Job's story, we need to look at the image of the satan found here. In Job, the satan is a member of God's court and functions like a prosecuting attorney; in fact, the word *satan* means "accuser." The Hebrew Bible uses this term for many different figures: the other side in a lawsuit (Ps. 109:6), an opponent in war (1 Sam. 29:4), and an adversary generally (Ps. 38:20). The satan is not the ruler of demons or the source of evil in the thought world of the Hebrew Bible. In Job, the satan serves in the heavenly entourage and remains subservient to God. Being the *satan* seems to be a task God assigns to various members of the heavenly court at different times, so it is not even a permanent job. By the time of the New Testament, ideas about Satan have changed significantly, but throughout the Hebrew Bible *satan* does not refer to an evil being who has rebelled against God. In the Job story, the satan only does to Job what God authorizes. This makes the problem that the book raises even more severe, because Job's troubles do not come from some evil entity who opposes God's will; rather, God grants direct permission to God's own emissary to inflict multiple catastrophes on Job.

Job's friends. In the story, God allows satan to devastate Job's property, kill his children, and inflict him with boils. After these tragedies strike, Job's friends come to visit (2:11-13). These friends represent and argue for the

BOX 8.2

JOB ARGUES WITH GOD

Read Job 31:3-37, noticing especially verses 3-8 and 35-37. What claims do you see Job make? What assumptions about the cause of suffering does he hold? What stance does he take in his complaint against God?

notion that bad things happen to people only when they have done evil. In accord with this perspective, they encourage Job to repent and seek forgiveness so that he will not have to suffer anymore (chs. 4–31). Even Job's wife tells him to curse God and die so that his suffering will end (3:9). But Job will not curse God and will not admit that he has done wrong, because he knows better (chs. 9, 27, 29, 31). He knows he has been righteous! He is so confident that he calls God on the carpet. He says he is willing to go to court; he is ready to sue God because he knows that he is being treated unjustly (ch. 13). When he finally gets a response from God, it is of no help. God says simply that Job has no standing to ask and that Job cannot understand God's ways (chs. 38–41). In all of this, Job remains faithful to God, even while challenging God, and to living a righteous life.

Divine justice and retribution. This story interrogates traditional ideas about divine justice and retribution. The notion that God punishes the wicked and blesses the good does not work in Job's case; it is simply wrong. This does not mean there is no truth to that equation, only that it does not always work. This more ambiguous understanding of the way things work fits the world as we know it. We know that the righteous regularly do suffer and that the wicked often prosper. But we also know that good people usually have more meaningful lives and the wicked suffer because of their deeds—usually, but not always. So what are we to think when we see someone suffer? Is it because they have done evil? The story of Job says, not necessarily. The writer of Job believes in the goodness and justice of God, but recognizes that the world does not always reflect that goodness and justice. In the end, this book proclaims that God is beyond human comprehension. We cannot always explain what happens to people by looking at whether they live as God requires. God's justice seems to demand that the righteous receive blessings and escape suffering, but we know that equation often breaks down.

No Resolution

Job offers no easy answers. In the end, God restores Job's fortunes; God gives him more children and restores his health (ch. 42). (Many scholars are convinced that this rosy ending is a

BOX 8.3

Read Job 38:1-18; 40:1-9. Chapters 38–41 are devoted to questioning Job's status and power, asking whether he has the right to raise the questions he raises about God's justice. Note the final response of Job in 42:1-6. What do you think of this conclusion of the discussion? Keep it in mind when we get to our study of apocalyptic literature (chapter 17) and its raising of similar questions.

late addition to the book.) But even this restoration does not explain how it can be right that he suffers as he does. The writer of Job simply leaves the question hanging because there is no straightforward answer. The problem of the suffering of the righteous has no resolution in Job.

On the other hand, the book does offer its main character as the proper response to adversity. When the righteous suffer, they must remain faithful. Sometimes people talk about Job as a person of great patience. In some ways, this misses the main way the book portrays him. Job is patient in his suffering mainly at the beginning; he soon challenges God directly and forcefully, demanding an account of God's actions. While we might disapprove of such challenges to God, they are manifestations of faith in Job. Job knows who God is, that God is a god of justice, and so he demands that God live up to that character. Job can challenge God in this way because he has so much faith in God. Faith is not resignation or cowering before God; faith trusts God and engages God in genuine conversation, even debate. So the outstanding characteristic of Job is his faithfulness rather than his patience.

Job, then, leaves readers with questions more than with answers. It is a book of the Bible that recognizes the injustices of life and offers no easy or clear answers about why they happen. It does, however, provide an example of the proper way to respond: it says that whatever troubles a person must endure, the proper response is to maintain faith in God. That faith may manifest itself in arguing with God, even accusing God of wrongdoing. But in the end, it sees no other place to turn because it is only God who sustains the faithful in the midst of suffering.

▶ Proverbs: Advice for the Good Life

The book of Proverbs has no story line; it is simply a collection of proverbial sayings, maxims by which to guide one's life. Tradition attributes the book to Solomon, that wisest of Israelite kings, but it is actually composed of proverbs (some of which may go back to Solomon) that were collected over the course of several centuries. It probably took the form we have now in the third century B.C.E.

A Context-Oriented Genre

A **proverb** gives a very narrow glimpse at reality. Proverbs are true if you say them at the right moment, but not if you apply them in the wrong setting. In English we have the proverb, "Look before you leap," but we also have, "You snooze, you lose." One of these proverbs urges caution and reflection before making a decision, the other advises quick action before an opportunity passes. Which is true? We know that each is true if you say it at the right moment, but both give bad advice at other times. This is the nature of proverbs, including those in the Bible. Consider what Proverbs says about bribes in 21:14: "A gift in secret averts anger; and a concealed bribe in the bosom [averts] strong wrath." This verse observes that bribes work, but the next verse says, "When justice is done, it is a joy to the righteous." These proverbs that appear next to each other both note a truth, but they stand in significant tension. One seems to recommend giving bribes; the other seems to reject bribes by advising readers to act justly. The book of Proverbs contains a number of these kinds of opposing statements. Thus the book's writers recognize the ways different circumstances call for different behaviors. As Ecclesiastes 3 says, "For everything there is a season. . . ."

The book of Proverbs, then, contains a series of generalizations to help readers guide their lives, as long as one reads them at the right moment. Sometimes these proverbs recommend certain behavior, and sometimes they just report an observation. So individual proverbs are not specific instructions that apply on all occasions and to all situations.

A guide for life. This collection of proverbs, however, is not random. The sayings are sometimes arranged by topic and sometimes by author. As a whole, the book tries to convince its readers to adopt a particular way of living. It does not threaten them with judgment if they resist, but does try to coax them into seeing that its advice gives the best way to live. The book's advice about how to live offers a manner of life that fits the way the world really is, and so helps readers cope with it. Sometimes you need to know that bribes work if you want to understand why things happen as they do. At the same time, you need to know that the righteous avoid this way of conducting business. So the book wants to inform readers about how things really are, even as it tries to form their character. Reading the book as a whole, then, we see it trying to persuade readers to adopt a particular way of life (rather than enforce it through threats), a way of life that fits the world that God has made.

BOX 8.4

AKKADIAN WISDOM TRADITIONS

Another part of the international wisdom tradition on which Israel drew was from Mesopotamia, written mostly in Akkadian, the language of Assyria and Babylonia. Like other nations, they had groups of proverbs. Among the Akkadian proverbs still preserved are: "As long as a man does not exert himself, he will gain nothing" (the equivalent of our "No pain, no gain"); "The one who expects to be dead soon says, 'Let me eat up all I have'; the one who expects to get well says, 'Let me economize'"; and "As a wise person, let your understanding shine modestly, let your mouth be restrained, your speech guarded" (adapted from the translation of Robert H. Pfeiffer in *Ancient Near Eastern Texts*, ed. Pritchard, 425–26).

▶ Ecclesiastes: All Is Vanity

Provenance

The book of **Ecclesiastes** opens by identifying its author as "the son of David, king in Jerusalem," which most take to mean Solomon, the ideal sage of Israel; but most scholars think the book was composed long after his death. In this literary guise, however, the book has the old sage give advice about how to understand life. In parts it reads like an essay or a speech, in others like a collection of sayings. The book seems best suited to the setting of a school in which a wise old teacher passes on advice about how to make sense of the world and have a meaningful life.

Vanity of Vanities

The writer of Ecclesiastes has a somewhat bleak outlook on life. The regular refrain is: "**Vanity** of vanities, all is vanity." This is the writer's poetic way of saying that life is absurd. The writer says he has attained the wisdom available to humans only to discover that it is futile, just as success is. He believes that God has predetermined life, which he sees has an inescapable rhythm, and that humans must live within the limits God has set. Still, he believes that God is good, and so humans should enjoy the world God has given them; people should put themselves into their work and enjoy their recreation (2:24; 5:18-19; 9:7-10). Human lives may not have the cosmic significance we would like to give them, but we can still enjoy what God gives us.

The Purpose of Life

In spite of this apparent pessimism about life, human existence does have purpose in this book. The summary in the book's final verses reads: "Fear God, and keep his commandments; for that is the whole duty of everyone." Many scholars think this ending was inserted into the book sometime after its original composition, because it has a different perspective from the one that dominates the preceding material. Yet the book's canonical form (the way it appears in the Bible) includes these concluding remarks that shape the way we read the whole book. With the current ending, the book says that humans may not be able to figure out all of God's judgments and deeds, but they can have a life of meaning if they seek that meaning by doing God's will. So while the writer's judgments about the limits of human life are sobering, there is good to life.

▶ Esther: Veiled Providence and the Origin of a Feast

The book of Esther is a charming tale, full of intrigue and irony. It is a story about Israelites in exile, and more broadly about living in the Diaspora (that is, outside Palestine). Its genre is not that of the Wisdom literature; it is more like a novella, but we treat it here because of its outlook. This book never mentions God, and its lack of any account of divine action sets it apart from most other books of the Hebrew Bible but makes it more like what we find in the wisdom tradition. Further, it has no mention of the ancestors, Moses, or David, not even of the exodus or Sinai. Despite its silence about God, the book seems to believe in divine providence and divine justice.

The Book's Purpose

The story of Esther provides the basis for the Jewish feast of Purim. Many think that this feast emerged during or soon after the Babylonian exile. It is celebrated near the time of the Persian New Year. Thus, many hold that the feast was begun as a way of helping the exiles avoid participation in the Persian pagan celebrations. While the story is probably earlier, the book seems to have been written sometime in the third or early second century B.C.E.

A contest. The story is set in Susa, the winter home of the emperor Ahasuerus (who is Xerxes I, 486–465). When his wife publicly disobeys him, he exiles her and holds a contest to choose a new queen. A member of the court, Mordecai, is Jewish and the foster parent of Esther, whose

BOX 8.5

FEAST OF PURIM

The feast of Purim is the only Jewish festival that is not a religious celebration. This festival is held in the month of Adar on the Jewish calendar (February to March on the secular calendar) and commemorates the escape of Jews from a pogrom in the time of the Babylonian exile. The book of Esther provides the etiological tale (a story that provides an origin) for this feast. Many nonfactual elements of the story lead scholars to recognize that it is not a historical account.

Hebrew name is Hadassah. Mordecai tells her to conceal her Jewish identity while participating in the contest. She eventually wins and is made queen of Persia—still, no one knows she is Jewish.

A plot. Meanwhile, Mordecai hears of a plot to assassinate the emperor and saves the emperor by reporting it. But Mordecai subsequently makes an enemy of a powerful official, Haman, by refusing to show him deference by bowing when Haman passes by. Haman decides to get revenge by killing not only Mordecai, but all of the Jewish people. Haman, the archetypical villain, tricks the king into signing a decree that sets a day on which everyone throughout the empire is allowed to kill Jews and take their possessions. As the story is told here, the king's decrees are irrevocable. This is one of the fictional aspects of the story, but an important one for the progress of the story.

Haman casts lots to determine what day to schedule the massacre. Casting of lots was a common form of divination. It is something like rolling dice, with the various symbols and numbers telling something about the future. The holiday Purim gets its name from this act (and what will eventually happen on that day); the Akkadian word for lots is Pur.

Informing the queen. When Mordecai hears of the decree, he goes to Esther—who has not heard this news even though she lives at the palace. When she does hear of it she does not want to act. The rule of the court was that no one could enter the king's presence without being summoned and she had not been called for a month. Any person entering the king's presence without a summons would be executed unless the king held out his scepter. Mordecai responds to her legitimate concern by telling her that she and her family would die unless she took action and concludes, "Perhaps you have come to royal dignity for just such a time as this" (Esther 4:14). She tells him to have all the Jews fast for her and she devises a plan. At this point, Esther stops being a passive character in the story and becomes the dominant force in events to come.

A banquet. Esther goes to the king, who receives her graciously. When he asks her what her request is, she invites him and his advisor Haman, the enemy of the Jews, to a banquet the next day. The king accepts the invitation. On the night before the banquet, Haman becomes newly enraged at Mordecai for not bowing and builds a seventy-five-foot gallows on which to hang him. At the same time, Ahasuerus cannot sleep and so has the royal record of the last few years read to him. He is reminded that

BOX 8.6

A HIDDEN PRESENCE?

While God is not mentioned in the Hebrew version of Esther, what do Esther 4:13-14 and 9:24-28 suggest about God's presence?

Mordecai saved his life and that he has never thanked Mordecai properly.

The next morning the king calls Haman and asks him what the king should do to honor someone. Assuming the king would honor him, Haman proposes an elaborate public proclamation, with the person wearing a crown and riding the king's horse. The king likes the idea and tells Haman to do that for Mordecai, even telling Haman to lead the horse and make the proclamation. Unable to refuse, he performs this humiliating act and goes home in shame. Just then, the messengers arrive to take him to Esther's banquet.

Reversal of fortune. On the second day of the banquet, the king again asks what Esther wants. This time she asks him just to let her and her people live, because there is a plot to kill them all. The somewhat inebriated king becomes very angry and asks who would do such a thing. Esther points across the table and says, "this wicked Haman!" (7:6). Frightened, Haman begs Esther for mercy, but gets none. The king has Haman hanged immediately (and ironically) on the very gallows he had built to hang Mordecai. Then Ahasuerus gives all of Haman's possessions to Mordecai and elevates him to the position formerly held by Haman.

A new decree. Since the earlier decree allowing the murder of Jews could not be revoked, the king now issues a new decree: on the same day as the proposed massacre, Jews may assemble, arm themselves, and kill anyone who tries to do them harm. With this new decree and the rise of Mordecai to such a high position, no one dared to harm the Jews that day. So the Jews were saved from destruction. When all of this action is over, Mordecai sends a letter to Jews throughout the Persian Empire telling them to remember this day. The text explains where the name Purim comes from and says Jews adopted it, observing it as a custom to commemorate these great events. The feast is still celebrated today.

Interpreting the Story

Diaspora life exemplified. This clearly fictional tale gives us an interesting glimpse into being Jewish in the Diaspora in the Hellenistic era, and it makes some important points. First, it is interesting to note that the minority community of the Jews is represented and saved by a woman. Thus, the oppressed people are represented by a member of society who was always marginal in Hellenistic society. Her position in the story exemplifies the way Jews of the Diaspora of the fourth through the second centuries B.C.E. lived in two cultures. Even her name symbolizes the struggle: Esther is probably derived from Ishtar, a Babylonian goddess.

Absence of Torah observance. In this dual culture setting, the Torah's instructions about food, Sabbath, and marriage are absent. Indeed, her identity as a Jew is unknown to the king and others in his court. (This absence of Torah regulations is similar to what we see of the leading character in the book of Judith, but very different from the book of Daniel.) Nothing about being Jewish keeps her (or Mordecai) from participating fully in the Persian court. The later additions to the book in Greek that are a part of the LXX express concern about this. They have her say that she does not drink wine from which a libation has been offered to the gods and that she abhors her marriage to a non-Israelite (Additions to Esther C 14:14-18). Thus, the struggle to determine how to live as the people of God and the multiple answers that question received are evident in the literary history of this book.

Additions to the book. These latter Greek additions to the book are also concerned that the story does not assign God an active role. So they insert God into the story in various places. For example, God gives Mordecai a dream that figuratively tells him what "God had determined to do" (Additions to Esther A 11:12). Thus, they give the story a different theological outlook. The canonical Hebrew version, however, assigns God no active place. Even when Esther has Mordecai tell everyone to fast for her, she does not explicitly ask for prayers. God never emerges from the background. Even as the book tells people to celebrate the feast, it is for the way they gained release from their enemies (14:22).

God's providence. Such a limited role for God as an active participant in events of the world is similar to much that we have seen in the Wisdom literature. Still, the book does seem to let God's providence serve as a backdrop. Some interpreters even think that Mordecai alludes to God's providence when convincing Esther to act, saying that if she does not help, such rescue will come from "another quarter" (4:14). Further, a strict—if ironic—justice also functions in this book. Haman dies on the very gallows he prepared for committing an atrocity; those who plotted against the Jews were killed on the appointed day, rather than the Jews they had plotted against.

Without ever mentioning God, this book provides its readers with ways to think about how to live in the world as people of God, trusting that God's providence remains even when it seems inactive. It gives a reason for the feast of Purim that assures them of goodness in life within the ambiguity of their setting.

▶ Conclusion

The Wisdom literature of the Bible looks at life from a perspective that differs from most other parts of the Bible. It scrutinizes life's difficulties and limits; it explores those times when things are not what they should be. While these books offer no simple answers to life's difficult problems, they do provide a balance within the

BOX 8.7

GREEK ADDITIONS

The Greek version of the book of Esther that appears in the Septuagint has several more chapters than the Hebrew version. Most scholars think these chapters were added later, though some think the Greek version represents a different telling of the story. Among the most outstanding features of these additions is the more active role they give God and the attention they give to Torah observance.

biblical witness that acknowledges that the pattern set out in Deuteronomy does not always work. This perspective affirms that righteous living usually brings blessing, but not always. When these exceptions come, the wisdom tradition counsels faith and obedience because its authors remain confident in the ultimate justice and mercy of God. These writings, then, offer their readers comfort when things in life are not fair, when simple answers will not suffice. They even try to show how complications of life can point believers to God. God remains the source of all good things and all order in the world, even when the individual lives of the faithful seem to spin out of control. These writings contend that trusting in God makes for the best life, even in difficult and unfathomable times.

▶ LET'S REVIEW ◀

In this chapter, we learned that:

- The Wisdom literature views the world and the place of God in it differently from other biblical texts
- The Wisdom literature questions the Deuteronomistic pattern of explaining events
- The Wisdom literature relies on general revelation
- Esther gives God no direct role in the affairs of the world

▶ KEY TERMS ◀

Ecclesiastes
Feast of Purim
Job
Proverb
Providence
Satan
Theodicy
Vanity
Wisdom literature

▶ QUESTIONS FOR REVIEW ◀

8.1 What themes that are typical of Israelite literature does Wisdom literature not include?
8.2 What ideas about the way things happen in the world does the book of Job challenge?
8.3 How do the writers of the wisdom tradition think God relates to the world?
8.4 What is the practical purpose of the book of Esther?
8.5 What view of the presence of God do we see in Esther?
8.6 What do we see about the different ways Jews related to non-Jewish culture through Esther and the later additions to it?

▶ FOR FURTHER READING ◀

Richard J. Clifford, *The Wisdom Literature*, Interpreting Biblical Texts. Nashville: Abingdon, 1998.

James L. Crenshaw, *Old Testament Wisdom: An Introduction*, rev. ed. Louisville: Westminster John Knox, 1998.

Katherine Dell, *The Book of Proverbs in Social and Theological Context*. Cambridge: Cambridge University Press, 2009.

Michael V. Fox, *Character and Ideology in the Book of Esther*, 2nd ed. Grand Rapids: Eerdmans, 2001.

Roland E. Murphy, *The Tree of Life: An Exploration of Biblical Wisdom Literature*, 3rd ed. Grand Rapids: Eerdmans, 2002.

Leo G. Perdue, *Wisdom and Creation: The Theology of the Wisdom Literature*. Nashville: Abingdon, 1994.

———, *Wisdom Literature: A Theological History*. Louisville: Westminster John Knox, 2007.

9 Israel's Response to God
The Psalms and the Song of Solomon

IN THIS CHAPTER WE'LL EXAMINE THE BOOK OF PSALMS AND THE SONG OF SOLOMON:

- Psalms
  - Israel's response to God
- Song of Solomon
  - A love poem

The Psalms contain Israel's response to God; they come from and address all sorts of occasions and aspects of human life. Some give thanks for blessings, others complain about God's absence, and still others ask for a future blessing. The Psalms are human words addressed to God. This distinguishes them from most of the rest of Scripture, which intends to provide believers with a word from God to humans. In the Psalms we hear Israel's search for and the people's experience of God; we hear something of the inner life or spiritual experience of their ancient authors. And since the particular psalms in our Bibles were collected and saved for use in public worship, we can assume that their words resonated with the larger community. So these books provide a glimpse into the spirituality of ancient Israelites.

The Psalms reveal a deep experience of God's presence in the lives of the people who wrote them. The authors know God and experience God in ways that show they have a personal relationship with God. Today we sometimes hear Christians say that ancient or first-century Judaism was a religion of formalism based on legal demands, rather than on the covenant and a personal relationship with God. One reading of the Psalms should dispel that false idea. The authors of these songs know God personally and depend on the presence of

God for meaning in their lives. They are willing to bring their most intimate thoughts—even the ugliest parts of themselves—before God, knowing that God will not turn them away.

▶ The Psalms: Poetry of Praise and Lament

The Collection and Its Structure

Taking shape. The collection of Psalms found in the Bible took shape largely between 400 and 200 B.C.E. This is a time after the returned exiles had completed their rebuilding of the temple in Jerusalem. They created this collection, in part, to provide material for worship at the temple, and perhaps in synagogues as well. In some ways this collection of psalms functioned like a hymnal in a church today by giving the congregation common words to express their thoughts and to offer praise to God. By 100 B.C.E. the collection was basically what we have now, and it was being recognized as Scripture.

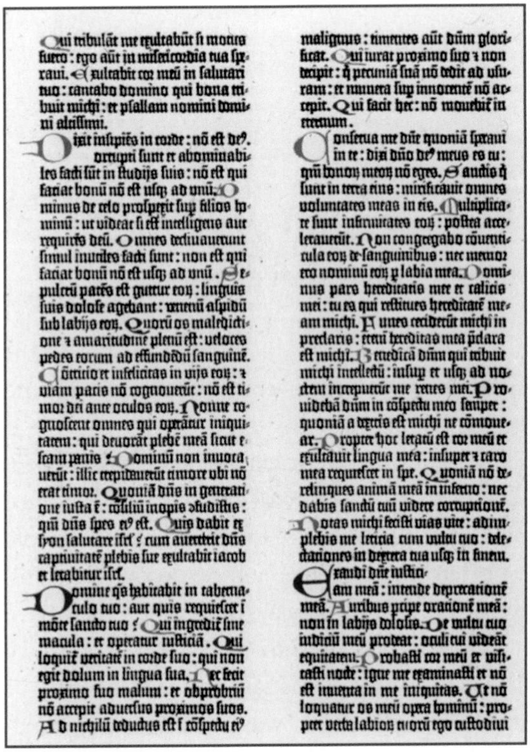

FIGURE 9.1 **PSALMS IN THE GUTENBERG BIBLE**

The Gutenberg Bible was the first book of any considerable size to be printed with moveable type. These Bibles were printed in the 1450s.

Project Gutenberg

The structure. As it appears in the Bible, the **Psalter** (as the collection of Psalms is known) is divided into five books: Psalms 1–41; 42–72; 73–89; 90–106; 107–150. These divisions seem arbitrary because they do not represent themes, a particular kind of psalm, or any other clear ordering principle scholars have been able to agree upon, though some characteristics do appear in most of the books (for example, four of the five end with a doxology and each has a mixture of laments and hymns). Many scholars think they were divided into five books to reflect the number of books in the Torah (Pentateuch), though this does not help us understand why particular psalms appear in one book rather than another. Part of the reason we remain unable to discern the design behind the divisions may be that the collection is the work of multiple editors. Perhaps at some point each book had some thread that held it together, but as various psalms were added to the collection the thread was obscured and finally lost.

The Psalms as Hebrew Poetry: Parallelism

The Psalms show us something about the structure of Hebrew poetry, as do some sections within the prophets because they contain several literary tropes and much traditional imagery. Hebrew poetry, as was the case also with Greek poetry, is structured according to meter or rhythm. There is less attention to rhyming the ends of lines, and more to how many syllables or beats are in each line. It is the use of such cadences that sets poetry apart from prose in Hebrew. One of the important tools of Hebrew poetry in the Psalms is **parallelism**, a technique that thematically and structurally connects thoughts with two or more lines.

Synonymous parallelism. A common type of parallelism found in the Psalms is **synonymous parallelism**. This literary device repeats in a different way the same thought or idea in two consecutive lines. Psalm 19:1-2 provides good examples. Verse 1 reads:

> The heavens are telling the glory of God;
> And the firmament proclaims his handiwork.

Both of these lines assert that the created world reflects and makes known the nature of God. Line one says that the regions above the earth carry out this function; line two says that the vault above the earth (that they thought held rain or the stars) does the same thing. Verse 2 has a similar pair:

> Day to day pours forth speech,
> and night to night declares knowledge.

These lines assert that this knowledge of God reveals itself constantly; line one says this happens in the day, line two that it continues throughout the night. Thus, while the second line does not really express a new thought or reveal a new piece of information, the repetition provides emphasis and poetic balance and beauty.

BOX 9.1

SUPERSCRIPTIONS FOR PSALMS

Some of the psalms have superscriptions (notes written before they begin) that give instructions about how to play them (for example, "with stringed instruments" [Psalm 4], or "for flutes" [Psalm 5]), or name the author of the psalm, commonly mentioning David (for example, Psalms 3–32, 34–41).

Parallelism of contrast. Antithetical parallelism constitutes a second kind of parallelism. Here the second line states the opposite of the idea in the first line, basically articulating the other side of the coin. Psalm 18:27 provides a good example:

> For you deliver a humble people,
> but the haughty eyes you bring down.

These lines give a picture of God's response to humility and its opposite, pride (similarly see Ps. 138:6). Together the two lines paint a fuller image of the same notion about God's response to human attitudes.

Synthetic parallelism. A third sort of parallelism, **synthetic parallelism**, has the second line expand the idea of the first. So we read in Psalm 89:27:

> I will make him my firstborn,
> the highest of the kings of the earth.

In this verse, the second line specifies what it means when God makes David God's "firstborn." Such explanations help guide the readers' interpretation of the statement in the first line.

The psalmists sometimes combine types of parallelism so that three lines incorporate two of the types. Keeping these patterns in mind helps us understand the Psalms because they guide the way we interpret them. We do not need to look for a major new point in each line, but often just a new way of expressing the same basic thought (or its complement or opposite). While these patterns sometimes seem repetitious to us, it is a style that promotes easy memorization. Since most people would not have had a copy of the text and could not have read it if they did, and since these psalms played a part in the community's worship, employing devices to aid memory became important.

Types of Psalms

Our survey of the Psalms will look at a few distinctive kinds of psalms.

Psalms of praise. Psalms of praise exalt various characteristics and acts of God. They celebrate God's power as seen in creation or in sustaining the world or the people of Israel. In addition to taking delight in God's nature itself, these psalms also call on others to praise God for all God does and is. Psalms 8, 19, 66, 100, 114, 117, and 150 number among these psalms of praise. Though a somewhat distinct type of their own, enthronement psalms belong with psalms of praise or with royal psalms because they offer praise to God for serving as Israel's king and so protecting Israel from their enemies and showering blessings on them (e.g., Psalms 29, 47, 93).

> BOX 9.2
>
> **A PSALM OF PRAISE**
>
> What does Psalm 100, a psalm of praise, suggest about how the people are related to God? How would you compare this with the sentiment expressed in Psalm 23?

Thanksgiving psalms. Similar to the psalms of praise, **thanksgiving psalms** offer God thanks for having saved or having blessed the person who sings. Sometimes this is a general thanksgiving for the goodness of life (Psalm 65) or for God's constant presence as a help (Psalm 138). At other times, the singer gives thanks for something more specific, such as recovering from a serious illness (Psalm 30). These psalms extol the power of God and God's willingness to help in times of distress. Psalm 23 belongs in this category of psalms; it gives thanks for the ways that God cares for the needs of God's people. Such psalms also offer us a glimpse into the function some sacrifices had at the temple. Rather than being sin offerings that are required, these psalms reveal that people brought sacrifices as thanksgiving offerings and as testimony to what God had done for them (for example, Psalm 116). So offering sacrifices could be a joyous response to the goodness of God.

Royal psalms. Royal psalms celebrate various moments in a king's career; for example, they may give God thanks for a victory (Psalms 18, 20, 60) or ask God to bless a royal wedding (Psalm 45). Some offer thanks for the way God assures the king's victory, and so, by extension, blesses God's people (Psalms 2, 110). Some of these psalms seem to serve as part of a king's coronation, as they ask God to bless the king with particular gifts and traits (e.g., justice, mercy, help for the poor). While thanking God for endowing their ruler with these virtues, such psalms also exhort the king to adopt those behaviors (Psalm 72). Psalm 101 even has the king promise God that he will rule justly. Thus these psalms see the monarchy as God's will, and as a means God uses to bless the people.

Psalms of lament. Beyond celebrating and giving thanks, some psalms express Israel's sorrow and grief. **Lament psalms** deal with both national or communal loss (Psalms 60, 80, 137) and personal tragedy or trouble (Psalms 7, 13, 17, 120). These psalms describe the person's grief and express sorrow; then they ask God for help, even giving reasons why God should help them. They often cite God's own nature as the basis for their plea for help. In Psalm 88 the request for help remains implicit, as the author just complains to God about his circumstances. In the midst of these expressions of sadness, the writers also confess their sins and ask for forgiveness. This happens most famously in Psalm 51, which according to tradition was written by David after the prophet Nathan confronted him for taking Bathsheba and killing her husband. David confesses and repents, while he expresses sorrow for his sin and its consequences.

The cursing psalms. The **imprecatory psalms**, which belong among the lament psalms, are rather disturbing. These psalms hurl curses at one's enemies and ask God to do them all sorts of harm. Some ask God to kill those who oppose the writer, others speak of the joy the authors would feel at seeing the children of their enemies killed (Psalms 109, 137). These are not sentiments we expect to find in the Bible. We must remember, however, that the psalms are expressions of people's experience that they bring before God. We often try to hide the ugly side of our feelings, thinking we cannot expose them to God. The psalmists were people who trusted God enough to express their most violent and unjust feelings in God's presence. These psalms give voice to the anguish that oppressed, aggrieved, and disadvantaged people feel. They do not give permission for believers to kill children in retaliation or to attack enemies; they simply express what many, perhaps all, of us feel when we suffer unjustly. These psalms bare the souls of the faithful before God, pouring out these ungodly thoughts in the safest place, the presence of God. The rest of the psalms paint a portrait of God that does not allow God to act in the ways the imprecatory psalms ask God to act. Thus, while these psalms express hatred, they do not authorize it as an attitude that can remain part of the lives of God's people.

Didactic psalms. The final kind of psalm we will consider has a teaching function. The **didactic psalms** intend to teach those who hear and repeat them what God wants in the lives of God's people. Psalm 1 contrasts the ways of the righteous and the ways of the wicked, urging those who hear it to choose the way of godliness. Such psalms prescribe this way of life as the way to please God, and so the way to receive God's blessings (Psalms 32, 37). One of these teaching psalms deserves special note, Psalm 119. This psalm that praises and gives thanks for the law (hence also classified as a Torah psalm) is an **acrostic**: there is a stanza for each letter of the Hebrew alphabet and each line within that strophe begins with that letter. Such artistry manifests a kind of love for the law that shows Israel did not experience the law as a terrible burden, but as a blessing from God.

▶ Song of Solomon: "Love Is Stronger Than Death"

Although the Song of Solomon (also known as Song of Songs and Canticles; the Hebrew title means "the greatest song") is not one of the Psalms, it is included in this chapter because it is poetry and its genre is different from other books. Two of its names come from the book's first verse that includes a title for it: "The Song of Songs, which is Solomon's." This whole book is a love poem, complete with loving, even sensuous, descriptions of both lovers. Including this kind of poetry in the Bible has made many people uncomfortable. So some have read it as an allegory of the love God has for Israel. Christians have sometimes read it as an allegory of God's love for the church. These readings try to avoid having a love poem in the Bible. Yet the nature of the poem remains obvious to all who read it.

This is a poem that affirms, even celebrates, sexuality. Here sexuality is a gift from God. The poem also transcends much of the patriarchal system of arranged marriages, as these two lovers find each other outside the bounds of that system. The man and woman express their attraction in loving and sensual descriptions of each other.

The Song of Solomon, then, rejoices in our humanity and physical nature. It implicitly rejects the notion that spirituality is found in denying our physical nature. It finds blessings in the way God has made human beings, including our sexual nature and desires.

BOX 9.3

OTHER TYPES OF PSALMS

These include:

- Enthronement hymns, celebrating the kingship of God (96, 97, 99)
- Wisdom psalms, meditations on life (73, 112)
- Pilgrimage psalms, sung by pilgrims en route to the temple in Jerusalem (hence overlapping with songs of Zion) (122)
- Songs of Zion, celebrating the glories of Jerusalem (48, 76, 84)
- Hymns of the sacred history of Israel (78, 105–106)

BOX 9.4

SEX IN THE BIBLE

Read Song of Solomon 1:1-8; 8:6-7. What does this suggest about sexuality when you remember the rules about extra-marital sex found throughout the Bible?

▶ Conclusion

The sample of Israelite poetry we find in the Psalms and the Song of Solomon shows great range and depth. They also demonstrate great appreciation for both the spiritual and the physical aspects of life. The Psalms evidence

FIGURE 9.2 **AN EXPRESSION OF SEXUALITY**

This fourteenth-century B.C.E. Eyptian relief in gilded wood suggests a prelude to an intimate encounter between King Tutankhamen and Queen Ankhesenamen. Art Resource

a depth of devotion to God that disproves any view of ancient Judaism that sees it as a legalistic religion. The Psalms show a people who bare their souls, even the darkest parts, to God. They possess an intimate relationship with God that assures them that God will not reject them because of these kinds of thoughts and feelings. Therefore, they experience the type of relationship with the Divine that every religion strives to attain. Thus the Psalms have become classics of Western culture.

The presence of the Song of Solomon in the canon suggests that Israelite spirituality included all spheres of life. Thus this sample of poetry provides a glimpse of the aesthetic side of Israelite culture.

▶ LET'S REVIEW ◀

In this chapter, we have learned:

- The Book of Psalms is a collection of material used in worship at the temple
- The Psalms are Israel's response to God
- Psalms use various poetic structures
- There are multiple types of psalms
- About the Song of Solomon
  - —A love poem
  - —Celebrates sexuality

▶ KEY TERMS ◀

Acrostic
Antithetical parallelism
Didactic psalms
Imprecatory psalms
Lament psalms
Parallelism
Psalms of praise
Psalter
Royal psalms
Synonymous parallelism
Synthetic parallelism
Thanksgiving psalms

▶ QUESTIONS FOR REVIEW ◀

9.1 How are the Psalms different from the poetry in the prophetic writings?
9.2 Name three kinds of psalms and tell about their distinctive characteristics.
9.3 Why do you think the editors of the Psalter included the imprecatory psalms?
9.4 What does the Song of Solomon say about human nature?

▶ FOR FURTHER READING ◀

William P. Brown, "Psalms, Book of," in *New Interpreter's Dictionary of the Bible*, ed. Katharine D. Sakenfeld, 4:661–80. Nashville: Abingdon, 2009.

Nancy L. deClaissé-Walford, *Introduction to the Psalms: A Song from Ancient Israel*. St. Louis: Chalice, 2004.

Rolf A. Jacobson, editor. *Soundings in the Theology of Psalms: Perspectives and Methods in Contemporary Scholarship*. Minneapolis: Fortress Press, 2010.

Patrick D. Miller, *They Cried to the Lord: The Form and Theology of Israelite Prayer*. Minneapolis: Fortress Press, 1994.

Roland E. Murphy, *Wisdom Literature and Psalms*, Interpreting Biblical Texts. Nashville: Abingdon, 1983.

10 Between the Testaments
From Alexander the Great to the Time of Jesus

IN THIS CHAPTER WE WILL LEARN ABOUT THE PERIOD AFTER THE WRITINGS OF THE HEBREW BIBLE WERE COMPLETED:

- Alexander the Great and Hellenization
- Maccabean Revolt
- Judean independence
- Emergence of important religious groups within Judaism
- Roman domination
- Atmosphere of political unrest

The world changed dramatically between the return of Judah from exile in the fifth century and the birth of Jesus. New rulers from new directions arrived on the scene and new religious and political movements were born. We cannot understand Jesus or what it meant to be a Jew in Palestine in his day without knowing something about the political and social world into which Jesus was born. We took a glance at the political changes of this era in chapter 7 when setting the context for Daniel; now we need to fill out that picture. Still, we will only touch on the highlights that help us understand the New Testament and its times.

As we saw in chapter 6, when the Judahites returned from exile in Babylon, they remained under foreign domination. The new ruling empire was Persia (roughly equivalent to modern Iran), whose policy was to encourage the repatriation of peoples the Babylonians had exiled. Thousands of Judahites, but not the majority, chose to return to their homeland. Many hoped God would establish an independent Jewish state that wielded significant power in the region. Such hopes, however, were not fulfilled as large empires continually dominated the region of Palestine.

▶ Alexander the Great and Hellenization

Alexander the Great conquered all that we now think of as the Middle East, along with parts of North Africa, Turkey, and some of southern Europe in the fourth century B.C.E. His empire extended from Greece to the border of India. It was the largest empire the ancient world had known, but it did not last long. Alexander died at a young age in 322 and left no heirs. So his empire was divided among his generals, only two of whom will concern us: **Ptolemy** and **Seleucus**. Ptolemy ruled the areas of North Africa (primarily Egypt), Palestine, and parts of Lebanon (that is, through the Bekaa Valley); and Seleucus took control of the areas east and north of Ptolemy's territory and established his capital in Damascus (thus his realm is often called the Syrian kingdom).

FIGURE 10.2 **GENERAL LYSIMACHUS**
Lysimachus was a general of Alexander the Great and ruler of western Asia Minor after Alexander's death. *Cities of Paul*

FIGURE 10.1 **ALEXANDER THE GREAT**
Coin with head of Alexander the Great, fourth century B.C.E. Lexington Theological Seminary

These two generals, along with the rest of Alexander's successors, continued Alexander's program of hellenization (fostering Greek culture). This plan helped them rule because it moved their territories toward a common culture, so that their subjects had less reason to revolt. While a number of indigenous populations made some bids for independence, most accepted many aspects of Greek culture: Greek became the language of commerce and education; many cities adopted the central Greek educational institutions; and Greek styles of art and customs began to dominate the cultural landscape.

The Gymnasium

Among the most important institutions Alexander and his successors introduced in their conquered lands was the Greek **gymnasium**. In classical Greece the gymnasium was the central educational institution for upper-class boys; it served as the approximate equivalent of high school through the first few years of college. After finishing at the gymnasium, a person could go on to take instruction to become a doctor or lawyer, or return to the family business. In this school, students studied Greek literature, math, rhetoric, and warfare, since these students would become the officers if a war broke out. Their day also included physical education—in the nude, just as contestants were in the ancient Greek Olympics. (The word *gymnasium* means place of nakedness.) When the conquered areas accepted this institution, it accelerated their acceptance of Greek culture.

Throughout the regions Alexander's successors ruled, the children of wealthy people (nearly the only children who received a formal education) attended the gymnasia in their regions or cities. Since the language and culture of the governing power was Greek, those who wanted to be economically and socially

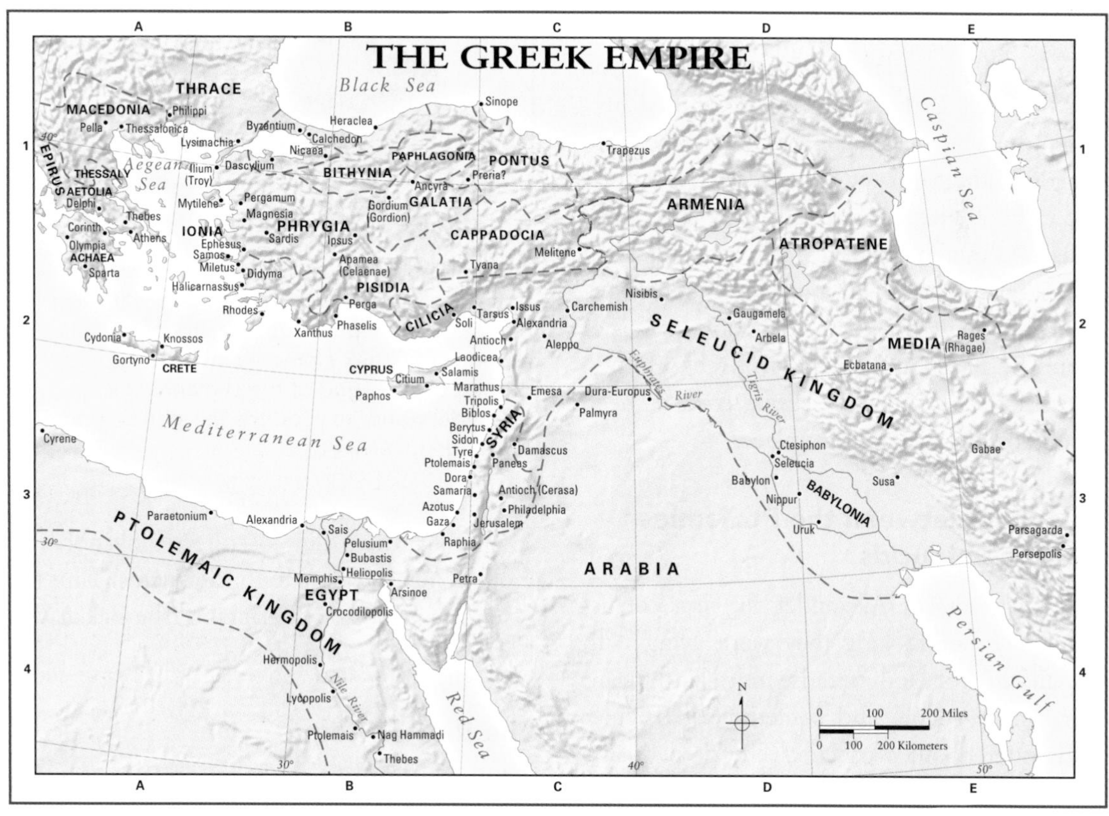

MAP 10.1

successful had to adopt, at least publicly, many aspects of Greek culture. So the sons of the rich went to the gymnasium to learn Greek culture and ways.

Greek Religion

Another way Greek culture infiltrated the indigenous cultures was through religion. The new rulers brought Greek gods to their conquered lands, but did not impose the worship of those gods, nor did they prohibit the worship of gods already there. Rather, they introduced the Greek gods as manifestations of the same gods the peoples were already worshiping; they mixed or combined the identities of the gods so that a person did not even have to add the worship of a new god, just recognize that the god who had a particular function in their region was the same god Greeks had worshiped by a different name. For example, in Egypt the highest god in the pantheon was **Amon-Re**, the sun god. The Ptolemies asserted that the Greek **Zeus** and Amon-Re were really just different names for the same god. So soon there are references to Zeus-Amon-Re, and soon images of Amon-Re have him appear in Greek clothes. These kinds of changes seem to have been accepted fairly well in most places.

FIGURE 10.3 **SERAPIS**

A hybrid god of the Hellenistic world. Ptolemy I, the successor of Alexander the Great who ruled Egypt, emphasized worship of Serapis. He introduced Greek elements into the appearance of the Egyptian god of the sun and Apis, god of the underworld, to produce this patron god of Alexandria. *Cities of Paul*

Palestine between the Ptolemies and the Seleucids

The successors of Alexander did not coexist peacefully. Before long they were vying with one another for land, because more land meant more tax revenue, and sometimes particular lands offered other benefits. The descendants of Ptolemy and Seleucus fought over control of Palestine. The Ptolemies retained control until 198 B.C.E., when they lost the region north of modern Saudi Arabia to the Seleucids. Thus the Seleucids gained rich farmland (the Bekaa Valley) and seaports of Palestine.

The Rise of Rome

While such conflicts continued in the east, a new power had arisen in the west: Rome. By the beginning of the second century B.C.E. the Romans had begun to expand their power into Turkey. Seldom did they send an army to conquer a nation unless invited by a neighbor. Rome entered several of what we might call mutual protection treaties with the small regional kingdoms that had achieved independence in Asia Minor (modern Turkey). Of course, the small number of forces those nations could provide Rome was inconsequential, but these treaties extended Rome's influence into new areas. When Rome did intervene in a situation, it often retained substantial control over that area, though not necessarily direct governance. Still, these areas sent Rome tax money that supported its growing power.

FIGURE 10.4 **ANTIOCHUS IV**

This coin is a tetradrachma. Art Resource

Antiochus IV and the Jews

Antiochus IV Epiphanes assumed power in the Seleucid realm (Syria) in 175 after his brother Seleucus IV Philopator was assassinated. Kings who needed money in this period often turned to one of three options: go to war to gain a higher tax base, raise taxes, or take money from temple treasuries (which often contained large sums of money and expensive objects). Antiochus opted for both more wars and robbing temples.

Jason. In the midst of these troubles, the area around Jerusalem, now called **Judea**, caused Antiochus notable problems—including resistance when he wanted the money in the temple treasury. In 174 Jason, the brother of the high priest in Jerusalem, approached Antiochus with a proposal (2 Macc. 4:7-10). If Antiochus would declare Jason the high priest—an office that had political as well as religious functions in this period—Jason would initiate a campaign of hellenizing Jerusalem and the surrounding area. In his need for money, Antiochus took a bribe and agreed to Jason's proposal. This created problems in Judea because the office of high priest was a lifetime appointment. But since Jason was at least a member of the high-priestly family, the unrest was contained.

A gymnasium in Jerusalem. Jason began his hellenizing efforts by establishing a gymnasium to promote acceptance of Greek culture among the elite, and he put it within sight of the temple. This made his actions doubly unacceptable to a large segment of the population because it offended some who worshiped at the temple to see the gymnasium as they left or arrived at the temple—and imagine that they happened to look down from the Temple Mount to the field while P.E. class was in session!

Jason's rapid and aggressive moves to hellenize Judea made him very unpopular, but a solution presented itself to Antiochus in 171. That year another wealthy resident of Jerusalem, Menelaus, offered him a bribe to attain the office of high priest. Again, Antiochus accepted. Menelaus knew this would agitate the population of Jerusalem because he was not even of the proper lineage to be high priest, so he sent his brother to make the announcement. His brother was killed in the ensuing riot, but when order was restored, Menelaus assumed his post as high priest.

Civil war in Judea. Still needing money, Antiochus attacked Egypt (the Ptolemies). Again, however, Rome intervened and saddled Antiochus with even more debt. During the course of the war, a rumor circulated in Jerusalem claiming that Antiochus had been killed. Since the elites knew that whoever was high priest when the next king secured power would probably be confirmed in that post, civil war broke out in Jerusalem. Jason and his allies attacked the forces of Menelaus, and a third group appeared on the scene, a group our sources call "the Pious." This group rejected the hellenization that both Jason and Menelaus had imposed and wanted to restore things to what they were before this intrusion.

Angry about his defeat, and marching through Judea to return home to Damascus with an army of battle-hardened veterans, Antiochus arrived in Jerusalem to find the civil war in progress. He slaughtered thousands, plundered the temple, and returned Menelaus to power. But the unrest did not end. So in 167 Antiochus sent a general named Apollonius to Judea to put an end to the rebel activity. Early in his suppression of the resistance, Apollonius killed many Jews in Jerusalem on the Sabbath, when he knew they would not be prepared to fight (2 Macc. 5:24-30).

The Pollution of the Temple and the Maccabean (Hasmonean) Revolt

Since Antiochus believed that the unrest in Judea stemmed from its residents' religion, on about **December 15, 167 B.C.E.**, he outlawed observance of the religion of the Torah (e.g., Judaism) in Judea. He established the cult of Zeus in the temple by erecting a statue of Zeus and sacrificing a pig on the altar. Furthermore, he forbade parents to circumcise their sons, forbade observance of the Sabbath, and destroyed as many copies of the "books of the law" as he could find (1 Macc. 1:45, 48, 56). Apollonius found an encampment of those fleeing to avoid breaking the law. They refused to defend themselves or fight a battle because it was the Sabbath, which they refused to violate by engaging in battle. Apollonius said, "Fine, but we don't keep the Sabbath." Then he slaughtered the whole group (Josephus, *Jewish Antiquities* 12.6.2). This episode demonstrates just how committed to obeying God the Pious were. Given such depth of faith and commitment, it is no surprise that the troubles in Judea did not abate.

Just to make sure that no one could claim to be observant, and so try to foment rebellion on that basis, Antiochus set out to make everyone sacrifice to an idol. To do this he sent soldiers to towns throughout the region to make each person comply. More than a few decided that one sacrifice was not so bad. But when the soldiers came to Modein, not far from Jerusalem, things did not go smoothly. When the first resident offered to make a sacrifice to another god, an old priest named Mattathias leapt out and killed him. The book of 1 Maccabees recounts these events and says that through this action, Mattathias demonstrated his "zeal for the law" (1 Macc. 2:26). This act began the Maccabean Revolt.

Judas rededicates the temple. Mattathias escaped capture in the riot that followed his daring act and became the first leader to bring together the various bands of the Pious throughout Judea so that they formed a united front against the Seleucid Empire. When Mattathias died just a few months after his initial act, his son Judas assumed leadership of the movement and achieved incredible success. Using techniques of guerrilla warfare, he regained control of the temple and a section of Jerusalem in just three years, even though a garrison of Syrian troops remained stationed in the city. In 164 they cleansed and rededicated the temple to God and reestablished the sacrifices to God there. Hanukkah still commemorates this rededication of the temple at the time of the Maccabean Revolt.

BOX 10.1

SOURCES THAT TELL OF THE MACCABEAN REVOLT

Our knowledge about the Maccabean Revolt comes largely from 1 and 2 Maccabees, books in the Apocrypha that clearly support the actions and ideology of the Maccabean rulers. The Jewish historian Josephus also tells of many of these events. One of the most dramatic tales from this period comes from 4 Maccabees. This book tells the story of seven brothers and their mother who are all tortured to death by Antiochus IV Epiphanes because they refuse to violate God's law.

BOX 10.2

HANUKKAH

The retaking and rededication of the temple is still celebrated in Judaism with the Feast of Hanukkah. That feast lasts eight days to commemorate the purification of oil to use in the temple menorah. In the story, the little bit of purified oil that remained (only one day's supply) miraculously lasted the eight days required to purify new oil. In the New Testament, this feast is known as the Feast of Dedication (John 10:22-42).

▶ The Move toward Jewish Independence

Jonathan. Antiochus's successor (who came to power perhaps by assassinating Antiochus) granted Jews religious freedom and allowed Judas to retain some power. Soon, war broke out afresh, and Judas was killed in 160 (Josephus, *Antiquities* 12.9–13.1). His brother Jonathan took over as leader of the movement and gained new concessions over the course of his tenure. By 153 all of Judea was under his control. He was able to advance his position because the Seleucid Empire was itself unstable. Jonathan sided with the winner in a civil war, and for his loyalty was made high priest and civil governor. He became so powerful that the Seleucid king had him assassinated in 143. The final son of

BOX 10.3

JEWISH GROUPS OF THE FIRST CENTURY

Speaking of the first century B.C.E., Josephus says:

> "At this time there were three sects among the Jews, who had different opinions concerning human actions; the one was called the sect of the Pharisees, another the sect of the Sadducees, and the other the sect of the Essenes."
>
> Josephus, *Ant.* 13.171

Mattathias, Simeon, then came to power and retained leadership until his death in 134. He also amassed more power, political independence, and land (Josephus, *Antiquities* 13.2-7).

The priesthood and the Essenes. Jonathan's rise to the office of high priest caused problems in Judea. The initial uprising that led to the Maccabean Revolt started when priests from the wrong family assumed that post. Since the **Hasmoneans** (the family name of the Maccabeans) were not in the high-priestly line, some found Jonathan's assumption of this position problematic. This was probably when the **Essene** movement known from the Dead Sea Scrolls came into existence. This group abandoned worshiping and serving in the temple to protest the improper way the temple was being operated. They were a community with priests at their core who looked forward to a time when temple services would be conducted correctly. They envisioned their leadership assuming the post of high priest and bringing temple worship into conformity with what they thought God wanted. Their hopes were never realized, but their departure from the temple signals the significant differences that existed among Jews who were trying to be faithful to God in this period.

The Pharisees. At about the same time, and perhaps for similar reasons, another group broke away from the Pious. The **Pharisees** were more of a lay movement, while the Essenes were at least initially a priestly movement. The Pharisees did not isolate themselves from society as the Essenes did, but formed an opposition group to the ruling powers. So they, like the Essenes, had both political and religious

BOX 10.4

THE "WICKED PRIEST"

The Essene commentary on Habakkuk begins its description of the Maccabean ruler who takes over as high priest by saying: "This refers to the Wicked Priest who had a reputation for reliability at the beginning of his term of service; but when he became ruler over Israel he became proud and forsook God and betrayed the commandments for the sake of riches" (1QpHab 8).

The conflict between the Teacher of Righteousness and this ruler is mentioned in the next column of the commentary: "This [Hab. 2:8b] refers to the Wicked Priest. Because of the crime he committed against the Teacher of Righteousness and the members of his party, God handed him over to his enemies."

reasons for separating themselves from the Hasmoneans. We will discuss the Pharisees and their religious views after a survey of political events.

John Hyrcanus and independence. When Simeon died, his son John Hyrcanus (134–104) became ruler of Judea and the surrounding area. John took advantage of Syria's weakness to declare independence by stopping the payment of tribute (c. 129). He also expanded his borders so that he controlled most of Palestine as an independent king. Finally, for the first time since the sixth century, there was an independent Jewish state in Palestine.

Hasmoneans and Sadducees. By this time, the Hasmoneans had clearly adopted political goals. That is, their interests went far beyond securing the right to worship God as they believed Jews should. Indeed, John Hyrcanus's kingdom was in many ways a typical Hellenistic kingdom. Official documents were written in Greek and his political supporters were the children of the people his grandfather, Mattathias, had opposed. His political allies came from the segment of society that gave rise to the **Sadducees**, the other religious party we hear so much about in the New Testament.

▶ Roman Domination of Palestine

Pompey

Within twenty years of John's death, assassinations and intrigues designed to attain the throne plagued the Jewish nation. In 66 a civil war broke out that neither side seemed able to win. Fatefully, both sides appealed to Rome to take

CHART 10.1

THE MACCABEAN LEADERS

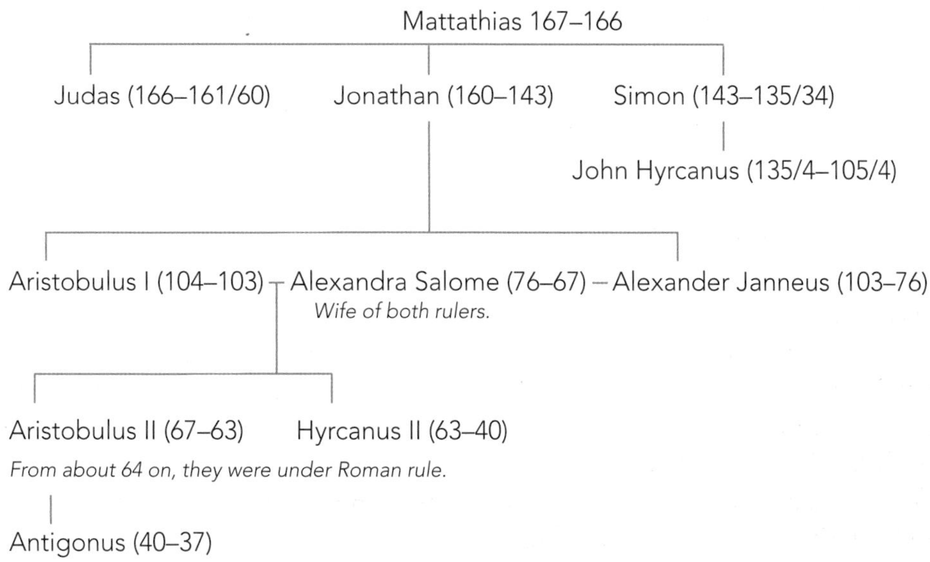

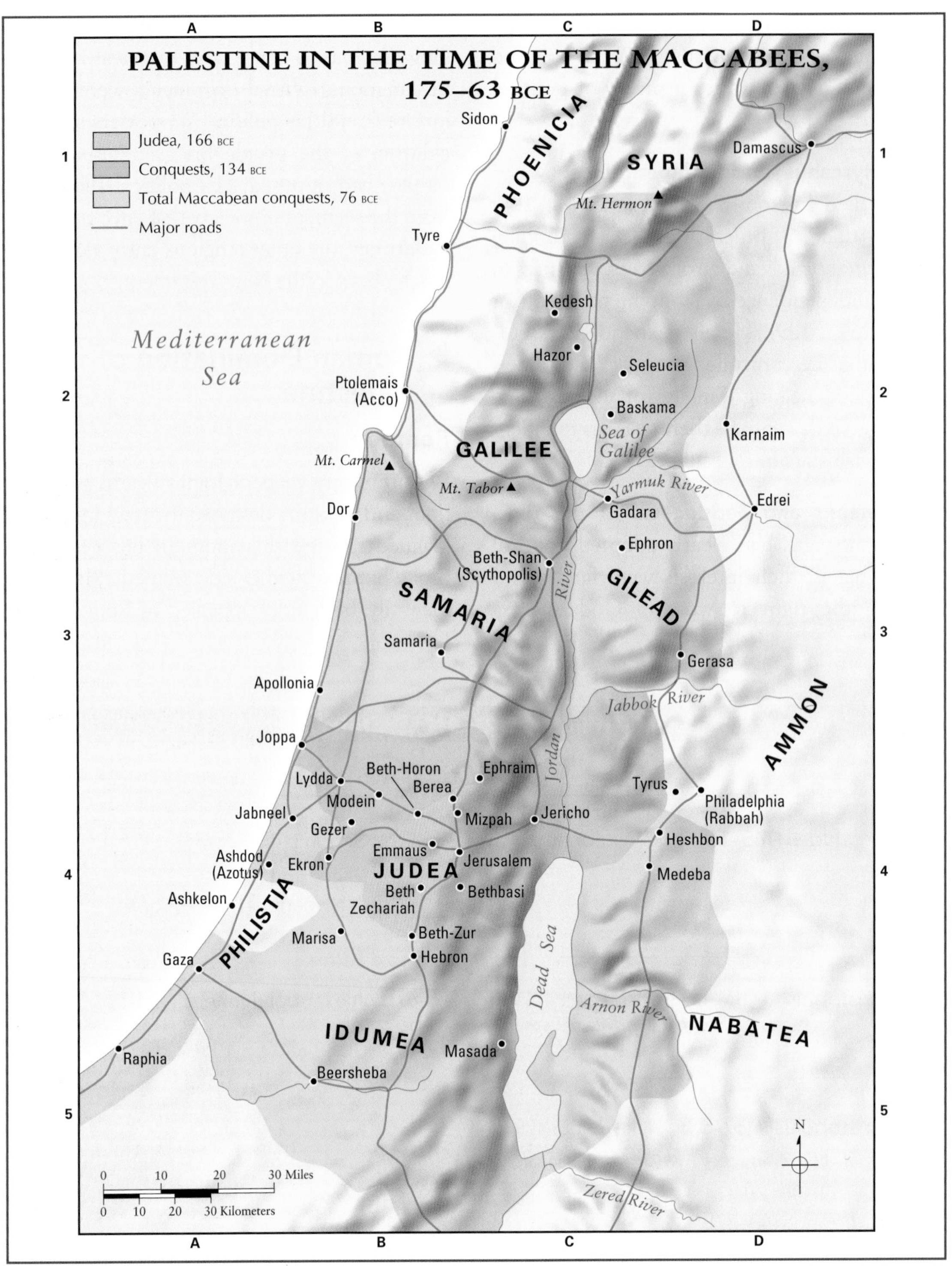
PALESTINE IN THE TIME OF THE MACCABEES, 175–63 BCE
Judea, 166 BCE
Conquests, 134 BCE
Total Maccabean conquests, 76 BCE
Major roads
A
B
C
D
1
2
3
4
5
Mediterranean Sea
Sidon
PHOENICIA
SYRIA
Damascus
Mt. Hermon
Tyre
Kedesh
Hazor
Seleucia
Ptolemais (Acco)
Baskama
Sea of Galilee
Karnaim
GALILEE
Mt. Carmel
Mt. Tabor
Yarmuk River
Edrei
Dor
Gadara
Ephron
Beth-Shan (Scythopolis)
River
GILEAD
SAMARIA
Samaria
Gerasa
Apollonia
Jabbok River
AMMON
Joppa
Jordan
Lydda
Beth-Horon
Ephraim
Berea
Tyrus
Philadelphia (Rabbah)
Modein
Jabneel
Mizpah
Jericho
Gezer
Heshbon
Emmaus
Ashdod (Azotus)
Ekron
JUDEA
Jerusalem
Medeba
Beth Zechariah
Bethbasi
Ashkelon
PHILISTIA
Marisa
Beth-Zur
Hebron
Gaza
Dead Sea
Arnon River
NABATEA
IDUMEA
Masada
Raphia
Beersheba
N
0 10 20 30 Miles
0 10 20 30 Kilometers
Zered River

MAP 10.2

their side as a way to win the struggle. When Rome chose a side, it sent troops to enforce the decision, and in 63 **Pompey** (the famous general in the triumvirate with Caesar and Crassus) took Jerusalem. The Roman victory in Jerusalem signaled the end of an independent Jewish state.

In his victory tour through the city Pompey entered the temple, even the most holy place that symbolized the immediate presence of God. Although he did not plunder the temple, entering its sacred (and forbidden) areas soured relations between Jews in Judea and Rome—and there was little respite for the next two hundred years. The great desecration of the temple by Antiochus was too recent for Pompey's tour not to seem like a repeat performance. Furthermore, since Pompey's victory also ended Judean independence, the people hated the Roman presence. It was almost like turning the back clock a hundred years because Rome placed Judea under the governor of the province of Syria, whose headquarters was in Damascus (the capital of the former Seleucid Empire)—it just felt too much like a return to the days before the Maccabean Revolt.

Antipater and Antigonus

As time passed, some Hasmoneans gained a bit of power in Judea by helping Roman causes in the region, but the real power remained in the hands of the governor of Syria. When Antipater, the governor of Syria, died in 43 B.C.E., however, there was a momentary power vacuum because the Romans had not yet confirmed his two sons to succeed him. A final Hasmonean, Antigonus, saw in this moment an opportunity to regain independence for Judea. He had one of Antipater's sons assassinated, but the other escaped to Rome to receive confirmation from the senate.

Meanwhile, Antigonus made himself high priest by deposing his uncle. (To legitimate this move, he cut off his uncle's ear so that he had a visible physical defect, which disqualified him from serving as high priest.) Thus Antigonus controlled both the political and religious institutions in what he declared to be an independent Judea.

Herod the Great

The Romans, however, appointed Antipater's son ruler of the region and sent troops to help him establish his position. When he returned to Judea with these troops, he quickly won the war and killed Antigonus. Thus began the reign of **Herod the Great**, the person the Gospel of Matthew has on the throne when Jesus is born. These events happened a mere forty years before the birth of Jesus—so some people who lived through Herod's assumption of power by defeating the last of the Hasmonean line would have been alive at the time of Jesus' birth.

Herod's building program. The Gospel of Matthew presents Herod as an evil ruler, and in some ways he was. In other ways, however, he helped his subjects. By ingratiating himself to the Romans, he gained a good deal of political independence and the Romans granted him the title of king (though he, of course, paid tribute to Rome) and expanded the territory he ruled. He took on huge building projects, creating harbors to enhance sea trade and public buildings for everyone's use. He also built enormous palaces and military fortresses for himself. Among his many important accomplishments

FIGURE 10.5 **REMAINS OF HEROD'S PALACE**

This residence, near Jerusalem, is just one from which Herod ruled. The ostentatious character of this palace is evident from the large fountain in the center of the courtyard. Such a use of water in an arid region was a show of wealth. Jerry Sumney

in the region, perhaps the most notable was his sponsorship of the massive renovations of the temple in Jerusalem. Under his reign, it became a vast complex that took up several city blocks and was multiple stories tall. This magnificent structure took most of his reign to build.

Herod's offenses. As Herod gave the modern equivalent of millions (probably billions) of dollars to this work, he also outraged the faithful by committing various offenses along the way. For example, he decided to put a statue of a Roman eagle over one of the temple's gates, a move that not only violated the patriotic sentiments of the people but also the command not to have any graven image. Riots ensued and Herod suppressed them violently. He met any opposition with swift and disproportionate retaliation—and that included people within his household who fell under suspicion.

Late in his life Herod seemed to become delusional, thinking that there were plots to depose him everywhere. He suspected several members of his household, and so had them executed. On his deathbed he gave orders for his three sons to be killed. While this order was not carried out, it shows how ruthless Herod could be, even as he lay dying. It is easy to see why Matthew could envision him ordering the slaughter of all the children in the Bethlehem area (Matt. 2:16).

While Herod seems to have had some Jewish ancestry, he was not observant of the faith.

FIGURE 10.6 **TOWER OF PHASAEL**

Built by Herod the Great in memory of his brother who was killed by the last Hasmonean to try to take power in Jerusalem. Jerry Sumney

This bothered many of the people who thought he should be more sympathetic to some of their causes because of his ethnic connections with them. Overall, Herod was very unpopular with the general population of Judea. For them his cruelty outweighed any good he may have accomplished.

After Herod

At Herod's death, the Romans divided his territory among his three sons: Herod Antipas, Philip, and Archelaus. These three sons governed most of Palestine during the early years of Jesus' life. They ruled with varying degrees of success.

Herod Antipas administered Galilee and the southern areas east of the Jordan River until 39 C.E. Philip ruled the land in northeast Palestine, including what is today the Golan Heights and the eastern part of Syria until 33/34. Archelaus governed Judea and Samaria, but was such a bad ruler that the Romans deposed and banished him in 6 C.E. These areas were then made part of the province of Syria and administrated by a series of Roman procurators (the title of governors of smaller regions) who answered to the governor of the province. In the year 26 Pontius Pilate assumed this office and governed until 36.

BOX 10.5

HEROD AND THE BIRTH OF JESUS

Herod the Great died in 4 B.C.E. Matthew has Jesus born two years before Herod's death. Luke, however, has Jesus born when Herod's son Archelaus rules in Judea, as the reference to this census of Quirinius (Luke 2:2) indicates. Each Gospel writer gives his date for Jesus' birth to help establish specific elements of Jesus' identity: Matthew implies that Jesus belongs among royalty by having the king be worried about him; Luke shows that Jesus' birth is important beyond Judea by connecting it to an event that is part of the broader world.

FIGURE 10.7 **HEROD'S PALACE AT MASADA**

The fortress on this mountain was the place of the last stand of the Jewish fighters in the revolt against Rome in which the Jerusalem temple was destroyed in 70 C.E. The fighters here held out against the Romans for four years after the destruction of the temple. Marshall Johnson

The Jewish-Roman War

Given the region's recent memory of independence, it is not surprising that there was political unrest in Palestine. Furthermore, it was near the eastern edge of the empire, and so had contacts with nations that had managed to resist Roman takeover. Some among the faithful also continued to look for God to fulfill the prophets' promises of a kingdom of David. Moreover, some procurators engaged in extravagant economic exploitation of the people, taxing them far more than what Roman tribute demanded.

After many smaller uprisings over several decades, a full-scale revolt broke out in Palestine in 66. It lasted four years, but was finally crushed by the Roman army. Near the end of this revolt, the Romans sacked Jerusalem and destroyed the magnificent temple it had taken Herod so long to build.

Even this did not end all hopes for an independent Jewish state. **Bar Kokhba** led a final revolt in 132–135 that may have been provoked by the emperor Hadrian's plan to make Jerusalem a pagan city. Following the suppression of

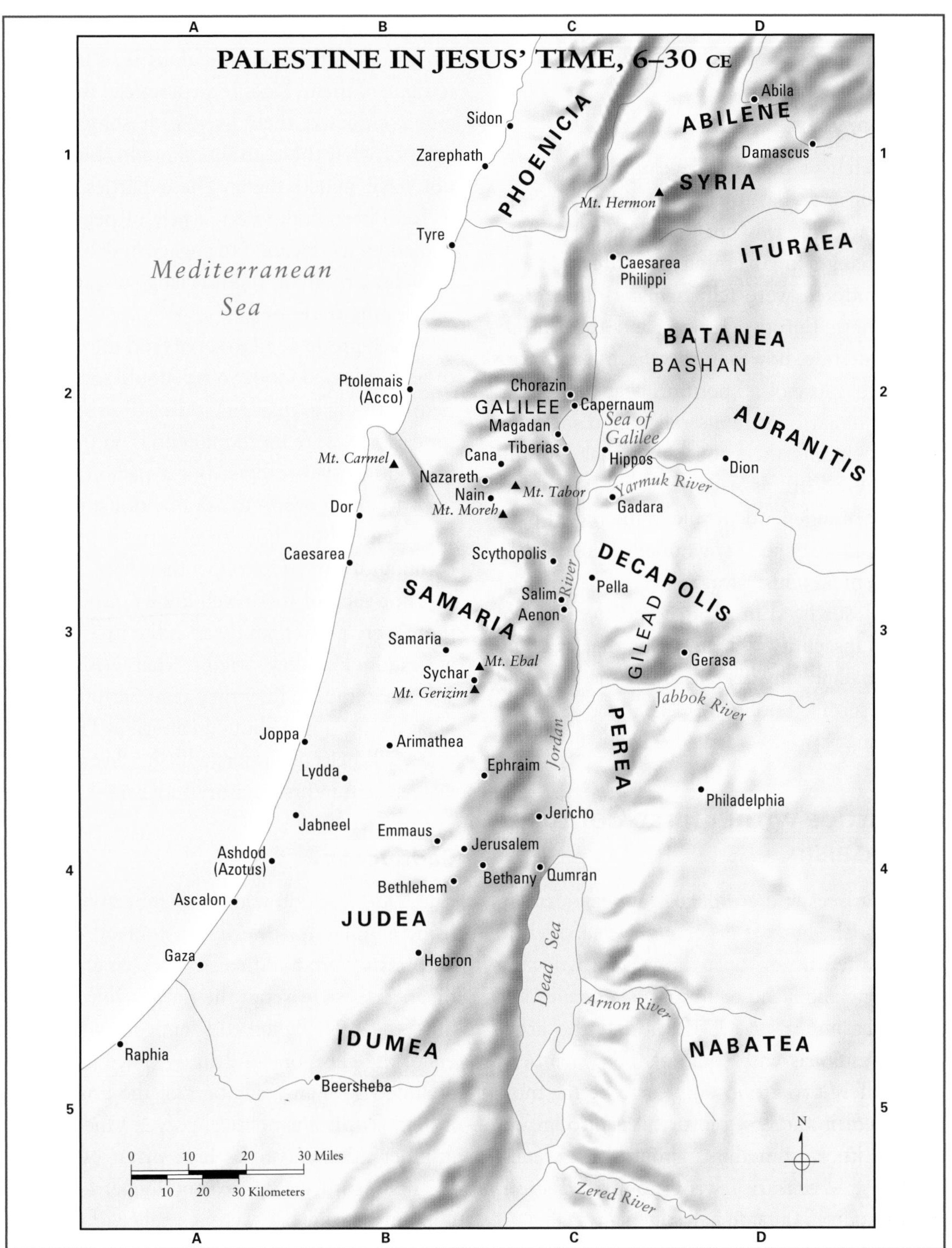
PALESTINE IN JESUS' TIME, 6–30 CE
A
B
C
D
1
2
3
4
5
Sidon
Zarephath
PHOENICIA
Abila
ABILENE
Damascus
SYRIA
Mt. Hermon
Tyre
Caesarea Philippi
ITURAEA
Mediterranean Sea
BATANEA
BASHAN
Ptolemais (Acco)
Chorazin
Capernaum
GALILEE
Magadan
Sea of Galilee
AURANITIS
Tiberias
Hippos
Dion
Mt. Carmel
Cana
Nazareth
Mt. Tabor
Yarmuk River
Nain
Gadara
Mt. Moreh
Dor
Scythopolis
DECAPOLIS
Caesarea
Pella
SAMARIA
Salim
Aenon
River
GILEAD
Samaria
Mt. Ebal
Gerasa
Sychar
Mt. Gerizim
Jabbok River
Jordan
PEREA
Joppa
Arimathea
Ephraim
Lydda
Philadelphia
Jericho
Jabneel
Emmaus
Jerusalem
Ashdod (Azotus)
Bethany
Qumran
Bethlehem
Ascalon
JUDEA
Dead Sea
Gaza
Hebron
Arnon River
IDUMEA
NABATEA
Raphia
Beersheba
N
0 10 20 30 Miles
0 10 20 30 Kilometers
Zered River

MAP 10.3

this revolt, Rome ordered all Jews to leave the region of Judea.

Summary

This sketch of political developments in Palestine suggests that it was a troubled place. In some ways, this was not distinctive. The continual changes in governing structures that Palestine suffered were felt in many other areas of southern Europe, Turkey, and the Middle East. Palestine, however, may have been more volatile because of its position near the border of the Roman Empire, its religious distinctiveness—including the expectation that faithfulness to God brings national success—and its memory of independent rule in the recent past, to say nothing of suffering under some less than competent administrators.

So Jesus lived in an area and in a time of political insecurity. Remembering that will help us understand why his talk about the kingdom of God sounded political and dangerous in the ears of many.

▶ Parties within First-Century Judaism

The Pharisees and Sadducees appear often in the Gospels, but we never get a clear picture of who they are or what they teach. Knowing something about these groups will enhance our understanding of the Gospels and the arguments Jesus has with some of their members. While these two groups appear to be the most prominent in the first century, it is also important to know something about the Essenes, another first-century Jewish group, and about Jews who lived outside Palestine.

The first thing to note about the three Jewish groups is that most religious Jews belonged to none of them. Most Jews practiced their faith and conducted their lives with some knowledge of what these groups thought, but would not have joined them. These parties seemed to have been composed largely of people who had enough education to engage in debates that drew on a reservoir of knowledge of earlier and developing traditions.

Each group tried to serve God the way they thought pleased God. So we should see them as people trying to discern God's will in their own time. Some were more influential on the larger population than others, but a person did not need to join a group to ask one of its members for advice about how to observe a particular commandment or to follow their lead.

For each of these well-known groups (and there were more than three in the first century) we will look at their origins, what writings they saw as Scripture, how they read Scripture, and what they thought about an afterlife. These features will help us understand the diversity that was present in first-century Judaism.

Sadducees

The Sadducees drew their membership largely from among the priestly aristocracy, but not all priests were Sadducees. They emerged as a distinctive party about the time of John Hyrcanus (134–104), when they appear as supporters of the Hasmonean dynasty. Since the group included so many members of the aristocracy, it held significant political power. One of their number often served as high priest (which by the first century B.C.E. was no longer a lifetime appointment). They were a smaller group than the Pharisees in the first century and were less influential with the larger population, but they wielded significant political influence (Josephus, *Antiquities* 13.10.5-6).

Their Scripture. The Sadducees argued that only the Torah (the Pentateuch) should serve as the authority for what to believe and how to live. They said that the other books—the prophets, Wisdom literature, Deuteronomistic History, and so on—were good reading and helpful, but not authoritative. Thus one might gain encouragement or insight from them, but they were not determinative guides for how to live faithfully. The Sadducees' definition of the canon (that is, group of authoritative texts) or the Bible sets them apart from most other Jews of their day and helps explain why some of their beliefs differed from fellow Jews.

Their reading of Scripture. The Sadducees' method of interpreting the Torah was also distinctive. They read the texts quite literalistically, rejecting interpretations (particularly the Pharisees') that made new demands by the way they applied the texts to their day. Reading a text literally made eminent sense for priests who needed to follow instructions about proper procedures for offering sacrifices, but it also meant that the texts offered little guidance in some areas of their lives. While twenty-first-century people identify literalistic reading with conservative religious beliefs and political outlooks, it worked in just the opposite way for the Sadducees. Being consistent literalists allowed fuller participation in a new setting because there were no commands about the new issues that arose. A modern example might be that a consistent literalist could snort cocaine because there are no commands against it in the Bible (though one might cite biblical instructions that require a person to obey the government as a command that prohibits use of that substance—but not all governments have such laws). When not reading as a literalist there could be many reasons to reject cocaine use, but the most literal reading does not. The Sadducees' literalism allowed them to participate more fully in cultural Hellenism than some other Jews. After all, there were no commandments, for example, against learning Greek or studying Homer. (Of course, many Pharisees also knew Greek and Homer.) Overall, their literalistic reading permitted them to practice their faith with fewer impediments to participation in and acceptance of the surrounding non-Jewish cultures (Josephus, *Antiquities* 13.10.5-8).

No afterlife. Finally, because they said only the Torah was authoritative, the Sadducees did not believe in a long-term afterlife. The Torah offers no hope for an extended and meaningful afterlife. Throughout most of the Hebrew Bible the dead go down into Sheol, where there is no presence of God and no goodness to life. From there, the dead seem to fade out of existence (Pss. 6:4-5; 30:9; 88:1-12; Isa. 38:18). This was the Sadducean view of the afterlife (Jospehus, *Wars* 2.8.14; Acts 23:6-8). It not only cohered with the dominant view of the Torah, it also fit their social position. Proportionately, more people who experience the world as a harsh and difficult place look forward to a better life after this one, while the wealthy and dominant do not need God to balance the scale by giving them good things in an afterlife. The Sadducees were primarily the powerful people; their position in society was evidence that their families

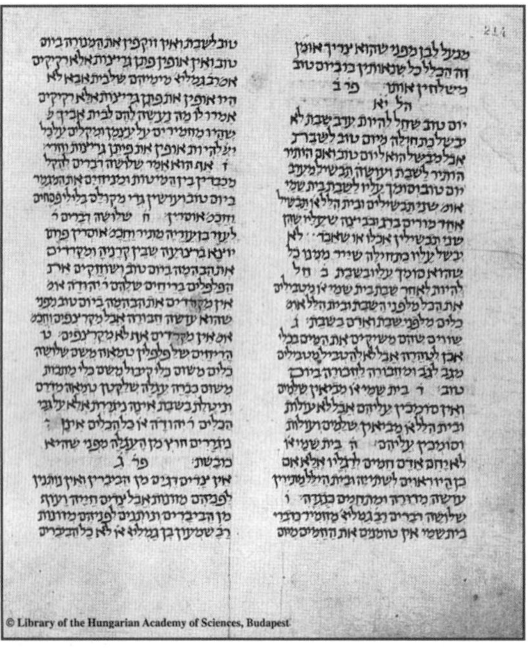

FIGURE 10.8 **THE MISHNAH**

From the Kaufman manuscripts. Probably dating from the early thirteenth century, this manuscript is considered one of the most important, nearly complete (missing only one page) manuscript of the Mishnah. Library of the Hungarian Academy of Sciences

had been faithful to God, and the continuance of their descendants in the halls of power was what they envisioned as the reward for their faithfulness. In this they were again consistent with the dominant view of the Torah.

Their end. While the Sadducees were a powerful political force in Jerusalem throughout most of the first century, the fall of the temple and the restructuring of Judea's government in 70 C.E. dramatically diminished their importance—there was no temple to operate and they were removed from their political offices. Within a few years of the temple's fall, the Sadducees faded from the scene permanently. Other groups would prove better suited to preserve Judaism through yet another crisis.

Pharisees

Their origin. The Pharisees probably grew out of the Pious who fought in the Maccabean Revolt. They parted ways with the Hasmoneans at about the same time the Essenes broke with the ruling house, perhaps also over concerns about the Hasmoneans assuming the post of high priest. The Pharisees focused their efforts on the study and teaching of Scripture and were revered for their scholarship and expertise in the interpretation of the sacred texts. Beyond this, they were known for their faithful observance of the law as a way to serve God. Their faithfulness and expertise in Scripture lent them powerful authority and more influence than either of the other groups (Josephus, *Antiquities* 13.5.9; 13.10.5-8).

Their Scripture. The Pharisees held that the Torah, Prophets, and Writings (the three divisions of the present-day Jewish Bible) were all authoritative for determining what proper beliefs and practices were within Judaism. This immediately distinguished them from the Sadducees because it meant that they had a much larger Bible, and one that included ideas that did not appear in the Torah.

The Oral Torah. The Pharisees' method of interpreting and applying Scripture was also quite different from the Sadducees'. The Pharisees preserved a body of tradition known as the Oral Torah that they claimed went all the way back to Moses; Moses not only wrote the Law, but also began interpreting it. Some even said the first parts of the Oral Torah were given to Moses on Mount Sinai.

The Oral Torah was a continually growing tradition of interpretation that incorporated sayings of previous generations and brought them into conversation with newer understandings. These preserved sayings and interpretations often included contradictory instructions, making clear that there was no one Pharisaic way of thinking about any issue; rather, there was a continuing conversation about how to live for God, with different pious and thoughtful people arriving at differing conclusions (Josephus, *Antiquities* 13.10.6; Mishnah, *Avot* 1). Much of this tradition was recorded in the Mishnah, a guide to Jewish life compiled around the year 200 C.E. Through this tradition, the Pharisees sought to make the Law relevant for their day; that is, they tried to discern how Jews in their day should live to be faithful to God and the covenant.

A fence around the Law. This interpretive tradition often intentionally required more than the Law did because the Pharisees wanted to be certain that they did not violate God's commandments. They spoke of building a fence around the Law that assured those who observed it that they would not violate God's instruction. This was an expression of their love of God and their determination to live within the covenant. Most of their interpretations imposed little or no extraordinary burden on most people because they incorporated instructions about how to live that were simply part of the cultural pattern of Jewish life in Palestine. They drew everything into their religious life, so that everything they did was part of their service to God.

BOX 10.6

THE TRADITION ABOUT THE ORAL TORAH

Mishnah *Avot* (which means "fathers") 1.1 relates the tradition of how the Oral Torah came to the people of the first and second centuries C.E.: "Moses received the Law from Sinai and committed it to Joshua, and Joshua to the elders, and the elders to the prophets; and the prophets committed it to the men of the Great Synagogue. They said three things: Be deliberate in judgment, raise up many disciples, and make a fence around the Law."

We all follow many rules that no one bothers to write down but that all of us know we must obey. For example, there is no rule in most college student handbooks that says students cannot come to class naked, yet nearly everyone wears clothes to class. In 1992, however, Andrew Martinez, a student at Berkeley, started attending class naked as an act of protest. It took a few months for school officials to make him stop because there was no written rule that prohibited that kind of political statement. The Pharisees would not have had that problem; they would have incorporated that cultural norm into their tradition if they thought anyone might violate it. Thus many of their rules imposed no burden beyond adhering to cultural norms, even though they discussed some small details.

Keeping the Law. The New Testament sometimes presents the Pharisees as teachers who tried to make the Law harder to observe, but that was not their intention—just the opposite. They wanted to make it *possible* to keep the Law when one was not sure what it required. Did some of them prescribe practices that few, except their own circle, would be able to observe and that they violated? Of course, but that can be said of every religious group, just as one can find hypocrites in every Christian denomination. We should not let the improper behavior of a minority become the way we characterize the whole group (just as you would not want the worst person in your church or organization to stand for what you are all like). The Pharisees were doing in their time what people of faith must do in every generation: seek the best way to live as God's people. Jesus engaged the Pharisees in debate about whether they had come to the proper conclusions, but he did not reject what they were trying to do or even the way they went about it.

The afterlife. Since the Pharisees included the book of Daniel (a book that clearly assumes an afterlife) among their authoritative texts, they believed in an afterlife with rewards and punishments—at least for some people (Dan. 12:1-3; Josephus, *Wars* 2.8.14; Acts 23:6-8). There was no one position on this topic, as was often the case with Pharisees. Some envisioned something akin to reincarnation; others believed in realms of punishment and reward. Christian ideas about heaven and hell grew out of some Pharisaic views. As we noted in connection with the Maccabean Revolt, ideas about an afterlife with long-term rewards and punishment flowered as the faithful thought about the fate of martyrs. At first, the fuller afterlife with rewards and punishments was thought to extend only to the very faithful (particularly martyrs) and the very wicked (compare 4 Macc. with Ps. 88:1-12). But as time passed, the tradition extended an afterlife to more and more people until it included everyone. Such ideas about personal existence made room for apocalyptic thought (that is, what we find in the book of Revelation) to flourish.

The Pharisees worked among people who belonged to no particular religious party, trying to help them live faithful lives, even as they maintained disagreements among themselves on particular points. They set a high standard of behavior with their own personal conduct by conforming their lives to what they understood to be God's will for them, and they called others to serve God faithfully (Josephus, *Wars* 2.8).

Their influence. Today's Judaism owes much to the diligent work of Pharisees. In the wake of the disastrous destruction of the temple by the Romans, Pharisees were able to maintain their faith because they had carved out a way to serve and honor God through the way they lived their lives outside the sacred precinct. While the loss of the temple was devastating, it did not prevent them from knowing God's presence and pursuing God's will through the study of Scripture. The later rabbis, on whom later Judaism explicitly builds, were the intellectual descendants of these faithful Pharisees.

Essenes

We noted above that the Essenes emerged as a protest movement when one of the Maccabeans accepted appointment to the high priesthood.*

*Alternatively, the split may have come because the Maccabeans refused to make the person who became

FIGURE 10.9 **CAVES ABOVE THE QUMRAN SETTLEMENT**

The Dead Sea Scrolls were found in the caves around the settlement. Marshall Johnson

In the beginning, they were a separatist group composed mostly of priests, but as time passed they attracted a number of members from beyond the priesthood. The core group of the Essenes was more like a monastic group than either the Pharisees or Sadducees. This inner circle of devotees withdrew from political life and worship at the temple because they found its leadership, and so its worship, unacceptable to God. Thus to participate in it would mean to join in acts that were displeasing to God, and so incur condemnation.

Their communal life. Most scholars think that this core monastic (and celibate) group lived near the Dead Sea in a compound at Qumran from about 150 B.C.E. until 68 C.E. At Qumran priests were preeminent; all leadership posts were held by priests, who kept themselves ritually pure so they were ready to lead worship at the temple. To join this inner group, a person had to pass exams that covered aspects of religious knowledge and one's own morality. Those who passed these tests entered a two-year period of probation. At the end of that time, those who chose to stay gave their assets (except what their family would need to live on after their departure) to the group.

No more than about two hundred of these core members occupied the Qumran compound, while first-century writers estimate the total number of Essenes to be four thousand. An ancient manuscript known as the Damascus Document (CD) seems to belong to the broader Essene movement. This book develops rules for how to live as a married person in a normal community, even as it works from the same basic beliefs found in the Dead Sea Scrolls. The Qumran community may have functioned as something like a religious retreat center for the group, with members traveling there for instruction and edification.

Their Scripture. Like the Pharisees, the Essenes accepted as authoritative the Torah, Prophets,

---

the leader of the Essenes the high priest. Of course, any such refusal may have been simultaneous with their own acceptance of the post.

BOX 10.7

DEAD SEA SCROLLS REFERENCE SYSTEM

Each scroll found at Qumran is given a designation that tells several things about it. The initial number indicates the cave in which the document was found. Then the letter Q shows that it is from Qumran. The following letter comes from the first Hebrew letter in the text, which is followed by letters that indicate something of its content. The number at the end refers to the column within the scroll that a passage comes from. For example, 1QpHab 8 indicates a scroll that came from cave 1 at Qumran. The P indicates that it is a pesher, that is, a sort of commentary on a biblical book. "Hab" shows that it is about Habakkuk. And the number 8 means the citation comes from column 8.

and Writings, as well as some other texts, especially those composed by leaders within their movement. In fact, fragments of every book in the Hebrew Bible except Esther have been found among the Dead Sea Scrolls.

Their reading of Scripture. A principal Essene method of interpretation is known as *pesher* interpretation, which applies what a text says directly to one's own time. The Essenes focused their interpretive efforts on the prophets, relating prophecies—particularly those that called for the victory of the righteous and the downfall of the wicked—to the immediate past, present, and future. They were convinced that these prophetic texts spoke of things happening in their time. They accepted these interpretations in part because they came from an authoritative interpreter of Scripture, the founder and leader of their community whom their various writings call "the Teacher of Righteousness."

This method assumes that present readers live in the time of fulfillment, the moment when God is about to fulfill all prophecy. The Essenes thought they were living in the days when God would set all things right. Any prophecy that predicted a victory for God's people they applied to themselves and looked for its fulfillment in the very near future, maybe the next few days or weeks. This meant that they would take charge of the temple so that proper worship of God would be restored. But they envisioned a larger battle of good against evil, a battle in which angels and demons participate with humans—this was a war for control of the world.

Ritual purity. The Essenes at Qumran maintained constant ritual purity so they would be ready to engage in this holy war and to assume their positions in the temple without delay. Since they were the only faithful people, even within Israel, they needed to be ready to take up arms with the heavenly hosts to fight against the powers of evil. They were the frontline human troops in this battle. In a document known as the *War Scroll*, they even specified the names of various regiments. So they were ready for the decisive act of God that would reorient the world to make it what God wanted it to be. In this reorientation, God would put their group in charge of the temple and the world order.

Interpretation, reinterpretation. This outlook also led them to adopt the pesher method of interpreting the Bible. The method may seem

BOX 10.8

"THE TEACHER OF RIGHTEOUSNESS"

Some documents from Qumran call the founder of their community "the Teacher of Righteousness." One Qumran document describes the founder's arrival like this: "But God considered their deeds, that they had sought Him with a whole heart. So He raised up for them a teacher of righteousness to guide them in the way of His heart" (Damascus Document 1.10-11, which is also in 4Q266 and 4Q268 found at Qumran). Interpreting Habakkuk 2:1-2, the Qumran commentary on this prophet (1QpHab 7.4-5) says, "this refers to the Teacher of Righteousness to whom God made known all the mysterious revelations of his servants the prophets." (Translations from Michael Wise, Martin Abegg Jr., and Edward Cook, *The Dead Sea Scrolls; A New Translation* [San Francisco: HarperSanFrancisco, 1996].)

strange at first, but many people still read the Bible in this way. People who read Revelation to find or interpret current events or to predict that the end of the world is imminent (for example, the Left Behind Series or Jack Van Impe, to name just two of many) adopt the method used at Qumran. The Essenes were not alone in using this method. As we will see in the next chapter, Matthew adopted the same method of reading when he applied passages in the Hebrew Bible to the life of Jesus.

When the end did not come as quickly as the Essenes thought and the Teacher of Righteousness died, they began reinterpreting his readings of Scripture. They continued to believe that the great act of God was near, but thought they had misunderstood some of their leader's interpretations.

The afterlife. Given their acceptance of the prophetic writings as authoritative and their view of the dominance of evil in the world, it is no surprise that the Essenes believed in an afterlife with rewards and punishments. Though they were marginalized in the present, they believed God would reward them for their faithfulness in the next realm—whether they died of natural causes or were killed in the great battle. They spent little time describing that future existence because they remained focused on the ways God would restructure the present world.

The end of the Dead Sea sect. The community at Qumran was destroyed in 68 C.E., when the Roman army moved through the region to establish its siege of Jerusalem. Given the Essenes' talk of engaging God's enemies in battle, the Romans were unlikely to leave this enclave in place. This was about the time they hid their library (what we know as the Dead Sea Scrolls) in the caves near their compound where the scrolls were found in the 1940s. Once the central community was destroyed, the Essenes faded. While people who shared much of their outlook continued to influence both Judaism and emerging Christianity, the group itself soon ceased to exist.

Judaism outside Palestine

The groups we have discussed so far all flourished within Palestine. But in the first century C.E. more Jews lived in the **Diaspora**, that is, outside Palestine, than in Palestine. Yet many Jews

FIGURE 10.10 **THE OLD CITY OF JERUSALEM TODAY**

The Dome of the Rock, an Islamic shrine, is visible on the mount where the Jewish temple once stood in the heart of the ancient city. Wikimedia Commons

living outside Palestine continued to be interested and active in the affairs of Palestine. For example, observant Jews in the Diaspora continued to send a contribution to the temple (the temple tax) annually. The prominent groups in Palestine probably also had some presence in Jewish communities beyond Palestine, as the example of the apostle Paul indicates. He was a native of a city in Turkey, yet identifies himself as a Pharisee. Furthermore, the first-century Jewish writers who tell us about the various parties within Palestine lived outside its borders when they wrote: the philosopher Philo of Alexandria lived all his life in Egypt, and the historian Josephus had lived outside Palestine for many years when he wrote about these parties. So the ways Jews in Palestine differed on the matters we have discussed probably mirrors the kind of diversity present among non-Palestinian Jews.

Cultural challenges. Jews living in the Diaspora faced different questions because of the different cultural environments in which they lived, but they would have engaged many of the same kinds of methods and strategies their Palestinian counterparts used to think about how to be faithful. The writings of Philo show that Diaspora Jews were engaging questions about how to be observant and were coming to varying conclusions. He explained how he thought a person should read and obey the biblical texts, and mentioned people whose understandings he found unacceptable. So Jews in the Diaspora thought about how to be faithful, did so in some communication with the groups in Palestine, and came to differing opinions. There was no single way to live the Jewish faith in the first century.

The Septuagint. The common language among Diaspora Jews was the same language that dominated the whole Middle East following the sweep of hellenization: Greek. Though the religious language of Judaism continued to be Hebrew, few Jews spoke or read much of it. So they needed a translation of the Bible into Greek to facilitate knowledge of the biblical texts. That translation is known as the Septuagint (LXX), a work mostly completed in the second century B.C.E. It enjoyed wide acceptance and became the means by which many in the Jewish community knew the Bible. It also became the Bible of the early church.

BOX 10.9

THE "TEMPLE TAX"

As a way of supporting and retaining a connection with the temple, Jewish men sent a contribution of a half-shekel each year. This was one of the few collections of this type that the Romans allowed. This offering is now sometimes referred to as the *temple tax*.

The synagogue. Both inside and outside Palestine, Jews worshiped most often in **synagogues**. Most Jews within Palestine seldom went to the temple (at most four times a year), and many outside Palestine never got there or perhaps saw it only once in their lifetime. So while most Jews supported the temple and its daily sacrifices, they were hardly ever present to witness them or participate directly in them. The synagogue served as their usual place of worship and religious education (among other social and civic activities). Even residents of Jerusalem worshiped and learned the faith in synagogues more often than at the temple. Many cities, both in Palestine and in the Diaspora, had several synagogues. Thus the synagogue was a central religious and cultural institution for the Jewish community from perhaps as early as the sixth or fifth (though the archaeological evidence appears only in the third) century B.C.E. forward.

▶ Conclusion

Our survey of groups within Judaism demonstrates that it was a diverse religion in the first century C.E.; some scholars even prefer to talk about the *Judaisms* of the first century. Jews held different views about many things, even as they shared foundational beliefs in God and God's covenant with them. This review of the political, social, and religious environment of the fifth through the first centuries offers a glimpse into the backdrop of the world of Jesus. Political tensions were high throughout Palestine for most of Jesus' life. And Jesus was born into a religious community that possessed a rich diversity of thought and conversation about how to live for God. Jesus, as an observant Jew in the first century, interacted with various people who held the kinds of views we have described—and we have not talked about all of the known groups. He engaged various people in discussion and debate about how to be a faithful Jew. When he disagreed with them, the discussion was still about how observant Jews should live out their faith. What Jesus taught and how he lived situated him within these discussions about how to be faithful to God as an observant Jew.

▶ LET'S REVIEW ◀

In this chapter, we learned about the time between the return from Exile and Jesus:

- Hellenization
  - —Alexander the Great
  - —His successors
  - —The Seleucids and Ptolemies
  - —Antiochus IV
- Maccabean Revolt
  - —Mattathias
  - —Judas
  - —Jewish national independence
- Roman dominance
  - —Pompey
  - —Herod the Great
  - —Jewish-Roman war
- Origins and teachings of religious groups within Judaism
  - —Sadducees
  - —Pharisees
  - —Essenes
- Diaspora Jews
  - —The Septuagint
  - —The synagogue

▶ KEY TERMS ◀

Alexander the Great
Amon-Re
Antiochus IV
Bar Kokhba
December 15, 167 B.C.E.
Diaspora
Essenes
Gymnasium
Hasmoneans
Herod the Great
Judea
Pharisees
Philo
Pious
Pompey
Ptolemy
Qumran
Sadducees
Seleucus
Septuagint
Synagogue

▶ QUESTIONS FOR REVIEW ◀

10.1 Why did Alexander and his successors promote hellenization?
10.2 What led to the Maccabean Revolt? What was its purpose?
10.3 How is the development of various religious parties in Judaism related to the political developments after the success of the Maccabeans?
10.4 Why did the people of Judea hate Herod?
10.5 Why were there so many revolts in Judea during this period of time?
10.6 Compare the origins of the three main religious parties in Palestine.
10.7 Compare what the three main religious parties in Palestine identified as authoritative Scripture and how they went about interpreting those recognized texts.

▶ FOR FURTHER READING ◀

Shaye J. D. Cohen, *From the Maccabees to the Mishnah*, Library of Early Christianity. Louisville: Westminster John Knox, 2006.

John J. Collins, *Between Athens and Jerusalem: Jewish Identity in the Hellenistic Diaspora.* New York: Crossroad, 1983.

Paul V. M. Flesher, "What Did a Synagogue of Jesus' Time Look Like?" Bible and Interpretation Website 2011

http://www.bibleinterp.com/opeds/fle358001.shtml

Lester L. Grabbe, *Judaic Religion in the Second Temple Period: Belief and Practice from the Exile to Yavneh*. New York: Routledge, 2000.

Jodi Magness, *Stone and Dung, Oil and Spit: Jewish Daily Life in the Time of Jesus*. Grand Rapids: Eerdmans, 2011.

Wayne O. McCready and Adele Reinhartz, eds. *Common Judaism: Explorations in Second Temple Judaism*. Minneapolis: Fortress Press, 2011.

James D. Newsome, *Greeks, Romans, Jews: Currents of Culture and Belief in the New Testament World.* Philadelphia: Trinity Press International, 1992.

George W. E. Nicklesburg. *Jewish Literature between the Bible and the Mishnah*, 2nd ed. Minneapolis: Fortress Press, 2010.

Michael E. Stone, *Ancient Judaism: New Visions and Views*. Grand Rapids: Eerdmans, 2011.

Anthony J. Tomasino, "Diversity and Unity in Judaism before Jesus," Bible and Interpretation Website 2004 . http://www.bibleinterp.com/articles/Tomasino_Diversity.shtml

James C. VanderKam, *The Dead Sea Scrolls Today*. 2nd ed. Grand Rapids: Eerdmans, 2010.

PART 3

What Is the Story of the New Testament?

11 The Gospels
Their Composition and Nature

THIS CHAPTER DESCRIBES IMPORTANT ISSUES IN THE STUDY OF THE NEW TESTAMENT GOSPELS:

- Genre, recognizing that the Gospels are interpretations of Jesus' life
- The question of the historical Jesus

The books that eventually formed the New Testament were all written between the years 50 and 125 C.E. They come from various authors and differing perspectives. While they all believed that God had acted in a new and world-changing way in Jesus, they understand that action in distinctive ways. Their books illustrate some of the ways the church's self-understanding developed in its first decades and show us some of the questions and problems its members faced as they established communities that based their relationship with God on Christ.

The earliest church had to think about how the new act of God in Christ related to God's prior acts of the exodus from Egypt and God's covenant with Israel. After all, every member of the earliest church was and continued to be an observant Jew who worshiped at the synagogue and the temple. They clearly did not think that the beginning of the church meant the end of God's relationship with Israel, because they continued their practice of Judaism. But they did have to rethink the meaning of that identity when large numbers of non-Jews became members of the church. Even then, Jewish church members did not abandon their observance of Judaism. Furthermore, all church members interpreted the meaning of Jesus' life, death, and resurrection through the Scriptures that Christians now call the Old Testament or Hebrew Bible, along with some books now in the Apocrypha and Pseudepigrapha (which was the full extent of their Bible). Thus they wrestled with difficult issues as they thought about the place of the church in relation to Judaism.

▶ The Origin and Nature of the Gospels

Date and Provenance

We begin our survey of the New Testament by looking at the Gospels. The first of the Gospels (probably Mark) was written thirty-five to forty years after the death of Jesus. This is some twenty years after the earliest New Testament writing (1 Thessalonians) was written, but since the Gospels tell the foundational stories of the church, we begin with them rather than with the earliest books.

Their purpose. The Gospels were not written simply to preserve the sayings of and stories about Jesus; rather, they intend to give those stories and sayings specific meanings. These stories do not come directly from Jesus himself, but from people who believe he is the Messiah and God's Son. The Gospels are not eyewitness accounts; they do not come from people who were present when Jesus did or said the things they record. In fact, Luke tells us that he did research: he read other accounts of Jesus' life (including the Gospel of Mark), listened to the stories that preachers told about Jesus, and talked to eyewitnesses (Luke 1:1-4). This is the way Matthew and Mark went about their work as well. (The Gospel of John seems to have been put together a bit differently; see below.)

BOX 11.1

GOSPEL

The word *gospel* is a translation of the Greek word *euangelion*, which means "good news." In some contexts it even meant news of a victory in battle or in athletic competition (for example, in Philostratus, *Life of Apollonius* 5.8). *Euangelion* was also used by the imperial cult to summarize the good things, such as fortune and salvation, that the emperor brought to the empire. So when the church used this word, it carried an implicit subordinating of Rome to Christ.

Oral Tradition

The early church remembered and passed on orally many stories about Jesus and many things that he said. Very soon after his death, believers began shaping sayings and stories that various people remembered into forms that were easy to memorize. Some people collected sayings of Jesus and sorted them into categories, sometimes organizing them so that the last part of one saying reminded the reader of the first part of the next saying. Other times they put similar sayings together; for example, the Beatitudes were put in a list and parables with similar themes were grouped together. In these and other ways, the earliest church remembered and preserved teachings of Jesus and the stories from his life.

Parallels and Varieties of Meanings

People often tell the same story in different ways, and two people who watch the same event may describe it in distinctive ways. Similarly, people told the same stories about Jesus in various ways. Who they were and what perspective they spoke from often determined what parts of the story they emphasized or left out. At the same time, they gave the same story different meanings. They might agree on what happened or on what Jesus said, but still arrive at very different ideas about what that event or saying shows that believers should do or think.

Of course, we know from experience how one story can be given many meanings. Perhaps you know a person who has a favorite story that they manage to tell in many settings, each time making it fit (at least somewhat). Or you can think of the different meanings people give significant events. Just think of the many ways people interpreted the attacks on the World Trade Center and Pentagon on September 11, 2001: some said it was punishment for the immorality of the United States; others said it was because of injustices the United States had imposed on other nations; and still others said it was an act of evil people that had nothing to do with the actions of the United States. The issue here is not whether any of these is correct, but only that a single event can be given many interpretations.

Multiple meanings. Even within the Gospels the same story sometimes has rather different meanings. For example, Mark 7 and Matthew 15 contain a story that has Jesus engage in a debate with some Pharisees about the interpretation of some ritual purity regulations. After the public part of the exchange, Jesus further explains his position to his disciples in private. After Jesus says that it is not what goes in the body that makes a person unclean but what comes out, Mark adds that this saying means that believers can eat all foods—that is, that the **kosher** food laws do not apply to the church (7:19). When Matthew tells this story in his Gospel, he has read Mark's version but does not think it means that the kosher laws no longer apply for the Jews in his church. So he removes Mark's explanatory remark because, for him, the story shows how to interpret such laws correctly, not that the church can abandon them. As we will see below and in our discussion of the Letters of Paul, the church had to think long and hard about how to apply the Mosaic law in the church. For now, we simply note that the same story could be given rather different meanings.

BOX 11.2

SAME STORY, DIFFERENT MEANINGS?

Compare Mark 7:18-20 with Matthew 15:16-18. How do you see each writer giving a meaning to the same saying of Jesus?

Directed meaning. The Gospels were written in part to limit the meanings people could give to stories about Jesus or to things he had said. They intend to show that a story or saying has a particular meaning, and by implication not some other meanings. The writers put their stories in particular contexts and in a particular order to lead readers to understand them in a certain way. They also, when they think it is necessary, tell the readers what a story means by adding an interpretive comment (as we just saw Mark do) or by noting that the disciples did not understand the full meaning of what Jesus said until after the resurrection. The Gospels are more interested in giving the stories particular meanings than in providing precise historical accuracy.

Theological Accounts

Like the narratives of the Hebrew Bible that relate the life of Abraham and his descendants and the stories of the Israelites, the Gospels are theological accounts, not history texts. They tell their stories as they do to make theological points, not to give more accurate accounts of facts. The Gospels assume that their readers are already familiar with many, probably most, of the stories they recount, so their task is not to introduce or even preserve those stories but to interpret them. These writers want their accounts of what Jesus said and did to provide their readers with a proper understanding of Jesus. They do not want to tell what happened (since the readers already know), they want to tell what it means that Jesus did or said a particular thing. The Gospels are thoroughly theological documents.

One can tell that they do not intend to be historical writings, but rather theological interpretations, by comparing some of their stories. One example will have to suffice here. Matthew, Mark, and Luke all tell a story about Jesus returning to his hometown after becoming famous for his preaching and healing in the region of Galilee (an area in northern Palestine that borders the western side of the Sea of Galilee). While the crowd initially appreciates his return, it eventually turns on him. Matthew (13:53-58) and Mark (6:1-6) place this story in the middle of Jesus' ministry in Galilee, where it makes good sense in the flow of the narrative. Luke, however, makes this the very first story he tells about the ministry of Jesus (4:16-30); in fact, he makes this episode the story that sets out a central theme in Jesus' ministry. He moves it out of chronological order to do this—he makes it the first event in the ministry of Jesus. After he tells this story, Luke begins telling the stories that Mark put before it. The way Luke moved the story of Jesus' return to Nazareth demonstrates that his intention is to give not accurate chronology, but religious instruction. He wants to tell readers what the ministry of Jesus means more than he wants to get factual details correct.

▶ The Search for a Historical Jesus

There are four Gospels in the New Testament (rather than one) because each provides a different perspective on the meaning of the life, death, and resurrection of Jesus. Each provides an angle on understanding his ministry and work that the others do not. If the point were simply to get correct factual data, we would not have four. Having four complicates questions about historical accuracy because readers have to think about which report of an event is correct when they differ. The Gospel writers (often called **evangelists**, a word that means those who tell good news or a **gospel**), however, would say that questions about historical accuracy miss the point. They want readers to know how God worked through Christ and what that means for their relationship with God. They care little for providing correct historical detail.

Perspectives on Jesus

Over the last few decades, there has been another resurgence of interest in "the **historical Jesus**," that is, in finding detailed, accurate historical information about what Jesus did or said. Often some of the results of such research flash

BOX 11.3

TATIAN'S *DIATESSARON*

The first extant attempt to harmonize the Gospels into a single coherent running narrative of the life of Jesus is the *Diatessaron* of Tatian, completed in about 172. *Diatessaron* means "through the four." This attempt at harmonization shows that the early Christians recognized contradictions in the narratives of the four Gospels.

across the headlines near an important religious holiday, claiming to be some new revelation. Those supposed new discoveries are nearly always subjects New Testament scholars have been discussing for many years—nothing new at all. Groups such as the Jesus Seminar and many individual scholars have combed through the New Testament Gospels and other sources in an attempt to construct a life of Jesus that is objective and factual. Such attempts began in the eighteenth century. Using the tools of modern history, researchers have repeatedly tried to arrive at a clearer picture of what Jesus was "really" like. But these attempts have produced very different, even contradictory, images of Jesus, in part because these accounts are never objective.

An objective life of Jesus? No one can write an account of any historical figure that is strictly objective. The discipline of history has recognized for decades that no one can write an objective history of an event or a person. All historians must make choices that skew the picture of the events they narrate. Just deciding that some events are irrelevant or inconsequential for understanding a person or event means that a prior interpretation is already determining the outcome. Scholars who try to construct an objective life of Jesus are doomed to failure because they always think and write from a nonobjective standpoint. Even when we work as a group, the group's perspectives and those of its individual members will limit what we see and skew our vision.

Furthermore, events are too rich for anyone to report everything that goes on, and observers report only from their own perspective. Even eyewitness accounts necessarily fail to be strictly objective because witnesses must always choose what details to leave out and which to include.

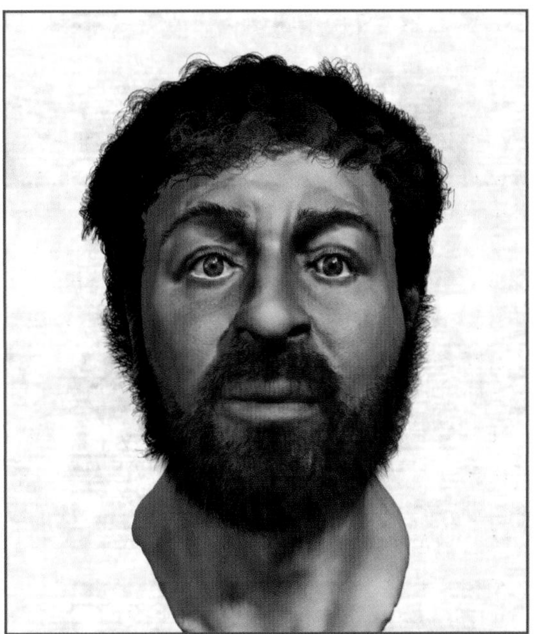

FIGURE 11.1 **THE MEDITERRANEAN JESUS**

This representation of Jesus is closer to what he probably looked like than those images based on Europeans or other peoples. BBC

So when historians begin their work, they are already dealing with sources that are only telling the story from their own perspective—and that is the case even if there are eyewitnesses, which we do not have for events in Jesus' life.

History and faith. Beyond this, one of the motivations for much historical Jesus research is to present a Jesus who differs from the images found in the Gospels. Seemingly believing that they have produced an objective account of Jesus' life, some researchers think their account should be the one Christians look to for guidance about what Jesus thought, and so what believers should think. This way of proceeding, however, confuses history and faith. Faith is a stance that adopts a particular perspective on events and people. Just as the prophets of Israel gave a religious interpretation of events in their day, so the Gospel writers provided their communities with a theological text; the evangelists wrote books that gave interpretations of Jesus' life.

Unavoidable interpretation. Knowing the facts does not tell a person how to interpret them. Even if a historian were to overcome all the problems inherent in searching for the precise historical facts about Jesus' life, this information would not tell us what we should believe about Jesus or whether we should believe *in* him. The evangelists wrote their Gospels to a certain extent because there were competing interpretations of Jesus. While first-century believers and nonbelievers could agree on many facts about the life of Jesus (for example, that he was executed by the Romans), they did not agree about what those facts meant.

An episode from the Gospels demonstrates this point well. Matthew 12:22-32 reports that a crowd witnesses Jesus exorcising a demon. Many in the crowd see that healing and think Jesus must be "the Son of David." But others in the crowd who witness the same event conclude that Jesus is in league with the devil. The two groups see the same occurrence and both acknowledge that the person has been healed, but the question about the event's meaning remains. The issue was not what happened, but what the happening meant. So even if historians could determine precisely what happened throughout Jesus' life, the question of meaning would remain. Historical investigation might establish what happened, but it cannot determine what the church should believe about Jesus. Once we recognize this crucial point, studies of the historical Jesus become much less important for the faith of people in the church. The church's faith does not rest simply on the historical Jesus of Nazareth, but on the interpretation given that life by the early church, particularly in the writings of the New Testament. Thus what we find in the Gospels is precisely what the church needs: an interpretation of Jesus' life that shows how God was present and active in that life in a unique way.

BOX 11.4

FACTS AND INTERPRETATIONS

Read Matthew 12:22-24. Notice that everyone agrees about the facts. What is it that they disagree about?

The facts remain. All of this does not mean that historical facts have no importance. A central part of the Christian proclamation is that God was present in a real person. That there was a Jesus is very important—and no credible historians doubt that there was such a person. Indeed, nearly all historians agree that he was known as a Jewish healer and teacher who was seen as a political problem by the authorities and was executed by the Romans around the year 30. Furthermore, we can know the broad outlines of the kind of person Jesus was because his life produced the early church. Only a person who valued love and honored God above all else could generate the kind of community that has the values the early church proclaimed. Jesus was an observant Jew who called people to repent and orient their lives toward service to God. But we cannot know, and the church does not need to know, with certainty the precise details of what he did on a particular day or even exactly what he said on particular occasions. The Gospels have him say little, perhaps nothing, that other good Jewish teachers of the time had not already said. Of course, the church and the writers of the Gospels saw him as much more than a teacher, not because they had different facts but because they understood those facts in a particular way. Those facts revealed something to them that others did not see about the unique presence of God in Jesus. Most of this understanding of his life and ministry, however, came to his followers only after their experience of his resurrection.

FIGURE 11.2 **JESUS CASTING OUT DEMONS**

This painting by James Tissot (c. 1890) portrays the story of Jesus allowing the demons that possessed the man to go into a herd of pigs. The possessed pigs then throw themselves into the Sea of Galilee. See Mark 5:1-20. Art Resource

▶ The Synoptic Gospels and John

The first three Gospels of the New Testament (Matthew, Mark, and Luke) are known as the **Synoptic Gospels** because they have the same basic outline for the life of Jesus. They all have Jesus begin his ministry in Galilee and then expand it to include the surrounding area. Following this they give a lengthy account of a single trip to Jerusalem from which he never returns.

Then they relate the story of Jesus' rejection, arrest, and execution in Jerusalem. While they differ in many of the details, they have Jesus say and do many of the same things. These features distinguish the first three Gospels from the Gospel of John. John has Jesus spend a good deal of time in Judea (the area around Jerusalem), making three trips to the region during his ministry. Few of the same stories appear in John that appear in the other Gospels, and John has many episodes that the others do not recount.

Sources of the Gospels

Markan priority. Part of the reason for the differences between John and the Synoptics lies in the resources the writers had available. Most New Testament scholars think that Matthew and Luke both read Mark before they wrote their Gospels and adopted his outline for their accounts of Jesus' life. John, on the other hand, may have known of them but did not rely on the other Gospels to fill in his story of Jesus' life. Instead, John built on traditions known through the person that it calls the "Beloved Disciple," but more on that later.

BOX 11.5

THE SEARCH FOR THE HISTORICAL JESUS

The numerous differences between John and the Synoptics constituted part of the motivation for the initial searches for the historical Jesus. Those searching for the historical Jesus were trying to determine whether John or the Synoptics were closer to historical fact. However, since both John and the Synoptics give interpretations rather than strictly historical accounts, our comparison should be between what each wants its readers to believe about Jesus.

BOX 11.6

THE COMPOSITION OF JOHN

While the Gospel of John attributes its basic content to the Beloved Disciple (see John 21:24), the book went through some editing before it took the shape it has in the canon. Some scholars now argue that the author(s) of John had read Mark. Even if this is the case, its account does not rely on Mark the way the other Synoptics do.

A sayings collection. Matthew and Luke used more sources than just Mark when they wrote their Gospels. Among the other materials and traditions they used, most scholars think they had a written collection of sayings of Jesus that we call **Q** (that probably comes from the German word *Quelle,* "source"). No one has a copy of this document, but by compiling the sayings that appear in both Matthew and Luke, scholars can develop a rough idea about what it probably contained. Most think that some sayings of Jesus that Matthew and Luke have in common are so much alike (sometimes the wording is exact) that the similarity could not be the result of common **oral tradition**; they must have had access to copies of the same written source. As we saw above, this way of collecting material to compose their Gospels fits the way Luke says he went about the task of writing.

FIGURE 11.3 **SERMON ON THE MOUNT AND HEALING OF LEPERS**
This fresco, which is in the Sistine Chapel, shows two events from the life of Jesus (Cosimo Rosselli, 1439–1507). In this way it portrays Jesus as both a teacher and a healer. Wikimedia Commons

▶ Analysis and Faith

Christians sometimes worry that analyzing where the Gospels got their information about Jesus threatens their faith, but such analysis does not pose a threat to believers, because this study does not deny that God speaks through these texts or suggest that their writers misunderstood Jesus. Rather, they worked in much the same ways the prophets did. The evangelists experienced the presence of God in Christ and produced in written form the kinds of beliefs about him that were held in the church, the beliefs that had come to them from apostles and other members of the earliest churches. Their statements of these beliefs helped the church retain those beliefs and guard itself against ideas that they saw as dangerous. By the beginning of the second century there were many writings from church members that gave interpretations

> *BOX 11.7*
>
> **LUKE AND HIS SOURCES**
>
> What does Luke 1:1-4, the Gospel's introductory paragraph, tell you about the way he went about preparing to write his Gospel? What three kinds of sources does he name as places that he got information about Jesus?

of the life of Jesus and stories of various apostles, among other things. But very early in this period, these four Gospels began circulating as a group and resonated with the faith of so many in the church that they were accepted as guides for what Christians should believe. Thus it was the judgment of a wide spectrum of the faithful that these Gospels spoke God's word in ways that other accounts of Jesus' life and teaching did not. So, however the evangelists went about the task of writing, the church discerned that God had spoken through them. Questions about how the writers did their work poses no challenge to the claim that God speaks through them.

▶ Conclusion

The Gospels are not the kinds of writings that most people imagine; that is, they are not simple eyewitness accounts of what Jesus said or did. As we have seen, the Gospels are much more than this. They are theological accounts of Jesus' life that draw on a variety of sources to present sophisticated narratives designed to help the readers in their faith communities understand Jesus in the ways the writers think are most helpful. The evangelists draw on written and oral sources for the stories they tell about Jesus. They know that the same story can yield many meanings, so they work to limit those meanings by the ways they shape their accounts of events

BOX 11.8

THE Q SOURCE

The hypothetical document Q is composed primarily of the material in Matthew and Luke that does not appear in Mark. Although no copies of Q are extant, such a document seems the best explanation for how Matthew and Luke could have so much material in common, including even the precise wording. An example of this appears in Matthew 9:37-38 and Luke 10:2. The wording is precisely the same throughout this saying of Jesus; only the introductions to the saying differ. We can see the ways that the Gospel writers sometimes expanded on a saying in Q by comparing Matthew 10:16 and Luke 10:3. Both draw on Q, but Matthew both deletes things from it and adds to it:

Matthew 10:16

See, I am sending you out like sheep into the midst of wolves; so be wise as serpents and innocent as doves.

Q

Go on your way. See, I am sending you out like sheep into the midst of wolves.

Luke 10:3

Go on your way. See, I am sending you out like lambs into the midst of wolves.

CHART 11.1

HOW THE GOSPELS WERE COMPOSED ACCORDING TO THE TWO SOURCE HYPOTHESIS

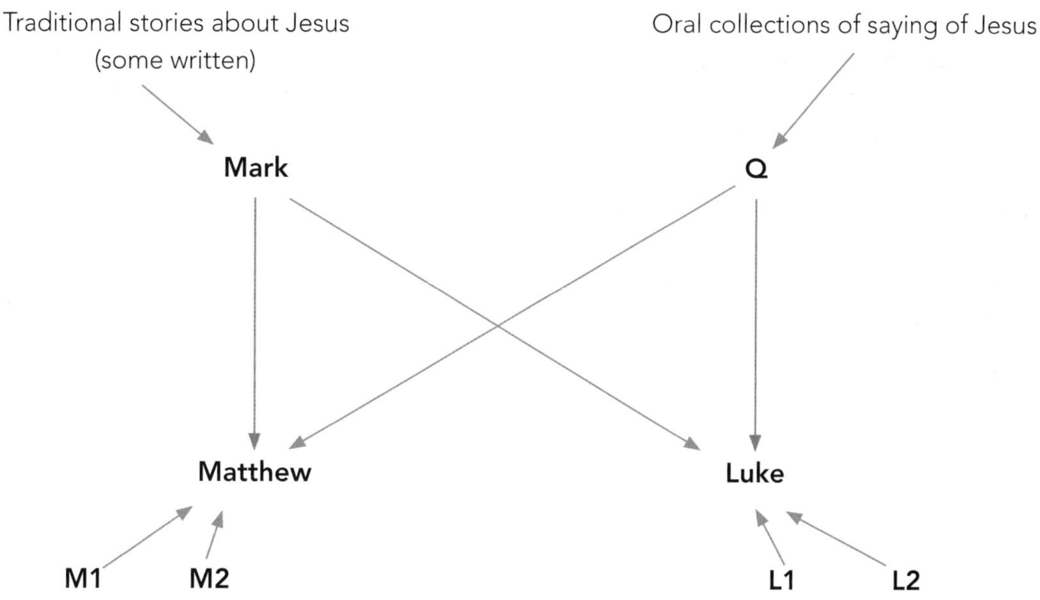

M1 and M2 designate material found in Matthew that came from a source that only he uses. This accounts for material not found in Mark or Q. Similarly, L1 and L2 designate sources Luke uses that contain material not found in Mark or Q.

in Jesus' life. The evangelists' intentional sculpting of their stories does not mean their stories are less useful for the purposes they intend—that is, building a particular kind of faith in their churches. For us, recognizing that they do this is simply one way of acknowledging that no one gives an objective account of a life or of significant events; it is simply not possible. Even if it were possible, such an account would be less valuable than the accounts we have because all events are open to multiple meanings. With the Gospels, we see the ways a large body of the early church came to understand the importance of Jesus.

We have also seen that the Gospel of John is quite different from the Synoptics. This is the case, in part, because John relies on a different body of sources. Of course, he gives the stories from his sources his own interpretation—an interpretation that is distinctive among the New Testament Gospels. Thus the four Gospels, those that are relatively similar and the one more different, give us multiple windows into how the early church saw God working in Jesus.

▶ LET'S REVIEW ◀

In this chapter, we learned about the nature and composition of the Gospels:

- The Gospels as theological, not historical, works
    - Oral tradition
    - Multiple meanings of a single story
- The question of the Historical Jesus
    - Attempts to get behind the Gospels' theological accounts
    - Problems with trying to write an objective account of the life of Jesus
    - Relationship between faith and history
- The relationship among the Synoptics
- The relationship between the Synoptics and John
- Sources for the Gospels
    - Oral sources
    - Q

▶ KEY TERMS ◀

Evangelist
Gospel
Historical Jesus
Kosher
Oral tradition
Q
Sabbath
Synoptic Gospels

▶ QUESTIONS FOR REVIEW ◀

11.1 Why do the various New Testament Gospels tell the same story about Jesus in different ways?

11.2 Compare the stories the Gospels tell about Jesus to the stories Genesis tells about its important characters.

11.3 What does Matthew 12:22-32 show about the influence of interpretation on how a person tells about and understands an event?

11.4 Which Gospels are called the Synoptic Gospels? Why are they given that designation?

11.5 Discuss how the Watson essay in For Further Reading helps you evaluate various claims of people about the historical Jesus, especially the more sensational ones.

▶ FOR FURTHER READING ◀

James L. Bailey and Lyle D. Vander Broek, *Literary Forms in the New Testament: A Handbook*. Louisville: Westminster John Knox, 1992.

Marcus Borg and N. T. Wright, *The Meaning of Jesus: Two Visions*. San Francisco: HarperSanFrancisco, 1999.

John Bowker, *Jesus and the Pharisees*. Cambridge: Cambridge University Press, 2008.

Rudolf Bultmann, *Jesus Christ and Mythology*. New York: Scribner, 1958.

Richard A. Burridge, *Four Gospels, One Jesus?* Grand Rapids: Eerdmans, 1994.

Craig A. Evans, *Jesus and His World: The Archaeological Evidence*. Louisville: Westminster John Knox, 2013.

Paula Fredriksen, "From Jesus to Christ: The Origins of the New Testament Images of Jesus," Bible and Interpretation Website 2000 http://www.bibleinterp.com/articles/fredricksen_JesustoChrist.shtml

Richard A. Horsley, *Jesus in Context: Power, People, and Performance*. Minneapolis: Fortress Press, 2008.

Richard A. Horsley, *The Prophet Jesus and the Renewal of Israel: Moving Beyond a Diversionary Debate*. Grand Rapids: Eerdmans, 2012.

Philip Jenkins, *Hidden Gospels: How the Search for Jesus Lost Its Way*. New York: Oxford University Press, 2001.

Luke T. Johnson, *The Real Jesus: The Misguided Quest for the Historical Jesus and the Truth of the Traditional Gospels*. San Francisco: HarperSanFrancisco, 1996.

Leander E. Keck, *Who Is Jesus? History in Perfect Tense*. Columbia: University of South Carolina Press, 2000.

Craig Keener, "Will the Real Historical Jesus Please Stand Up? The Gospels as Sources for Historical Information about Jesus," Bible and Interpretation Website 2010 http://www.bibleinterp.com/articles/keener357924.shtml

Amy-Jill Levine, *The Misunderstood Jew: The Church and the Scandal of the Jewish Jesus*. San Francisco: HarperOne, 2006.

Wayne A. Meeks, *Christ Is the Question*. Louisville: Westminster John Knox, 2006.

K. F. Nickle, *The Synoptic Gospels: An Introduction*, rev. ed. Louisville: Westminster John Knox, 2001.

Mark Allan Powell, *Jesus as a Figure in History*, 2nd ed. Louisville: Westminster John Knox, 2013.

R. H. Stein, *The Synoptic Problem: An Introduction*. Grand Rapids: Baker, 1987.

Francis Watson, "Inventing Jesus' Wife," Bible and Interpretation Website 2012 http://www.bibleinterp.com/articles/wat368023.shtml Discuss how this helps you evaluate various claims of people about the historical Jesus, especially the more sensational ones.

12 Four Views of One Jesus
Mark, Matthew, Luke, and John

IN THIS CHAPTER WE WILL LOOK AT FOUR VIEWS OF JESUS CONVEYED BY THE FOUR GOSPELS:

- Mark
  - Jesus as God's Son
- Matthew
  - Jesus as Messiah
- Luke
  - Jesus' mission to the poor
- John
  - Christ as preexistent Word

One of the reasons the four New Testament Gospels differ from one another in the ways they present the meaning of the life, death, and resurrection of Jesus is that they address churches composed of rather different people with different needs and traditions. Thus they show us something of the diversity that existed among the early believers in Christ. Because of who they were, various churches practiced the faith in different ways (for example, Jews in the church continued to observe the Sabbath, but non-Jews did not). Cultural differences influenced the way various church members lived and determined the kinds of interpretations of Christ that were most meaningful. There was a basic coherence in the core of their beliefs, but what they emphasized and how they lived out their faith differed. So when the Gospels' writers give differing interpretations to stories about Jesus or sayings from Jesus, they do this to meet the needs of their churches. As we survey the Gospels, we will see important differences. For believers, this range of interpretations of the person and work of Christ provides the church with a richer understanding of his significance for the ways he provides a relationship with God.

FIGURE 12.1 **THE FOUR EVANGELISTS**

The four are presented as their traditional symbols: Matthew as a human (or angel), Mark as a lion, Luke as an ox, and John as an eagle. See Revelation 4:7. Art Resource

▶ Mark: The Coming Reign of God

As we have noted, Mark was probably the first of the four New Testament Gospels. Its account of the ministry of Jesus set the pattern for the ways Matthew and Luke would present their interpretations of Jesus. Mark was written for a church that was composed predominantly of non-Jews; he gives special attention to Jesus' dealings with non-Jews because he wants his readers to recognize that the life of the Jewish Jesus has importance for them. There is a whole section in Mark (5:1—8:21) in which Jesus performs parallel miracles for Jews and **Gentiles**. For Mark, this demonstrates that Gentiles had an important place in Jesus' ministry, even though that ministry was conducted mostly among Jews.

Mark, like all the Gospel writers, tells his stories in the order he does and in the ways he does to make theological points. He arranges the flow of his narrative so that even the order in which he puts events conveys important theological assertions. Often materials are put together to produce a common theme. So we cannot simply read individual episodes and get the full picture Mark wants readers to see; we must read the book as a whole. Comparing the ways the Gospels tell the same story or noticing what they include or leave out can help us identify some of the themes and emphases of each writer.

Beginnings

The kingdom of God. Mark begins his Gospel with the baptism of Jesus by **John the Baptist**, calling this the "beginning of the good news [gospel*] of Jesus Christ, the Son of God" (1:1). By taking this as his starting point, he focuses the readers' attention on the ministry of Jesus as the place one comes to understand the church's message about him. After telling of Jesus' baptism, Mark records what he sees as the core of Jesus' preaching: repent because the **kingdom of God** is near (1:14). This mes-

*The word *gospel* means "good news" (Greek *euangelion*).

sage presents a number of challenges. First, it calls hearers to reorient their lives (repent) in the light of what God is doing in the world. Mark does not explain what must change, but that will become more obvious as the story progresses. When Mark speaks of the "kingdom of God," it implies that those who accept this message must put membership in this domain above political allegiances. Speaking of the church in this way caused it problems because the Roman Empire sometimes heard it as a challenge to its dominance. While Mark's record of Jesus' use of this expression does not constitute a frontal assault on Rome, it does challenge all other loyalties—including those to Rome or any government. We must remember that Jesus uses this language in a region where political unrest is common. So he seemingly meant to offer a challenge, implying that identifying with him relativizes all other claims.

BOX 12.1

KINGDOM OF GOD

While the expression "kingdom of God" seems harmless today, in the first century it would have sounded dangerous. The establishment of God's kingdom signals that the will of God has become the dominant reality in the world. Seen from the perspective of believers, this implies the overthrow of present world powers. When those powers hear of this other kingdom, they recognize the implicit threat, particularly since Rome claimed that the gods supported their domination of the world.

The nearness of the kingdom. In this introduction of Jesus' preaching, Mark says Jesus proclaims that this kingdom is "near," an expression that admits some ambiguity: it might mean that it is in close proximity or that it is coming soon. Mark perhaps wants to have it both ways. For him, the presence of Jesus means that the kingdom is near so that having a relationship with Jesus brings a person into that domain. He also means that the kingdom is coming soon; Jesus proclaims that God is about to act in a dramatic way to establish a realm in which people do God's will. So he announces God's intention to act and implies that God will do this through Jesus.

Son of God and Son of Man. This first sentence also introduces the central way that Mark identifies Jesus when it calls him "the **Son of God**." Jesus himself does not claim to be the Son of God in Mark, but instead uses the ambiguous expression "**Son of Man**" (for example, 2:10, 28), which could be translated "son of a human." This title could mean simply that he is a human being, but more likely it draws on some developing traditions that began as early as Daniel. Perhaps it relates to Daniel's story of the three men being put into a furnace. In this story, God saves them from being burned alive and as others look into the giant furnace they see not only the three men, but also a fourth person who "has the appearance of a god," or literally, "like a son of a god" (3:25). The expression "son of a human" more certainly goes back to the visions of Daniel in which he sees a person "like a son of a human being" coming in the clouds to establish a kingdom for God on the earth (7:13-14).

Various writers within the apocalyptic tradition (the tradition that produces books like

BOX 12.2

SON OF MAN

Read Daniel 7:13-14. In the New Revised Standard Version, look at the footnote attached to "human being" in verse 13. (*Aram* is an abbreviation for Aramaic, the language in which this part of Daniel is written.) What do you think it means for Jesus to call himself "son of man" in the Gospels, when you see this previous use of this title?

Revelation) developed this image into a figure who will bring God's kingdom into the world in a dramatic and cosmic event. Mark brings together the ideas that Jesus is Son of God and Son of Man, so that being the Son of God includes being the Son of Man. Although most people Jesus meets do not recognize that he is the Son of God, demons sometimes do (5:7). The one person who finally recognizes that Jesus is the Son of God is a Roman soldier who watches him die. This points us to the importance of Jesus' death in Mark. For Mark, only a witness to that event can discern who Jesus really is.

Jesus Begins His Ministry

Exorcism. In Mark the first miracle Jesus performs is an **exorcism** (1:23-28). In the ancient world there was a well-known literary tradition of exorcism stories. Many people in the ancient world were credited with being able to exorcise demons. As these stories were usually told, they involved an argument between the demon and the exorcist in which each tries to gain the advantage over the other. Knowing the identity of the demon was sometimes important in being able to send it away. In Mark's exorcism story, the demon or unclean spirit has the advantage of knowing precisely who Jesus is, yet he is powerless. There is no real argument or verbal jousting; Jesus simply tells the demon to shut up and sends him away. Jesus is so powerful that the demon obeys immediately. This way of telling the story emphasizes how mightily God works through him. Even more, it demonstrates that the coming of God's kingdom means the defeat of evil. Demon possession represents an intimate and dominating manifestation of the power of evil in the world. Jesus is able to dispatch that power without breaking a sweat. So the first thing Mark tells us about God's rule in the world is that it will overcome evil.

This is part of Mark's presentation of Jesus as a person of action and power. Although we know the story will lead to Jesus' execution, which does not seem a proper ending for a powerful person, Mark creates an image of Jesus that makes him seem like an important person. In the Gospel's first section, Mark's favorite transition from one story to the next is the word *immediately.* As soon as Jesus finishes doing something, "immediately" the next thing begins. This imprecise designation gives the impression that Jesus is constantly in demand. He has to sneak off before dawn to get in a word of prayer, and even then the crowd is looking for him before he gets back (1:35-38). He cannot even get a nap in his disciples' boat without being awakened to calm a violent storm on the lake (4:35-40). Then all the time Jesus is making his way to Jerusalem, Mark says that things happen "on the way." That is,

BOX 12.3

OTHER EXORCISTS

Examples of exorcism are found in a number of writers from this era. Lucian, a second-century satirist, describes an exorcism. Though he thinks such things are foolishness, he tells us what one is like.

> For my part, I should like to ask you what you say to those who free possessed men from their terrors by exorcising the spirits so manifestly. I need not discuss this: everyone knows about the Syrian from Palestine, the adept in it, how many he takes in hand who fall down in the light of the moon and roll their eyes and fill their mouths with foam; nevertheless, he restores them to health and sends them away normal in mind, delivering them from their straits for a large fee. When he stands beside them as they lie there and asks: "Whence came you into his body?" the patient himself is silent, but the spirit answers in Greek or in the language of whatever foreign country he comes from, telling how and whence he entered into the man; whereupon, by adjuring the spirit and if he does not obey, threatening him, he drives him out. Indeed, I actually saw one coming out, black and smoky in colour.
>
> (Lucian, *Lover of Lies* 16; trans. A. M. Harmon, Loeb Classical Library [Cambridge, Mass.: Harvard University Press, 1921], vol. 3)

The Jewish historian Josephus mentions a root found in an area of Palestine that has the ability to exorcise demons (*Jewish War* 7.6.3). In his history of the Jewish people he gives this account of an exorcism:

> God also enabled [Solomon] to learn that skill which expels demons, which is a science useful and sanative to men. He composed such incantations also by which distempers are alleviated. And he left behind him the manner of using exorcisms, by which they drive away demons, so that they never return; and this method of cure is of great force unto this day; for I have seen a certain man of my own country, whose name was Eleazar, releasing people that were demoniacal in the presence of Vespasian, and his sons, and his captains, and the whole multitude of his soldiers. The manner of the cure was this: He put a ring that had a root of one of those sorts mentioned by Solomon to the nostrils of the demoniac, after which he drew out the demon through his nostrils; and when the man fell down immediately, he abjured him to return into him no more, making still mention of Solomon, and reciting the incantations which he composed. And when Eleazar would persuade and demonstrate to the spectators that he had such a power, he set a little way off a cup or basin full of water, and commanded the demon, as he went out of the man, to overturn it, and thereby to let the spectators know that he had left the man; and when this was done, the skill and wisdom of Solomon was shown very manifestly.
>
> (*Antiquities* 8.2.5; trans. William Whiston, *The Life and Works of Flavius Josephus* [reprint, Grand Rapids: Kregel, 1960])

A similar demonstration (though here a statue rather than a cup of water) that the demon is leaving is required by the exorcist in Philostratus's *Life of Apollonius* 4.20.

FIGURE 12.2 **EASTERN SHORE OF THE SEA OF GALILEE**

Much of the ministry of Jesus was conducted in the regions surrounding the Sea of Galilee (which is really a large lake). The eastern shore was in the Decapolis, a predominantly Gentile area, while the western shore was in Galilee, a predominantly Jewish area. Art Resource

Jesus is on the move—places to go, people to meet. If Mark were trying to give this impression of Jesus today he would have Jesus with a cell phone, a Bluetooth receiver on his ear, and a full PDA, all of which he is using at the same time, while hailing a cab.

In parables. Mark gives a surprising meaning to Jesus' use of **parables**. We usually think of parables as a way Jesus tried to make his message understandable for his audience; Mark sees them differently. Jesus tells few parables in this Gospel, and Mark groups most of them together in chapter 4. After Jesus compares God's kingdom to a person who plants a field, everyone is puzzled. When Jesus is alone with his close circle of followers, they ask him what it means. He explains it to them and then tells them that his parables hide his message from people who are not part of his group. For Mark, a person either has the perspective that faith brings or Jesus and his teaching remain incomprehensible. Of course, Mark spends his whole Gospel trying to help his readers come to the faith that makes understanding Jesus possible. Interestingly, it seems that this is the moment when Jesus credits his disciples with understanding him best. As we will see, from this moment on they seem to understand him less and less clearly.

The Messianic Secret

Another surprising feature of Mark is the way he has Jesus react when people recognize who he is: he regularly instructs them, often vehemently, not to tell anyone. When Jesus asks the disciples who they think he is, Peter replies, "You are the Messiah." Jesus responds by ordering them not to tell anyone (8:27-30). Similarly, at the **transfiguration** (when Jesus becomes shiny and has a conversation with Moses and Elijah) Jesus tells the three disciples who were with him not to tell anyone about it (9:9). And when demons shout that they know he is the Son of God, he silences them (1:24; 3:11-12). Furthermore, when Jesus performs a miracle, he often tells the person not to tell anyone who did it (3:43). This characteristic of Mark's presentation of Jesus is known as the **Messianic Secret**. In many places Matthew and Luke follow Mark in having Jesus not allow people to say who he is.

Concealing his identity. Mark seems to have Jesus hide his identity so that he is not misunderstood. Jews of the first century had varying ideas about what the messiah might be and do. Included among those views of messiahs were some who thought he would restore the temple to proper worship, and others who believed he would be a military leader. Neither these nor any other conceptions of a messiah, however, fit what the church came to say about Jesus. No one prior to the church thought the messiah would be a poor artisan whom the Romans executed. So the church significantly redefined the mission and identity of the messiah. Perhaps, then, Mark reflects Jesus' reticence to give the wrong impression by allowing people to make proclamations about his identity before his mission was complete. After all, when Peter confesses that Jesus is the messiah and Jesus immediately predicts his death and resurrection, Peter explicitly rejects the idea that God's messiah would be killed by the Romans. Jesus then rebukes him severely (calling him Satan; 8:22-33).

More than a miracle worker. Perhaps Mark is also concerned that people not simply identify Jesus as a wonder-worker; he wants to be sure the message of Jesus receives the proper attention and so does not allow claims about his exalted identity to overwhelm his teaching. In any case, Mark and all the Synoptic Gospels have Jesus be careful about what titles people assign to him. The only exception to Jesus' practice of prohibiting such acclamations follows his healing of a Gentile, a person who would have no expectations about a messiah. He commissions this person to go tell everyone what God had done for him (4:19-20).

Torah Observance

Even though Mark is written for churches that are predominantly Gentile and so do not observe many of the commands that make Jews distinctive, he still presents Jesus as a person who observes the law. Jesus argues with others about *how* to be observant, but he always keeps the law as he interprets it. When Jesus disagrees with some about how to observe the Sabbath, that does not mean he no longer keeps it. Some other religious teachers think the way he interprets the law is dangerous, but all participants in the discussion agree that keeping it is the right thing to do.

Mark presents Jesus in this way even as he has Jesus authorize the eating of non-kosher food (7:14-23). Mark's non-Jewish church members do not keep those food regulations because they are not Jewish. Note too that it is Mark's interpretation of this exchange, not a direct saying of Jesus, that allows his churches to ignore the food laws. Meanwhile, Jesus instructs Jews he meets to keep the law (for example, 3:43-44; 10:17-22). So Jesus remains observant to the law and calls other Jews to keep it, even as he opens ways for Gentiles to serve God as Gentiles.

Disciples and Misunderstanding

Mark's presentation of Jesus' inner circle of disciples is also distinctive. Jesus singles out twelve disciples as his closest followers early in his ministry (3:13-19). These twelve represent the reconstituted tribes of Israel, and by symbolic extension the whole people of God. Readers might think that these twelve disciples would understand Jesus better than anyone, but that does not seem to be the case in Mark. **The Twelve** are among the people Jesus says will understand the parables, but then they misunderstand nearly everything about Jesus and his ministry, including his parables. When Jesus stills the storm on the lake, they ask one another who this person is (4:35-41). When they see Jesus walk on the water, they fail to understand how he could do that (6:45-52). They also cannot figure out what it means when he miraculously feeds thousands of people (6:30-44; 8:1-10).

Their misunderstanding grows as the narrative continues. When Jesus tells them he must go to Jerusalem and be killed, they first say he has misunderstood (this is when he calls Peter Satan; 8:31-33). At the transfiguration, Peter suggests that they build places not just for Jesus but also for Elijah and Moses (9:2-8). Then after the transfiguration, they still do not get it when he tells the three with him that he is going to Jerusalem to be killed and then raised, but now they are afraid to ask what he means—after all, they do not want to be called Satan (9:9-10). The next time Jesus tells them he is going to be killed, they get into an argument about who gets the highest government position in the new kingdom (9:30-37).

The key to understanding. The downhill slide of the Twelve continues through the end of the book. After again missing the point when Jesus predicts his death and resurrection, they have another argument about who should get the best job in the royal court (9:35-45). In the end, they all desert him when he is arrested and Peter ends up swearing that he does not know Jesus (14:43-72). None of them witnesses the crucifixion and none comes to the tomb. The last we see of them they have deserted and denied Jesus.

From weakness to apostleship. This is a strange way to present the Twelve. The readers know that after the resurrection these men become the people who proclaim the message of Christ and are willing to die for him.

Some interpreters suggest that Mark presents the Twelve in this way because his church has undergone a time of persecution, during which some succumbed to the pressure and denied their faith. Once the crisis has passed, they want to rejoin the church. So the church must decide how to respond to people who denied their faith to save themselves from some suffering (whether that was economic pressure or physical punishment). Mark's answer comes in the form of his narrative, a story in which the disciples closest to Jesus suffer a severe lapse of faith. After their weakness, everyone knows they become mighty witnesses for Christ. We never see the risen Jesus explicitly receive them because they never reappear in the story, but all of Mark's readers know that the disciples who deserted Jesus became the apostles. Mark's presentation of the Twelve implies that his church should take back those who repent, even if they had a significant lapse in faith.

FIGURE 12.3 **MODEL OF A RECONSTRUCTION OF HEROD'S TEMPLE**

This was the temple in operation in the time of Jesus. This reconstruction shows the massive size of the temple complex. (The model is in the Holy Land Hotel in Jerusalem.) Wikimedia Commons

The Passion

Mark devotes nearly five of his sixteen chapters to Christ's **passion** (the week that leads up to his crucifixion). Thus he gives this aspect of Jesus' ministry more importance than any other. So much of Mark is focused on the passion story that it led one nineteenth-century commentator to call this Gospel a passion narrative with a long introduction (Martin Kähler). Mark, then, sees the death and resurrection of Christ as the culmination of Christ's ministry and the part of that ministry that gives meaning to the rest. However much this emphasis on Christ's death makes present-day readers uncomfortable, Mark sees it as the key to understanding everything else. In this Mark is consistent with other New Testament writers, all of whom see the death and resurrection of Jesus as the event that contains the key to understanding who Jesus is and what his life and ministry mean. The earliest church could make Jesus' death central because it was followed by the resurrection. When it seems that the ministry of Jesus has been nullified by a defeat, God raises Jesus and so vindicates the life and message of Jesus and provides the guarantee that Jesus is God's presence in the world.

▶ Matthew: Messiah and Interpreter of the Law

The Gospel of Matthew is written for a rather different audience than Mark, so it emphasizes different things and talks about Jesus from a different perspective. Matthew follows the basic outline of Jesus' career that we saw in Mark: his ministry starts in Galilee, then expands to the surrounding area before Jesus begins his one trip to Jerusalem, where he is executed. Matthew, however, expands the story in several ways, most notably by adding stories about Jesus' birth and about appearances of Jesus after his resurrection, and by including a lot more of Jesus' teaching. This last feature has made Matthew a favorite of the church for centuries.

A Jewish Audience

Jesus as Messiah. The churches Matthew writes for are predominantly Jewish, though they have many non-Jews in them as well. We can tell he writes for a Jewish audience in many ways. First, the primary way Matthew identifies Jesus is as the Messiah. Emphasizing this understanding of Jesus only makes sense if Matthew is writing to people who have some expectations about a messiah.* Second, Matthew emphasizes the importance of keeping the law. Not only does Jesus observe the law, but he is also its authoritative interpreter and he commands others to keep it (we will come back to this point).

The "kingdom of heaven." Finally, we can tell that Matthew wrote for a largely Jewish audience by the way he refers to the realm of God's rule; instead of calling it the "kingdom of God," as Mark and Luke do, he usually calls it the "**kingdom of heaven**." By using this expression, Matthew avoids naming God directly. By the first century, many Jews observed the command not to take God's name in vain (one of the Ten Commandments) by not using even the word *God*. Instead, they used various circumlocutions (indirect ways) to refer to God. A common way to do this in the second century was to replace "God" with something such as "the Holy One, blessed be he." So Matthew is attentive to this sensibility when he minimizes the use of "God" by replacing it with "heaven."

Ancestry and Birth

The genealogy. Matthew begins his Gospel with a genealogy of Jesus and an account of his conception and birth. Unlike Mark, Matthew provides this narrative to construct Jesus'

*As we noted in connection with the prophetic writings, "messiah" simply means "anointed." Anyone God appoints to a task is in some sense a messiah. Matthew and the early church, however, come to give the title a more specific meaning.

BOX 12.4

JESUS AND THE LAW

What do you think Matthew 5:17-19 says about how Matthew's church relates to the Law to have Jesus say that those who teach it will be great in the kingdom of heaven?

identity. More than in Mark, Matthew wants to designate Jesus as the Messiah. While Mark uses this title for Jesus, it does not carry the weight for him that it does for Matthew. The genealogy in Matthew gives Jesus a Jewish pedigree that goes all the way back to Abraham himself. It also traces Jesus' lineage through the kings of Israel. In this way, Jesus stands in the royal line and so is qualified to be the messianic king who inherits King David's throne.

Conception and birth. Matthew's story of Jesus' miraculous conception and birth identify Jesus as God's immediate presence in the world, the one the name Emmanuel (Hebrew for "God with us") truly fits. The birth or **nativity narrative** of Matthew tells of the escape of Jesus, **Mary**, and **Joseph** to Egypt. They flee there because **Herod the Great** wants to kill Jesus after the **magi** (ancient astrologers) come to Herod looking for the child whose astrological signs designate him as a king (2:1-6). Since Herod has no new son, he views this unknown child as a threat. When he cannot find him, he takes the drastic step of killing all the children under two years old in the region of Jesus' birth (2:16-18). (We noted in chapter 10 how ruthless Herod the Great was when he thought someone threatened his position, so this episode is not out of character for him.) The most important point for Matthew in this narrative is that the magi, Herod, and the Scriptures all signify that Jesus is a king—even though he is born to poor parents. Thus Matthew emphasizes the royal aspect of Jesus' messianic identity as he begins his Gospel; these early elements of Matthew indicate that Jesus is the proper king of God's coming kingdom.

Jesus' Teaching: The Sermon on the Mount

After Jesus and his family return to Palestine (following Herod's death; 2:19-23), Matthew skips ahead to the baptism of Jesus by John the Baptist (3:13-17) and then follows the order of events in Mark, but breaks off the narrative several times to have Jesus teach for an extended period. The first of these breaks is also the most famous: the **Sermon on the Mount**. Matthew is telling stories about what Jesus does and then says, "After he sat down, his disciples came to him. Then he began to speak, and taught them, saying . . ." (5:1-2). Then comes the Sermon on the Mount. At the end of this long discourse, Matthew says, "Now when Jesus had finished saying these things, . . ." and he picks up the narrative where he left off (7:28). Matthew got most of this teaching of Jesus from Q, that written account of Jesus' sayings that had at first been passed on orally. Matthew uses material from Q to construct the five discourses of Jesus that he inserts into his account of Jesus' ministry. In this way, Matthew provides his readers with more of what Jesus taught. This also shows that Matthew thinks it is important to see Jesus as a teacher.

The authoritative interpreter. Matthew's Sermon on the Mount reveals some important things about his view of Jesus. This sermon helps Matthew identify Jesus as the authoritative interpreter of the law for the church. Just as the Essenes at Qumran had an authoritative interpreter of the Bible, so does the church. Matthew has Jesus affirm the validity of the law for the church by having him say explicitly that he has come not to abolish the law but to fulfill it, that is, to actually live by it. Furthermore, Jesus says that those who teach and observe the law will be great in the kingdom of heaven (5:17-20). Then Jesus proceeds to give the proper interpretations of various commands in the law.

A stricter demand. Christians have often said that Christ came to free people from keeping God's law and that Jesus made it easier to live for God. But this perspective violates Matthew's understanding of the ministry and message of Jesus. When Jesus gives his interpretations of commandments, they never get easier; rather they become more demanding! The first command Jesus interprets is, "Do not murder." Jesus says this command expects more than that you must refrain from murder. The intent of the command is that you not keep hatred in your heart. If you hate others, Jesus says God wants you to straighten out this relationship before you come to worship God (5:21-26).

Jesus interprets the command that prohibits adultery to mean that you must not harbor thoughts about sex with someone you are not married to (5:27-32). Then he says that the command against swearing falsely means that you must always tell the truth so that no one ever needs you to swear an oath because they know you are so honest (5:33-38). When he interprets the "eye for an eye" command, he says it means you must not respond in kind to the evil someone does to you (5:38-42). And the "love your neighbor" command intends you to identify all people, even your enemies, as your neighbors and so love them (5:43-47).

The intention of the commands. With these interpretations, Jesus reveals the true intention of the commands—and none of them makes the law easier to keep. The command about murder was never intended only to stop murder, according to Jesus, but also to lead a person to get rid of the attitudes that lead to murder. Jesus makes this same kind of move with all the commands he interprets here. As the authoritative interpreter of the law, Jesus says that these commands prohibit both the acts and the ways of thinking that lead to them. The commands are clearly in force, but now with their deeper meaning revealed. So Jesus does not do away with the law, he explains how to keep it as God intended.

Relevance for the church. Matthew knows that non-Jews in the church do not keep the Sabbath and some other commands that were given only to Jews, but this does not mean that the law is no longer relevant for the church. The law remains the guide for the church's life; it shows what God wants from God's people, and thus Matthew makes sure that his readers know how Jesus interprets it so they can live as God expects.

The Beatitudes. The Sermon on the Mount also contains other teachings that help form the lives of Jesus' followers. **The Beatitudes** appear at the beginning of this discourse (5:3-11).

BOX 12.5

THE BEATITUDES

When you read the Beatitudes in Matthew 5:3-12, you may notice that those who are "blessed" in these statements are not enjoying the "good things" in life. What understanding of existence do you think makes statements like these possible?

These proverbial sayings outline the manner of life that believers in Christ are to adopt, even as they show that the values of God's kingdom are not the same as the values of the outside world. There are few rewards in the economic, social, and political systems of the world for the meek, or those who try to be righteous or merciful, or who suffer persecution because of their faith. Yet Matthew makes these the virtues Christians should adopt.

The Lord's Prayer. Matthew also gives his account of the **Lord's Prayer** (or as it is sometimes called, the Our Father) in the Sermon on the Mount (6:9-13). This prayer both honors God and asks God to sustain one's own life and act to make the world what God wants it to be. When Matthew has Jesus pray that God's kingdom may come, he is probably praying for an end-time event that completely reorients all the structures of the world.

Much of the rest of the Sermon on the Mount invites people to begin to live according to the values that God's reorientation of the world would institute. Thus Jesus exhorts people to be prepared for judgment by being forgiving, acting in ways that please God, and devoting their lives to God's service. Such are the instructions Jesus gives to those who would follow him.

Other Discourses

The other discourses in Matthew have their own themes and emphases. The second discourse (9:35—11:1) focuses on how disciples, particularly those who teach, should conduct their lives and what they should expect as responses to their message. The third time Matthew gives an extended account of Jesus teaching is in 13:1-58. In this discourse Jesus tells and explains parables that describe the often hidden nature of the kingdom and its great value. The fourth discourse (18:1—19:2) gives extended attention to relations within the community of believers, including the importance of bringing others into the church and how the church should settle disputes among members. The final discourse (24:1—26:2) is addressed only to the disciples. It focuses on the end of time, with particular emphasis on judgment and the importance of being prepared for it. This discourse and other statements of woes and judgment provide a preview of the judgment that Matthew says Jesus will dispatch at the end of time. This judgment includes both condemnations for the wicked and disobedient and blessings for the faithful. Bringing judgment is an essential feature of the message and mission of Jesus for Matthew because it is an enactment of God's justice. All the Gospels have judgment play an important role in the work and teaching of Jesus.

These extended discourses are not the only places where Matthew includes teachings that do not appear in Mark. And besides the material from Q, Matthew includes teaching of Jesus that Mark included in his Gospel (for example, the parable of the Sower). The significant amount of space Matthew devotes to Jesus' teaching through these speeches indicates just how much importance he gives that teaching.

Fulfillment Citations

One of the most outstanding features of Matthew is his use of **fulfillment quotations** (sometimes called formula quotations), places where Matthew introduces a passage from the Hebrew

FIGURE 12.4 **SHOP FLOORS, SEPPHORIS**

The city of Sepphoris is about five miles from Nazareth in central Galilee. These mosaics are evidence of how much Herod Antipas (son of Herod the Great) spent making this city a showcase of his realm. Some have even speculated that Jesus or his father Joseph may have worked as carpenters in this building campaign in Sepphoris, but there is no direct evidence to support this idea. Jerry Sumney

Bible with the expression, "This was done to fulfill what was spoken [or written] by the prophet." Sometimes he identifies the prophet, but often he does not. Matthew uses these statements from the Hebrew Bible to connect Jesus with Israel's hopes for a renewed relationship with God, as many Jews, especially those in the apocalyptic movements, believed there had been an incomplete restoration between God and Israel, especially after the fall of the Second Temple. Matthew further uses these biblical texts to provide the means by which to interpret who Jesus was and what he accomplished for God's people. Sometimes these statements are attached to Jesus' actions (for example, 8:17, where Jesus healing people fulfills a Scripture), and sometimes to events that just happen around Jesus (for example, 2:17-18, when Herod kills the babies around Bethlehem). Such quotations all indicate that Matthew sees God acting in the life of Jesus in ways that mirror the ways God had been present with Jews of previous generations.

Prophecy and fulfillment. When Matthew says that something "fulfills" a Scripture, he does not necessarily mean that the prophet predicted what would happen in Jesus' life. Indeed, none of the "prophecies" Matthew quotes was originally about Jesus; none of the prophets thought they were talking about someone who was to be born when or how Jesus was. Rather, Matthew reads the prophets and finds new meaning in them because of who he understands Jesus to be. At the same time, his thinking about Jesus' identity takes clearer shape as he interprets that life through his reading of Scripture. One example will have to suffice to illustrate this.

Retrospective interpretation and levels of meaning. When in his birth narrative Matthew has Jesus' family go to Egypt and then return, Matthew says the trip fulfills this Scripture, "Out of Egypt I have called my son" (2:15). This is a quotation of Hosea 11:1. The Hosea

BOX 12.6

VIRGIN IN ISAIAH AND MATTHEW

The Septuagint translated the Hebrew term Isaiah uses to refer to the young woman who was to have a child in Isaiah 7 with a more specific term than Isaiah uses. The term Isaiah uses can mean a woman with no sexual experience or simply a young woman. The Greek word in the Septuagint, *parthenos*, always means a virgin. Matthew seems to draw on the Septuagint's translation when he quotes this Isaiah passage to talk about Mary (1:23).

passage, however, it is not a prediction at all; rather, it is an account of past history. Speaking for God, Hosea recounts how God had called the Israelites, whom he calls "my son," out of slavery in Egypt. This act should have led them to trust God and be faithful to God, but instead they worshiped other gods. This passage in Hosea is an indictment, not a prediction of some good thing to come. But when Matthew reads about "my son" he thinks of Jesus, whom he knows to be God's son par excellence. So he applies the statement to Jesus. (He also thinks of Jesus as the son who responds properly to God's blessings and so fulfills this responsibility for God's children who had failed—finally God has an obedient son.)

Matthew knows that Hosea was not talking about Jesus, but that does not stop him from hearing a statement about Jesus. Matthew, along with many readers of his day (Philo of Alexandria is a good example), saw multiple levels of meaning in texts. There were literal meanings, and then there were hidden allegorical or spiritual meanings that only some people were able to discern. Matthew discovers new meanings of texts because of his belief in Christ. The way he treats these texts does not fit the ways we think texts should be read, but he is employing well-known first-century methods of interpretation. So while these texts from the Hebrew Bible were not predictions that prove who Jesus was, they do serve as ways Matthew and others in the early church came to understand Jesus.

Testing the interpretations. We do not use such methods today because they are uncontrollable; people could say a text meant nearly anything, and it would be hard to say they were wrong. Today we try to use methods of interpretation that can be tested by others so that our readings do not simply reflect our own inclinations and prejudices. This does not mean that the church cannot celebrate Matthew's use of these methods. Through them Matthew has helped the church develop its faith in Jesus and to keep that faith connected to the God of Israel. So when these fulfillment texts are read on Christian holidays, Christians can be glad that they have come to understand God's acts in Christ through them. At the same time, Christians should avoid seeing these texts as predictions that somehow prove who Jesus is.

Passion and Resurrection

Distinctive details. As noted at the beginning of our discussion of Matthew, this Gospel includes stories about encounters with the resurrected Christ, as well as an account of Jesus' birth. Mark only reports that an angel tells the women at the tomb that Jesus was raised and ends by saying they did not tell anyone. Before getting to **resurrection appearances**,

BOX 12.7

MULTIPLE MEANINGS

The Gospel writers were not alone in seeing multiple meanings in earlier texts. As we saw in chapter 3, Jewish interpreters such as Philo found multiple meanings in the biblical texts. Other Christian writers read similarly for more than one meaning. Near the beginning of the third century, Origen explicitly sets this out as the way to read the Bible: "Just as the human being consists of body, soul, and spirit, so in the same way does the scripture, which has been prepared by God to be given for our salvation" (*On First Principles* 4.1.11 [Greek version], trans. Frederick Crombie, *Ante-Nicene Fathers,* ed. Alexander Roberts and James Donaldson, vol. 4 [reprint, Grand Rapids: Eerdmans, 1956], 359).

Matthew expands some elements of the trial of Jesus beyond what we read in Mark. Only Matthew has the famous episode in which the Roman governor **Pilate** washes his hands of any responsibility for Jesus' death (27:24-26). Matthew is also the only Gospel that tells of Judas's remorse and suicide (27:3-10; Acts 1:18-20 also tells of it). Following Jesus' death, only Matthew has the rulers of Jerusalem get Pilate to post guards at his tomb (27:62-66). Of course, Matthew is also the only one who says those guards spread false rumors about the disciples stealing the body of Jesus (28:11-15).

Resurrection appearances. When the women see the resurrected Christ, Matthew has them report their experience to the disciples and tell them that Jesus said to meet him in Galilee (28:9-10). Once the disciples return to Galilee, Matthew closes his Gospel by having the resurrected Christ appear briefly to the disciples to tell them that God has given him all authority in all parts of the cosmos, so they should proclaim the message about him to the whole world (28:16-20). This appearance and commission implies that their relationship with Jesus has been restored after they deserted him at his trial. Their failure is not mentioned, but Jesus' instruction to them assumes they are and will be faithful to him. Matthew is the only Gospel that records the admonition, often called the Great Commission, to spread the message

BOX 12.8

PREDICTIONS AND THE GODS

Christians should avoid saying that the passages in the Hebrew Bible that Matthew (and then many after him) cites are actual predictions of Jesus. Just because there were some who thought they were predictions does not prove they came from God. After all, in the first century people believed that various gods provided some information about the future (for example, Apollo at Delphi), even if it was often rather vague. So to say that something was predicted in the ancient world did not show that the prediction came from the God of Israel. Even New Testament writers (at least tacitly) assume that other beings could give reliable predictions of the future or correct insights (see the story in Acts 16:16-19).

FIGURE 12.5 **ISRAELITE TOMB, FIRST CENTURY**

This is one of many tombs in the same cave. Bodies would be placed on the ledge in front of the arched recess for a year. Then the remains would be gathered and placed inside the recessed area, often in an ossuary (a box for bones, perhaps we could say a type of coffin). Jerry Sumney

about Jesus throughout the world. Significantly, this commission includes telling people to obey what Jesus had commanded (which includes his interpretation of the law).

Summary

The ways Matthew expands the story found in Mark adds new understandings of Jesus. Matthew establishes new links between Jesus and the previous acts of God in Israel's history through his fulfillment quotations. He also helps Jewish believers in Christ think about how to live faithfully as people who both believe in Christ and live out that faith by remaining observant Jews. For Matthew, membership in the church does not take one out of Judaism; rather, Jesus' teaching helps them know how to live within Judaism as they recognize the new thing God has done in Christ.

Matthew identifies Jesus as God's obedient son, who demonstrates how God's people should respond to God's blessings. This relationship to God is first established through the story of the virgin birth and continues through the Hosea passage Matthew cites that refers to God's son. This combination of elements gives Jesus a unique relationship with God, a relationship that Jesus lives up to by being obedient to God's will—even being willing to die as part of that obedience.

Importantly, Jesus is the Messiah through whom God is present and working to call the world to conform to God's will. Of course, Matthew has redefined all expectations of God's Messiah. This figure is now the authoritative interpreter of the law and God's king who commands God's heavenly army (see 26:52-56 and the claim to possess all authority in the Great Commission). As the Messiah and King, he is also the one who will come from the heavens in judgment (26:63-64). All of this makes faith in and obedience to Christ of primary importance for Matthew.

▶ Luke: Compassion and Justice

Distinctive Emphases

Luke has his own themes and emphases as he explicates the identity and significance of Jesus, even as he also follows Mark's basic outline of Jesus' ministry. Like Matthew, Luke adds stories about Jesus' birth and some postresurrection appearances—more of both than Matthew. Luke wrote for a predominantly Gentile church, so he does not focus his attention on some of the themes that were important for Matthew. The central way Luke thinks about Jesus is as the Son of God, though with a somewhat different meaning than what we saw in Matthew or Mark. Luke is also concerned about fulfillment of Scripture, but again in a distinctive way. Perhaps the most distinctive thing about Luke is his emphasis on the attention Jesus gives to the poor, an emphasis that is present in many explicit and subtle ways, as we will see.

Preparation

The conception and birth of John the Baptist. Luke begins his narrative even earlier than Matthew. Instead of starting with the announcement of Jesus' birth, he begins with the promise of the birth of John the Baptist (1:5-25). Thus God has a hand in the immediate preparation for Jesus' work and ministry by intervening for an elderly childless couple and defining John's lifework even before his birth. (We should not miss the parallel between this story and the many stories of barren women in the Hebrew Bible, with special reference to Hannah and her son Samuel in 1 Samuel 1.)

The story of the angel's announcement to **Zechariah** that he would have a son is intentionally a bit humorous. The old priest is offering incense at the temple when the angel appears with the announcement. Zechariah is skeptical (maybe he thought the incense was a bit thick and he was hallucinating) and so asks for a sign, which the angel agrees to give. Unfortunately, the sign is that the old man would not be able to speak until the child was named—not exactly the sign he was hoping for, I expect. Then his wife **Elizabeth** does become pregnant.

Elizabeth and Mary. While Elizabeth is pregnant, the same angel appears to Mary and asks her to have God's baby (1:26-38). She agrees and decides to visit her cousin Elizabeth, John the Baptist's mother-to-be (1:39-56). When Elizabeth sees her, the baby kicks and she takes this as a sign that there is something special about Mary. Mary then breaks out with the poem known as the **Magnificat** (to which we will return) and tells Elizabeth of her pregnancy. She stays with Elizabeth three months before returning home.

Naming John the Baptist. After the birth of John, the day to name him finally arrives (1:59-66). Elizabeth is in charge since Zechariah is still mute (people seem to think more than this is wrong with the old man because they do not initially include him in the naming process). When Elizabeth declares that his name will be John (as the angel had instructed), the relatives think it is a bad choice and so decide to ask poor old Zechariah. Then he writes on a piece of paper that the child's name is to be John. Immediately he can speak again. His first words are a poem of thanksgiving (perhaps not the first thing that would have come out of the mouth of many of us) now known as **the Benedictus** (1:68-79).

The Birth and Childhood of Jesus

Luke then jumps to the story of Mary and Joseph's trip to Bethlehem, where they are unable to find a room (2:1-7). Matthew's story assumes that the couple lives in Bethlehem (since the magi find them there nearly two years after Jesus' birth), but Luke has them travel from northern Palestine to this town just south of Jerusalem. When Jesus is born, angels tell the news to local shepherds who go and find Jesus lying in the feeding trough of a barn (2:8-20). On their way home after a week in Bethlehem, Mary and Joseph take Jesus to the temple, where two people, a man and a woman, recognize that he is the one who will bring salvation to God's people (2:21-40).

Differing emphases. This birth story is very different from the one Matthew tells; the stories have different characters who do different things. Their different accounts reflect the writers' differing emphases. Matthew emphasizes the royal character of Jesus not only by explicitly having the magi call him a king, but also by having these wealthy people bring him expensive gifts. Matthew even has King Herod worry about losing his throne to Jesus. No wealthy or important people appear in Luke's story because he stresses Jesus' mission to the poor and lower class. First he focuses attention on the women (who were generally not seen as men's equals in the first-century Mediterranean world). While Matthew tells of an angel visiting Joseph, Luke recounts the angel's visit to Mary instead. Furthermore, the first person to recognize the special nature of Jesus is Elizabeth (at least it is her interpretation of the movement of her fetus), another woman. A woman is also one of the first two who recognize Jesus as the savior when he is taken to the temple as an infant. Additionally, instead of having wealthy magi, who can get an unannounced audience with the king, visit Jesus, Luke has third-shift shepherds witness the baby's arrival.

The Magnificat. This different array of characters signals that Luke will give us a different perspective on the mission of Jesus. But there is even more in the birth narrative that makes this difference clear. Mary's poem, the Magnificat, announces this theme. This poem, which is more likely a composition of Luke than of Mary (such a composition would have been quite a

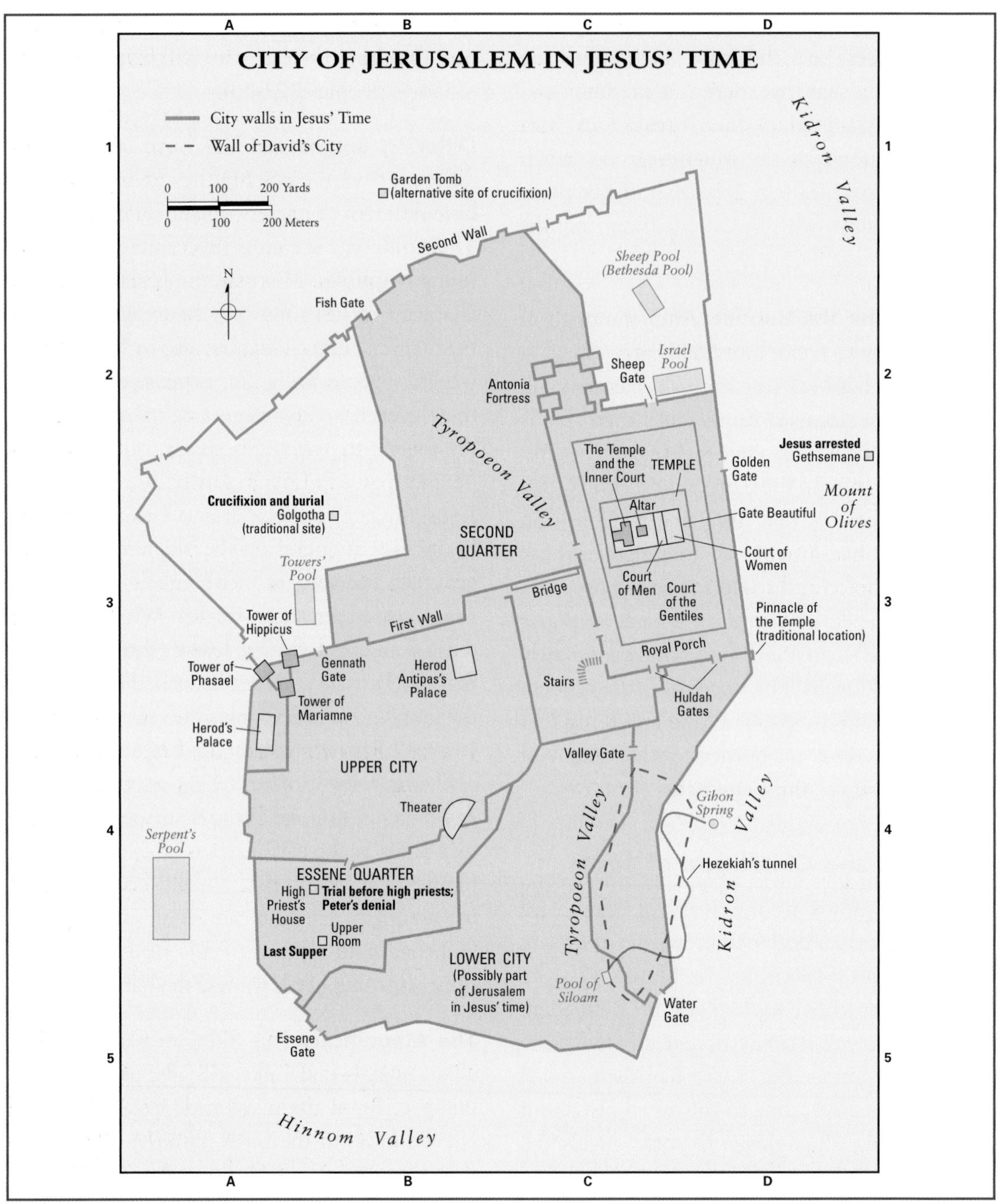
CITY OF JERUSALEM IN JESUS' TIME
City walls in Jesus' Time
Wall of David's City
0 100 200 Yards
0 100 200 Meters
N
A
B
C
D
1
2
3
4
5
Kidron Valley
Garden Tomb
(alternative site of crucifixion)
Second Wall
Sheep Pool
(Bethesda Pool)
Fish Gate
Israel Pool
Sheep Gate
Antonia Fortress
Tyropoeon Valley
The Temple and the Inner Court
TEMPLE
Golden Gate
Jesus arrested
Gethsemane
Mount of Olives
Altar
Gate Beautiful
Crucifixion and burial
Golgotha
(traditional site)
SECOND QUARTER
Court of Women
Towers' Pool
Court of Men
Court of the Gentiles
Bridge
Tower of Hippicus
First Wall
Pinnacle of the Temple
(traditional location)
Royal Porch
Tower of Phasael
Gennath Gate
Herod Antipas's Palace
Stairs
Huldah Gates
Tower of Mariamne
Herod's Palace
UPPER CITY
Valley Gate
Gihon Spring
Theater
Serpent's Pool
Hezekiah's tunnel
ESSENE QUARTER
High Priest's House
Trial before high priests;
Peter's denial
Upper Room
Last Supper
LOWER CITY
(Possibly part of Jerusalem in Jesus' time)
Pool of Siloam
Water Gate
Essene Gate
Hinnom Valley

MAP 12.1

feat on the spur of the moment), defines the mission of Jesus as one that will bring down the proud and wealthy, but will elevate the weak, poor, and hungry. Luke uses this poem to point readers to an important element of his understanding of the meaning of Jesus' ministry.

Theological accounts. The different ways that Luke and Matthew tell of Jesus' birth demonstrate how thoroughly theological their accounts are. They tell of his birth in their different ways because they want their readers to see different things about the identity and purpose of Jesus. When celebrations of Christmas combine the two accounts (as usually happens, because we often see the shepherds and the magi visiting Jesus together), they minimize or miss the distinctive points of each account. It is important for Matthew to point out the royal nature of Christ; he presents Christ as God's king who rules over the whole cosmos. On the other hand, Luke wants to insist that Jesus identified himself with the poor and has the alleviation of their suffering as a central concern of his mission. The early church held that both Luke and Matthew were right. Thus they saved these two very different accounts of Jesus' birth, because both told an important truth about Jesus. Without each of these accounts, the church's understanding of Christ would be diminished.

BOX 12.9

THE MAGNIFICAT

The poem Luke has Mary recite in Luke 1:46-55 is one of the most famous parts of the New Testament. When you read that passage, what themes of Luke do you see being emphasized?

Jesus' childhood. Luke is the only New Testament Gospel to include a story about Jesus' childhood, though there are plenty of more fanciful stories in apocryphal Gospels that were written in the second and third centuries. Luke tells of Jesus and his parents going to Jerusalem for the Passover celebration when he was twelve (2:41-51). When it is time to go home, unbeknown to his parents, Jesus stays behind to discuss religious matters with teachers in the temple. Thinking he is with relatives, Mary and Joseph begin their trip home. When they cannot find Jesus that night, they return to Jerusalem and look for him frantically for three days before finally finding him in the temple, where he had been amazing the teachers with his questions and answers. Mary asks him how he could do such a thing to them. Jesus responds, "Did you not know that I must be in my Father's house?" This response could be construed as less than respectful, so Luke comments that Jesus went home and was obedient to his parents. The point Luke makes with this story is that Jesus already knows he is God's Son, even as a child of twelve.

Baptism and Genealogy

After this one episode from Jesus' childhood, Luke skips forward to Jesus' baptism by John, and so the beginning of his ministry. But before starting his account of that ministry, Luke inserts a genealogy after Jesus' baptism, implying that it should shape our reading of Jesus' ministry (3:23-38). Luke traces the lineage of Jesus all the way back to Adam, rather than stopping at Abraham as Matthew had. Luke constructs this genealogy to contribute to his interpretation of Jesus, just as Matthew had done with his. Luke does not stop his list of Jesus' ancestors with Abraham, because Luke's audience is predominantly non-Jewish, so establishing the authentic Jewishness of Jesus is not as central a concern. By tracing ancestors all the way back to Adam, Luke suggests that Jesus, and by implication his work and mission, are relevant for everyone in the world.

Differences from Matthew. Luke's genealogy is different from Matthew's in another important way. While Matthew traced the lineage of Jesus through the kings of Israel to show that Jesus was the legitimate king, Luke takes a different route. The only king Luke names among the ancestors of Jesus is David. After David the genealogies of Matthew and Luke are completely different, except for one other name that appears in both, Zerubbabel, until they get to Joseph. They have such differing accounts because they want to convey different points with these lists of ancestors. Luke has little interest in portraying Jesus as the messianic king, and so does not relate Jesus to the Israelite kings. Luke helps his readers identify Jesus with the poor by giving him ancestors who did not sit on the throne, but were from among the people.

BOX 12.10

LUKE AND WORLD EVENTS

One of the ways Luke shows that the ministry of Jesus is relevant for the whole world is to connect things in the life of Jesus to various events in the world. For example, he notes that the birth of Jesus takes place in connection with a census decreed not just by the governor of the region, but by the emperor (2:1). Similarly, Luke dates the beginning of John the Baptist's ministry by the reign of the emperor and the term of the Roman procurator, as well as by who ruled other nearby regions and who was high priest (3:1-2). Thus the ministry of John and Jesus are connected to the entire world and all spheres of life.

Unique sonship. Luke's genealogy traces Jesus' ancestors back beyond even Adam by saying that Adam was the "son of God" (3:38). So the definitive ancestor for Jesus is God. The story of the virgin birth makes Jesus God's son in an even closer way. So Jesus' most distant ancestor and his most immediate progenitor is God. Thus Jesus is the son of God in a unique way.

For Luke, Jesus as the Son of God has a more intimate relationship with God than anyone else does. Jesus is the fulfillment of the destiny of humankind; what God wanted with Adam comes to fruition in Jesus. But Jesus does more than realize the relationship with God that God wants with humanity; Jesus is also the one through whom that relationship is made possible for others. Thus Jesus' sonship is not exhausted by his intimacy with God; his sonship includes bringing others into the proper relationship with God.

Jesus' Ministry

Luke begins his account of Jesus' ministry by expanding and moving the story of Jesus' return to Nazareth after he had gotten famous (4:14-30). As noted earlier, Luke knows that Mark tells this story in the middle of Jesus' Galilean ministry but moves it to the beginning of his account of Jesus' ministry to make it the theme-setting episode for the whole of that ministry. Once Luke has told the Nazareth story, he takes up the outline of Jesus' ministry that he got from Mark. Luke introduces the Nazareth synagogue incident with just two verses that say Jesus got famous and then went home (4:14-15), so that the narrative can make some sense as a story line. But Luke's shifting of the story into this place demonstrates that he has a theological, rather than chronological, agenda; his point is to show what the life and ministry of Jesus mean, not to get the historical details correct.

The sermon at Nazareth. Luke's account of Jesus' preaching at his hometown synagogue is more than twice the length of the story found in Mark. Luke adds both a Scripture reading and an interpretation by Jesus that turns the crowd against him and sets out a central theme of his ministry. Jesus reads a selection from Isaiah 61:1-2 that he combines with a piece from Isaiah 58:6:

> The Spirit of the Lord is upon me,
> because he has anointed me to bring good
> news to the poor.
> He has sent me to proclaim release to the
> captives
> and recovery of sight to the blind,
> to let the oppressed go free,
> to proclaim the year of the Lord's favor.
> (Luke 4:18)

After reading this, Jesus says, "Today this scripture has been fulfilled in your hearing" (4:21). At first, everyone is pleased because Jesus is announcing that God is about to bring them relief from their troubles, whether it is their oppression by the Romans or other difficulties. But then Jesus tells two stories from biblical history (the healing of Naaman, a military officer of an enemy, and Elijah's feeding of a Gentile widow) to indicate that the people God is acting to rescue are not those in the synagogue. Rather, the captive and oppressed in this reading are the people the faithful see as outside their circle, the undesirables (in the interpretive stories, not members of the people of God) who the people present look down on. When the congregation realizes that Jesus is saying that God is about to save the people that the righteous see as outside the circle of God's primary concern, they become angry and throw Jesus out of town.

Concern for the poor and the oppressed. This episode defines Jesus' ministry by having Jesus say that the poor, the oppressed, and the ill are the real focus of God's salvation. This explicit statement is repeated one other time in an episode that Matthew also relates. In that text, John the Baptist has been arrested and sends messengers to Jesus asking if he really is the Messiah (Matt. 11:2-6). Jesus sends them back with this message, "Go and tell John what you have seen and heard: the blind receive their sight, the lame walk, the lepers are cleansed, the deaf hear, the dead are raised, the poor have good news brought to them" (Luke 7:22). Since Matthew also has this story and quotation, it was probably part of the common tradition about Jesus, but Luke makes it a central feature of his ministry.

We have already seen how Luke's nativity story reshapes the tradition to focus on women and the poor. Luke also tells some stories that do not appear in the other Gospels that point us to his concern for the poor and marginalized. One of these unique traditions is the conversation between Jesus and the thief on the cross, where Jesus says the crucified man will be with him in paradise (23:39-43). Another episode found only in Luke is the parable of the Rich Man and Lazarus (16:19-31). Lazarus is a poor beggar, a street person covered with sores who lives near the rich man's mansion. In this parable, both men die, but they have very different fates: the rich man is condemned, while Lazarus goes to paradise. The troubling feature of the story is that the rich man is not condemned for any particular sin or shortcoming. His problem is that he is rich! This alone is apparently enough to bring him condemnation. At the same time, nothing good is said about Lazarus's character or faith; he was just poor and so gains admission to paradise. We might want to say the rich man was condemned for not helping the poor, but the text does not say so. This disturbing parable exaggerates Luke's point: God's salvation especially targets the poor.

The Good Samaritan. One other example will have to suffice to illustrate this theme, the parable of the **Good Samaritan** (10:25-37). This way of naming the parable would have been an oxymoron for many Jews of Jesus' day because Jews and Samaritans did not get along—there were no *good* Samaritans. The ancestors of Jews and Samaritans were related, and in the first century they had similar Bibles and competing interpretations and traditions. In part because they were so close to one another (ethnically, theologically, and geographically), there was a mutual and deep dislike and distrust. We need to keep this cultural backdrop in view as we hear this narrative.

An expert interpreter of the law comes to test Jesus by asking what he needed to do to inherit eternal life. Jesus asks him what the law says he should do, to which the man replies, "Love God and your neighbor." Jesus says, "That's right, go do that." Then the man, worried about such a broad command, asks Jesus who his neighbor is. Jesus responds by telling a parable about a man beaten up, robbed, and left to die. Two people who serve in the temple pass him by, but then a Samaritan stops to help. He gives the man first aid and takes him to a local inn, telling the keeper that he would pay the bill on his return trip. Jesus then asks who acted like a neighbor to the injured person. The lawyer, of course, says it was the one who helped him. The episode ends with Jesus saying the equivalent of, "So, go be like a Samaritan." Luke has made an enemy the hero of this parable; the unacceptable outsider is the one who pleases God.

Hobnobbing with tax collectors and sinners. These stories and the way Jesus regularly associates with "tax collectors and sinners" makes the people who are unacceptable to others the primary beneficiaries of Jesus' work and ministry (5:29-32). It is not that God does not

BOX 12.11

THE BEATITUDES AGAIN

Like Matthew, Luke also has a series of "blessed" attitudes in a sermon of Jesus. What emphases of Luke do you see when you compare Matthew 5:3-12 with Luke 6:20-22? How might the warnings in Luke 6:24-25 help Luke emphasize the teaching he wants readers to hear?

FIGURE 12.6 **THE GOOD SAMARITAN**

Jan Weenix (1640–1719). This painting depicts the parable of Jesus in which two religious officials fail to help a robbed and beaten man, but then a Samaritan stops to help him. Making a Samaritan (a person from an ethnic group that Jews disliked) the hero of the story was part of the shocking nature of this parable. Art Resource

want a relationship with others, but perhaps that they do not need the attention the poor and those who have turned from God need. Giving attention to these people constitutes an important part of the heart of Jesus' ministry for Luke. Jesus has come to restore to the poor and oppressed their proper dignity and integrate them into the community of the people of God.

Passion and Resurrection: A Divine Plan

Like Matthew, Luke is interested in showing that the ministry and passion of Jesus fulfill Scripture. But whereas Matthew had God acting in and around Jesus to accomplish God's purposes, Luke has Jesus work to fulfill Scriptures on purpose, as part of what he is supposed to do. Jesus says things like, "The Son of Man must suffer" (9:22) or "This scripture must be fulfilled" (22:37). Luke thinks there is a divine plan that is foretold and prefigured in Scripture that must be fulfilled. It is as though there is a script and Jesus knows his part and he must perform it. The plot is determined, now Jesus must play his part.

Through the eyes of faith. This plan was not obvious from reading Scripture and was not on the surface of the texts. Once again—just as it was with Matthew—the only way to discern the plan is to read Scripture through belief in Jesus. This becomes obvious even within the narrative of Luke. The disciples have not seen how Jesus' ministry fulfills Scripture, and so they are completely confused by his death. Then the resurrected Christ appears to them and Luke says he "opened their minds to understand the scriptures" (24:45). Without the experience of the resurrected Christ, the disciples cannot see the foreshadowing of Jesus' ministry in the Scriptures of Israel. So again, Luke is using the Hebrew Bible to help interpret Jesus and his ministry by inserting new layers of meaning; he is finding meanings that only people who already have faith in Christ are able to discern.

Unique aspects of the passion. Like Matthew and Mark, Luke devotes more time to Christ's passion than to any other part of his life or ministry. One unique aspect to Luke's account of Jesus' trial is his insertion of Herod Antipas (23:6-12). This Herod is the son of Herod the Great, who played a role in Matthew's birth narrative and who had financed the expansion and lavish refurbishment of the temple. Herod Antipas was still the ruler in Galilee when Pilate was governor in Judea and Jesus was put on trial. Luke has Pilate try to get off the hook of having to condemn Jesus by sending him to Herod because Jesus was from Galilee. Herod asks Jesus for a magic show, but refuses to get involved in the trial. All of this maneuvering gives Luke more opportunity to emphasize that Jesus was not a threat to the Roman Empire, a point Luke wants to highlight.

FIGURE 12.7 **CAESAR ON A COIN FROM CORINTH**

When asked whether faithful Jews should pay taxes to the Romans, Jesus asks his questioners whose image is on the coin. When they say it is Caesar's, Jesus says they should give to Caesar what belongs to Caesar and give to God what belongs to God (Mark 12:13-17; Matt. 22:15-22; Luke 20:20-26). The question about taxes is a trick question because some Jews believed God wanted a Jewish theocracy in Jerusalem, and so the concession of paying Roman taxes violated God's will. At least, they thought, paying those taxes showed that a person was not depending on God to bring that new kingdom immediately. Jesus evades the question with his answer, which implies that those who asked it (and all those who used Roman currency) were implicated in cooperating with the Romans by bringing Roman money into the temple precincts. *Cities of Paul*

Resurrection appearances. Luke provides more stories about the resurrected Christ than Mark and Matthew. In Luke the women find the empty tomb and talk with an angel, but do not see Jesus. That first happens in the strange story of the two people who were going home to Emmaus, a town not far from Jerusalem (24:13-35). While talking about the crucifixion of Jesus and how disappointed they were by it, another person joins them on their walk home. He explains that everything happened just as Scripture said it should. When the two men get home, they invite the stranger in to have dinner with them. Once dinner is prepared, they ask to stranger to pray before the meal. When he does, they recognize that it is Jesus and he disappears. These men then run back to Jerusalem and tell the eleven disciples what had happened.

While the disciples were discussing this, Jesus suddenly appears among them—and they are afraid he is a ghost (24:36-53). Jesus assures them that he is not a ghost by inviting them to touch him and by eating some fish. After some discussion and teaching, Jesus floats up into the sky and out of their sight.

A new and different body. These resurrection appearances signal that Luke envisions Christ's resurrection as something other than a resuscitation of a corpse; this new body is able to walk with people without being recognized, it can pop in and out of rooms, and even be mistaken for a ghost. Yet it can be touched and can eat. This is not like any body that anyone had ever seen. Luke and the early church saw the resurrection of Christ as the beginning of a new kind of life in the world. As they saw it, the resurrected Christ had the body that the saved would have in their afterlife with God. So the resurrection is more than a dead person waking up; it is the initiation of a new kind of existence that Christ both possesses and enables others to receive.

FIGURE 12.9 **BASE OF STATUE OF TRAJAN**

This inscription refers to Emperor Trajan as a god and as a son of god. *Cities of Paul*

The resurrection is no mere miracle for Luke; it is the beginning of a new era that brings with it a new way to exist in the presence of God. This is the point Luke's stories of the resurrected Christ try to convey.

Summary

Luke, then, introduces Jesus as the Son of God who will extend God's special care and concern to the poor and the marginalized. Jesus' identification with such people constitutes at least part of the reason the authorities distrust and crucify him. But God vindicates the ministry of Jesus through the resurrection and shapes that resurrection existence of Christ so that it is the pattern for all the children of God that follow Jesus. Through Christ, they become God's children and come into the new life with God that Christ's resurrection initiates. But Luke does not tell this whole story in his Gospel; he has a second volume, the Acts of the Apostles, in which he gives his characters speeches to explicate some of the theology that appears only in narrative form in the Gospel.

▶ John: Incarnational Christology

Differences from the Synoptics

As noted at the beginning of our discussion of the Gospels, John is very different from the other three. While Matthew, Mark, and Luke tell of only one trip of the adult Jesus to Jerusalem, John has multiple trips; while the Synoptics concentrate their attention on Jesus' ministry in Galilee, John has many more stories about Jesus in Jerusalem and the surrounding region. In fact, few of the stories that the Synoptic Gospels tell about Jesus in Galilee appear in John, and John has many stories about Jesus' time in Judea that the others do not tell.

The postscript. Another difference between the first three Gospels and John is what we know about their creation. It seems that Matthew, Mark, and Luke were each written by a single person who wrote what his particular church needed to understand the person and mission of Jesus. Even so, we do not know who those three people were. The ending of John, however, attributes much of what is found in this Gospel to the "**beloved disciple**" (21:20-24). Yet even the form of this attribution shows that others contributed to the final version of John, because the text says that these stories come from the beloved disciple and "*we* know that his testimony is true" (21:24). So someone other than this disciple wrote at least the conclusion to John.

Other editing. Most scholars think that the people who added the postscript also edited the book in other ways. They probably added some things and perhaps rearranged others. You can see this in places such as the end of chapter 14, where Jesus says, "Let's get up and go." But no one does. It is only after a long speech (his "I am the vine" discourse) that anyone gets up and leaves at 18:1. So it appears that the whole speech in chapters 15–17 was added after the basic story line was in place. Still, the editors who finished what the "beloved disciple" started had their understandings of Jesus shaped by this important teacher.

The "Beloved Disciple"

Though some have identified the "beloved disciple" as the apostle John, this seems unlikely. This Gospel has little interest in Galilee, the region John came from, and none of the stories in the other Gospels in which John or his brother plays a prominent role appears in John. The first time the "beloved disciple" appears in the narrative is at the Last Supper, where he is sitting beside Jesus (13:23-25). Judea seems to be this disciple's home; that is the reason he has so many stories about Jesus' ministry in that region.

Preexistence

John is the only New Testament Gospel that clearly teaches the **preexistence** of Christ. The prologue of John (1:1-18) asserts that Christ was with God before the creation of anything and that Christ worked as God's agent of creation. And though there are many ways it may be understood, John says that "**the Word**," what he calls the preexistent Christ, "was God" (1:1). Thus the Gospel begins by assigning to Christ the highest place possible. Such statements create difficulties for people who say they worship only one God—how could Jesus be "with God" and be God, and the people continue to profess that they worship only one God? In later years, the doctrine of the Trinity was devised to try to make sense of just such questions. The Gospel of John, however, offers no resolution of this matter.

Jesus and God

The prologue is not the only place that John identifies Jesus with God in the most intimate of ways. In several texts John has Jesus identify himself closely with God in various ways. In some places it is as simple as Jesus saying, "God works on the Sabbath and so I do too" (5:17-18), which his hearers interpret as a comment that makes Jesus equal to God. Elsewhere Jesus says, "I and the Father are one" (10:30). Finally, John phrases some statements of Jesus so he seems to claim divine identity. In conversation with some critics, Jesus says, "Before Abraham was, I am" (8:56-59). What is significant about this statement is that when God spoke to Moses at the burning bush, the name of God Moses is given is "I am." In some places when Jesus says "I am," the readers could understand the phrase to mean "I am he," or more colloquially "It's me" (8:24; 13:19). But cumulatively these oblique statements indicate that John wants readers to identify Jesus with God in an intimate and unique way. This identification of Jesus with God is John's central theological affirmation and the primary way he identifies

BOX 12.12

THE WORD AND WISDOM TRADITIONS

The way the Prologue of John talks about the Word's participation in creation parallels what some Jewish Wisdom traditions claim about personified Wisdom. Proverbs 8 says that when God created the world, Wisdom was "beside him, like a master worker" (see vv. 22-31). Such ideas about Wisdom were developed in Sirach (Ecclesiasticus), Baruch, and the Wisdom of Solomon (books in the Apocrypha).

FIGURE 12.8 **INSCRIPTION FOR NERO**

The remains of an inscription above these columns of the Parthenon call Nero a god and a son of god. The church's claims about Christ were challenges, at least implicitly, to such claims for an emperor.

Cities of Paul

Jesus. It is because of this divine element of Christ's nature that John asserts that salvation comes through him.

Jesus in charge. Because of this identity with God, Jesus is always in charge of his own destiny—even throughout the passion. Jesus tells Pilate that the only reason he has power to crucify Jesus is because God lets him have it (19:8-12). Then on the cross, rather than calling out in desperation, "My God, why have you deserted me" (as he does in Matthew and Mark), Jesus assigns a caretaker for his mother and dies only after completing all he was to accomplish and saying, "It is finished" (19:30). At the same time, however, John is careful to make clear that Jesus is human: he cries when others are sad (11:32-36) and must hide so people do not arrest him (8:58; 11:53-54) or make him a king (6:15).

A Different Kind of Teacher

Beyond the lofty and difficult theological affirmations about Christ, John also portrays Jesus as a different kind of teacher than what we see in the other Gospels. In the Synoptics, Jesus teaches with parables and short responses, almost quips. In John, however, Jesus has long conversations in which he first makes a cryptic statement that the other person misunderstands, Jesus responds by asking how they could misunderstand, and then he explains at length what he means. If you ask Jesus a question in John, you should be ready to take a seat because the answer is going to take a while.

Jesus and Nicodemus. The story of the teacher **Nicodemus** is a good example of this pattern (3:1-21). He comes to Jesus and says that he and others know Jesus is from God; Jesus responds by saying that to get into the kingdom of God a person must be born again. Nicodemus is taken aback by this abrupt and ambiguous statement and so asks how it is possible for a person to enter his mother's womb again. We miss part of the art of Jesus' statement because we are not reading in Greek. In Greek, Jesus' comment could mean born again or born from above. This does not make what Jesus says easier, but does leave it open to new meanings. After Jesus chides Nicodemus for not understanding, he explains that a person must receive God's Spirit from above and accept salvation through Christ and his death to be counted among God's people.

The woman at the well. The episode with the woman at the well is another example of this mode of teaching in John (4:1-30). As Jesus sits by a well with no bucket, a woman who does have a bucket comes to draw water. Jesus asks for a drink and then says that if she knew who he was she would ask him for running water. Our translations almost always translate Jesus' comment as offering her "living water," and that is a correct literalistic translation. But the phrase "living water" in ancient Greek meant "running water (our expression is also metaphoric since the water is not actually running, at least not as animals run). Of course, she understands his statement to mean running water and finds it remarkable since he had asked her for a drink and since he did not even have a bucket. Jesus then goes on to speak of proper worship of God; more particularly he says that a person does not need to be in a specific holy place to worship acceptably. So what begins as a strange and ambiguous statement ends up teaching an important lesson.

"The Jews" in John

A final feature of John shows just how important it is that his church knows they do not have to be in a particular location to worship God. John has often been seen as an anti-Semitic writing because of the way it talks about "the Jews." Using this label, John has this group oppose Jesus, hunt him, and be responsible for bringing him before Pilate. The first point to note in trying to understand the designation "the Jews" is that the author of John was himself Jewish. In a sense, he has adopted this expression to designate those within the family who disagree with him. For John, it is still good to be a descendant of Abraham (and on Isaac's side of the family; that is, not a descendant of Ishmael, and so a non-Jewish person).

The expression "the Jews" in John usually designates the civic and religious leaders of Jerusalem. Although he is not completely consistent in his use of the term, the author usually uses it to describe this group. John rejects their leadership because they have rejected the church's teaching and probably have ejected his church's members from their synagogues. A number of statements in John have convinced many scholars that the Jewish members of John's church have been expelled from their synagogues (see John 9:34-35, 16:1-2); that is, on this view John

BOX 12.13

TEXTUAL CRITICISM AND THE STORY OF THE ADULTEROUS WOMAN

Among the favorite stories of many people from the Gospel of John is the episode in which some people bring to Jesus a woman whom they say they caught in the act of adultery (there is no mention of the man). They ask Jesus whether they should impose the death penalty as the Law said they should. After a few moments, he tells the accusers they may impose this penalty, but the person with no sins has to throw the first stone. Since no one met this requirement (obviously), they left her alone (7:53—8:11).

The kindness and wisdom of Jesus exemplified in this passage are part of what has made it such a favorite. Unfortunately, this story should not be in John or any place else in the Bible. It is in none of the earliest copies of John and appears for the first time in a fifth-century manuscript. Such a story may have been an oral tradition about Jesus that someone eventually added to John. It appears in Bibles today because it was part of the manuscript tradition that the King James Version was based on, so it was included in that influential translation. Modern translations often set these verses off with some notation to let the readers know they were not part of John when it first began to circulate as an authority for the church.

has read his community's experience back into the story of Jesus. We need to remember that in the early years of the church's existence, Jewish believers in Christ continued to be members of their synagogues and to live as faithful Jews. The synagogue continued to be an important religious, social, and educational center of their lives.

Banned from the synagogue. The members of John's church, however, have been banned from their home synagogues. This was a painful—and unexpected—experience. We can easily understand why it happened, if we remember the exalted claims John makes about Jesus and the difficulty in holding those claims together with the commitment to worship only one God. However understandable their expulsion might be, John's church experienced it as persecution. As they saw it, they were being punished for believing the truth about God and God's Christ. The people these church members blame are the religious teachers who lead in the synagogues. These are the people who have done them harm and these are the people that John calls "the Jews." Again, we must remember that the writer of this epithet is also Jewish and that he values that heritage and religious experience. Still, John uses this name to designate those who oppose his church.

The most prominent narrative that leads scholars to understand the situation of John's church in this way is the story of Jesus healing the man born blind (John 9). Since Jesus healed the man on the Sabbath, some religious leaders accuse him of not observing the Sabbath and so of breaking the law. But other people think Jesus must be from God or he would not be able to heal congenital blindness. During their debate about this healing the leaders bring in the man's parents to ask whether he was really born blind and how he had come to see now. His parents respond by affirming that he was born blind, but will not comment about his new ability to see; they say, "ask him, he's an adult" (9:18-21). John then explains their refusal to answer by saying, "His parents said this because they were afraid of the Jews; for the Jews had already agreed that anyone who confessed Jesus to be the Messiah would be put out of the synagogue" (9:22).

Backward projection. New Testament scholars understand this explanation by John as a projection of his church's experience into the life of Jesus. That is, he envisions Jesus encountering the same kind of opposition the church experiences decades later. It seems unlikely that the ministry of Jesus (given that he attracted relatively few people and that it was of fairly short duration) would have attracted the kind of organized response John reports in 9:22. Besides, it would have been very unusual to expel people from a synagogue for claiming that someone was

FIGURE 12.10 **PRESENT-DAY SAMARITANS, MOUNT GERIZIM**

Mount Gerizim has been a worship center for Samaritans since at least the second century B.C.E. Today there are fewer than a thousand religious and ethnic Samaritans. The woman Jesus talks with at the well was a Samaritan. She asks Jesus whether people should worship in Jerusalem or on Mount Gerizim, the place Samaritans say the temple should be located. Getty

a messiah. As we noted in our account of the political situation in Palestine, many people had come forward claiming that God had anointed them to defeat the Romans and free Judea. Those who believed these claimants were not put out of synagogues; it violated no commandment or tradition to claim that a particular person was a messiah. So it seems unlikely that this episode recounts the actual response of leaders to Jesus' ministry during Jesus' lifetime.

John's church, however, not only claims that Jesus is the Messiah, but also that he is God's helper in creation and one who can identify himself as "I am." This definition of the messiah might well lead to expulsion from the synagogue. So it is not simply the claim that Jesus is Messiah, but the content John's church gives that assertion that provokes the painful experience of being put out of their synagogue.

BOX 12.14

THE *BIRKAT HA-MINIM*

Sometime probably after the Jewish Revolt of 132–135, a line was added to the liturgy of many synagogues that is known as the *Birkat ha-Minim*, the "Benediction against the Heretics." This prayer asks God to leave no hope for heretics and the wicked and to humiliate God's enemies and to find those praying innocent in judgment. The slanderers or heretics and wicked in this prayer are usually identified as Christians and Sadducees. Some earlier scholars dated this statement to the first century and so surmised that it might be a reaction to the teaching of the church for which the Gospel of John was written. Since it was probably composed after the Gospel of John, it seems unlikely that its insertion was the cause of the expulsion of John's church from the synagogue. Some scholars nevertheless see this prayer as an explanation for these statements in John.

Repercussions. John's labeling of his and Jesus' opponents as "the Jews" has had terrible repercussions throughout the history of the church. Once the church was predominantly Gentile, many read John as an indictment against all Jews (rather than a dispute in which all participants are Jewish, as it is in John). Such readings of John have produced anti-Semitism and supported the persecution and killing of Jews. We must reject all such uses of John and remember that they rest on misreadings of this Gospel. John clearly does not intend to indict all Jews, because *he is one*, as are most members of his church. John is in the middle of an argument with fellow Jews about how to understand the messiah and Jesus. His pain at being on the side that was ejected from the synagogue led him to say harsh things about those on the other side. Unfortunately, those harsh words and the label he chose for his antagonists have led to even worse consequences. A better understanding of John's historical context can help put an end to these poor interpretations and their evil consequences.

Resurrection Appearances

Mary and Thomas. Among the differences between John and the other New Testament Gospels are John's resurrection stories. It is still Mary Magdalene who discovers that Jesus has been raised and who first encounters him, though she does not immediately recognize him (20:1-18). The first time Jesus appears to the disciples, Thomas is not present (20:19-29). Thomas refuses to believe Jesus has been raised until he experiences it for himself, which is not until a week has passed. John is, then, the Gospel from which we get the image of the "doubting Thomas." After these appearances in Jerusalem, John shifts the scene to Galilee for his final resurrection story (ch. 21). The disciples have been fishing all night with no success. Jesus appears on shore and tells them to throw their nets on the other side of the boat. Once they do, the nets are so full they can hardly get them to shore. (Luke has his story of a miraculous catch of fish at the beginning of Jesus' ministry, in ch. 5.) After Jesus gives them some breakfast, he and Peter have the famous exchange where Jesus asks Peter three times (the same number of times Peter denied knowing Jesus outside Jesus' trial), "Do you love me?"

Both the doubting Thomas story and this appearance by the lake make clear that this resurrected Christ remains embodied. In the Thomas episode, Jesus tells Thomas to touch the wounds from the cross, and in the seaside story Jesus fixes food. Near the end of the first century, some in the church began saying that the risen Christ had no physical existence and others that even the earthly Jesus had not had a body. John wants his readers to be clear that Christ existed in bodily form, both before and after the resurrection.

Summary

John's portrayal of Jesus is quite distinctive: he sees Jesus as the incarnation of the preexistent Word of God, the agent through whom God created the world. The risen Christ then returns to his place in the heavens at God's side, as the unequaled means of attaining entrance into the presence of God. He identifies Christ as the most powerful of beings, the being who is one with God. Thus Christ is the one through whom John says all people have a relationship with God; the central mission of Christ is to bring God's salvation to humanity. Perhaps because of the way he envisions Christ's preexistent relationship with God or because of the conflict situation in which John's church finds itself, John is more explicit and emphatic than the other Gospels about the necessity of belief in Christ for a right relationship with God.

▶ Conclusion

The four New Testament Gospels, then, offer quite different ways to think about the life, death, and resurrection of Christ. The early church decided it was important to preserve and keep together these diverse ideas about the meaning of Jesus' life. There were many other Gospels being written and many other ways to understand who Jesus was and how he brings people into relationship with God. But the main body of the church (not some small group of officials chosen by an emperor working in a smoke-filled room) found these interpretations of Jesus to be those that brought life and meaning. Texts such as the *Gospel of Thomas* and the *Gospel of Judas* were written later than the New Testament Gospels and represent understandings of the world and God that most within the church found harmful. Whether it was their denial of the importance of bodily existence in the world, their exclusivism, or their belief in many gods, the developments they represent failed to resonate with most people in the church and violated the beliefs on which the church had been built.

The larger body of believers saw the four New Testament Gospels as the works that appropriately interpreted and preserved the teaching of Jesus and the apostolic teaching about Jesus. They read and used many other texts, but did not give them the authority accorded the Gospels that became part of the canon. The different perspectives found in these four tellings of the life of Jesus enrich the believer's understanding of him in ways that no single account could. So while having multiple accounts may create some kinds of problems (for example, historical differences), they also enhance the faith of believers by providing multiple ways to think about how God has been present in Christ and what God wants for the world.

▶ LET'S REVIEW ◀

In this chapter, we learned:

- How each of the canonical Gospels constructs the identity of Jesus in different ways
- How each Gospel intends to address the concerns and cultural understandings of different audiences
- How the images the Gospels use represent the differing theological emphases of each author
- How the multiple images of Jesus contribute to a richer understanding of the ways the church thought of him
- Mark—the earliest Gospel
  - —Jesus as God's Son who brings God's kingdom
  - —Must see the power and suffering of Jesus to understand him
- Matthew
  - —Jesus as Messiah
  - —Jesus as authoritative interpreter of God's law
  - —Fulfillment quotations
- Luke
  - —Jesus' mission to the poor and outcast
  - —Jesus as God's Son (with a nuance different from Mark)
- John
  - —Christ as preexistent Word of God
  - —Christ identified with God
  - —Jesus in control even in the passion

▶ KEY TERMS ◀

Beatitudes
Beloved Disciple
Benedictus
Elizabeth
Exorcism
Fulfillment quotations
Gentiles
Good Samaritan
Herod the Great
John the Baptist
Joseph
Kingdom of heaven
Lord's Prayer (Our Father)
Magi
Magnificat
Mary
Messianic Secret
Nativity narrative
Nicodemus
The passion
Pilate
Preexistence
Resurrection appearances
Sermon on the Mount
Son of God
Son of Man (of a human)
Transfiguration
The Twelve
The Word
Zechariah

▶ QUESTIONS FOR REVIEW ◀

12.1 Why do the four Gospels give different understandings of Jesus?
12.2 What does Mark mean when he has Jesus say that the kingdom of God is "near"?
12.3 How did a message of a coming kingdom sound in Roman-dominated Palestine?
12.4 Why do some scholars think Mark presents the twelve disciples as such failures?
12.5 Why are the genealogies of Matthew and Luke so different?
12.6 What are the main things Matthew wants readers to think about Jesus from reading the Sermon on the Mount?
12.7 What do Matthew's fulfillment quotations say about the way he reads the Hebrew Bible? Are there parallels among other groups within Judaism?
12.8 What does the Magnificat show about Luke's understanding of what the mission of Jesus is about?
12.9 Name some stories and sayings of Jesus that point to Luke's concern for the outcasts and the poor. How do these stories make these points?
12.10 Compare the ways Matthew and Luke talk about Jesus "fulfilling" Scripture.
12.11 What are some of the ways the Gospel of John has Jesus identify himself with God?
12.12 Compare the way Jesus teaches in John with the way he teaches in the Synoptics.
12.13 Discuss John's use of the expression "the Jews."

▸ FOR FURTHER READING ◂

Richard A. Burridge, *Four Gospels, One Jesus?* Grand Rapids: Eerdmans, 1994.

John T. Carroll, "Luke, Gospel of," in *New Interpreter's Dictionary of the Bible*, ed. Katharine D. Sakenfeld, 3:720–34. Nashville: Abingdon, 2008.

R. Alan Culpepper, *The Gospel and Letters of John*, Interpreting Biblical Texts. Nashville: Abingdon, 1998.

Joel B. Green, *The Gospel of Luke*, New International Commentary on the New Testament. Grand Rapids: Eerdmans, 1997.

———, *Methods for Luke*. Methods in Biblical Interpretation. Cambridge: Cambridge University Press, 2010.

Daniel J. Harrington, *What Are They Saying about Mark?* New York: Paulist, 2004.

Morna D. Hooker, *Beginnings: Keys That Open the Gospels*. New York: Morehouse Group, 1998.

———, *Endings: Invitations to Discipleship*. Peabody, Mass.: Hendrickson, 2003.

Philip Jenkins, "Hidden Gospels," Bible and Interpretation Website (No date but cites a 2001 book) http://www.bibleinterp.com/articles/hiddengospel.shtml

Donald H. Juel, *The Gospel of Mark*, Interpreting Biblical Texts. Nashville: Abingdon, 1999.

Frank J. Matera, *What Are They Saying about Mark?* New York: Paulist, 1987.

Pheme Perkins, *Introduction to the Synoptic Gospels*. Grand Rapids: Eerdmans, 2009.

Mark Allan Powell, *Methods for Matthew*. Methods in Biblical Interpretation. Cambridge: Cambridge University Press, 2009.

———, *What Are They Saying about Luke?* New York: Paulist, 1990.

Donald Senior, *The Gospel of Matthew*, Interpreting Biblical Texts. Nashville: Abingdon, 1997.

Gerard S. Sloyan, *What Are They Saying about John?* New York: Paulist, 1991.

F. Scott Spencer, *Salty Wives, Spirited Mothers, and Savvy Widows: Capable Women of Purpose and Persistence in Luke's Gospel*. Grand Rapids: Eerdmans, 2012.

Jay Williams, "Mark, The Gospel of Radical Transformation," Bible and Interpretation Website 2008 http://www.bibleinterp.com/articles/williams.shtml.

13 The Story Continues
The Acts of the Apostles

IN THIS CHAPTER, WE WILL LEARN ABOUT

- ▶ Luke's story of the church
  - ▷ Not a threat to the empire or a new religion
- ▶ The beginning of the church
  - ▷ First among Jews, then among Samaritans
  - ▷ The church faces opposition from its earliest days
  - ▷ Peter as apostle to the Jews
- ▶ Gentiles enter the church
  - ▷ The place of Gentiles in the church
  - ▷ Paul as apostle to the Gentiles
- ▶ Paul's arrest in Jerusalem and journey as a prisoner to Rome

The book of Acts tells the story of the church's beginning in Jerusalem and its spread throughout the ancient Mediterranean world until it reaches Rome. This book is a continuation of the Gospel of Luke; it even begins by saying, "In the first book, Theophilus, I wrote about all that Jesus did and taught. . . ." In important ways it continues the story of Jesus' life with God's people, even though Jesus' ministry is over. For Luke, even though Jesus is no longer present as he was before, Christ remains in the church's company spiritually.

▶ The Church's Beginning and Mission

Just as the Gospels tell their stories of Jesus' life to give their readers particular understandings of Jesus, so Luke tells his story of the church to lead readers to a particular understanding of the church and its message. That is, Acts is a theological account of the church's beginnings; Luke is more concerned to provide a correct understanding of the church than he is to get the historical details just right. Luke selects the stories he tells and tells them the way he does to shape his readers' ideas about the church and to show how God is present and active in the church.

Luke's stories about the church include a number of sermons and speeches by various characters. Of course, these are not tape recordings. As we saw with speeches and interchanges between Moses and God in Exodus and Numbers, the speeches of Acts are inserted for the benefit of the readers. Luke uses these speeches to express his views, to make more explicit what the narrative implies in the way it tells its stories. While no one would have remembered a whole sermon or speech, Luke could interview people who were present and so might recall what the theme was and even some main points. Luke then did what all historians of the first century did: he took that sketch and filled in what he thought the person could have said. As he did this, he filled the speech with the points he himself wanted the readers to hear.

MAP 13.1

The ascension. Luke begins the book of Acts by backing up a bit to retell the story of Jesus' ascension into heaven after the resurrection. In this account, Jesus continues to appear to his disciples for over a month (forty days) and at the end of that time tells the disciples to wait in Jerusalem for God's Spirit to come on them after he is gone. Finally, he commissions them to be witnesses to him throughout the world and then ascends in a cloud.

Pentecost

Acts has the remaining eleven from Jesus' inner circle select a replacement for Judas so that they can again represent the gathering of the whole people of God by paralleling the full number of the tribes of Israel (1:12-26). Then they wait for guidance about what they are to do. They do not have to wait long; the action begins during the **Feast of Pentecost**, about a week after Jesus' ascension. Pentecost is a Jewish feast that comes fifty days after Passover to celebrate the harvest and the giving of the law to Moses. It was a pilgrimage feast, so there were thousands of visitors in the city.

BOX 13.1

PILGRIMAGE FEASTS

There are three traditional Jewish pilgrimage feasts, religious events for which Jews went to Jerusalem, the site of the temple: Passover, Pentecost, and the Feast of Booths. These festivals have both seasonal meanings and connections to the story of the exodus. Passover celebrates the escape of the Israelites from Egyptian slavery, particularly the time when the firstborn of all the Egyptians died, but the firstborn of Israelites who performed the proper rituals were spared. Passover is also a spring New Year festival. Pentecost celebrates the giving of the law to Moses and is an autumn harvest festival. The Feast of Booths celebrates God's care of the Israelites while they were in the wilderness and is another harvest festival.

A spiritual experience. While the disciples of Jesus are gathered during this feast, the Spirit of God comes on them suddenly and in dramatic fashion (2:1-41). Luke says that it looks as though little flames appear above the head of each disciple and that they begin to speak in languages they had never studied, the languages of all those visitors to Jerusalem. The whole thing creates such a stir that it leads some people to think they are all just drunk. When **Peter** gets some order restored, he asserts that they are not drunk; rather, God's Spirit (the same Spirit that made prophets weird) was causing them to act like this. He then preaches the first Christian sermon and the church comes into existence when people accept his message and receive baptism with the promise of forgiveness and receiving the Spirit. Luke says that over three thousand people joined the church that day.

Peter's sermon. In this first sermon, Peter interprets the disciples' experience of the Spirit and the life, death, and resurrection of Jesus as the fulfillment of prophecy, particularly prophecy about God's intimate presence with God's people in the **last days** (that is, in the eschatological era). Peter says that the hopes of God's people are being fulfilled in Jesus and those who believe in him.

This sermon, then, identifies the church as the community in which the special presence of God resides; in fact, it comes to live in every believer. This coming of the Spirit, in turn, is a sign that a new time of God's presence in the world has begun. God is doing something new, living among God's people in more intimate ways than ever before—and all of this is mediated through the risen Christ.

The "last days." All the emphasis of Acts on the time of the church as the last days may seem odd. It may also have seemed odd to some who first read Acts because it was not written until near the end of the first century. That means that for seventy years people had been saying they were living in the "last days." That's a lot of last days! But this does not deter Luke—and neither would the subsequent two thousand years—because he sees the "last days" as an era marked by ways God lives among God's people more than he views it as a particular number of actual days. The central meaning of his talk of last days lies in his conviction that God has acted decisively in Jesus to begin to accomplish God's purposes for the world. That act of God in Christ is the beginning of an act, and an era of time, that will be completed only at the end of time.

FIGURE 13.1 **PENTECOST**

Drawing from a twelfth-century manuscript of the Latin Bible. The Day of Pentecost (a Jewish pilgrimage feast) is the day on which the church began. According to Acts 2, it was at that festival that the Holy Spirit came into the disciples and others in their company so that they were able to speak in languages they had never learned. Luke says the Spirit looked like a flame over the head of each person. Art Resource

BOX 13.2

THE LAST DAYS

In Acts 2:14-21, Peter is defending the activities of the group gathered on the day of Pentecost. He explains how it is that people of all languages can understand what is being said. He asserts that this event happens because God's Spirit has come on those who believe in Christ. How do you think his quotation of the prophet Joel helps him explain what is happening?

▶ The Growth of the Church and the Admission of Gentiles

The first half of Acts relates stories that tell of the church's phenomenal growth and the beginning of persecution in Jerusalem and the surrounding regions. Throughout this part of Acts, everyone in the church is Jewish and remains an observant Jew, as well as being a member of the church. Church members continue to observe the Sabbath and worship at the temple; some of their church meetings are even held in the temple. It seems they gave little thought to offering church membership to non-Jews. But that changes with the story of **Cornelius** (Acts 10).

Cornelius: a decisive change. Luke's account of the conversion of Cornelius is a turning point in the book, a linchpin in his story of the church. This story is so important that he gives three accounts of it: he tells the story, has Peter immediately tell it to others in Jerusalem, and then has Peter tell a short version of it a few chapters later. This episode carries so much weight because it authorizes the church's mission to Gentiles, a mission it had not previously envisioned, at least not clearly.

Peter's visions. At the start of this pivotal story, Peter has gone to Joppa, a seaport thirty-five miles from Jerusalem, to preach. While there, one afternoon he has the same vision three times (10:9-16). In his dream he sees a sheet that contains all sorts of animals Jews are not allowed to eat, and a voice from heaven tells him to kill and eat them. Peter, being an observant Jew, refuses, saying he had never eaten unclean food and was not about to start! Then the voice says, "What God has made clean, you must not call unclean." While Peter is trying to figure out what this means, some men come to the house he is visiting and tell him about their boss, a Roman centurion named Cornelius. Cornelius

BOX 13.3

WORSHIPING IN THE TEMPLE

When you read Acts 3:1 and 5:12-13, where do we find the apostles? What does this suggest about the relationship of the earliest church and the worship at the temple?

is an unusual Roman; he worships God (though probably not only God), gives generously to the poor, and may even have helped support the local synagogue. These men tell Peter that an angel appeared to Cornelius, instructing him to send someone to bring Peter who would tell him what God wanted him to do (10:17-23).

The Spirit descends on Cornelius. Peter is now confused about the meaning of two visions—his and Cornelius's—because he has no idea what to say to Cornelius. (Remember, all people in the church are Jews and everyone assumed that a person had to be Jewish to be in the church.) But Peter goes with them the next day (10:23-48). When they arrive at Cornelius's house, the centurion, who has gathered a crowd to hear Peter, comes out to meet them and to thank Peter for coming. Peter begins by saying that he should not be there, but has come in response to the visions. Apparently not knowing what else to do, he begins to tell them about Jesus and his role in judging the world and forgiving sins. As Peter is preaching, the Spirit comes on Cornelius and the others there just as it came on the people at Pentecost. Peter is shocked that God's Spirit could inhabit Gentiles, but takes it to mean that they can join the church without converting to Judaism. So he says essentially, "Well, if God takes them, I guess we should too."

Gentiles and Jews in the church. This is a radical step for the church because it means there are ways to live out one's faith other than being an observant Jew. The church would wrestle with the question of how Gentiles could be counted among God's people without converting fully to Judaism for many decades, even centuries. How was it possible for people to be pleasing to God if they did not do what the Bible commanded of God's people? We will see **Paul** grapple with this issue in some of his letters. For him, Gentiles must remain Gentiles (and Jews remain Jews) because requiring Gentiles to become Jews implies that God is only the God of Jews, rather than the God of the whole world. Remaining Gentiles means that they do not observe the law in the same ways Jews do.

The reaction. While Acts does not provide the same kind of explicit theological reasoning we find in Paul's letters (missives that were written in the midst of the controversy), Luke shapes his stories to explain the admission of Gentiles. After Peter baptizes Cornelius and the other Gentiles in Caesarea, he returns to Jerusalem, where news of his exploits has already arrived (11:1-18). The Jerusalem church is not happy that he baptized a Gentile without requiring him first to come into Judaism. Luke has Peter repeat the whole story about the visions and the coming of the Spirit. Once the people hear that God's Spirit came on the Gentiles before Peter baptized them, they accept their admission as the will of God. The crucial point is that bringing Gentiles into the church was an act of God. The way and the timing of their reception of the Spirit were proof that God wanted things to happen as they did. Luke makes the comparison with Pentecost to show that God has again acted in an unexpected way as a part of God's new presence in the last days.

Luke will mention the Cornelius story again in his account of a conference held in Jerusalem to decide whether Gentiles should convert to Judaism to be in the church (15:7-11). So the controversy did not end after their initial acceptance into the church. The reason for the renewed controversy will be evident when we get to that part of Luke's story.

Peter's Leadership

To this point in Acts, Luke has focused attention on Peter. Peter preaches the first sermon, is the first to heal someone, one of the first to be imprisoned for the faith, and a central figure in the Jerusalem church. But after the Cornelius episode he recedes from the scene. By the time Acts is written, Peter is known more specifically as the apostle to the Jews because both historically and in the Acts account he conducts his ministry primarily among Jews. This makes it particularly important that he is the apostle who admits Cornelius into the church. Peter, the leading figure among church members who are Jewish, not only approves of having Gentiles in the church who do not convert to Judaism, he is the person who baptizes the first Gentile. Telling the story in this way secures the place of Gentiles (as Gentiles) in the church.

FIGURE 13.2 **JESUS RESCUING PETER**

This manuscript illustration (by Daniel of Uranc, 1433) depicts the story of Peter asking Jesus to let him walk on water, just as Jesus was walking on water during a storm. At first, Peter is able to do it. But after he becomes frightened by the storm, Jesus must rescue him from drowning (Matt. 14:22-33). Art Resource

▶ Paul: Apostle to the Gentiles

The martyrdom of Stephen and the introduction of Paul (Saul). Once the door is open to a mission to Gentiles, the leading characters of Acts change. While Peter played a central part in nearly every episode in the first half of Acts, Paul becomes the central character in the last half. Acts introduced a man named **Saul** (Paul) in the story of the martyrdom of **Stephen**, one of the episodes—and a long one—in which Peter is not dominant. In this story, a deacon named Stephen preaches a long sermon that accuses the people at the temple and their ancestors of being unfaithful to God. The speech enrages some people of Jerusalem so much that they stone him for blasphemy (6:8—8:1). He is

BOX 13.4

THE MARTYRDOM OF STEPHEN

After Stephen has preached a sermon that accuses the worshipers at the temple of unfaithfulness, Acts 7:54—8:1 recounts his martyrdom. What echo of what Jesus says in his crucifixion do you hear from Stephen? What major character is introduced in this story? Why do you think he is introduced here?

the first person in Acts to be killed for the new faith and so is known as the first martyr of the church. Saul shows his approval of this stoning by holding the coats of the men who throw the rocks. A few episodes later, we hear that Saul is expanding his work of persecuting the church by going to Damascus (9:1-2).

Paul Turns to Christ

But on the way to Damascus, Acts says, Saul has an experience of the risen Christ that changed his life (9:3-22). Christ appears in a bright light and asks why Saul is persecuting him. Saul responds by asking who he is talking to. The voice responds that it is Jesus and that Saul should go on to Damascus, where someone would tell him what he needed to do. In Damascus Saul becomes a member of the church and, whether he is aware of it then or not, embarks on the path to becoming the apostle to the Gentiles. His name also changes to Paul, and from this point forward Luke continues referring to him as Paul. The rest of Acts chronicles Paul's mission to expand the church throughout Asia Minor (modern-day Turkey) and then southern Europe, until he eventually arrives in Rome, where only a fledgling community of Christians lived and where his energies remained focused on preaching to Gentiles.

Paul the Missionary

After remaining in the region of Damascus for a few years (perhaps three), Paul begins working with **Barnabas** as a missionary of the church in Antioch (ch. 13). They become so successful at starting churches in what is now southeast Turkey that it appears there are soon nearly as many Gentiles in the church as Jews (ch. 14). When there were only a few Gentiles in the church, they could be seen as a sign of God's concern for the world, and even an indication of the open-mindedness and generosity of the Jewish church members. After all, these Gentiles were granted access to the blessings of God

BOX 13.5

DUAL NAMES

Many Jews in the first century had a Jewish name and a Roman name. Examples of this practice in the New Testament include Silas, also known as Silvanus (the Latin name), who was a coworker with Paul; Joseph Barsabbas, also known as Justus, who was the unsuccessful candidate to take Judas's place among the Twelve (Acts 1:15-26); and a person mentioned in Colossians named Jesus, whose Latin name was Justus (4:11). This was probably also the case for Paul, which was his Roman name, while his Jewish name was Saul.

BOX 13.6

PERSONAL INFORMATION ABOUT PAUL

Paul tells us some things about himself in his letters, but many of the things commonly believed about Paul come only from Acts, not from Paul himself. Paul tells us that he was from the tribe of Benjamin and an observant Pharisee who persecuted the church (see Phil. 3:4-6). Acts adds that he was from Tarsus, was a Roman citizen, and that he studied with the famous rabbi Gamaliel. These data are less certain than what Paul says about himself because they come from a source written several years after his death.

that had been promised to and through Israel. But when the number of Gentiles in the church increased—they even constituted a majority in some churches—questions about identity arose. The church had to think about what sort of movement it was. Most had seen it as a movement within Judaism, but if its membership includes more Gentiles than law-observant Jews, it becomes nearly impossible to maintain this view.

The Jerusalem Conference and a Momentous Decision

The Antioch church's tremendous missionary success among Gentiles leads to the **Jerusalem Conference** (or council; ch. 15). Paul and Barnabas (the senior partner in Paul's first mission work) go to Jerusalem to discuss whether Gentiles had to convert to Judaism to be in the church. Paul and Barnabas had established predominantly Gentile churches in several places that did not require its Gentiles to begin observing the laws that made Jews so distinctive in the ancient world (e.g., Sabbath and kosher food regulations). Paul and Barnabas tell the leaders gathered in Jerusalem that they had seen God's Spirit come on Gentiles and remain with Gentiles who did not fully convert to Judaism. Then Peter, who here makes one of his only appearances in the second half of Acts, says that he was there when the Spirit came into Cornelius and so he knows it is God's will to admit them without full conversion to Judaism. This is the view that wins the day, and so the church as a whole accepts the idea that Gentiles should remain Gentiles, even as they have become part of the people of God.

BOX 13.7

PHARISEES

Pharisees were among the members of the Jerusalem church. When the Pharisees appear in the Gospels, they are usually presented as people opposed to Jesus and his understanding of how to practice the faith. But that stereotypical characterization did not hold true for all Pharisees. Some were even open to the message that the church proclaimed about Jesus. We see this from the account of the Jerusalem conference in Acts 15. Luke notes, without seeming to think it calls for an explanation, that some members of the church who were Pharisees were present for that meeting.

FIGURE 13.3 **THE AREOPAGUS, SEEN FROM THE ACROPOLIS**

This is the location that has traditionally been identified as the place where Epicurean and Stoic philosophers asked Paul to address them while in Athens (Acts 17:22-33). By the first century, however, the council composed of those philosophers met in the market below this hill. Art Resource

Gentiles in the church. One of the main purposes of Acts is to support the belief that Gentiles are fully members of the church without fully converting to Judaism. They must adopt the ethics of Judaism, worship only the God of Judaism, and read its Scriptures as authoritative. But they do not become **proselytes** of Judaism (by receiving circumcision and keeping the Sabbath, the food laws, and some other parts of the law that make Jews distinctive) in order to be numbered among the people of God. They join Jewish members of the church in communities that ground their primary religious identity in their faith in Christ.

Church and Empire

In Acts Luke is also anxious to help readers defend themselves against the charge that the church is an enemy of the Roman Empire. The church made claims about Jesus that sounded threatening to the power structures of the day; among other things, they said Jesus was the king and Lord who was bringing a kingdom into the world. This sounds like a revolution—and Jesus

BOX 13.8

THE JERUSALEM CONFERENCE

As Acts describes the beginning of this conference in 15:1-5, what does the author tell us the central question is? What larger question does that issue stand for? Who are the people who raise this issue? Are you surprised to find them in the church?

had been executed as an insurrectionist. Not only this, they also withdrew from civic life. As part of their commitment to worship only God, Christians were absent from ceremonies that asked the gods to bless their city—which would have included nearly all civic occasions. So they seemed to lack patriotism. Even more, they held strange and unauthorized meetings where they talked about this new king and they began to behave differently; some of these groups even had women as their leaders. They seemed quite subversive, or at least suspicious.

Nero and persecution. As early as the year 62, **Nero** singled out the church for persecution by blaming its members for the fire that devastated the capital city. Though few probably thought

FIGURE 13.4 **THE PARTHENON ON THE ACROPOLIS, ATHENS**

The Parthenon was a temple to the goddess Athena, built in the fifth century B.C.E. Marshall Johnson

Christians were actually responsible for the fire, they were a suspect group. This active, government-sponsored persecution was rare in the first several decades of the church's existence. On the other hand, they did suffer sometimes severe economic and social disadvantages. For example, their commitment to worshiping one God meant that they excluded themselves from many settings in which business transactions were conducted because many trade groups met in buildings associated with temples of various gods and ate food that had been dedicated to the god of the temple as part of their meeting. For small artisans and merchants, staying away from these meetings could well mean the difference between having enough to eat and sending your children to bed hungry.

BOX 13.9

TWO ACCOUNTS OF THE JERUSALEM CONFERENCE

Most scholars are convinced that the Apostolic Council depicted in Acts 15 is the same visit of Paul to Jerusalem described in Galatians 2:1-10. Questions arise about this because of the rather different ways the conference is described in the two sources. For example, Paul emphasizes his independence in Galatians, while the account in Acts seems to assume authority for the Jerusalem apostles. The differences in these tellings suggest that both Acts and Paul tell their story the way they do so that readers will understand the event in a particular way.

BOX 13.10

PAUL'S VERDICT—ALMOST

Acts recounts the conclusion of Paul's trial at Caesarea in 26:30-32. When you read that passage and the verdict Agrippa nearly pronounces, what important theme in Luke does it support?

By the time Luke was being written, Nero had instigated his persecution of the church in Rome. Even though few officials outside Rome launched a campaign to hunt down and arrest church members, the emperor's identification of them as a subversive group put them on the defensive. Thus the combination of Nero's persecution, the politically loaded language they used (for example, kingdom of God), and their separation from the civic life of their city and adoption of strange and countercultural behaviors all made them appear to be a dangerous and subversive group.

Paul Reaches Rome

To counter suspicions about the church, Luke has several characters go on trial before Roman judges and magistrates. In every case the Roman official finds the person not guilty. Believers are found guilty of offenses by various tribunals (for example, local courts), but never by Roman judges. Perhaps Acts ends as it does to keep this record intact. In the final part of Acts, Paul has been arrested and sent to Rome for trial. Acts concludes by saying he stayed there under arrest for two years. So readers never get to hear how his trial turned out. Most scholars think he was found guilty and executed, events Luke does

MAP 13.2

BOX 13.11

LUKE'S TENDENCIES

Scholars have long noted that Luke has certain tendencies in his presentation of stories about the church in Acts. For instance, he smooths over arguments so that life within the church looks more harmonious than other sources (such as Paul's Letters) suggest it was. An important tendency is the book's presentation of the Roman officials. While they are not necessarily sympathetic, they never find church members guilty of crimes. Believers may be convicted by Jewish or other local officials, but never by Romans. This is one of the strategies Luke uses to show that the church is not a threat to the empire.

not want to record. Thus he ends the story of the church with Paul preaching in Rome, even though he is under house arrest. The gospel has reached the capital of the world and is finding success. What a good place to end.

Luke thus leaves his readers on a high note: the gospel has gotten to Rome and is still on the move. Both the author and the audience know that the end of the book is not the end of the story; Luke begins the book by telling the readers he is continuing the story begun with the coming of Jesus and ends in the middle of the story of Paul's ministry. He seems to want readers to see themselves as the continuation of the story of Jesus' presence made known through the church.

▶ Conclusion

Luke's story of the beginning and initial years of the church is as thoroughly a theological account as was his story of Jesus' life. He begins by interpreting the beginning of the church as an eschatological event that changes the way God is present among God's people. He sees God directing the spread of the church to the first Gentiles and then throughout the Mediterranean world. While telling his story of the spread of the church, Luke also validates the apostleship of Paul by relating narratives that parallel events in his account of Peter's work as an apostle and by giving multiple accounts of Paul's Damascus road experience, interpreted as a call to be the apostle to the Gentiles. Luke's theological account also gives readers a way to argue that this new movement, the church, does not represent a direct threat to the empire. Thus Luke provides his readers with an interpretation of the church that supports their faith and gives readers a way to respond to outside criticism that could lead to more organized opposition.

FIGURE 13.5 **PAUL IN PRISON**

Rembrandt here portrays Paul under house arrest, as Acts says he remained for two years in Rome (Acts 28:30-31). Art Resource

▶ LET'S REVIEW ◀

In this chapter, we have seen that the book of Acts

- Offers a theological interpretation of the beginning and initial spread of the church
  - Pentecost
  - Time of the church as the eschatological time
  - Peter as the central character because he is the Apostle to the Jews
  - Admission of Gentiles
  - Paul and the church reach Rome
- Provides ways believers could argue that the church is not a danger to the empire
- Explains the admission of Gentiles into the church as full members without entering the Mosaic covenant
  - Place of Paul
  - The Jerusalem Conference
- Depicts Paul's arrest in Jerusalem and trip as a prisoner to Rome

▶ KEY TERMS ◀

Barnabas
Cornelius
Jerusalem Conference
"Last days"
Nero
Paul
Pentecost
Peter
Proselyte
Saul
Stephen

▶ QUESTIONS FOR REVIEW ◀

13.1 How does Luke understand the events on the day of Pentecost that mark the beginning of the church?

13.2 Why is the story about Cornelius so important in Acts? How do various elements of the way it is told support the point it wants to make?

13.3 Why does Luke in Acts have believers in Christ go on trial before so many Roman judges?

13.4 What does it mean to Luke to say that the church is an institution of the "last days"? Why is this important to him?

13.5 Why does Luke, writing near the end of the first century, give so much attention to validating the spread of the church to Gentiles?

13.6 Why is it important for Luke to have Paul reach Rome and why does Luke stop the story before we know the outcome of Paul's trial? What does this tell us about Luke's purposes in writing Acts and about the literary and historical nature of Acts?

▶ FOR FURTHER READING ◀

Beverly Roberts Gaventa, "Acts of the Apostles," in *New Interpreter's Dictionary of the Bible*, ed. Katharine D. Sakenfeld, 1:33–47. Nashville: Abingdon, 2006.

———, *The Acts of the Apostles*, Abingdon New Testament Commentary. Nashville: Abingdon, 2003.

Jacob Jervell, *Luke and the People of God: A New Look at Luke–Acts*. Minneapolis: Augsburg, 1972.

Mark Allan Powell, *What Are They Saying about Acts?* New York: Paulist, 1991.

Earl Richard, ed., *New Views on Luke–Acts*. Collegeville, Minn.: Liturgical, 1990.

F. Scott Spenser, *Journeying through Acts: A Literary-Cultural Reading*. Peabody, Mass.: Hendrickson, 2004.

Joseph B. Tyson, "When and Why Was the Acts of the Apostles Written?" Bible and Interpretation Website 2011. http://www.bibleinterp.com/opeds/actapo358006.shtml

14 The Pauline Letters
Apostolic Advice to Early Churches

IN THIS CHAPTER WE WILL LEARN ABOUT CENTRAL THEMES IN PAUL'S LETTERS:

- 1 Thessalonians
  - The suffering of Christians and the second coming
- 1 Corinthians
  - Spirituality, ethics, worship, and the resurrection
- 2 Corinthians
  - Apostleship and leadership in the church
- Galatians
  - Gentiles as full members of the people of God
- Philippians
  - Leadership conflicts and claims about Christ's exaltation
- Philemon
  - Advice to the owner of a returning slave
- Romans
  - Travel plans and relations between Jews and Gentiles

After the Gospels and Acts, most of the rest of the New Testament is composed of **letters**. Letters are different from other kinds of writings in the Bible. Letters usually address a specific situation. Unless they are literary epistles or some form of public letter (like our letters to the editor or blogs), letters speak to a particular person or group of people who are in specific circumstances. The many letters authored by Paul are sensitive, then, to the communities he visited and to their distinctive situations. We will study these letters and the cities to which Paul wrote to while extending the influence of the early church.

▶ Letters: A Context-Specific Genre

One half of a conversation. We can think about letters as one half of a conversation. If you have ever read someone else's mail (perhaps a roommate) or had to hear half a conversation of someone on a phone, you know how hard it can be to make sense of one side of a discussion. When you only hear responses to questions or references to people you do not know, you cannot fully understand what the people are talking about.

When we read a New Testament letter, we are reading someone else's mail. The writer sent the message to a specific group of people trying to help them figure out how to live and what to believe as Christians. If it is hard to understand a letter written recently or one side of a conversation, it is much more difficult to comprehend the meaning of a letter written two thousand years ago. We often miss allusions to things they all knew about, we do not know the people they mention, we do not know much about the city they lived in, and we are not certain about what problems they faced or what questions they had. So we have to try to discover what issues these letters address. After all, the writers did not explain the problems they address because the recipients already knew about them. Since writers do not explain what the problem is, later readers have to reconstruct the problem from the answer. Of course, the same answer might be the response to several questions, and how we understand the question influences how we understand the answer. So we must read between the lines carefully.

FIGURE 14.1 **WEALTHY FIRST-CENTURY WOMAN**

When the author of 1 Timothy tells women not to braid their hair (2:9), it is probably because braided hair was a sign of wealth and he thought it inappropriate for people to exhibit their wealth when the church gathered for worship. Art Resource

Adapted to the Circumstances

In addition to those issues, the personalized nature of letters allows their writers to give advice that is only meant for the specific recipients of that letter. Sometimes the instructions we give one person are right, but would be wrong for another person. For example, when my daughter was three years old I told her never to cross a busy street without holding my hand. When she was twelve and standing at the same corner, I told her to wait for the "Walk" signal before crossing. When she was yet older, I simply said, "Be careful." I gave her seemingly contradictory advice, but it was the right thing to tell her each time. What had changed was the circumstances; she had changed and so different advice was appropriate.

We see the same kind of things in New Testament letters. In Paul's letters he gave each community the advice he thought they needed at that moment in their lives, and sometimes what he told one community contradicts what he told another. When Paul wrote the Corinthians, he told them that they could not contribute financially to support his ministry, saying it would violate his call to ministry to take their money. But when he wrote the Philippians, he thanked them for all the times they had sent him money. The reason Paul let one church give him money and not the other was because of what it meant to each church to support him. The Corinthians apparently thought it would mean that Paul would have to support the ideas of their leaders (no matter how outrageous), while the Philippians did not attach that idea to their gift. So while Paul gave contradictory instructions to these churches, they do not involve him in a contradiction of ideas (though that is not out of the question). His comments addressed the specific people to whom he wrote, not all people of all times.

How to read ancient letters. The very specific nature of letters generally, and the New Testament letters in particular, tells us something important about how to read them. People today cannot simply pick up these letters and apply their instructions directly to themselves, because we do not face the same circumstances these letters address. The instructions these letters contain are conditioned by general social and political situations, cultural norms, and specific problems. None of these are precisely the same for present-day readers. For example, one letter, 1 Timothy, instructs women not to braid their hair. That makes no sense to us, but in the first century wealthy women had elaborate hair styles that often involved a lot of braiding. Women of lesser means could not devote the time needed to have that style; nor could they afford the expense of hiring (or owning) someone to style their hair in that way. So that command is probably intended to instruct the wealthy not to distinguish themselves from other church members by flaunting their wealth. If the author of 1 Timothy were writing to churches today, he would have nothing to say about braiding, but he might give some instructions about how to dress if differences in wealth were causing problems in a church.

Culture-specific settings. All the instructions in the New Testament letters are conditioned by their cultural and community-specific settings. To understand what these letters are about we must always look at *why* a writer gives the instructions readers find in a letter, not just at the instructions themselves. Given that the letters address such specific times and places, Christians cannot assume that those instructions can be applied directly to the twenty-first century. Believers can, however, listen for guidance by seeing how these writers tell their readers to embody their beliefs about God and Christ in the ways they conduct their lives.

Letters as Pastoral Theology

The authors of these letters often give explicit reasons for the advice they offer. These authors frequently ground their instructions in who God is, how they believe God has acted in Christ, or how the Spirit is present in their lives. They advocate some ways to understand Christ, and reject others. They tell churches how the Spirit shows itself in their lives, and tell them what it does not do. The letters give their readers ways to understand the circumstances of their lives by interpreting them in light of what they believe about God and the world. These letters show us how the early Christians made sense of their beliefs. They are very much works of practical theology, examples of how their authors applied Christian understandings to the specifics of life. They often had the same kinds of questions Christians have today, even if those issues arose in a different form.

> *BOX 14.1*
>
> **CRITICAL INTRODUCTION REMINDER**
>
> Our survey of the Pauline letters will include the elements of a critical introduction for each letter. See Box 4.1 (page 50) for the things included in such an introduction.

For congregational reading. Paul wrote more letters in the New Testament than any other author. His letters were usually substitutes for a personal visit. When he knew there was a problem or thought a church needed some encouragement, he would try to visit them. But when that was not feasible, he wrote them a letter. All of his letters were intended to be read in front of the whole church—even those that seem to be addressed to an individual (notice how many people are mentioned in the greeting of Philemon, a letter written primarily to address a single person). So they are intended for a group of people, not just a single person. Still, they are personal, revealing his hopes and fears, as well as aids to help the recipients understand their lives as Christians.

Paul's authority. The semipublic nature of the letters suggests that Paul expects his churches to follow his teaching and instruction. He is the founder of the churches he addresses (except for Romans) and he understands himself to be an apostle, and so an authoritative figure in the church. Still, he expects his churches to think for themselves, not just do what they are told. So he has to convince them that his instructions and teachings are correct. Only occasionally does he rely on his commission as an apostle to tell them they must obey his instructions—and when he does resort to this tactic, it does not seem to work.

For each letter of the New Testament, we will discuss who wrote it, when it was written, and what problems or issues it addressed. We

FIGURE 14.2 **RECONSTRUCTED STOA (PORCH) OF ATTALOS, ATHENS**
This covered sidewalk included a continuous line of shops (see the wall and doors on the right in the photograph). Wikimedia Commons

can understand what we read in these documents only when we have some clarity about these matters.

▶ 1 Thessalonians

The Context

The earliest New Testament letter is probably 1 Thessalonians. It was written around the year 51 to a church in a city in northern Greece, one of the first places Paul preached in Europe. Paul's custom was to preach for a few months (perhaps as long as a year and a half) in a city and then move to a new city to start new churches. Such a quick departure meant that he left behind churches that had only been in existence for a short time. This could be problematic under any circumstances, but at that time it was particularly difficult because Paul was often the first believer in Christ to visit these cities.

The people in these cities had no idea what it meant to be in the church. As you might guess, a lot of questions and problems arose after Paul left town. Sometimes one of Paul's associates would stay behind for a while to help them, or some person from another city who was in the church would come to live there and so help them think about how to live out their new faith. But these fledgling churches still needed to hear from their founder.

Several months had passed since Paul had left Thessalonica, and he had made his way to Corinth in central Greece (Acts 18:1-5). When he got worried about that little band of believers in Thessalonica, he sent Timothy, a junior partner, to check on them. Timothy returned with good news and a couple of important questions from them. Paul then wrote 1 Thessalonians in response to the report from Timothy. While expressing his gratitude for their continuing faith and the way they had conducted themselves in his absence, Paul addressed two issues: (1) how could they make sense of being persecuted because of their membership in the

FIGURE 14.3 **THE ARCH OF GALERIUS, THESSALONIKI**

Galerius, emperor from 305 to 311, is known as the emperor who carried out one of the last Roman persecutions of Christians. Thessaloniki is the modern city; Thessalonica is the ancient one. *Cities of Paul*

church, and (2) what happens to church members when they die.

The Persecution and Suffering of the Believers

It was difficult for early Christians to understand why being in the church would lead to **persecution**. They joined the church because they were convinced that they should worship only the one God of Israel, the God who was God of the whole world. To do this, they had to cut themselves off from much of their old life: they could no longer participate in their family's worship gatherings or civic events (which always involved worship of a god), even business associations often involved worship of various gods. When they stopped worshiping the gods of the city, their neighbors got suspicious because the Christians seemed not to care about the well-being of the city if they were not willing to worship the god that protected it. Some people stopped doing business with believers, others treated them as the neighborhood pariahs. Overall, much of life got more difficult when a person joined the church.

Why is this happening? They were asking: Why does my conversion to worshiping only the most powerful God lead to having a worse life? Do these difficulties mean it was a mistake to abandon the other gods? Has God abandoned us? Are we doing something God is punishing us for? The church in Thessalonica needed an interpretation that made sense of the disadvantage and persecution they faced. At the general level, this is the question of why bad things happen to good people. This query is more pointed, though, because these good people are suffering precisely because they are doing right.

BOX 14.2

IT IS THE SAME EVERYWHERE

What kinds of parallels does Paul draw in 1 Thessalonians between the experience of the church in Thessalonica and that of Judea? Why do you think Paul points out this similarity?

Evidence of faithfulness. Paul tells the Thessalonians that their persecution is not a sign that God has abandoned them or that they were doing something wrong. Instead, he asserts that this has always been the pattern of life for the people of God. It was like that for the prophets of Israel, for Jesus, for the church in Judea, and for Paul. So in a sense their persecution is a sign that they are doing what God wants, and that they have maintained their faith indicates that God *is* with them. This explanation, of course, needs an explanation!

The powers that be. This interpretation of why the faithful face troubles builds on a broader understanding of the state of the world. Paul, along with all New Testament writers, assumes that the good world that God made has been corrupted by the forces of evil. Indeed, evil has taken control of the world and refuses to let it go. Furthermore, human beings cannot wrest it from those evil powers, and so are in many ways at their mercy. This may seem too dramatic and mythical for twenty-first-century people who like to think of themselves as the masters of their own fate, but it holds an important truth about our experience of the world.

Paul recognized and experienced the oppressive nature of the structures of power in his day. But he was convinced that the evil that dominates the world would not have the last word; rather, at some point God would intervene to establish justice. But this requires a dramatic reorientation of the cosmos, even the end of the world as we know it. Paul argues throughout his letters that God would act to vindicate the righteous, though they must endure, patiently awaiting that vindication until the end.

Conflicting values. Since evil dominates the world, God's faithful people should expect to suffer because the values they live by come into conflict with the way the world works. Their alternative manner of life and belief at least implicitly speaks a word of judgment against those who support the systems that control economic, social, and political life. But in the midst of their suffering they have assurance that they are on the right side. The early church saw the resurrection of Christ as the guarantee of God's vindication of the righteous. The death of Christ seemed to show the power of the forces of evil, but God's raising of Christ demonstrates that God can and will defeat evil. Paul believes that since God has raised Jesus, the suffering church members can be certain that God can and will vindicate them.

The example of Jesus. This understanding of the state of the world undergirds the early

BOX 14.3

THE POWERS TODAY

We know there are forces (though we do not personify them as often as first-century people did) that we cannot escape, though we do not like to think about it in these terms. All of us are implicated in economic, political, and social systems that abuse the less fortunate to benefit the privileged. Every time we buy a pair of shoes or groceries, we get them for the price we do because someone worked at wages most of us would consider unfair if it were offered to us.

Even if we are careful to buy fair-trade products we do not escape, because we have to admit that most of what we buy is not produced under those conditions. And even if we could escape direct purchases that involve unfair labor at some point in their production, we would have investments in retirement accounts that have fewer scruples because their goal is to make money. Should we decide to divest and make all small business loans to struggling entrepreneurs in developing nations, we would still have to pay our taxes, and some of that money goes to buy military equipment that imposes the interests of our nation over others (and, of course, buys non-fair-trade products).

There is no escape from this predicament because this is the way in which the world is structured.

church's theology because it provides a primary way to understand the death of Jesus. Throughout the New Testament the resurrection of Christ is seen as the sign that God was with Jesus and that the ministry of Jesus revealed the will of God. Jesus' rejection and death also gave the church its way to interpret its own suffering—believers are following in the footsteps of Jesus and receiving the same kind of treatment he received. By remaining faithful as he did, then, they also expect God to validate their lives by raising them to life with Christ.

Suffering is to be expected in this world. With this worldview as his starting point, we can understand why Paul is not shy about telling the Thessalonians that they should expect to suffer as Christians (2:14-15; 3:4). The forces of evil want to get these people back from God and keep them in their clutches. But these people have joined the other side by joining the church; they have joined the counterinsurgents who represent and work for the will of God in the world. As they labor to build an alternative community, the forces of evil resist them in many ways, some subtle but others explicit. Paul says believers can be willing to suffer for their faith because they know that God will more than make up for the difficulties they endure by giving them life when God acts to reclaim the cosmos.

Death and Resurrection

This understanding of the world and the suffering Christians must endure, however, also helped create the second problem that 1 Thessalonians addresses. Christians at Thessalonica were worried about the fate of believers who died before the end had come. They thought the world would end and Christ would return to reward the faithful before any of them had died. But now some had died, perhaps even some who had suffered for their faith.

Doubts. Many people in the ancient world thought that death was the end of all existence; that is, they did not believe in an afterlife (4:13—5:11). Even though there were stories about Hades and the underworld, many rejected belief in any such postmortem existence. The Christians in Thessalonica seem to be among those who doubted that there was life after death. Their understanding of Paul's preaching had been that Christ would return to vindicate their faith and reward their endurance before anyone in their church died. Given the combination of doubts about an afterlife and their suffering for the faith, they are worried about the fate of those who had died; had they endured problems for nothing? Had they accepted adverse treatment only to die with no response from God?

Death and the end of the age. While these seem like odd questions to us, we must remember that these people were among the earliest to believe in Christ and that Paul had only been with them a short time. In addition, Paul probably thought the end was coming soon. Given his experience of the world, particularly suffering persecution, he may have thought things had gotten so bad that God could not wait much longer to rescue the world. Besides, the beginning of this final act of God had already taken place: Christ had been raised. As the early church understood the resurrection, it was the beginning of the last days, the last period of history. As the decades passed they had to start

BOX 14.4

HADES

In Greek mythology Hades was the abode of the dead. Those in earlier times thought it was a gloomy place where the sun did not shine and where the remnant of the person had no consciousness and no mind. By the first century, some thought there might be some distinction between what happens to the good and what happens to the evil.

asking how long the "last days" would last! They have certainly lasted longer than any of them thought. So Paul's preaching included the warning that the last days were here, that this was the moment to turn to God. It apparently did not include discussion of what happens to believers who die before the end comes.

Believers who die before the end comes. Now Paul must clarify the situation for the Thessalonians. He asserts that those who die will miss none of the blessings of God. Imagining the end as a single day, Paul says that the dead are the first ones to join Christ in the new coming era of God's reign (4:16). He says the dead will participate fully in the coming of Christ (which scholars often refer to as the **parousia**, the Greek word that means "coming") and the resurrection, so their suffering will be vindicated. As he assures his readers about the certainty of God's act to reclaim the world, he also tells them that the timing is completely uncertain (4:2-3). They can know beyond doubt that God will act because God raised Christ, but they cannot know when it will happen. In fact, it will happen when they least expect it, so they must always be ready for it. While many have tried to predict when it will be, Paul says that is inscrutable—and ultimately unimportant. The more significant thing to know is that God does not allow injustice and evil to have the last word; rather, God will establish justice and love as the ultimate truth of existence. This is really the point of all talk about the end times in the Bible.

We have spent a great deal of time talking about a relatively small letter because it brings us our first look at many issues and presuppositions of other New Testament letters. We will not have the luxury to linger over other letters as we have over 1 Thessalonians. But with the background we have gained here the issues and questions of some of the others will be easier to grasp.

▶ 1 Corinthians

The Context

Not too many months after Paul wrote 1 Thessalonians, he left Corinth and set up his mission headquarters in Ephesus, an important coastal city in Asia Minor. From there he sent people to

BOX 14.5

HOPE AFTER DEATH?

Paul begins to addresses the concerns of the Thessalonians about fellow-believers who have died in 1 Thessalonians 4:13-14. What assurance does he give them that there is existence after death? Does that assurance work? Why or why not?

visit the churches he had established in Greece, and sometimes he traveled back there himself to encourage the people he had left behind. It was also from Ephesus that he wrote some of his letters, including 1 Corinthians (16:5-8). This is not the first letter (5:9 mentions an earlier one) that he had written to them, but it is the first letter to them that we possess. First Corinthians was written in about 53–54 in response to a letter some in the church wrote to Paul and a report brought to him from some members of the Corinthian church (probably those who delivered the letter). They tell him of a variety of problems and questions that have arisen since he had left.

Spirituality: A Central Issue

Perhaps the central issue that 1 Corinthians addresses is how to understand spirituality. Most members of the Corinthian church had been pagans until they came into the church, so their understanding of spirituality had been formed in that environment and their expectations about what it meant to have an experience of a god was shaped by that culture. In that

FIGURE 14.4 **ANCIENT CORINTH, RUINS ALONG A MAIN ROAD**

The city extended all the way to Acrocorinth (in the background), which served as a part of the city walls. Marshall Johnson

FIGURE 14.5 **GALLIO INSCRIPTION, DELPHI**

This inscription gives the date of Gallio's term as pronconsul in Corinth. Acts says that Paul was brought before Gallio on his first trip to Corinth as a missionary. The connection of this date with Paul's visit to Corinth supplies us with the clearest reference point for dating events in the life of Paul. Marshall Johnson

setting, experiences of a god, or the spirit of a god, were not only personal but also individualistic; the experience benefited only the person who had the encounter. Furthermore, such experiences empowered people to live powerful and successful lives. Some of these experiences were also thought to improve one's chance for an afterlife.

Rivalry and gifts of the Spirit. The Corinthians used this understanding of encounters with a god and the view of spirituality it assumes to develop their understandings of leadership and community relations. They argued that their church's leaders should be impressive people who were able to assert their will over others. With their view of spirituality, their gatherings for worship became contests over who had the best and most evidence of the Spirit of God. They believed that the Spirit gave them various abilities: it gave some the ability to impose their arguments and wills on others, it gave some new hymns of praise, and it gave some the power to speak in tongues. In this setting, **speaking in tongues** was an ecstatic experience in which they said the Spirit took control of them and they uttered things that came from the Spirit. They did not know what it meant, only that it came from God—only someone with the gift of interpretation could tell people what had been said in a tongue. Various members were using these abilities to demonstrate to others in the church just how spiritual they were.

The proper use of spiritual gifts. Paul rejects this way of using gifts that come from God; he redefines spirituality and what it means to have God's Spirit by giving it a communal focus. He argues that God's Spirit shows itself in a person's willingness to serve others and to use his or her gift(s) to enrich the life of the church, rather than to make himself or herself look important. He spends the first quarter of the letter trying to help them think about what leaders should be like, turning them away from the idea that the most impressive people are the best leaders. Because they are having a difficult time thinking about how to use these gifts from God, Paul gives them rules about how many people could speak in tongues at a worship service and how many could exercise other gifts, and under what conditions.

BOX 14.6

THE WORD OF THE CROSS

In 1 Corinthians 1–4 Paul is trying to redefine spirituality. He does so by calling his message the "word of the cross." This phrase makes the attitude of Jesus that led him to accept death as the pattern for all conduct within the church. He knows this is countercultural. When you read 1 Corinthians 1:18-26, do you see ways that Paul is acknowledging that what he is asking for contradicts what makes good sense in the rest of the world? How has this pattern already shaped their community?

The example of Jesus. For Paul, spirituality shows itself when people conform their lives to the example set by Jesus. More specifically, he says that the cross and resurrection of Jesus are the pattern for Christian spirituality because in submitting to the cross Jesus acted for the good of others rather than doing what was better for himself. This self-giving and subordinating one's own good for the good of the group was shown to be true spirituality by the resurrection. Paul was aware that having spiritual experiences is personally fulfilling and uplifting—he even tells of his own experiences that he says were very meaningful. But he argues that self-fulfillment or self-realization is not at the core of spirituality; rather, he identifies willingness to do what is best for others as the true measure of spirituality. However amazing the experiences or abilities are that people get from the Spirit, people are not spiritual unless they use those gifts to serve others.

Spirituality and morality. The Corinthians also thought that having God's Spirit meant that they could make their own decisions about morality. Paul agrees that the Spirit helps believers think about ethical matters, but he sets some limits because the Corinthians' behavior exemplified how hard it is to distinguish between what I want and what the Spirit tells me. This problem surfaces over matters of sexual ethics (ch. 5). Some at Corinth decided that the

BOX 14.7

GLOSSOLALIA

The technical term for "speaking in tongues" is *glossolalia*. Most understand this phenomenon as an ecstatic experience in which the speaker feels controlled by a power outside oneself that leads one to utter things one does not understand. This experience is found in many religions throughout the world, in ancient times and now. Christians who claim this experience say that it comes to them through the Holy Spirit. The church at Corinth had many people who claimed this experience, and Paul's instructions to them assume that they do not understand what they are saying. In fact, no one does unless the Spirit gives a person the power to interpret them. Luke perhaps sees this gift operating differently on the day of Pentecost. In that story, people from different places hear the message spoken in their native languages. This view of what happens with glossolalia, however, is unusual.

Spirit led them to believe that Christians could employ the services of prostitutes (6:15-16); others bragged that a member of their church was having an affair with his stepmother. They seemed to think that if they possessed God's Spirit their physical conduct was of no consequence. Paul rejects this behavior, telling them that God's Spirit could not guide them to these decisions because these expressions of spirituality violated the faithfulness and holiness of God.

Sexual ethics. These instructions do not suggest that Paul thinks bodily existence is detrimental to spirituality or that sex is bad—just the opposite. Paul insists that how people live is important because God is interested in the whole person, not just a soul or inner self but all the elements that make a person human. Paul's discussion of sex includes his assertion that sex within marriage is a gift from God (ch. 7). Although he thinks his life as a celibate is better for him and some others because he saw difficult times coming for the church and because it freed him to serve God less encumbered, he sees married life as God's will for most people.

Observing the Lord's Supper

The Corinthians also needed instructions about how to worship, including how to hold the ritual of the **Lord's Supper** (11:17-34). Paul writes in a time before different churches developed varying ways to understand and celebrate **Communion** or the **Eucharist**. When the Corinthians got together in one another's homes, they had a meal together that remembered and celebrated Christ's death and resurrection—the central events that they believed enabled their relationship with God. It seems to have included an entire meal in this early time because Paul says some people are full while others are hungry, and some are even getting drunk. The Lord's Supper (as Paul calls it) was supposed to be an occasion that reminded all members of their common commitments and helped them live together as a community of equals. But things had gone awry.

The social context. To understand the problem with the Lord's Supper, we need to think about what kinds of people were in the early church. The Pauline churches drew members from most parts of the economic spectrum found in a Hellenistic city. There were some wealthy people who owned large estates and were accustomed to deference from others, and there was a segment of the fairly well-off merchant class who had a relatively comfortable and stable life. But most of the members of Paul's churches came from among the poor and the slave populations of the city. This wide range of classes seldom came together for social or religious purposes, and each thought that the way the other classes approached worship was wrong. Think of the different expectations for worship that various segments of the population in America have now (just compare an Episcopal mass with a Pentecostal service). Such differences were probably even more dramatic in the first century; slaves (who were often slaves because they were captured in a war and so they were foreigners) and their masters usually had rather different religious practices, even though there was overlap. Not only did Paul's churches have people from these different classes with their different expectations, he expected everyone to be treated as an equal. The lowliest person in the church could become its leader; soon slaves would be leaders

FIGURE 14.6 **THE LAST SUPPER**
This is Leonardo Da Vinci's representation (1498) of the last meal Jesus shared with his disciples before his arrest and crucifixion. Wikimedia Commons

in some churches and women were already leaders in Paul's time.

The Lord's Supper and mutuality. The combination of so many social classes with the expectation that all were to be one created a number of difficulties for the early church, as we can see from 1 Corinthians. The Lord's Supper was supposed to be an occasion that reminded the people of what they shared and why they were all one, even as it helped create that unity by having all share in a common meal. But this was not happening at Corinth because the wealthy were beginning the meal before all the poor arrived, and by the time the poor got there the good food was gone. So they were making distinctions according to social class. This was a common practice at dinner parties in the culture, so the rich may not have thought it rude or inappropriate. But Paul says all must share the same meal at the same time because class distinctions have no standing in the church. Since all are equal before God, the church's practices must reflect that oneness.

The Lord's Supper and the Last Supper. Paul's instructions about the Lord's Supper includes a quotation of a tradition about its institution that has become one of the most commonly recited parts of the church's celebration of it (11:23-26). Paul says that during his last meal with his disciples Jesus took bread and wine, prayed over them, and interpreted them as remembrances of his death and resurrection. Working from this quotation, he tells the Corinthians that their meal together must remember those events in a way that recognizes that social and economic differences carry no weight in this community that honors Christ and exists because of what they are remembering. His instructions here may well have led the church away from including an entire meal as a part of its celebration of the Lord's Supper.

Questions about the Resurrection

In addition to these problems, the Corinthians also have some questions. One of these concerns the nature of the afterlife (15:35-57). Some seem to think that to be happy and close to God they must exist as bodiless souls in heaven. Many people in the ancient world saw the body as a detriment to spiritual life and communion with the gods. Paul rejects this view because he sees human bodies as creations of God that are part of what make human beings the things God intended them to be. For Paul, life as a material body is not inferior to life as a bodiless soul. In fact, he thinks that people can only experience the fullness of life that God wants for them if they have a body. So he argues that believers will be embodied people in heaven, that they will have bodies like the body God gave Christ at the resurrection. That is, the resurrected Christ is the sample of what believers will be like in heaven.

In his response to their questions about the afterlife, we again see the importance of the death and resurrection of Christ for Paul and the early believers in Christ (15:1-34). Paul cites it as the pattern for Christian spirituality and leadership, as the thing that binds them together as a church, and now as the preview of their life with God after death. At one point he says explicitly that the central confession of the church is that "Christ died for our sins" and "was raised" (15:3-4). When he makes this assertion, he says he is reciting a tradition that had been handed down to him, so this is not an understanding of Christ that originates with Paul. It is important to note that Paul writes 1 Corinthians only about twenty years after Jesus' death. His citation of this tradition shows that it was among the earliest ways that the church thought about Jesus.

Summary

First Corinthians gives us a glimpse into the early church. We see the kinds of problems they faced and how they tried to incorporate their new beliefs and commitments into their lives. They clearly struggled with how to live as believers in Christ in a world that held very different values and resented the changes they saw in those who joined the church. Paul deals with many issues in this letter that are still on people's minds: spirituality, leadership, relationships within the church and among social classes, sexual ethics, and life after death. This letter shows us how Paul uses his understanding of God and Christ to develop ways to think about various questions and to figure out how to live as a Christian.

▶ 2 Corinthians

The Context

A composite document. Most scholars think that 2 Corinthians is a compilation of multiple letters; some think an editor put two letters together, others that parts of as many as five or even six letters are found in this book. At least chapters 10–13 were written at a different time than the previous chapters, but all of the material included in 2 Corinthians was written between 55 and 57 and it all addresses a single problem. Perhaps the person who put the letters together thought it appropriate to do so because they all deal with a single issue.

Superior Christians? By the time Paul wrote the letters of 2 Corinthians, he had made a second trip to Corinth because they continued to have problems. His visit, however, did not go well. He found that some teachers, who claimed the title of apostle, had come to Corinth (chs. 11–12). They claimed to be superior to other Christians, including Paul. Specifically, they claimed that they had a larger measure of God's Spirit in them than other believers had. This spiritual gift gave them extraordinary spiritual experiences, the ability to work miracles, powerful speaking skills, and the ability to rise above the troubles of life. They said others in the church should, then, defer to their authority and support them generously. You can think of them as preachers who wear Gucci togas and travel in the latest model of Ferrari chariot, while telling others to sacrifice in their giving for the church. (The type remains all too familiar.)

The Corinthians' response. When Paul confronted them on his visit to Corinth, they rebuffed him and the church did not come to his defense. So he left, saying he would return shortly. But rather than coming back, he wrote them letters designed to bring them back to him without engaging in a direct confrontation with those other teachers.

BOX 14.8

THE "SUPER-APOSTLES"

Paul derisively calls the teachers he wants the Corinthians to reject when he writes the various letters of 2 Corinthians "super-apostles." These newly arrived teachers have been understood by scholars in many ways. The clearest thing we can say about them is that they arrived in Corinth with letters of recommendation from other churches. They claimed that the Spirit gave them the power to give impressive speeches, rise above the troubles of life, and have powerful personalities. Possessing the Spirit in this measure, they said, made them apostles that the church should support financially. Paul argues that these people misunderstand the Spirit and apostleship.

The Corinthians' readiness to accept these other teachers demonstrates that 1 Corinthians was not completely successful. Even if the church listened to some of the specific instructions (which seems likely), they had kept their old ways of thinking about spirituality and leadership. They still thought that God's Spirit made people impressive and powerful, rather than enabling people to endure difficulties with faith. That way of thinking made them susceptible to the claims these new preachers made. It was easier to claim someone as your leader who is impressive and fits the culture's definition of success than it is to identify yourself with someone who refuses to conform to those expectations.

FIGURE 14.8 **ISTHMUS OF CORINTH**

This view is from Acrocorinth. The narrow isthmus is all the land mass that connects the southern part of Greece (the Peloponnesus) to the northern areas of Greece. Jerry Sumney

other teachers. He calls the intruders "super-apostles" and says he is sorry he is so weak that he will not abuse the Corinthians. A whole section of 2 Corinthians is known as the "Fool's Speech" (11:1—12:13) because Paul asks them to listen to him even though he is being a fool. In this section he makes the claims of his rivals seem ridiculous, even as he says he can match and better all their claims. But he says it is foolish to evaluate leaders by whether they are powerful speakers, have impressive successes, and can make people do what they want. Christian leadership can only be evaluated, he says, by whether it conforms to the example of the crucified Christ.

The differences in understandings of Christian apostleship, ministry, and leadership between Paul and the rivals at Corinth stem from their different understandings of spirituality. The intruders think that the Spirit makes apostles and ministers superior to fellow Christians and immune to the troubles of life. Paul, on the other hand, says the Spirit enables leaders to be humble and retain their faith while they spread the gospel as they endure hardship for the good of the church.

▶ Galatians

The Context

Galatians addresses a completely different set of issues than the Corinthian letters. The basic issue Paul confronts in Galatians is the place of the law of Moses in the lives of Gentile Christians. Since this letter was probably written around 54–56, the church had been thinking about this issue for twenty years without coming to agreement about it—and Galatians shows Paul's frustration at the lack of progress. Our earlier discussion of Acts noted that this remained an issue into the beginning of the second century. Galatians is written during the period in which the argument about this issue was heated.

Circumcision, holy days, and food. Paul writes Galatians because some teachers were encouraging Gentile believers to be circumcised (5:2-12), observe Jewish holy days (4:10), and perhaps keep some kosher food regulations. Their main demand was that the Gentiles accept **circumcision**, a clear indication that a man was joining the Jewish community. Paul seems to think that the Gentile Christians do not understand that submitting to circumcision meant that they were committed to observing all the laws of the Torah, just as Jews kept them.

In some places various Christians said Gentiles could not be full members of the church unless they converted to Judaism through circumcision and observance of Torah, but we do not know what the Galatian teachers said the Gentile Christians gained by accepting these practices. Their proposal may have been intended only to make it easier for Jewish church members to remain in their synagogues since they would not have to explain how they could also belong to a religious group that did not keep God's law. Or perhaps the synagogue was afraid that extending some of their privileges (for example, absence from a city's religious observances) to these Gentiles might draw more attention to them and even end in having those privileges revoked. We just do not know why they advocated these practices.

Salvation threatened. Still, Paul is very upset when he writes Galatians because he believes that the salvation of Gentile believers is at stake. He says that if the Gentiles submit to circumcision, and thereby convert to Judaism, they will lose the relationship with God that they have through Christ. It is important to remember that

BOX 14.9

TWO GALATIAS

New Testament scholars have debated whether the Letter to the Galatians was written to churches in the traditional region of Galatia that is located in the central part of eastern Asia Minor or the large Roman province of Galatia that extended from this region to the southern coast. This difference matters not only because the people of the southern part of the province were culturally different from those of the original region, but also because it may affect the date of the letter. Paul says in Galatians that he has only been to Jerusalem twice since joining the church (1:18; 2:1). Those who want to keep this information compatible with the Acts account of Paul's life must have the letter written before the Jerusalem Conference (Acts 15). Paul traveled with Barnabas to southern Asia Minor early in his missionary career, but did not travel to the original region of Galatia until after the Conference. So if the letter is written to churches in the region of Galatia, its account of Paul's travels and those of Acts are irreconcilable.

FIGURE 14.9 **CAPPADOCIA**

This region of Asia Minor is in today's central Turkey. Note the entrances to the cave dwellings carved into the soft rock. This area is in the ethnic region of Galatia. Art Resource

Paul thinks it is good for Jews to remain observant Jews when they join the church. He thinks observing the Torah is an appropriate way for Jewish believers in Christ to live out their faith. But he also argues vehemently that if Gentile believers observe the law in the same way, they lose their salvation. He believes that when Gentiles are required to convert to Judaism to be in the church, it shows a lack of confidence in Christ to be a person's means to forgiveness and relationship with God. He also thinks that Gentiles converting to Judaism suggests that God is only the God of Jews rather than of the whole world.

Paul's Argument

Paul's basic approach to this problem in Galatians is to assert that those who rely on Christ's faithful obedience to God as their means to a relationship with God already have all the blessings someone might claim were gained through conversion to Judaism. He says they should know they do not need to take up Torah observance because they already have the Spirit of

BOX 14.10

THE TERM *JUDAIZER*

New Testament scholars have often used the term *Judaizer* to refer to members of the church who demanded that Gentiles accept full proselyte conversion to Judaism in order to be in the church. This term, however, is now offensive to many, particularly Jewish scholars, and it is inaccurate. This label makes it sound as though these teachers were trying to make the church Jewish, implying that it was something else before their influence. But since the church started as a community in which all members were observant Jews, these people were not trying to make the church Jewish—it was already thoroughly Jewish. What they opposed was losing a significant element of that identity of the church when others allowed Gentiles to become members without also becoming observant Jews.

God living in them (ch. 3). According to Paul, this presence of God in their lives is clear evidence that they are already fully God's people. He reminds them that the Spirit came into their lives through belief in Christ, and without circumcision and observance of Jewish holy days.

Abraham, father of believing Gentiles. Since Abraham is the progenitor of Jews, God's chosen people, Paul claims Abraham is also the ancestor of Gentile believers in Christ (3:6-29). He argues that Gentile believers are Abraham's heirs because they have the same kind of faith in God that Abraham had. Since Abraham is already their spiritual ancestor, they need no other connection to him or his descendants.

Baptism. Paul finally uses their own baptism to convince them they are already fully God's people. He identifies Christ as the descendant of Abraham par excellence and then asserts that in baptism believers are identified with Christ (3:16, 27-29). Thus, since they are one with Christ, they also are Abraham's heir and so the recipients of all of God's promises. He argues that it is through their identification with Christ that believers in him become children of God.

Summary

The whole of Galatians is devoted to the question of whether Gentiles are allowed to convert to Judaism. Paul insists that Gentiles remain Gentiles. At the same time, he wants Jews to remain Jews. Having observant Jews and nonobservant Gentiles in a single religious community is difficult. They have to think carefully about how to eat together and how to have various kinds of celebrations and services so that both the observant and the nonobservant could participate fully. When there is an inevitable conflict, Paul maintains that the church community is most important, so the unity of the church takes precedence over all other commitments. Thus, on some occasions, Paul thinks observant Jews might have to violate some Torah commands to have full fellowship with Gentiles who were not allowed to adopt some Torah laws (for example, circumcision and keeping the Sabbath). But beyond these moments that threatened the unity of the church, Jews in the church continued to observe the Torah.

Paul offers this complex way of incorporating Gentiles into the people of God because he believed that Christ was the means of the proper relationship with God for all people. Galatians is a powerful affirmation of Paul's belief that it is through Christ that all people are made right with God.

▶ Philippians

The Context

Paul wrote Philippians from prison (1:7, 13-14, 17). We are not sure where he was jailed, because he was arrested so many times for agitating unrest in the cities where he preached. The leading hypotheses put him in Ephesus (in Asia Minor, which is today's Turkey), Caesarea (in Palestine), or Rome. But he may have written it during an arrest that we know nothing about from other sources. The date of Philippians depends on where Paul was; it may be as early as 53–55 if he was in Ephesus or as late as 58–62 if he was in Rome. Fortunately, in this case knowing the precise date does not greatly influence our understanding of the letter.

BOX 14.11

THE CIRCUMCISION CONTROVERSY

Some believed that Paul taught that Gentiles should accept circumcision. A clear indication that the opponents of Galatians do not attack Paul's status as an apostle is that they claim to agree with him about a central point in the dispute. In Galatians 5:11 Paul says that some say that he still preaches that Gentiles must be circumcised to be in the church. Such a story might have gotten started because of some of Paul's practices. Paul did have Timothy circumcised because his mother was Jewish, while his father was a Gentile (Acts 16: 1-3). Here Paul's rule against Gentile circumcision did not directly apply. But it is easy to see why some might get the impression that Paul expected Gentile converts to eventually finalize their place in the church by accepting circumcision.

A Joyful Letter

Philippians is known for its emphasis on joy; Paul clearly has a good relationship with this church, takes pleasure in writing to them, and reminds them to "rejoice" or give thanks for the blessings God has given them (2:18; 3:1; 4:4). At the same time, they do have a problem, and Paul takes the occasion of this letter to give instructions about it and to warn them of another threat. Still, he is more pleased with this church than any other to which he writes a letter.

The Reason for Writing: Disputes among Leaders

It is not until near the end that Paul speaks explicitly of the central problem the letter has addressed. At the beginning of its final chapter, he asks two leaders in the church to settle their dispute and get along (4:2-3). The problem is serious enough that he asks other leaders to help them resolve the matter. He gives no hint about the nature of the dispute; he says only that he wants them to get along.

Christ's example of humility. Once we hear about that problem, the rest of the letter sounds a bit different—what seemed like generic instructions now address a specific difficulty. When Paul tells them to follow Christ's example by being humble and putting the interests of others ahead of their own, he has in mind most specifically how leaders should act (2:1-11). Of course, he would tell all Christians to behave in that way, but when we know that there is a conflict between leaders the instruction has a special poignancy. One of the ways he encourages them to resolve their problems is to remind them of his willingness to put their interests ahead of his own, an especially relevant point since he is in prison for the sake of the church when he writes. He also describes Timothy, whom he intends to send to visit them, as someone who is more concerned about their welfare than he is about his own (2:19-23). Paul's emphasis on unity and standing together in the face of opposition from outside the church also takes on special meaning when leaders are engaged in a dispute. He seems confident that these more mild and suggestive remarks will be enough to persuade his readers to act as they should.

Women leaders. Two important things emerge in his treatment of this problem. The first is that the two estranged leaders (named **Euodia** and **Syntyche**) are both women. This demonstrates clearly that Paul's churches had women leaders from the beginning. These women may have been more than leaders of local churches because Paul says both of them had engaged in the work of ministry with him. So they may have been members of his mission team at some point. Perhaps they engaged in this ministry only in Philippi, but either way they were approved and authorized leaders of the church. Any instructions we hear from Paul about the roles of men and women should be heard in the context of a group that has women among its leaders whom Paul recognized as legitimate.

A Christ "hymn." The second point involves what the early church believed about Jesus. When Paul gives Christ as his example of how Christians should put the interests of others ahead of their own, he quotes a hymnic liturgical statement that the church already knew (2:6-11). Someone other than Paul is probably the author of the piece, but Paul quotes it because it encapsulates an element of the church's belief about Christ that supports his exhortation about putting others first. This poetic insertion proclaims that Christ existed in heaven before the birth of Jesus and that his acceptance of the mission to come to earth was an act of obedience that involved accepting a self-humbling act. It also affirms that God has made Christ the ruler of the entire cosmos.

The exalted Christ. We often hear that it took the church several decades to begin to make

> *BOX 14.12*
>
> **PAUL USES PREVIOUSLY KNOWN MATERIAL IN HIS LETTERS**
>
> Paul inserts preformed confessional, hymnic, and liturgical material in several places in his letters. He does this to support his argument by citing things his readers already know and believe. His citation of those materials shows us later readers what the earliest church believed about Jesus, his relationship to God, and what he accomplished for humanity. Among these citations are Philippians 2:6-11 and Galatians 3:26-27.

the exalted claims about Christ that appear in more formulaic statements in the later creeds of the church. But this passage in Philippians demonstrates that the church made quite exalted statements about Jesus very early. Even if Philippians was not written until the year 60, this quoted material was composed some time before that. This means that within twenty-five years of Jesus' death Christians already understood him to be a preexistent being who existed "in the form of God." Claims about Christ's place as exalted ruler seem to be among the earliest beliefs the church confessed about Christ (as we see already in 1 Thessalonians, the earliest New Testament book), clearly from the time of the apostles and those who knew the earthly Jesus, so it is no surprise to find them here in Philippians.

A Jarring Interlude

Philippians has a section so distinctive that some scholars have argued that it is part of another letter that an editor inserted into the longer letter. In chapter 3 Paul suddenly veers off his discussion of putting others first to warn his readers not to listen to anyone who demands that Gentiles submit to circumcision (and so become Jewish proselytes) in order to be in the church. His tone changes and he excoriates those who promulgate such teachings—he even calls them dogs. This is quite a change in a letter that has been talking about rejoicing and joy and humility. But despite this sudden turn, it seems more likely that the section was part of the original letter, as some rhetorical and thematic studies of the letter suggest.

Privileges of Israel. In his brief aside, Paul says that he had all the advantages that being Jewish could boast or offer—and he thinks those advantages are substantial—but that he considered his relationship with God through Christ superior to what he had before. His reevaluation of those earlier privileges that accompanied his entering the church serves as his evidence that his Gentile church members do not need to become Jewish; he says they already have more than what they could get by joining that community. Believers in Christ have become the people of God through Christ rather than through the Mosaic covenant.

As it happens with other letters, much of what the later church has gotten from Philippians involves matters other than the letter's main point. Christology is not a major theme of Philippians, but the church has drawn extensively on what Paul says about Christ in this letter. Even though his quotation of the hymnic material is simply a supporting argument for his instructions about putting others first, it shows us what the church believed about Christ in its early days and so what enabled its members to risk a new direction in their lives and trust that God would make it worthwhile in the end.

▶ Philemon

The Context

Philemon is Paul's shortest letter; it often takes up less than a page in a Bible. While Philemon is the primary person it addresses, Paul greets the whole church of which he is a member. So while the letter speaks to a single person, Paul intends the whole church to hear his request. Of course, this makes it nearly impossible for Philemon not to comply. Paul is also in prison when he writes this letter (v. 13), but we cannot be sure where. This makes it impossible to give a specific date, but most scholars think it was written in the mid- to late 50s.

Slave and Master

This letter focuses on the single issue of the relationship between the slave **Onesimus** and his owner **Philemon**. Like many Christians in the first century, Philemon continued to own slaves. The church did not call for a sweeping reform of the slave system or even urge its members to free their slaves. The early church was in no position to institute a societal change, and it would have caused immediate suppression had they tried to subvert the slave system in the Roman Empire.

Societal distinctions. The beliefs of the church, however, were difficult to reconcile with owning slaves. One of the earliest confessions of the church was that in Christ the usual societal distinctions no longer give one status. So in the church one's sex, ethnicity, or social and economic status was not supposed to

FIGURE 14.10 **A COUPLE ON A DINING COUCH, SPARTA**

While men always reclined at a banquet, this was often not the case for women. They often sat at the foot of the couch. There would have been a small table in front of each couch that held the meal. Jerry Sumney

matter; women were leaders, slaves should be able to have positions of authority, and so on. This created some immediate problems in marriages and between slaves and masters. How could a wife or slave be the person with authority at church, but then be a second-class person at home? If a slave rightfully reprimanded her owner at church, what might the consequences be later? All sorts of tensions imposed themselves because the structure of society was so different from the values of the church.

Onesimus, runaway slave. Philemon addresses just this conflict. It seems likely that Onesimus has run away and has gone to Paul. There were provisions for slaves to seek mediation by making a plea for help to someone equal to or higher than their master in social rank. Perhaps this is what Onesimus did. Whatever the specifics, there were tensions between Ones-imus and Philemon that could have resulted in punishment for the slave.

Paul's Action and Advice

While in contact with Paul, Onesimus became a Christian. Paul then sends him home with this letter that makes a plea on his behalf. It explains that Onesimus has become a Christian and says that this must make a difference in how Philemon treats him; Paul says Philemon must receive him "no longer as slave but more than a slave, a beloved brother" (v. 16). Does this mean that Philemon should set him free? There is clearly significant tension between considering him a family member and owning him, but Paul also seems to ask Philemon to assign Onesimus to Paul. At the least Paul wants to keep Philemon from imposing any punishment on Onesimus.

This letter shows us the kinds of everyday problems the first-century church wrestled with. They saw the tensions between their beliefs and the way of life imposed on them by their culture, and they struggled to figure out how to live out their faith in that setting. We do not know with certainty what happened to Onesimus, but a tradition from the early second century suggests that he became a well-known leader of the church in Asia Minor.

▶ Romans

The Context

Romans is the only letter we have from Paul that he wrote to a church he (or one of his representatives) did not found. He writes to this church on a return visit to Corinth around the year 57. He tells the Romans that he plans to visit them after a trip to Jerusalem and he hopes they will support his mission farther west (15:31-32). Having started churches in the major cities in Asia Minor and Greece, Paul wants to expand his mission field to Spain (15:28). So part of the reason he writes the Roman church is to get them thinking about support for his mission. Since he has never been there, Romans includes an introduction to Paul's teaching that he thinks will recommend him to them.

Support for a mission to Spain. Because this letter does introduce Paul to the Romans, many readers have assumed that we find a more objective account of his teaching here because he is not addressing particular problems. Paul does, however, need to accomplish some important matters by the way he presents his teaching in Romans. First, this presentation needs to convince that church to support his mission to Spain.

Beyond that, the latter parts of this long letter seem to address actual problems in the church at Rome. So his presentation of his teaching in the earlier parts needs to set up those instructions. This is not very different from what Paul does in most of his letters; he uses theological points to address immediate issues.

Paul's church? Finally, one of the purposes of Romans is to claim this church for the mission of Paul. As the apostle to the Gentiles, Paul wants to represent all largely Gentile churches, including the church in Rome, when he makes his trip to Jerusalem. Paul is on his way to Jerusalem with a delegation from his churches to deliver funds he has collected from those churches to provide help to the impoverished church in Jerusalem. But this is more than a relief mission to Paul. He wants the contribution from his churches to express the unity of the church and hopes this aid from his churches will ameliorate some of the tensions between his

FIGURE 14.11 **MODEL OF THE ANCIENT CITY OF ROME**

The round structure on the left is the famous Colosseum. It was built late in the first century, after the deaths of Peter and Paul. Wikimedia Commons

predominantly Gentile churches and the mostly Jewish churches in Palestine. So his effort to include the Romans among his churches has in view this desire to represent non-Jewish Christians.

Dispelling misconceptions. In addition to all those things he wants this letter to accomplish, he probably also has to craft his message to counter what some of his rivals say about him. Paul was a controversial figure in the early church. His message of the inclusion of Gentiles in the church without having them convert to Judaism was not well received by all, as we have seen. As a result, some characterized his message as libertine or antinomian (that is, against having any rules about ethical behavior). We have also seen that some rivals thought his ideas about how to be an apostle were wrong and showed that he did not possess the proper qualifications to be an apostle. If he wants the Romans to accept him as their apostle, he will have to dispel these and other misconceptions about himself.

Israel's priority. Paul devotes the first half of this letter to an exposition of his teaching that he thinks will address all of these reasons for writing the church in Rome. The Roman church has a significant number of both Jews and Gentiles, so Paul stresses the importance of the gospel for both. All the while he affirms a priority for Israel that non-Jews must not forget; the spiritual blessings that all Christians enjoy have come to them through Israel. Paul thinks the Roman Gentile Christians need to be reminded of this debt, perhaps because they no longer recognize the value of their Jewish fellow believers in Christ.

BOX 14.13

ROMANS IS NOT A SYSTEMATIC THEOLOGY TEXT

For many years, scholars treated Romans as though it were more of a systematic treatment of Paul's theology and less a letter because this letter is addressed to a church Paul did not found. The purposes we have seen that Paul needs to accomplish with Romans, however, indicate that it is as conditioned by the particulars of the situation as any other Pauline letter.

The Edict of Claudius. Some members of the Jewish community was expelled from the city of Rome under the emperor **Claudius**, many think because of disturbances caused by arguments with the church (perhaps in the year 49). Before the Jews were forced out by the Edict of Claudius, the church in Rome included both Jews and Gentiles. While the Jewish Christians were gone, the remaining Gentiles developed their own ways of doing things and their own leaders. When the displaced Jews were allowed to return after the death of Claudius, those in the church went back to their old congregations hoping to pick up where they left off. It seems, however, that those churches were not so eager to grant the returnees their old places. The Gentiles had perhaps forgotten just how much they owed to the Jewish faith and the Jewish members of the church. So Paul reminds the whole church that the gospel is equally for all people, but for the Jews first.

Three Images of Salvation

Justification. Paul begins his self-introduction by giving three ways to think about how Christ establishes the right relationship between God and believers. The first image he uses, **justification**, is judicial. He initially argues that everyone is guilty before God because all have sinned, Jews by failing to keep the commandments of the Torah and Gentiles by violating their own consciences. If God were to exercise only justice, punishment is due to all. But since God is both just and merciful, God sent Christ as the one who faithfully obeys God. God then allows Christ's faithfulness to count for those who identify with Christ. Furthermore, God allows Christ's death at the hands of the evil world to expunge the transgressions of the guilty. In this way, God is shown to be both just and merciful.

Paul does not think that, in order to show mercy, God stopped being just. For Paul, God must maintain both of these characteristics or God is not worthy of worship. We often think of mercy as the opposite of justice, but it is not. (The opposite of justice is injustice, not mercy.) If God stopped being just, believers would not be able to trust God because God could act on a whim. Believers need God to be just as much as they need God to be merciful. Paul recognized that and so interpreted the life and death of Jesus with these judicial metaphors.

BOX 14.14

SALVATION?

Compare the language used for salvation in Romans 3:21-26; 5:1 and 6:17-18. Why do you think Paul uses such different language to refer to what he thinks Christ accomplishes? What does this multiple language suggest about the way he thinks about the human condition?

BOX 14.15

EDICT OF CLAUDIUS

In the year 49 (probably) the emperor Claudius expelled some Jews from the city of Rome. According to the Roman historian Suetonius, he did this because of riots in the Jewish section of the city at the instigation of "Chrestus." Most interpreters think this is a misspelling of Christ. If that is correct, this episode demonstrates that there were believers in Christ in Rome long before any apostle went there.

Reconciliation. Paul's second image for thinking about how Christ relates believers to God, **reconciliation**, is relational. He argues that people outside the church do not have the proper relationship with God because they turn their backs on God and have become God's enemies by the way they live. They begin to view God and God's will as their enemy and desire things that violate God's will for the world. But God reaches out to such people even though they have turned against God. In Christ God shows humanity a love that intends to bring reconciliation in spite of their hostility. Paul says it is unusual for someone to give his life for a good person, but that Christ gave himself while humanity was hostile. Since God has shown that kind of love, believers can be confident that God will maintain that relationship with them.

Freedom from sin through the Spirit: Redemption. Paul's third image for understanding the work of Christ, **redemption**, builds on the second; by people's hostility toward God they have allowed themselves to be captured by the power of evil and now they cannot free themselves. While humans were inescapably held hostage to sin, God not only defeats sin through the cross and resurrection of Christ but also sends the Spirit to live in believers to enable them to reorient their lives and so live for God. Paul's discussion is realistic enough to acknowledge that people do not completely stop sinning, because they still live in a world that is controlled by sin (the name by which Paul refers to the power of evil in this part of Romans). This world encourages people to live in ways that violate God's wishes for the world. So while he does not think that having God's Spirit means that believers are completely free of sin, he does believe the Spirit empowers them to live significantly different lives. In addition, he says they have the promise that when they fail, God forgives them through Christ.

Paul has now given three images to help his readers think about how Christ affects salvation: a legal metaphor, a relational metaphor, and a metaphor of rescue and empowerment. In all of these believers depend on God to act through Christ to invite people back to the place God intends for them. Since God is the primary actor in all of these metaphors, and in Paul's thought more broadly, these affirmations about God are encouraging only if people can trust God to remain committed to the promises God makes. The conduct of some Christians in Rome, however, places God's trustworthiness in question.

BOX 14.16

METAPHORS FOR SALVATION

Paul uses multiple images to describe the ways the work of Christ affects the relationship between God and humanity. These images include: justification (an image drawn from the legal sphere), reconciliation (a relationship image), and redemption (a commercial image). These multiple kinds of images indicate that all of them are metaphoric; Paul sees none of them as the literal way that Christ's life, death, and resurrection bring salvation. For Paul, what Christ accomplished was too large to be described in just one way.

The Place of Israel in God's Plan

The Gentile church members in Rome and elsewhere perhaps thought that the coming of Christ meant that God's **election** of Israel as a special people was over. Their mission had been accomplished, so there was no need for God to maintain a special relationship with them. Compelling evidence for the end of this relationship seemed to be that Jews were not accepting the gospel in the numbers that Gentiles were. Thus it looks as though that special relationship was over.

Paul thinks this interpretation of things is impossible because it would mean that God is not trustworthy. If God could choose and then abandon Israel, God could do the same thing to the church. If the salvation Paul has explained in the first eight chapters of Romans is truly good news, people must be able to trust God not to change God's mind about providing salvation through Christ. They cannot do this if God has a history of abandoning the people God has chosen in the past. So Paul devotes chapters 9–11 to trying to explain the place of Israel in God's plan.

Israel's election remains, but salvation is through Christ. Paul's discussion is dense and convoluted because he affirms two things that stand in tension with one another: Israel remains God's chosen people and all salvation is through Christ. The historical fact that most Jews did not accept the church's preaching of Christ makes it very difficult to hold to both of these assertions. Yet Paul insists that both must be true.

In some parts of these chapters he says that only some Jews, those who were faithful to God, were ever the chosen people, so those who are not saved can only blame themselves. In other places, he says that the small number of Jews who respond seems to indicate that God has forsaken Israel. Scholars are divided over the details of this section of Romans, and even over the basic conclusion Paul reaches. He says near the end that "all Israel will be saved" (11:26) because God's promises are irrevocable. It is not clear whether he means all Israelites (that is, Jews) will turn to the gospel or whether he has redefined "Israel" so that it means only those who respond to God with faith, but this affirmation about Israel is absolutely necessary for Paul.

In the end, Paul leaves the question in the hands of God. After all his discussion and his reaffirmation that salvation is through Christ and that Israel will be saved, he knows the tension remains. So he ends his discussion with a doxology that praises God's unknowable wisdom (11:33-36). In other words, he cannot quite figure it out and so leaves this mystery to be solved by God's wisdom.

BOX 14.17

PAUL IS NOT A SUPERSESSIONIST

Supersessionism is the belief that the covenant with Israel came to an end when the church began, that it was superseded. Paul rejects the notion that God would simply end a covenant God had promised to maintain; that behavior would make God less than trustworthy. Paul does think God has acted in a new way in Christ and that all salvation comes through Christ, but for him that must not mean that God has ended the covenant with Israel.

The Christian Life

The final section of Romans gives some instructions about how Christians must live. The beginning verses of chapter 12 set the framework for everything that follows; Paul asserts that believers should dedicate their whole existence to service to God, just as a sacrifice at the temple is given wholly to God. He then gives directions about various matters, focusing on relations within the church. He gives particular attention to the ways that Jews and Gentiles should live together in a single church, with each respecting the conscience of the other and recognizing that each has a distinctive and valid way to serve God.

Summary

In Romans Paul presents his teaching to introduce himself to a church that he wants to accept him and that he wants to influence. He gives the church in Rome different angles from which to understand his teaching and denies some accusations about his teaching that he expects they have heard. This presentation of his gospel has given later Christians a wide range of ways to think about what Christ has accomplished for those who come to faith in him. Paul's use of metaphors from the court room, relationships, and being captured gives expression to various experiences of the human situation and the way he believes Christ offers a solution to each.

So this letter has provided the church with important ways to understand the heart of its faith. Some have also, unfortunately, grounded anti-Semitic views in Paul's discussion of the unfaithfulness of some in Israel. The comments of Paul, himself a Jew, do not support such ideas. So Romans has proved itself to be a powerful force within the church, even sometimes for nefarious purposes.

▶ Conclusion

We have seen in this chapter how important it is to take account of the genre Paul decides to use when writing to his churches. His decision to write letters rather than some less personal and more general form of address shows that he intends his remarks, teaching, and instruction to be situational, that is, addressed to specific people and their immediate circumstances. Thus his instructions may seem contradictory because he thinks the members of one group need to live out their faith in specific ways because of their situation, while others will need to act in other ways because their circumstances and their identity demand a different action. As we have seen, his letters address not only very different people, but also very different problems. To understand his letters clearly, we need to reach some understanding of the various problems his different churches faced. Paul's choice of the letter genre and the different problems he addresses when writing to various churches show that he does not intend the specifics of his instructions to be immediately applicable to other situations.

Paul's letters give us our earliest glimpse of the wide range of problems and questions that the first generation of believers in Christ faced as they tried to determine what this new faith meant. Their questions range from what to think about Christ's presence in the world to what happens to people when they die; from how to treat people in different social classes to whether they can eat food dedicated to another god; and from how to dress in church to what kinds of sexual morality the faith demands. Paul's responses to these and other issues powerfully shaped that generation and nearly all subsequent developments of the church's faith. As we have seen, some of those uses of Paul's letters were harmful. Other uses of these letters, however, have contributed to advances in human rights and numerous causes of justice.

▶ LET'S REVIEW ◀

In this chapter we learned about:

- The importance of genre and historical setting for each letter
- 1 Thessalonians
  - —Interprets the suffering of Christians
  - —Quells concern about believers who die before the Second Coming
- 1 Corinthians
  - —Defines spirituality in a new way
  - —Responds to a series of questions about ethical issues
  - —Responds to a series of questions about behavior within the church, particularly in worship
  - —Discusses the nature of resurrection existence
- 2 Corinthians
  - —Composed of multiple letters
  - —Main topic is the proper understanding of apostleship and leadership in the church
- Galatians
  - —Addresses questions about what Gentiles must and must not do to be fully members of the people of God
- Philippians
  - —Addresses a conflict between two leaders in the church, both of whom are women
  - —Incorporates a piece of preformed liturgical material that shows how early the church made claims about Christ's exaltation
- Philemon
  - —Deals with the return of a slave to his owner
- Romans
  - —Paul writes to a church he has never visited
  - —He introduces himself and his teaching in a way designed to include them among his church during his upcoming visit to Jerusalem and to persuade them to support his mission to Spain
  - —Paul sets out different ways to understand what Christ accomplished for humanity's relationship with God
  - —Paul urges Jewish and Gentile believers to value one another when their practices come into conflict

▶ KEY TERMS ◀

Circumcision
Claudius, Edict of
Communion
Ecstatic experience
Election
Eucharist
Euodia
Justification
Letters
Literary epistle
Lord's Supper
Onesimus
Parousia
Persecution
Philemon
Reconciliation
Redemption
Speaking in tongues
Syntyche

▶ QUESTIONS FOR REVIEW ◀

14.1 What are some of the reasons it is difficult to understand clearly the message of an ancient letter?

14.2 How does recognizing that some writings within the New Testament are letters influence how you think about the advice they give?

14.3 Why does one Pauline letter give advice that seems to contradict what he says in another letter?

14.4 Why did it create problems when people in Paul's churches stopped worshiping gods other than the God of Israel?

14.5 How does Paul interpret persecution for the Thessalonians?

14.6 What kind of definition of spirituality does Paul give the Corinthians?

14.7 How does Paul describe the afterlife for believers in 1 Corinthians?

14.8 How can you tell that 1 Corinthians was not as convincing to its recipients as Paul had hoped?

14.9 Describe the problem that Galatians addresses. What is Paul's basic response?

14.10 What does Philippians demonstrate about the place of women in the earliest Pauline churches?

14.11 What does Philippians show about how long it took for the church to begin to make rather exalted claims about Christ?

14.12 What combination of purposes leads Paul to write Romans?

14.13 What does Paul think the justice of God demands as a response to people doing evil?

14.14 What does Paul say about the election of Israel in the time after Christ?

▶ FOR FURTHER READING ◀

R. S. Ascough, *What Are They Saying about the Formation of the Pauline Churches?* Mahwah, N.J.: Paulist, 1997.

Jouette Bassler, *Navigating Paul: An Introduction to Key Theological Concepts*. Louisville: Westminster John Knox, 2006.

J. Christiaan Beker, *The Triumph of God: The Essence of Paul's Thought*. Minneapolis: Fortress Press, 1990.

Charles B. Cousar, *The Letters of Paul*, Interpreting Biblical Texts. Nashville: Abingdon, 1996.

Neil Elliott and Mark Reasoner, *Documents and Images for the Study of Paul*. Minneapolis: Fortress Press, 2010.

Paula Fredriksen, "From Jesus to Christ: The Origins of the New Testament Images of Jesus," Bible and Interpretation Website 2000. http://www.bibleinterp.com/articles/fredricksen_JesustoChrist.shtml

Victor P. Furnish, *Theology and Ethics in Paul*, New Testament Library. Reprint of 2nd edition. Nashville: Abingdon, 1968. Louisville: Westminster John Knox, 2009.

Richard A. Horsley, ed., *Paul and Empire: Religion and Power in Roman Imperial Society*. Harrisburg, Penn.: Trinity Press International, 1997.

Amy-Jill Levine and Marianne Blickenstaff, eds., *A Feminist Companion to Paul*. Feminist Companion to the New Testament and Early Christian Writings 6. New York: T. & T. Clark, 2004.

Abraham J. Malherbe, *Paul and the Popular Philosophers*. Minneapolis: Fortress Press, 1989.

Wayne A. Meeks, *The First Urban Christians: The Social World of the Apostle Paul*. New Haven: Yale University Press, 1983.

Wayne A. Meeks and John T. Fitzgerald, *The Writings of St. Paul*, 2nd ed. Norton Critical Edition. New York: Norton, 2007.

Calvin J. Roetzel, *The Letters of Paul: Conversations in Context*, 5th ed. Louisville: Westminster John Knox, 2009.

Alan F. Segal, *Paul the Convert: The Apostolate and Apostasy of Saul the Pharisee*. New Haven: Yale University Press, 1990.

Todd D. Still, ed., *Jesus and Paul Reconsidered*. Grand Rapids: Eerdmans, 2007.

Stanley K. Stowers, *Letter Writing in Greco-Roman Antiquity*. Library of Early Christianity. Philadelphia: Westminster, 1986.

Jerry L. Sumney, "Who Are Those 'Servants of Satan'?" Bible and Interpretation Website 2000 http://www.bibleinterp.com/articles/PaulOpponents_Sumney.shtml

Jerry L. Sumney, ed. *Reading Paul's Letter to the Romans*. Resources for Biblical Studies. Atlanta: Society of Biblical Literature Press, 2012.

Jerry L. Sumney, *Paul: Apostle and Fellow Traveler*. Nashville: Abingdon, 2014.

N. T. Wright, *Paul in Fresh Perspective*. Minneapolis: Fortress Press, 2008.

Magnus Zetterholm, *Approaches to Paul: A Student's Guide to Recent Scholarship*. Minneapolis: Fortress Press, 2009.

15 The Disputed Pauline Letters
Continuing Advice in Paul's Name

IN THIS CHAPTER WE LEARN ABOUT OTHER LETTERS ATTRIBUTED TO PAUL:

- 2 Thessalonians
- Colossians
- Ephesians
- 1 and 2 Timothy, Titus (Pastoral Epistles)

Some of the letters written in Paul's name were not actually written by Paul. These letters are often called the "disputed letters" because interpreters argue about who wrote them. Alternatively, they are sometimes called the **Deutero-Paulines**, which means the second series of letters written in Paul's name. A text written in the name of another person is referred to as a **pseudonymous** writing. While the practice of writing in another person's name sounds distressing to us, it was not uncommon in the first century. One way that many writers tried to extend the influence of an important teacher was to write in that teacher's name. Examples of it abound from this period; people were still writing letters in the name of Socrates three hundred years after he was dead. When writers took another person's name, they generally sought to apply that person's ideas to a new situation. At the same time, pseudonymity (assuming the name of another person) allows the writer to throw the weight of the revered person behind their own views. They did not view producing a pseudonymous document as dishonest, but more as expanding the tradition when a new problem arose.

Critical scholars are about equally divided over whether the real Paul wrote Colossians and 2 Thessalonians, though recently a few more seem to lean away from thinking Paul wrote them. A bit larger percent (perhaps 60 percent of the total) continue to think Paul wrote 2 Thessalonians, while about 40 percent think he wrote Colossians. A large majority is convinced that Paul did not write Ephesians, and 90 percent of critical scholars contend that Paul did not pen 1 and 2 Timothy and Titus. Interpreters find differences in vocabulary and style in the disputed letters, but more importantly their outlook and theology are somewhat different from what appears in the undisputed Pauline letters. Since these letters come from a later time, the problems they address are often somewhat different from those Paul addressed, and the churches that receive the later writings are quite different because their members are second- or third-generation Christians. The instructions the later letters give assume different things about the churches they address than what Paul could assume. Some of the problems sound familiar from the earlier letters, but the way in which they come up often seems different.

That these letters come from unknown authors who only use Paul's name makes them no less important as we try to understand early Christianity and no less authoritative for the church. Christians should remember that we do not know who wrote many books of the Hebrew Bible or even who wrote the Gospels, but they remain guides for the church. And while having people write in another person's name is troubling to twenty-first-century readers, the early readers found here an authentic extension of Paul's teaching and, more importantly, a word from God.

BOX 15.1

PSEUDONYMITY

In the ancient world, many people wrote various kinds of texts in the name of an authoritative figure who had died. The word for this is pseudonymity, which means literally "false name." The writer gained status for his writing by claiming it was written by the other person. Most apocalyptic literature was pseudonymous, often claiming to be written by people who lived hundreds or thousands of years before the book was actually written. While people today might describe this as fraud, in the ancient world it was seen as a way to bring the message of that ancient person into a new setting, or at least use that person's authority to argue for a particular view. Many religious people and philosophers used this technique. It was widely practiced and did not carry the stigma plagiarism does today.

▶ 2 Thessalonians

The Interim and the End

If 2 Thessalonians is pseudonymous, it was perhaps written as early as the year 65, and so within two or three years of Paul's death, but it may have been significantly later. Still it would have been within the first century and not later than when the letters of Paul began to be collected. The basic problem this letter confronts involves claims about what blessings Christians can possess before the **second coming** of Christ. As we have observed before, the church saw the

BOX 15.2

PARTIALLY REALIZED ESCHATOLOGY

The early church believed that the last days, the eschatological era, dawned with the life, death, and resurrection of Christ. But the fullness of the end had clearly not come, because the will of God was not dominant in the world. Still they believed they had some of the blessings of the end time. One of the most outstanding of these was the immediate presence of God in their lives through the Spirit. The belief that people can possess some gifts of the end time before the end arrives is called partially realized eschatology.

death and resurrection of Christ as the beginning of the last days. In this time of waiting for the final conclusion of all things at the return of Christ, believers enjoy some blessings of the end time. Perhaps the most outstanding of those gifts from God is the presence of the Holy Spirit in the life of each believer. Soon disputes arose between Christians about what blessings Christians had now and even over what powers the Spirit gives them in the present.

The teachers 2 Thessalonians opposes claim more gifts and blessings than the letter's author thinks Christians can possess in the present time (2:1-12). The outlook 2 Thessalonians opposes is an example of what is known as **overrealized eschatology**. These teachers contend that they, but not all Christians, have received a measure of God's Spirit that enables them to live above the troubles of life; this allows them to live closer to what God promises for everyone at the end. These teachers also say that since they have this extra portion of the Spirit, the rest of the church should recognize them as its spiritual leaders and support them financially.

What must happen before the end. The author of 2 Thessalonians caricatures this view by saying they claim that the Day of the Lord had already come (2:2). Then he shows that it could not have come yet because they know

BOX 15.3

ASSUMPTIONS OF TRANSLATORS

Read 2 Thessalonians 2:1-3 in the NRSV or the NIV. Now compare that with the same passage in the KJV. Notice the difference in the timing about the "day of the Lord." Many interpreters who thought that Paul wrote 2 Thessalonians soon after 1 Thessalonians assumed that both letters must address the same problem. Since it is clear that the letter's recipients want to know why the Second Coming of Christ has taken so long, the interpreters asserted that this was the problem 2 Thessalonians addressed. So even though the grammar of 2 Thessalonians 2:2 says that some people are saying that the day of the Lord has already come, translators who worked on the KJV and some subsequent translations thought they had to make it agree with the problem addressed in 1 Thessalonians. This passage shows how the interpretations of the translators can influence their translations. Such examples show why it is important to consult more than one translation when engaging in serious study of a biblical text.

FIGURE 15.1 **BRONZE COIN, THESSALONICA**

Minted during the Roman imperial period. The obverse (left) depicts Tyche, the goddess of fate or fortune, and the reverse (right) depicts Kabiros, a dying/rising god worshiped in Thessalonica.

Cities of Paul

that certain things must take place first. This discussion is one of the places some people turn to predict when the world will end, even though the real point of the passage is to assure its readers that the end has not come. The writer tells the Thessalonians that the **"man of lawlessness"** (or "lawless one"; 2:7-10) must be set loose before the end comes, but is still being held back by someone. These statements are intentionally veiled, but would have been clearer to the original readers than to us.

Misguided interpretations. The original readers knew who the "man of lawlessness" and the "restrainer" were, as the writer says explicitly in 2:5-6. Scholars often identify them with various Roman emperors, while more popular interpreters say they are various people from their own time, for example, Russian leaders or American presidents or Hitler—the list is almost endless. These popular interpreters identify the characters from 2 Thessalonians (and combine them with material from the book of Revelation) to predict that the end is coming soon. But when the international leaders such interpreters identify with the characters mentioned in 2 Thessalonians lose power or die, these readers immediately identify the figures in 2 Thessalonians with someone else.

We should notice two things about these kinds of readings. First, they use the text to do the opposite of what it was supposed to do: it was written to assure the readers that the end had not come and that it would be a while before it did; those who attach contemporary people to the figures in the text do so to say that the end is near. Second, and more importantly, the readings that use 2 Thessalonians to predict an imminent end of the world miss an important point in the text. The writer says that his original readers already know who these characters are, so they must be people who lived in the first century. The argument against the other teachers carries much more weight if the readers know who the man of lawlessness is. If they do not, it does them no good to be told the end has not come because he is still being held back. After all, if they do not know who he is, how can they be sure he is still being held?

Troubles before the end. The writer of 2 Thessalonians, along with the other New Testament writers, believes that the world will get worse before God finally acts to make all things right (1:5-10). The talk about the release of a lawless force that will fool people with the power of Satan fits this way of thinking about what is to come (2:8-10). For the early Christians, the world will finally get so bad that God will act in a drastic fashion to reorient everything in the cosmos because God cannot let such evil go on interminably. God's justice will require God to act then, but now God exercises patience so that as many as possible have time to abandon evil and return to God.

Living responsibly. The author of 2 Thessalonians directs his readers away from speculation about the timing of the end and toward how to live responsibly in the present time as they remember that God's judgment will come eventually. He also denies that some people have such a large measure of the Spirit that it allows them to escape life's problems. He instructs readers to reject the claims of such super-spiritual people and to stop giving them money. Thus this book contributes to the ways Christians think about the present life, spirituality, and the timing of the end.

▶ Colossians

Colossians is perhaps the first letter written in Paul's name after his death. This letter has Paul talk about his suffering for the whole church, particularly for those he had never met. This could be appropriate if he were alive because he did not personally found the church at Colossae; rather, another person from his mission team (perhaps Epaphras; see 1:7; 4:12-13) had been its founder. But the language the letter uses is more powerful if Paul has already suffered a martyr's death.

Purpose and Content

Colossians was written to oppose some teachers who had begun to say that Christians have not been forgiven of their sins and do not have a proper relationship with God unless they have visionary experiences (2:18). In their visions, these teachers say they see angels worshiping and they want the church to adopt some of the practices of the angelic worship that they witness. They have also adopted certain practices that facilitate attaining this kind of experience and expect other Christians to adopt them so they can secure their place with God. The writer of Colossians does not oppose visions as such; Paul himself had multiple visions and other ecstatic experiences. What he rejects is the idea that *everyone* must have visions and that they are necessary for salvation.

A Christ liturgy. Like Philippians, this letter cites previously written liturgical material that speaks of the exalted Christ (1:15-20). The poetic piece in Colossians makes Christ the one through whom God created and now sustains the world. Thus it presents Christ as a preexisting being who lived with God before the creation of anything in the cosmos. Colossians uses these claims about Christ as evidence that believers in him do not need the spiritual experiences the other teachers promote, because they have been brought into Christ through baptism. He says that their salvation is secure because they have identified with Christ and so enjoy the greatest spiritual blessings through their association with the most powerful being of the cosmos.

Baptism and newness. Colossians uses metaphors taken from **baptism** to make many of its most important points (2:11-12, 20; 3:1, 9-11, 14). In the first century, baptisms were immersions that symbolized the death, burial, and resurrection of Christ, and the end of one way of life for the one baptized and the beginning of a new one. Colossians assumes that people who receive baptism are old enough to recognize their need for salvation. Infant baptism becomes common many years after Colossians was written, so this writer simply assumes that all his readers remember their baptism. Colossians says that in the ritual of baptism one becomes identified with Christ and receives forgiveness from sins and the proper relationship with God.

The letter uses metaphors from the turning point of baptism to tell the readers to reflect in their behavior the new life they have been given in their baptism. They do not exhibit this new life in dramatic displays of spiritual experiences, but by living virtuous lives in community with one another. The writer enumerates the general virtues they should adopt and then gets so specific that he gives instructions about how each person should live given his or her social status (3:1—4:1).

BOX 15.4

IMAGES OF AN EXALTED CHRIST

Compare Philippians 2:6-11 with Colossians 1:15-20. Both passages quote poetic material (often identified as hymns) that was recited in churches. While Philippians records what believers were saying about Christ by the mid-50s (20 years after the death of Jesus), Colossians comes from about a decade later. Do you see any changes in the ways the church was talking about Christ? What kinds of continuities do you see?

Spiritual living. In this discussion about Christian spirituality, Colossians says that to "seek the things that are above" (3:1; or to "Set your minds on things that are above," 3:2) means living in the proper manner in all aspects of life. Being spiritual means adopting a way of being that is consistent with having been identified with Christ. This includes ridding oneself of some kinds of behavior—the writer lists sexual sins, anger, and slander among these (3:5-9). Colossians says that Christians do not need exciting personal experiences, but a confidence in their relationship with God that enables them to live out the virtues of holiness, compassion, humility, meekness, and love (3:12-14). Such a life of virtue in a secure relationship with God is the full spiritual life Colossians wants Christians to seek.

▶ Ephesians

Ephesians was probably written a bit after Colossians because its author seems to have used some phrases and themes copied from Colossians to formulate his message. In addition, it addresses the question of the relationship between Jews and Gentiles in the church from a different perspective than what we find earlier in the letters that come from Paul's lifetime.

FIGURE 15.2 **PAUL AT EPHESUS**

Gustav Doré (1832–1883). This woodcut illustrates Acts 19:17-20, "When this became known to all residents of Ephesus, both Jews and Greeks, everyone was awestruck; and the name of the Lord Jesus was praised. Also many of those who became believers confessed and disclosed their practices. A number of those who practiced magic collected their books and burned them publicly; when the value of these books was calculated, it was found to come to fifty thousand silver coins. So the word of the Lord grew mightily and prevailed." Catholic Resources for Bible, Liturgy, Art, and Theology

The Relationship of Gentiles and Jews in a Unified Church

The issues Ephesians addresses do not spring from issues that are as specific as those in the other Pauline letters. Ephesians seems so general that some have even thought it was composed as a cover letter for the first collection of Paul's letters. Though that seems unlikely, it does bring together many themes from those letters as it develops a theological basis for unity within the church.

By the time of Ephesians, Gentile Christians had begun to wonder about the necessity of retaining their connections to the church's Jewish heritage. This is very different from Paul's day, when Jewish believers were discussing what Gentiles needed to do to be part of the church. Ephesians argues that all of the church must maintain its connection to the historic people of God, Israel.

The church as cosmic body. Ephesians makes its case for the unity of the whole church by developing a view of the church that draws on previous ideas from Paul and from Colossians but also pushes beyond them. In the letters Paul certainly wrote, he talks about individual, local congregations as the "body of Christ." He uses that metaphor to urge the Corinthians to see the value in the gifts that each person brings to the group. When the author of Colossians speaks of the church as the **body of Christ**, he uses the image to designate Christ as the church's cosmic head (1:18, 24; 2:19; 3:15). As its head, Colossians sees Christ as the church's authoritative leader and the one through whom it derives its identity.

Ephesians fills out Colossians' vision of the church as Christ's body by detailing the connections between Christ and the church. This writer talks about the ligaments of the body being linked to its head and of growing into the proper height as Christ's body (4:15-16). This intimate connection between the cosmic Christ and the worldwide church demands unity among the various parts of the body. Ephesians asserts that this unity already exists because all Christians believe in the same God, have the same Spirit in their lives, confess the same things about Christ, experience the same baptism (as the ritual of admission to the church), and look forward to the same salvation (4:4-6, 13). What they need to do is recognize their unity in the face of what seem like important differences. But such differences pale in comparison to everything they share.

BOX 15.5

IDENTICAL PHRASES

Several phrases appear in both Colossians and Ephesians. For example, both say their readers were "dead in their trespasses" (Col. 2:13; Eph. 2:1, 5). To see more extensive parallels, compare Colossians 3:12-13 with Ephesians 4:1-2 and Colossians 3:16-17 with Ephesians 5:19-20. In other places Ephesians seems to take expressions in Colossians and give them a new meaning. For example, while Colossians 1:22 says that God has "reconciled you in the body of his [that is, Christ's] death," Ephesians 2:16 says Christ has "reconciled both groups [that is, Jews and Gentiles] to God in one body."

BOX 15.6

A SERIES OF ONES

Read Ephesians 4:4-6. Remembering that this letter wants to help the Jews and the Gentiles in the church continue to value one another, what kinds of bases for their togetherness does this passage provide?

The need to acknowledge unity. The immediate reason the letter recites all these reasons for the church's unity is to maintain and strengthen the ties of the church to its Jewish heritage. Since by this time there are more Gentiles in the church than Jews, the author argues powerfully that the non-Jews are members of the same community as Jewish believers and share the same experience of God through Christ. While tensions still exist between the Jewish church members who remain Torah observant and the Gentiles who are not (but he does not seem worried that Gentiles will take up the Torah), the author of Ephesians argues that the two groups must recognize that they are a single community of God's people despite those glaring differences (2:11—3:6).

The author urges the church to recognize the depth of its unity. The church's unity does not lie in having all the same ritual practices or in adopting the same ways to live out the faith. The early church included people of different ethnic groups (most obviously Jews and

FIGURE 15.3 **LIBRARY OF CELSUS IN EPHESUS**

Built 110–135 C.E., the library is also the tomb of a Roman governor of the province of Asia. The library reportedly held over twelve thousand scrolls, making it one of the largest libraries of the time. *Cities of Paul*

non-Jews) who embodied the gospel in very different ways. Some kept the Sabbath, some did not; some adhered to kosher food laws, some did not; Paul accepted money from some, and not from others. Paul and the author of Ephesians affirmed the validity of the differing practices, but always asserted that more important things held them all together in a single church. Ephesians says straightforwardly that the church's unity comes from having faith in the God that the church knows in Christ and from its members accepting this God's gifts through baptism. Whatever differences there are among different groups of Christians, these commonalities make them all one in the midst of their significant diversity.

▶ 1 and 2 Timothy, Titus (the Pastoral Epistles)

Setting and Purpose

The letters of 1 and 2 Timothy and Titus together are often called the **Pastoral Epistles** because they give instructions to associates of Paul about how to conduct their work as pastors. Since these pseudonymous letters were probably written after Paul's death, they do not actually address the people named as their recipients. They do, however, tell their readers how to organize their churches so that they can hold on to the gospel that the apostles preached. That is, they are concerned about church offices and governance structure as a way to keep out what they see as false teaching.

A number of scholars think these three letters were written at the same time by the same person and meant to be read as a group from their inception. Others, however, think that they address somewhat different issues and that 2 Timothy was not written by the same person who composed the other two. We will look at these texts individually.

1 Timothy

Interpreting the Torah. The main issue 1 Timothy addresses involves how Gentile Christians should interpret and keep the Mosaic law. Even though this letter comes from near the end of the first century, there are still questions about how the church should read the Bible. At this point, the primary Bible of the church is still the Hebrew Bible. It obviously has many commands (for example, do not work on the Sabbath) that most people in the church, since they are Gentiles, do not observe. (The church had not begun to call Sunday the Sabbath at this point. The Sabbath is actually Saturday, as the early church knew because so many of its members observed the Sabbath at their local synagogue.) It was hard to claim that the books of the Bible give instruction about how to live and understand God and then say that you do not really try to obey some of its commands.

Disputes over marriage and foods. The teaching 1 Timothy opposes wants to apply some aspects of the law directly to the Gentile members of the church that the author thinks must be handled differently. The author of 1 Timothy affirms the goodness of the law, while arguing that Gentile Christians should not directly observe some parts of it (1:6-8). There are also some people who advise Christians not to marry and to abstain from certain foods (perhaps the foods prohibited by the kosher food laws; 4:3). Some interpreters think these teachers tell people not to marry because they think that the body is evil and so must be severely restrained. Others think those who reject marriage are women who have gained significant freedom in the church by remaining single. To marry would put them under the authority of a man in the first-century social order, so they preferred to stay single. Some interpreters think an order of single women called **"widows"** had emerged and was amassing considerable power in the church (5:3-16). If this is the case, the author of 1 Timothy thinks some of their teaching is dangerous and so he wants them to marry and give up their teaching positions.

The role of women. Given his perception of the situation, the author of 1 Timothy instructs this church not to allow women to teach in the church (2:12) and gives qualifications for leaders that require them to be men (3:1-13). The author requires these men to exhibit the characteristics that the surrounding culture recognized as appropriate for leaders. These instructions are quite different from what we find in earlier letters. Paul does not place the restrictions on women that we find in 1 Timothy, and his construction of leadership is more countercultural than 1 Timothy's. At the end of the first century, the church found itself in a place that was different from where it had been forty years earlier. The author of 1 Timothy believes that his instructions about the qualifications for leadership and more conformity to cultural expectations will help the church live with less opposition from outsiders and be able to stave off the ill effects of false teaching.

As we read these repressive instructions, particularly for women, we must keep in mind that we do not know the circumstances 1 Timothy addressed as clearly as its author did. We started our discussion of the Pauline letters saying that none of them was written to people in the twenty-first century, so Christians cannot apply them directly to our time. In our cultural context, what 1 Timothy says about women and qualifications for leadership seem offensive. Again, how Christians today embody the gospel must be different from what we read in the New Testament because we live in a very different world.

Christians should also remember that this is not the only witness in the New Testament about women in leadership. Paul's mission team and his churches clearly had women leaders. But a group of female leaders in a particular setting near the end of the first century began teaching harmful ideas and adopting a way of life that the author of 1 Timothy believed was detrimental to the church as a whole. Their conduct evoked the reaction we see in this letter. His reaction to them, unfortunately, came to be the primary lens through which the church developed its

BOX 15.7

QUALIFICATIONS FOR LEADERS

We have noted that the Pastoral Epistles are concerned to set up structures of authority to help the church maintain beliefs that they think came from the apostles. Think about 1 Timothy 3:2-7 in this context. Beyond maintaining the apostolic teaching, what does this passage suggest about how leaders should relate to the outside world?

BOX 15.8

THE OFFICE OF WIDOW

Many New Testament scholars think that the widows 1 Timothy talks about constituted an office in the church that undertook various duties of ministry, including some teaching. Women who held this position were apparently supported financially by the church. Such an office might have offered women more freedom than they would have in most other circumstances in that period. These widows had grown so powerful in the churches 1 Timothy addresses that the author feels the need to curb their power by giving regulations that limit membership and what kinds of ministry they can provide. Particularly, he wants to limit their role in teaching.

governance structures and the place of women within them, as though these instructions were universally valid for all situations. But just as Paul's refusal of support from the Corinthians is not an indication that no minister or priest should ever accept money from a church, so the directives in 1 Timothy that were developed to deal with a specific occasion do not give direct instructions for Christians today (unless they also want to disallow braiding hair and tell ministers that they cannot accept pay).

2 Timothy

Faulty eschatology. The problem 2 Timothy deals with concerns expectations about the end times. Just as we found in 2 Thessalonians, some people are claiming "that the resurrection has already taken place" (2:18). It remains unclear whether they deny an afterlife or simply claim to possess in the present some powers or measure of the Spirit that the author of 2 Timothy thinks are available only after death or at the end of time. Instead of recommending that the church adopt institutional structures to repel this teaching, 2 Timothy calls attention to Paul's life. This letter has Paul present his life, including his current imprisonment and impending martyrdom, as an imitation of the life of Jesus. The pseudonymous author then recommends imitation of Paul as the way to maintain faithfulness to the correct teaching. If you want to know what to believe, 2 Timothy thinks you should listen to what Paul says; but when that is not sufficient, believers should call to mind Paul's manner of life to determine what they should think or do.

The author of 2 Timothy has Paul reject and condemn in no uncertain terms the people with wrong eschatology (2:18-19). At the same time, this Paul urges gentleness and kindness in the treatment of adversaries (2:25-26; 4:16). To follow Paul's example in 2 Timothy is to be humble and gentle, to accept suffering for the church, and to stand for the truth. There are several references to the coming judgment in 2 Timothy (1:8-12, 18; 2:10-12; 4:1-2, 8, 14, 16, 18). The letter does not mention it just to frighten those who might do wrong but to affirm that there is a future with God. The faithful do not need to worry about God's verdict because they are in Christ, and the multiple references to the judgment make it all the more natural to believe in that future with God—this in the face of a teaching that may deny that there is any future resurrection.

Examples of faith. Second Timothy reminds readers of the importance of having examples to follow and of being examples for others. Paul is the primary example the letter sets forward, but it also pictures Timothy's mother and grandmother (1:5) as people through whom Timothy came to faith. The letter alternates between naming good and bad examples, with the implication that the readers should follow the example of some people and avoid being like others. So believers are called to imitate those who believe correct teaching and whose lives conform to what God wants. At the same time, they are to become the kinds of people who teach the faith by the way they live.

Titus

Gentile Christians and the Torah. The letter of Titus returns us to the issues and perspectives of 1 Timothy. In Titus the primary issue is the place of the law's cultic purity regulations in the lives of Gentile Christians. We cannot tell what those who want more adherence to these directives think Christians gain from them, but the author of Titus contends that Gentiles must not adopt those practices.

Titus's solution to the threat of this teaching is to appoint leaders who are able to refute those who advocate that message. The first thing this letter does after the customary thanksgiving for the readers is to have Paul tell Titus to appoint leaders (1:5-9). He gives a list of qualifications that includes moral character and the ability to refute false teachers. Once the letter authorizes this structure, it immediately proceeds to castigate false teachers (1:10-16).

FIGURE 15.4 **THE PALACE OF MINOS ON CRETE**

Partial reconstruction. This palace dates back nearly two thousand years before Christ. It shows that a very developed civilization thrived on the island of Crete from the time of the Bronze Age. The writer of Titus has Paul say that he left Titus on Crete to appoint leaders in the churches. Art Resource

Societal expectations. Then the author turns to various groups among the recipients (2:1-10). He gives instructions about ethics and relations within the church to Titus, then to older and younger men, then older and younger women, and finally to slaves. The directions given these various groups encourage each to conform to societal expectations, saying that such behavior will keep others from defaming the church. So this letter is concerned about how outsiders view the church. Perhaps the writer thinks the church will be able to minimize the troubles its members face if the behavior of its members remains consistent with cultural expectations when possible.

After addressing various groups within the church, the author returns to the main topic: rejecting false teachers (3:9-11). He assures his readers that their salvation is secure without the new requirements. Finally, he tells Titus that after he repeatedly tries to convince them, he should put out of the church anyone who continues to hold the wrong view of the law.

▶ Conclusion

The concern about proper teaching that we see in Titus, the Pastorals, and the New Testament letters generally does not suggest that these writers were narrow-minded or control freaks. Rather, these authors recognized that what people believe influences how they live. If we believe our bodies are evil or of no concern to God, we may decide to engage in self-destructive behavior or to neglect responsibilities that support bodily health for others. If we think God loves one ethnic group more than another, we will probably treat others as less than human—as history has shown us repeatedly. What we believe matters!

The issues these letters engage may not seem urgent or even worth arguing about from a distance of two thousand years, but they usually grew out of what the authors thought the differing views said about God, Christ, and the meaning of being God's people. When we read them in this light, we are better able to understand their vehemence and their insistence that the church understand God in some ways rather than others.

▶ LET'S REVIEW ◀

In this chapter we learned about:

- Pseudonymity
- The question and significance of the authorship of New Testament writings
- The kinds of problems and issues the second generation of church members faced
- 2 Thessalonians
  - —Overrealized eschatology
  - —The "Man of Lawlessness"
- Colossians
  - —Opposes those who say only those who have certain spiritual experiences have salvation
  - —A poetic statement about the person of Christ
  - —Asserts the sufficiency of identification with Christ in baptism for salvation
- Ephesians
  - —Unity of Jews and Gentiles in the church
  - —Church as the cosmic body of Christ
- Pastoral Epistles
  - —All three call for more church structure and hierarchy to fight alternative teachings
  - —1 Timothy
    - Opposes an alternative way of interpreting the Torah
    - Opposes the leadership of women
  - —2 Timothy
    - Opposes overrealized eschatology
  - —Titus
    - Opposes Gentiles observing the law's cultic purity regulations

▶ KEY TERMS ◀

Angelic worship
Baptism
Body of Christ
Cultic purity
Day of the Lord
Deutero-Paulines
Eschatology
Man of lawlessness
Pastoral Epistles
Pseudonymity
Second coming
The "widows"

▶ QUESTIONS FOR REVIEW ◀

15.1 What did it mean when the people 2 Thessalonians opposes said, "The Day of the Lord is here"?
15.2 When is it most likely that the "man of lawlessness" lived? What makes you think so?
15.3 What meanings does Colossians draw out of the ritual of baptism?
15.4 How does Colossians say one's spiritual life comes to expression?
15.5 What is the basic topic of Ephesians? What do the tone and perspective of this discussion tell you about the date of the book?
15.6 How did the position of the "widows" influence what 1 Timothy says about women in roles of leadership?
15.7 How does 2 Timothy use examples of good people and bad people?
15.8 Why does 2 Timothy think various members of society should conform to cultural expectations?

▶ FOR FURTHER READING ◀

J. Christiaan Beker, *Heirs of Paul: Paul's Legacy in the New Testament and in the Church Today.* Minneapolis: Fortress Press, 1991.

Bruce Chilton, "James, Jesus' Brother," Bible and Interpretation Website 2002, http://www.bibleinterp.com/articles/Chilton_James.shtml.

Raymond F. Collins, *Letters That Paul Did Not Write: The Epistle to the Hebrews and the Pauline Pseudepigrapha.* Wilmington, Del.: Glazier, 1988.

Lewis R. Donelson, *Colossians, Ephesians, 1 and 2 Timothy, and Titus*, Westminster Bible Companion. Louisville: Westminster John Knox, 1996.

Mark Harding, *What Are They Saying about the Pastoral Epistles?* Mahwah, N.J.: Paulist, 2001.

Amy-Jill Levine and Marianne Blickenstaff, eds., *Feminist Companion to the Deutero-Pauline Epistles.* Feminist Companion to the New Testament and Early Christian Writings 7. New York: T. & T. Clark, 2003.

Wayne A. Meeks and John T. Fitzgerald, *The Writings of St. Paul,* 2nd ed. Norton Critical Edition. New York: Norton, 2007.

16 Hebrews and the General Epistles
Messages for Broader Audiences

THIS CHAPTER INVESTIGATES HEBREWS AND THE GENERAL, OR CATHOLIC, EPISTLES:

- These letters are written to a wider audience than the Pauline letters
- Hebrews
- James
- 1 and 2 Peter
- 1, 2, and 3 John
- Jude

The letters of James, 1 and 2 Peter, 1, 2, and 3 John, and Jude are known collectively as the Catholic or General Epistles because they address a broader audience than the Pauline letters. Instead of being written to a single church or the churches in a single town, they are written to larger groups, for example, all Jewish Christians outside Palestine (James) or all the churches in Asia Minor (1 Peter) or even to everyone who believes in Christ (2 Peter). These larger audiences do not suggest that these letters apply literally to all Christians everywhere and always any more than the Pauline letters do. Each of these letters takes up specific problems and issues that their authors thought a particular segment of the church or the church in a particular region needed help with. They give their instructions in the cultural and religious setting of the first and second centuries while the church continues to wrestle with how to understand God and Christ and how to live as Christians in what was sometimes a physically hostile world. So as we read them, we must continue to look for the

BOX 16.1

THE TERM *CATHOLIC*

While we often associate the word *catholic* with a particular church, its basic meaning is "universal" or "general." Thus the New Testament books called the Catholic Epistles are those written to a more general audience, in comparison with the specific audiences Paul's Letters address.

theological bases of the immediate directives they contain. This task helps all readers understand the early church better and helps believers think about how to live out those beliefs in the present.

Most New Testament scholars think all these letters are pseudonymous, that is, they were not written by the authors to whom they are attributed: James was not written by James, 1 Peter was not written by Peter, and so on. The possible exceptions are 2 and 3 John. The greetings in those letters identify their sender as "the elder." Since we do not know with certainty who "the elder" is, he may well have written these short dispatches. All of the Catholic Epistles (with the possible exceptions of 1 and 2 John) were written after their purported authors were dead. As we observed in relation to letters written in Paul's name, other writers adopted the names of these church leaders because the later writers believed they were saying what the person they claim wrote the letter would have said had he been there. Writing in the name of an apostle also gave the letter more authority than it would have had coming from anyone else.

▶ Hebrews

Even though it is not one of the Catholic or General Epistles, I will also discuss Hebrews in this chapter because it addresses a broad audience and is not one of the Pauline letters.

Authorship, Form, and Style

The book of Hebrews is not really a letter. It does not have the form of a letter, not even an introductory greeting that names the author and audience, though the author did append a closing like a letter's closing. Hebrews is more like a theological article or perhaps a closely reasoned (and really long) sermon that is written in more sophisticated Greek than any other New Testament book. It comes from a highly educated person and demands careful attention from its audience.

Some early traditions named Paul as the author of this work, while others rejected that idea. This dispute is reflected in the book's position in the canon: it is the first book after those that have Paul's name on them. Current scholars are unanimous in saying that Paul did not write it because both the writing style and the theological content are very different from Paul's. Many people have offered speculations about who its author might have been; guesses include Luke, Apollos, Barnabas, and Priscilla. We simply do not know who wrote it, only that the church found its teaching important to preserve and so gave it a place in the New Testament.

Hebrews is a rich but difficult book. Its style of argumentation fits expectations of the first century, but is sometimes hard for twenty-first-century readers to follow. Still, there is no mistaking the centrality it gives Christ and the exalted position it assigns him in relation to God and as the mediator of salvation to the world. The most difficult thing about Hebrews for many present-day readers is the way it compares Judaism and Christianity.

The Superiority of Christ

The book begins by affirming that God has been present in many ways through the prophets. This statement and many others affirm that God's voice has been heard authentically in Israel and among the Jewish people, including in their sacrificial system at the temple. Both the writer and the audience of Hebrews are Jewish. The writer is very familiar with the writings that make up the Hebrew Bible and with Jewish worship practices, and he expects his readers to know about these things. This author knows the value of the relationship with God that Israel has possessed, and he acknowledges the validity of the covenant of Moses and the efficacy of the **temple sacrifices**. However, each time he affirms the value of something within the Mosaic covenant he says, "But."

The primary purpose of Hebrews is to compare the blessings a person enjoys as a member of the covenant of Moses with the superior blessings one has in Christ. The voice of God was proclaimed by the prophets, but now God speaks more clearly through Christ (1:1-4). For this writer the Jerusalem temple is just a shadow of the heavenly temple, where an eternal and sinless high priest, Jesus, makes the earthly priests unnecessary (chs. 9–10). The sacrifices at the temple worked but had to be repeated, but the sacrifice of Christ is valid forever.

Hebrews uses these comparisons to convince fellow Jewish believers in Christ not to abandon their faith in Christ and the church (5:11—6:12; 10:23-25). Perhaps some have begun to question their faith in Christ because the end has not come, so they are considering leaving the church. The delay of Christ's second coming and their suffering of alienation from other Jews and the wider community while they wait may have made them think they were wrong about Christ. The primary reason some seem to be considering leaving the church is persecution. These believers have continued to suffer from economic and social persecution (see 10:32; 13:12-13). Under these conditions, the author of Hebrews knows that some people are considering giving up their membership in the church. He wants to refocus their attention so that they think more about what they are gaining and less about their struggles. But this encouragement also comes with a threat. This writer says that if they leave the church,

BOX 16.2

THE BIBLE OF THE AUTHOR OF HEBREWS

The author of Hebrews clearly knows Jewish tradition and ritual very well, yet his citations of Scripture usually come from the Septuagint, even when the Septuagint differs from the Hebrew text. An exception to this is Hebrews 10:30. The author of Hebrews may have known some of the other Greek translations of the Hebrew Bible (or parts of it) available in the first century, or even known some Hebrew. In any case, this writer clearly knows the books of the Hebrew Bible well.

they leave their relationship with God. Perhaps he uses such a dramatic contrast because many had experienced a relationship with God within Judaism before they joined the church. But he urges them to remain because they now possess better promises than they had before joining the church. He reminds them of the end-time blessings that he says belief in Christ brings. He argues that these benefits outweigh the losses they are enduring now. He also asserts that these end-time benefits are not available outside of the church, not even in Judaism.

Dangers of triumphalism. The argument of Hebrews is difficult for us because many Christians today are reticent to assert that Christianity is better than other religions. Such claims have been used to slaughter millions, so many Christians want to stay far away from ideas that have too often led to tragic and evil acts. The message of Hebrews is often distorted when used by those who perpetrate hate or justify harassment because they use it to assert that Judaism has no value. The author of Hebrews, however, affirms that the faith of Israel is valid and of great value (ch. 11). If this is not the case, his argument that Christ brings something better would be significantly diminished.

Readers of Hebrews must keep these dangers in view, even as they hear his writer claim exclusive benefits for those who believe in Christ. Throughout the New Testament, writers claim that Jesus is the clearest and best revelation of God; it was part of the church's message from its earliest days. But many of the New Testament writers make those claims without the numerous and explicit claims, or even the kinds of comparative claims, we find in Hebrews. Jews who joined the church obviously thought they gained something (and Paul says this explicitly in Philippians 3), but many express a continuing appreciation for their participation in the Mosaic covenant that seems absent from Hebrews.

Hebrews takes the tone it does to try to keep Jewish believers in Christ (and remember, he is Jewish) from leaving the church in the face of persecution. The author sometimes simply claims superiority for the church and sometimes threatens those who leave it with losing their relationship with God and the end-time exaltation to a life with God. Hebrews is another case that exemplifies the importance of remembering who the audience and recipients were; this is a discussion among Jews, not between Jews and Gentiles. When an argument is within the family, we often express ourselves with more vehemence and less caution than we might in a broader setting. Perhaps the writer of Hebrews has done the same thing.

BOX 16.3

THE IMAGERY OF HEBREWS

Hebrews draws extensively on the cultic imagery of the Hebrew Bible, for example, priesthood and temple, to describe how the actions of Christ provide a means of relationship with God. Paul draws on a wider range of images to speak of the human problem and how the work of Christ addresses it.

Christ as Mediating Priest

This book gives the church an exalted vision of Christ and what he accomplishes for the

BOX 16.4

HEARING THE WORD OF GOD

Read Hebrews 1:1-2. How do you see it maintaining crucial connections with the experience of God within the Jewish community? How do you see it looking to something new?

world. For this writer, Christ is the clearest revelation of God the world has or will receive. By adopting the temple imagery, the author of Hebrews envisions Christ serving as the one most qualified to enter God's presence to intercede for the people and the gift that the people offer to God (that is, Christ is both priest and offering; chs. 7–10). For this book, Christ is the only way to the proper relationship with God now and for eternity—and, the author asserts, that relationship is worth any difficulties a person may have to endure in life (10:19-39; 12:1—13:16).

▶ James

Author, Date, Form, and Recipients

This book was seemingly written near the end of the first century. Most consider its purported author, James, to be the brother of Jesus. Like Hebrews, this book does not read much like a letter; it opens with a greeting, but does not have the concluding elements of an ancient letter (greetings to others, a closing wish, and so on). James is a collection of **ethical exhortations**. Even though this book is pseudonymous, some think it contains material from actual sermons of James. Perhaps someone collected those comments and put them into something that resembles a letter as a way to preserve his teaching.

Again like Hebrews, the intended recipients may be Jewish members of the church, particularly those who live outside Palestine. Alternatively, when James addresses the "twelve tribes" (1:1), he may have the whole church in mind because he now sees the church as the renewed people of God. Nothing beyond the greeting points to a specifically Jewish audience.

"Be Doers of the Word"

James gives instructions about a wide range of behaviors and attitudes. Some instructions are

BOX 16.5

JAMES, THE BROTHER OF JESUS

Not long after the beginning of the church, the apostle James, the original leader of the Jerusalem church (the mother church of all Christianity), who had been one of the original disciples of Jesus, was martyred. The person who took his place as leader of that church was James, the brother of Jesus. According to the Gospels, none of the members of Jesus' family was among his followers. Still, soon after his death, Acts has Jesus' brother in one of the most important positions in the earliest church. The early church also recognized James as an apostle, even though he had not been one of Jesus' closest followers. The only other person accorded this status without being counted among the Twelve was Paul.

FIGURE 16.1 **YOUTH SERVICE PROJECT**

Member of a church youth group repairing the homes of the poor and elderly. The book of James insists that faith is not really faith unless it is seen in actions such as helping the poor. Chad Snellgrove

as general as resist temptation and live your faith, don't just talk about it (as he says it, "be doers of the word, and not hearers only"; 1:22). He also gives very specific instructions, such as don't say bad things about one another (4:11) and don't get angry easily (1:19). James is particularly concerned about the way the church treats the poor. He repeatedly warns readers against showing partiality to the wealthy and instructs the wealthy to give up their status for the good of others (2:1-13; 5:1-6).

Faith and works. The book of James is known best for its assertion that "faith without works is dead" (2:17). This statement is part of an exhortation to put one's faith into action; he says that if your life does not show that you have faith, then you do not really have faith. James says that if faith just means believing that there is a God, having it makes you no better than demons because they also believe that God exists.

Most New Testament scholars think that James phrases this statement the way he does to oppose it to Paul's assertion that justification (gaining the proper relationship with God through forgiveness) is by faith, without the works of the law. James either thinks Paul's way of stating this could lead to people saying it does not matter how believers live or he has heard some people say it means that. So he frames his exhortation to reject that interpretation of Paul's teaching.

These statements from James and Paul sound very different, even contradictory, but the two ideas are quite similar. The difference comes in the way each uses the word *faith*. In James it means assenting to particular beliefs; in Paul it usually means adopting both certain beliefs and the manner of life and way of understanding the world that goes with them. For Paul, faith includes an attitude of dependence on God, and a commitment to live as God's person. James, though, thinks the way Paul says this is an opening for people to reject any moral demands as part of the Christian way of life.

James and Paul have very different emphases, but both see morality as a necessary component of being in the church. They differ, however, in the way they express this. James thinks it is important to make the point by separating it from the word *faith;* Paul reasons that you can make the point by including ethical behavior in what it means to have "faith." They are not saying precisely the same things, but neither do they contradict each another in substance.

The book of James provides an emphasis on morality. It contains so little explanation of any other kinds of teaching that Martin Luther questioned whether it should be in the Bible. But the book's insistence that Christians' lives must be a demonstration of their beliefs remains an important message for believers.

▶ 1 Peter

Author, Date, and Theme

This letter addresses "the exiles of the Dispersion." Like James, this language draws on imagery taken from the history of the Israelites; this designation of non-Jewish Christians tells its readers to interpret their life situation through the lens of Israel's experience of being taken from their homeland. He supports this outlook in the closing of the letter by calling Rome "Babylon," the place the people of Judah were taken in the exile. So the pseudonymous author envisions the church as a people who are in a foreign land. The values and lives of Christians are not at home in the world as it exists. This perspective helps the readers of 1 Peter understand why they suffer persecution—they are aliens in a foreign land, even though they live in the neighborhood in which they grew up.

Since this letter was probably written near the end of the first century, Peter had been dead for about thirty years. The writer uses Peter's name to encourage the Christians in what is now Turkey who are enduring persecution because of their faith. Since Peter himself suffered and was martyred for the faith, the author knows that his testimony will be particularly effective because he has already gone through what he now encourages the readers to endure. The letter refers explicitly to Peter's suffering to remind the recipients that he understands their position and to give them an example to follow. The letter also reminds them that Christ suffered at the hands of the outside world.

BOX 16.6

AN IMPORTANT ETHICAL ISSUE

One of the ethical issues James deals with extensively is the treatment of the poor. How do you see James 2:2-5 addressing this issue in a way that is countercultural? What is the basis for this way of treating the rich and poor in the church?

BOX 16.7

ETHICAL EXHORTATION

Exhortation includes more than providing instructions about the right way to live. It also offers encouragement and support designed to help the recipient be able to live up to the demands given in the instructions. In the New Testament, this support might remind the recipients of what had been done for them or of the identity God had given them, in addition to reminding them that God's Spirit enabled them to live as they should. This exhortation might also include threats about what would happen if the instructions were ignored.

FIGURE 16.2 **CRUCIFIXION OF PETER**

Filippino Lippi (1481–1483). Tradition says that when Peter was about to be crucified, he asked to be crucified upside down because he felt unworthy to be executed in the same way Jesus had been executed. Wikimedia Commons

The Tension between Church and World

The writer wants to comfort the readers as he encourages them to remain faithful in spite of persecution. He reminds them of all God has done for them and assures them that they truly are God's people. As we have noted in connection with the Pauline letters, it is hard to reconcile the belief that you have joined God's people and now serve God as God wants with the experience of suffering because you belong to the church. So 1 Peter assures its recipients that this is often what happens to God's people because the evil that presently controls the world tries to injure them in order to tempt them to desert their relationship with God.

This letter sets up a sharp distinction between the church and the rest of the world. The church and the world are opposing forces and there can be no reconciliation between them; people must choose one or the other, they cannot give allegiance to both. The author of 1 Peter gives voice to the recipients' experience of the world. They know that joining the church brought trouble to their lives and remaining in it continues to do so. The author tries to help them remain faithful by identifying them as foreigners, as people who belong to another race,

BOX 16.8

PERSECUTION AND IDENTITY

It is clear from 1 Peter 4:12-13 that the church this letter addresses has been experiencing persecution. Think of how this experience might lead to the understanding of their place in the world that we see in 1 Peter 2:11. What does this identity suggest about the way the author wants the readers to relate to the outside world?

nation, and people. They are displaced people who are suffering because of who they are.

It is not enough simply to tell these people that they have made themselves foreigners; the author of 1 Peter must also affirm that this new identity is worth the suffering it brings. So he reminds them of the salvation that awaits them at the resurrection. With imagery drawn from baptism he focuses their attention on the promise of God's blessings in that later time, even as their new identity demands faithfulness and holiness in the present.

The letter of 1 Peter, then, provides believers an interpretation of their present suffering and reminds them of the identity that Christians possess in the present world. It stands as a constant reminder to believers that the values of one's culture are not those of the church or God's kingdom. This letter urges Christians to be distinct from those around them, even though that invites a clash of values in which believers suffer and are disadvantaged. He can urge his recipients to face these problems courageously because the salvation God gives them in Christ more than makes up for the struggle.

▶ 2 Peter

Form and Date

The author of 2 Peter assumes this pseudonym and writes to all Christians claiming to be the apostle, who is about to die. So it serves as something like a farewell address. This is probably the latest book included in the New Testament. It was written around the year 125 and its author notes that churches are already having a hard time understanding Paul's letters (3:15-16). This author also quotes from the Apocrypha, those books that were part of the Septuagint (the second-century B.C.E. translation of the Hebrew Bible), but did not become part of the Bible of Judaism.

BOX 16.9

SOURCES USED BY THE AUTHOR OF 2 PETER

The author of 2 Peter is familiar with the developments of early biblical stories that appear in the books of the Apocrypha. When the author of 2 Peter alludes to material from books of the Apocrypha, he does not seem to distinguish them from other biblical writings. Places at which 2 Peter is at least familiar with the same traditions as those in apocryphal books and is perhaps dependent on them include the list of deeds of God's judgment in 2 Peter 1:4-10, which is much like Wisdom of Solomon 10:4-8, and 2 Peter 1:7, calling Lot a righteous man, as does Wisdom 19:17. Even beyond the Apocrypha, 2 Peter draws on ideas also found in the collection of writings known as the Pseudepigrapha. The mention of angels being thrown into deepest darkness (2:4) draws on the same tradition found in *1 Enoch* 10.1-8. In addition to these lesser-known sources, 2 Peter clearly draws material directly from the New Testament book of Jude.

The Certainty of the Return of Christ

The main point of this letter is to assure its readers that the second coming of Christ will happen someday. The promise of Christ's return was now almost a hundred years old, and nothing had changed about the world. Some had begun to question whether it would ever come; perhaps they say that Christians already possess all the spiritual blessings God has to offer, though that is not clear. The main problem is that they deny the future coming of Christ. This author vigorously affirms belief in a second coming of Christ that accompanies the end of the world.

Personal attacks and caricatures. This is a rather harsh letter by our standards. The writer accuses the people who do not think there will be a future coming of Christ with all kinds of immorality and unfaithfulness. He paints a very unattractive picture of them, their morality, and their motives—he even calls them irrational animals (2:12). The kinds of accusations he makes about them are probably quite exaggerated. In this period of history, arguments between schools of thought and even in court cases regularly included accusations about the character of the person or people on the other side. Most of the time these were caricatures, or even completely false. But lawyers, speech writers, and even philosophers were trained to include these accusations so that people would be less inclined to listen to the other side. The author of 2 Peter accepts this way of arguing against a teaching that he thinks is very destructive to the church.

In his attempt to help his readers continue to believe in the second coming, he asserts that those who doubt it will face God's condemnation in the end. He assures the recipients of this letter that the promises of the God who made the world are secure; if God has promised the return of Christ, it will happen. Then he reframes the question about time. He says that while a hundred years seems like a long time to us, for God it is just the blink of an eye. As he says it, "with the Lord one day is like a thousand years, and a thousand years are like one day" (3:8). So when God says that Christ will return soon, what might seem like a long time by human reckoning is only a moment by God's account. Therefore, what seems like a long delay should not be taken as evidence that it will not happen.

A motivation for moral behavior. This writer goes on to say that certainty about the future coming of Christ should also motivate believers to live holy lives because that coming will include an evaluation of their lives as well as the lives of unbelievers. He uses the conviction that judgment is certain, then, to motivate Christians to live morally. While this sounds like a threat, it is more a reminder that they must live up to the identity God has granted them because they remain accountable to God for what God has given them.

The letter of 2 Peter deals with a question that the church has faced in every subsequent generation: When will the end come? This book has no specifics, and probably does not think anyone can give any. It has a message

BOX 16.10

WHAT COUNTS AS SCRIPTURE?

What does 2 Peter 3:15b-16 suggest about how this writer thinks about the letters of Paul? What does this suggest about when those letters began to be collected?

BOX 16.11

SHIFTING ESCHATOLOGICAL EXPECTATIONS

When the earliest believers interpreted the resurrection of Jesus as the beginning of the last days, they expected the end of those days to come quickly. As years became decades, it became clear that the end was not coming as quickly as they had at first thought. Yet the importance of having a decisive response from God to the evil of the world did not wane. It became clear in their thinking that what was important was not the timing of God's act but its certainty. Thus the way they expressed their eschatological hope changed. They stopped saying so often that the end was *near* and started saying that its coming would be *sudden*. This subtle yet vital change allowed them to continue to emphasize the necessity of living properly always and to maintain that certainty about God's coming justice.

that is much more important for believers than questions about timing. It says that God's future reign and judgment are certain. They should, therefore, constantly inform how people live their lives. The certainty of God's reward of the faithful and response to evil is more important than when God chooses to do it. However many years intervene, 2 Peter says Christians must live with the confidence that God will eventually establish justice and reward the faithful.

▶ Jude

Author, Date, and Recipients

The author of Jude addresses his letter to all Christians. The pseudonymous writer introduces himself as Jude, the brother of James, to claim a connection to an apostle and so increase the authority of his message. This letter was written around the close of the first century and sometime before 2 Peter because the latter seems to copy some parts of Jude. This letter clearly comes from a time after the original apostles have died because Jude calls his readers to remember what they had said.

The harshness that we observed in 2 Peter comes in part from Jude. Jude charges his opponents with all kinds of immorality and compares them with notorious evildoers from the Hebrew Bible and Jewish tradition to make

BOX 16.12

THE IMPORTANCE OF APOSTOLICITY

The greeting of Jude shows how important it was for a message to be associated with an apostle to be received as authoritative. The author of Jude claims to be the brother of James, which also makes him the brother of Jesus. Instead of claiming this connection with Jesus, Jude chooses to call himself "a servant of Jesus Christ and brother of James." The connection to Jesus does less to establish his authority than his connection to James, because apostles were recognized as the people authorized by Jesus to provide the correct interpretation of his words and deeds.

sure his readers do not want to be associated with them. In the same vein he predicts their coming condemnation. But even while he rails against them, he holds some hope for them to repent. As he comes to the end of his letter, the writer instructs the church to try to rescue these people, even while hating the filth that is the result of their sin (v. 23).

▶ Keeping the Torah

This book comes from a different perspective than most we have seen in the New Testament. While Paul writes to Gentile believers telling them they are not allowed to receive circumcision, keep the Sabbath, and adopt Jewish dietary regulations, Jude writes against people who do not keep enough of the law. The author of Jude seems to belong to the church in Palestine that continued to observe the law as faithful Jews. His accusations about the immorality of the teachers he opposes is probably quite exaggerated; their real failure is to keep the law as this writer thinks they should. Jude makes this the equivalent of gross immorality, perhaps because he believes that is where this teaching will lead.

The book of Jude helps us see something of the diversity of the early church and the church that developed the canon of the New Testament. Here is a book that comes from a branch of the church that continued to keep the Mosaic law, while most New Testament books come from the stream of the church that did not allow Gentiles to keep the law. These traditions are quite different from one another. Paul did not encourage Jews to give up their observance of the law unless it interfered dramatically with their fellowship with non-Jewish church members—which it did not do very often. Still, the early church included branches that differed significantly in their practice of the faith. The inclusion of Jude in the New Testament suggests that both were faithful ways to embody the gospel. This may give present-day readers a way to think about the diversity of the church today. The inclusion of Jude within the New Testament suggests to believers today that there are multiple ways of practicing the faith that are legitimate and faithful.

▶ 1 John

Date and Origin

The letters of 1, 2, and 3 John all seem to come from the same community, the group that also finished the Gospel of John. Scholars are led to this conclusion by how similar the vocabulary and outlook of these letters are to the Gospel of John. Given the issues that 1 and 2 John address, the three documents seem to have been written sometime around the year 100.

Purpose and Themes

The opening and closing characteristics of a letter are missing from 1 John, so it is not really a letter. It is an essay or perhaps an extended sermon that has a fairly specific focus. It wants to oppose a teaching that some in the author's church have begun to believe and advocate. This teaching has led them to break off from the church of which the author of 1 John is a leader.

The author of 1 John interprets the willingness of the advocates of the competing teaching to leave the church as a lack of love for fellow Christians. Perhaps the argument between those who remain with the writer and those who left was so vicious that the things said suggest a lack of love for those on the other side. In a conflict that involves a significant theological issue, this writer says that no one who lacks love for fellow Christians can know the truth about God.

However the debate was conducted, the author of 1 John both accuses the other side of a lack of love and emphasizes love as a feature of God's character. He says that love is so central to who God is that if a person lacks love for others, it shows that he or she does not know or have a relationship with God.

At the same time, the writer of 1 John fiercely denounces the other side; they do not just lack love, he calls them the antichrist. He says that if they were really God's people, they would not have left his church. So the vitriolic rhetoric seems to come from both sides, as those on each side believe they are arguing for the truth about Jesus.

The dangers of Docetism. The teaching 1 John opposes is called **Docetism**, the belief that Jesus did not have a physical body but was only a nonbodily presence on earth. While many today have trouble making sense of the claim that the human Jesus was divine, Docetists believed firmly that he was divine (or at least from one of the highest spirit realms), which meant that he could not be human or have a body composed of the matter of this realm. Docetists thought that the divine nature would be defiled if it came into contact with the matter that makes up the world. So if Jesus was divine, he must have been present in a way that did not involve actually touching the things in this world.

Docetism is known from both its later opponents and from some Docetic writings that still exist. Some Docetists were also **Gnostics**, but not all Gnostics were Docetists. This belief does, however, fit well the usual Gnostic devaluation of the world. Most Gnostics thought the world was a lowly place from which they wanted to escape; they saw it as the creation of a low and ignorant being who mistakenly thought he was powerful. This lack of power, usually along with some malevolence, made this world a bad place where ignorance and evil reign. It is easy to see why people with such beliefs would be inclined to Docetism because they would not want the divine Christ tainted by this world. The author of 1 John does not oppose Gnosticism more generally (though we would expect he would have opposed it had he known it), only the specific teaching of Docetism.

The author of 1 John sees Docetism as a serious threat to the church because it distances God from the world and diminishes the connection between Christ and Christians (notice that he says Christians will become like Jesus at the second coming [3:2-3]). He battles the danger of Docetism by pointing to the experience of the disciples with Jesus. Writing as the apostle John, he begins this treatise saying that he had real physical contact with Jesus. He saw and touched Jesus. So you can be sure that his teaching about the real physical nature of Jesus is true (1:1-3). Later he says that the test of truth is whether a person confesses that "Jesus Christ has come in the flesh" (4:2).

BOX 16.13

LOVE AND THE ANTICHRIST

Compare the sentiments in 1 John 4:7-11 and 1 John 2:18-19. How do you think the author held these two things together?

FIGURE 16.3 **IMAGE OF CAESAR ON A COIN**

The obverse (front side) of this coin, from Thessalonica, calls Caesar god (*Caesar theos*). The refusal of Christians and Jews to grant this title to Caesar set them apart from most others in the empire and became part of the reason they were persecuted. *Cities of Paul*

Christian virtues. While the problem with Docetism is what motivated this author to compose 1 John, he spends even more time commanding his readers to be loving in imitation of God. In part this is a rebuke of those who have left his church, since he attributes their departure to a lack of love as well as to their Docetism. But he also dwells on the topic of love to instruct his audience about how they should act in the midst of their debates about this theological issue. He says they must always act with love that reflects the way God has loved them.

In addition, this writer exhorts the readers to live righteously. He celebrates the grace that all believers receive in Christ, but also insists that they put sin out of their lives as evidence that they have received God's salvation. He tells them they must be sinless, but also says that anyone who claims to be sinless is lying. While he wants Christians to strive for sinlessness, he does not want them to despair when they do sin. Just when he says they must not sin, he adds that when they do sin Christ intercedes with God for them (3:4-10). So while resting securely on God's grace, he insists that Christians live ethical lives.

The writer of 1 John shows concern for both proper teaching and ethical living. He insists that the church hold correct beliefs about Christ and that its members put sin out of their lives and act out of love for others. This author knows there is a connection between what we believe and how we live; indeed, he demands that connection. This book also sets out what this writer believes everyone in the church must confess about Christ: that he is uniquely the Son from God and that he was genuinely human. This drawing together of the divine and human shows how much God values this world and so provides a reason for the importance of ethical living. God's immediate and intimate presence in the world reveals that God cares about what happens here, so Christians must live in a way that demonstrates God's love for the world.

▶ 2 John

Author and Intended Readers

The author of the short letter of 2 John identifies himself simply as "the elder" (v. 1), that is, one who holds a leadership position in the church. If this person did not also write 1 John, he knows it well because he follows some of its themes and echoes its instructions. "The elder" writes to "the elect lady and her children." We can see that this metaphor refers to a church by the final greetings in the letter, where the elder sends the recipients greetings from "the children of your elect sister" (v. 13). So he calls each congregation an "elect lady" and names the members of that church the children of that lady.

Themes

Two themes dominate the thirteen verses of this letter: the need to love one another and a warning against Docetists. Just as we find in 1 John, the elder makes the command to love one another fundamental; it is the command that should guide all of life. He is equally insistent that the readers reject those who say Jesus did not have a physical body, telling them not to welcome such people into their houses. "Welcoming" here involves more than giving them a cup of coffee; he means allowing them to teach or have a base of operation in someone's home.

This last command could be an effective tool against the spread of Docetism, because Christian missionaries and teachers who went from town to town often stayed with a member of the church. The church would support teachers with food and other needs as they lived in someone's home. The author of 2 John tells his readers not to extend this support to anyone who teaches Docetism.

This little letter gives us a glimpse of life in the early church. We see a person who is probably a prominent leader of one congregation giving instructions to another congregation that he thinks will listen to him. He is concerned that Christians believe the right things about Christ; for him this is essential. But he is also adamant that they act in love, even in the midst of controversy; he even sees adherence to correct teaching as an act of love.

▶ 3 John

Author, Date, and Destination

"The elder" wrote 3 John at about the same time he wrote 2 John, probably around the year 100. He writes 3 John to Gaius, the leader of a church in another city, to shore up support from Gaius and to commend Demetrius, another leader and probably traveling preacher, as a reliable teacher and ally. At the same time, the elder warns Gaius about Diotrephes, another church leader, who had refused support to some agents of the elder who had visited his church.

BOX 16.14

THE OFFICE OF ELDER

One of the earliest positions of leadership in the church was that of "elder." As early as Paul's Letter to the Philippians, he singles out the elders to mention in the letter's greeting. This leadership position was probably modeled after a leadership position in the synagogue. There seems to be significant development in the way the position is understood by the time we get to the Pastoral Epistles. Those letters give specific instructions about qualifications and duties of elders. In 2 and 3 John, "the Elder" who is the author of these letters seems to hold a position that he expects to be recognized beyond his own congregation.

Purpose

This conflict over recognizing leaders and teachers is probably related to the issue of Docetism. While that topic does not come up explicitly, Diotrephes' rejection of the elder's emissaries probably also means that he allows others, of whom the elder does not approve, to teach.

This letter shows what kind of turmoil often accompanies arguments over correct doctrine. It does not suggest that such arguments are not necessary, only that they often have unintended and unpleasant consequences. This letter does exhort Christians to be hospitable to one another, even as they engage in doctrinal disputes.

▶ Conclusion

The Catholic Epistles show us the issues and problems that faced the second and third generations of Christians. They were trying to make sense of their new faith as they encountered the world and its values. They were negotiating an understanding of themselves that further defined their beliefs about God and Christ and designated how they should live in relation to both the outside world and within the church. They demonstrate that the church continued to encompass diverse views, though within some parameters that most saw as inviolable. The writers of these missives defended their views passionately, but also tried to do so with kindness, believing that even the act of defending particular beliefs is an act of love for those considering the other teaching and for those who (mistakenly in their view) have already adopted that teaching. These writers regularly call their readers to accept the teaching of the apostles, sometimes saying this explicitly and sometimes writing in the name of an apostle. These books clearly designate the apostles as the teachers the church must look to for its understanding of how God is known in Christ.

▶ LET'S REVIEW ◀

In our survey of Hebrews and the Catholic Epistles we learned about:

- The settings in which the church set out its identity in the late first and early second centuries
- The things the authors of the Catholic Epistles saw as problems for the church of this era
- Hebrews
    - Not really one of the Catholic Epistles—or even a letter
    - Constantly compares the good things in Judaism with the good things members of the church possess
    - Asserts the superiority of faith in Christ
    - Intends to provide support for people enduring persecution
- James
    - A collection of ethical exhortations
    - Emphasizes the importance of living out one's faith commitments

— Is concerned about some interpretations of Paul's teaching

- 1 Peter
  — Written to help readers endure persecution by assuring them of future blessings
  — Makes a sharp distinction between the church and the rest of the world
- 2 Peter
  — Latest book in the New Testament
  — Argues for certainty of Second Coming of Christ, despite its unexpected delay
- Jude
  — Claims to be written by the brother of an apostle (and of Jesus)
  — Contains harsh polemic against those who interpret the Law differently
  — Calls on Jewish believers in Christ to continue to keep the Law
- 1 John
  — Opposes Docetism
  — Identifies love as a central Christian virtue
- 2 John
  — Opposes Docetism
  — Expects readers to be loving and at the same time to refuse hospitality to those who teach harmful things
- 3 John
  — Encourages support for leaders who welcome teachers who have proper teaching

▶ KEY TERMS ◀

Dispersion
Docetism
"The elder"
Exhortation
Gnostics
Sacrifice
Second coming

▶ QUESTIONS FOR REVIEW ◀

16.1 Discuss the literary form of the book of Hebrews.
16.2 Why does Hebrews evaluate the Mosaic covenant as it does?
16.3 Compare what James means by the word *faith* with what Paul means when he uses the term.
16.4 How does 1 Peter envision the way that members of the church relate to the world around them?
16.5 How does 2 Peter try to help readers believe in a second coming of Christ?
16.6 How is the perspective of Jude different from the Pauline letters?
16.7 What arguments does 1 John provide to lead his readers to reject Docetism?

▶ FOR FURTHER READING ◀

Bruce Chilton, "James, Jesus' Brother," Bible and Interpretation Website 2002, http://www.bibleinterp.com/articles/Chilton_James.shtml.

Lewis R. Donelson, *From Hebrews to Revelation: A Theological Introduction*. Louisville: Westminster John Knox, 2001.

Philip B. Harner, *What Are They Saying about the Catholic Epistles?* Mahwah, N.J.: Paulist, 2004.

Amy-Jill Levine and Maria Mayo Robbins, eds., *A Feminist Companion to the Catholic Epistles and Hebrews*. Feminist Companion to the New Testament and Early Christian Writings 8. New York: T. & T. Clark, 2004.

Darian Lockett. *An Introduction to the Catholic Epistles*. T. & T. Clark Approaches to Biblical Texts. Bloomsbury: T. & T. Clark, 2012.

David R. Nienhuis, *Not by Paul Alone: The Formation of the Catholic Epistle Collection and Christian Canon*. Waco, Tex.: Baylor University Press, 2007.

John J. Pilch, *Flights of the Soul: Visions, Heavenly Journeys, and Peak Experiences in the Biblical World*. Grand Rapids: Eerdmans, 2011.

17 Revelation
John's Apocalyptic Vision

IN THIS CHAPTER WE WILL LEARN ABOUT

- The genre of apocalyptic
- The purpose of apocalyptic
- The purpose of Revelation

The Revelation of John has been among the most abused and misunderstood books in the Bible. It has been used to frighten people and predict world events, although it was intended to bring comfort and assurance, as well as to encourage people who were suffering for their beliefs. As we read this book it seems strange and mysterious with its giant monsters (including dragons) and violent imagery. It is the only book many of us know that is like this. The people it was written for initially, however, were familiar with many books written in this style. It belongs in the category of literature known as **apocalyptic** (from the Greek word that means "revelation"). To understand the book of Revelation, we need to know something about this genre of literature and the way of thinking that lies behind it. Seeing other literature like it will help us understand why this book did not seem strange to its original recipients.

▶ The Apocalyptic Genre

This genre of literature developed from the Hebrew prophets, as their successors were influenced by the wisdom tradition and some non-Israelite ideas, especially some from Persia. The beginnings of Israel's use of such dramatic imagery appear in the first chapters of Ezekiel and the second half of Daniel. The original recipients of Revelation did not think Revelation was a strange document because they had read other apocalyptic writings that had the same kinds of descriptions of heaven (e.g., 1 Enoch 14.8-23), powerful beings, grotesque beasts (e.g., 2 Esdras 11:1-9), battles, scenes of judgment (e.g., 1 Enoch 102.1-11), and all that makes this book seem bizarre to us. These things are standard fare in apocalyptic writings, and this genre had been well-known for over a hundred years by the time John wrote Revelation.

The strange images in these books intend to convey a message from God that includes information that remains hidden from most people and is perhaps being revealed for the first time now. All these books predict that the end is near. They say God is about ready to act to stop the powers of evil that hurt God's people. Then God will also establish God's reign so that things will be as God intends them.

Predicting the Past

Most apocalyptic works are **pseudepigrapha**, that is, a work written by someone other than the person the book claims as its author. Most are written hundreds or thousands of years after the death of the purported author. By the first century, apocalypticists had written books in the names of Abraham, Enoch, Ezra, and many other characters in the stories of the Hebrew Bible. The value of pretending that these notable characters wrote them is in having those ancient people predict the future. If a

FIGURE 17.1 **FOUR HORSEMEN OF THE APOCALYPSE**

Palma Giovane (1544–1634). In Revelation 6, John tells of a vision in which four horses and riders appear in succession. Each horse and rider symbolize the devastation coming upon Rome and its inhabitants because of the way the empire oppresses the church and opposes the purposes of God.

Art Resource

book written in the first century has Abraham predict the future from Abraham's time to the first century, he appears to get it right because the events he predicts are really in the past when the book is written. Once Abraham (or whoever) gets over a thousand years of history correct, one expects he will get the next few years right as well. So when the book's author predicts that God is about to act, the prediction is credible because all the other predictions (which were not really predictions) have come true. The writers of these books are much better at predicting the past than at predicting the future. Scholars date many of these writings by when they start to. get history wrong. These ancient writers also all got the timing of God's catastrophic intervention in the world wrong because they proclaimed that the end of the world (or at least a complete reorientation of it) was near.

Symbolic imagery. These pretended predictions of world history (known as ***ex eventu*** [after the event] **prophecies**) demonstrate how we should read the imagery in this genre. These writers do not use open and straightforward names for the events and people of world history. Instead, they present them symbolically and in fantastic imagery that lets alert readers know who those historical figures are without calling them by name. For example, Daniel 8:5-8 talks about a giant goat with one horn coming from the west and flying across the earth without touching the ground. This goat conquers all the kingdoms in the Middle East, including the Persian Empire. From what follows, it becomes clear that this goat is Alexander the Great. But Daniel never calls him or any other ruler by name; rather, he uses these images that the author thinks the readers will be able to decode with little trouble.

This kind of imagery not only increases the dramatic effect, it also keeps the writer and readers safer. People under the Roman Empire (and before Rome under other repressive governments) could not openly predict its defeat at the hands of anyone, including God. To do so was to invite trouble and suppression, and probably execution. One could, however, write a strange book about various animals engaging in battles with an eagle (the symbol of the Roman Empire) being killed. The readers the book is intended for are supposed to

BOX 17.1

APOCALYPTIC AS GENRE AND WORLDVIEW

The term *apocalyptic* can refer to a way of perceiving the world or to a type of literature. The genre of an apocalypse usually has an angelic being bring a hidden message that reveals heavenly realities that help to explain the unjust circumstances that the recipient is experiencing. The book of Revelation is the only New Testament book written fully in this genre, though parts of others are (for example, Mark 13). Still, all New Testament writers have an apocalyptic worldview. They all see the world as a place that is dominated by evil to such an extent that only a catastrophic intervention by God can set things right. The apocalyptic worldview looks to this act of God to vindicate God's justice and the faithfulness of God's people.

FIGURE 17.2 **HEAVEN**

Jacopo Tintoretto (c. 1588). This image is the central part of one of the largest paintings ever done on canvas. It depicts Jesus and Mary, with the twelve apostles at their sides, occupying the region of Paradise above all other people. Art Resource

know what the author means, but it is hard to prosecute a person for such a book if one does not know the code. Writers of apocalyptic expect their readers to know how to read this sort of material. One of the reasons it is so difficult to read this material today is that most people simply do not know the genre and how to read it and its imagery. Once we recognize what kind of writing it is and read it as that genre should be read, we can make better sense of it.

A glimpse of transcendent reality. Using such imagery, these writings give their readers a glimpse of a transcendent reality that tells what the end will be like and how the supernatural world is affecting what is happening in our world. Apocalyptic writers see a connection between conflicts among spiritual forces and the status of earthly kingdoms and empires. When particular beings in that other realm are being successful, the empires they represent do well here. (Those empires, of course, also worship these beings.) The most basic conflict apocalyptic writers see is that between the powers who honor and obey God (for example, angels) and those who oppose God's will. Sometimes these evil powers are coordinated under a single ruler (such as Satan) and sometimes they do not seem to submit to a single ruler. However they are organized, these powers of evil have the upper hand at the moment.

Literature of Crisis

Apocalyptic writings appear in times of crisis. When the conflict is too great between what a community believes should be and what they actually experience, we often find apocalyptic. This experience of being deprived of what others have or of what you think you should possess is sometimes called "**relative deprivation**." You may not be destitute or on the verge of starvation, but you seem to have much less than others who are like you. Such circumstances often lead people to feel that they are in a crisis situation. In psychological categories we can think of it as **cognitive dissonance**. The people involved think there is simply too much disparity between the way things are and the way the group's beliefs suggest things should be. The problem becomes especially acute when the people see themselves as God's people and know they are suffering precisely for their belief in God. This suffering may not involve state-sponsored violence but rather economic disadvantage or social ostracism. We should not underestimate the long-term effect of such experiences, particularly when they might include depriving one's children of status or of enough to eat. When the persecution does involve state-sponsored violence and martyrdom, a group's faith can be pressed to the breaking point. When groups have these kinds of experiences, they often produce or read apocalyptic writings.

In such crisis situations apocalyptic writings try to assure those who are suffering that it is not all for nothing; God will act to set things right. God will vindicate their faith and punish those who abuse them. Apocalyptic writings serve to encourage the community to maintain its faith when the group's experience of the world seems to suggest that its beliefs are wrong.

BOX 17.2

THEODICY

Apocalyptic addresses the basic question of theodicy. In its simplest form, theodicy asks why bad things happen to good people. More generally, it is the question of why evil exists in a world created by a good God.

Justice and Judgment

The central theological purpose of apocalyptic literature among Jewish and Christian groups is to defend their belief in a God who is just, loving, and powerful. If God is these things, the world God made should reflect those characteristics of God. But it does not. In the experience of these people the world is unjust, especially for the people of God. The problem of the existence of evil in the world is always an issue theologians discuss, but it becomes an urgent question for you when you are the person suffering. At its heart, apocalyptic is a response to the problem of evil; it is a defense of the belief in the kind of God Jews and Christians say they believe in.

Apocalyptic defends this belief in God by asserting that God hates what is going on in the world as much as those who are suffering do and that God will make things right. Indeed, the situation is so bad that God will not delay taking action much longer; things have just gotten too bad for God to let it go on. Apocalyptic writers acknowledge that God is not in control of the world now, but say God is about to intervene on a cosmic scale to reassert control. While evil rules at the moment, God will soon take control and address the injustices committed by those evil powers and people. Then all will see that God is powerful and loving and just. That justice will be seen in God's rewarding of faithfulness and punishing of wickedness. Judgment is a necessary part of this scheme because God must be just.

Justice in 2 Esdras. The importance of justice appears explicitly at the beginning of 2 Esdras, a book in the Apocrypha. In this book, the supposed author, Ezra, asks God to explain why the nation of Judah is still in exile. He acknowledges that they did evil, but then says that the Babylonians who conquered them are even worse. How is it fair, he asks, for the worse nation to punish the better—and that on a long-term basis? An angel comes with the response that if Ezra can accomplish one of three tasks, then God will answer him. The tasks are humanly impossible (bring back a day from the past, weigh fire, measure a blast of wind); they are the same kinds of tasks God gave Job to silence him. But Ezra refuses this challenge and refuses to be silenced. He says he does not want to know about those kinds of things, but rather he wants an explanation for what happens to him every day! God gave him a brain, he argues, and so owes him an account that makes sense of this experience (2 Esdras 3:28—4:52).

God responds to this bold demand by granting Ezra a series of visions that explain how the righteous will be blessed and the wicked punished. The point to notice is that the starting point for the whole discussion is a question about the justice that should be evident in the world (because a just God should make a just world), but is in fact missing. Ezra says God owes him an explanation for the overwhelming injustice of the world. This demand is at the core of apocalyptic literature.

FIGURE 17.3 **THE LAST JUDGMENT**
Michelangelo (1475–1564). This fresco (1537–41) in the Sistine Chapel depicts Christ as the judge of all people. Wikimedia Commons

Interwoven injustice. While we usually want to deny or ignore it, a bit of reflection on our inability to stop being involved with processes that implicate us in injustice shows that the world is fundamentally unjust. (See the discussion of 1 Thessalonians above.) This often works to our advantage because it means we get

BOX 17.3

2 ESDRAS 3:30-31A; 4:22-25

I have seen how you endure those who have sinned, and have spared those who act wickedly, and have destroyed your people, and protected your enemies, and have not shown to anyone how your way may be comprehended. . . .

Then I answered and said, "I implore you, my lord, why have I been endowed with the power of understanding? For I did not wish to inquire about the ways above, but about those things that we daily experience: why Israel has been given over to the Gentiles in disgrace; why the people whom you loved has been given over to godless tribes, and the law of our ancestors has been brought to destruction and the written covenants no longer exist. We pass from the world like locusts, and our life is like a mist, and we are not worthy to obtain mercy. But what will he do for his name that is invoked over us? It is about these things that I have asked."

more than our share of resources and get them cheaply. It means some of us are secure and comfortable at the expense of the less advantaged. This injustice is woven so tightly into the fabric of our economic, social, and governmental structures that we cannot escape it even if we want to. Those who wrote apocalyptic were experiencing the brunt of that injustice and they wanted to tell their readers what God would do about it. But even beyond the usual injustices of the world, these communities were suffering more precisely because they were God's people. Apocalyptic writers assured readers that this experience of oppression and injustice would not be the last word. God will act to compensate them for their suffering and to repay those who abuse them.

These writings' use of extravagant imagery contributes to their persuasiveness. They address people who face overwhelming problems that they know are beyond their control. They know that the social, cultural, and governmental structures are so powerful and pervasive that they are inescapable. In the first century the Roman Empire found many ways to present their power as undefeatable. Beyond a military presence, they built government buildings that dwarfed other civic structures as a way to impose their presence and imply that they were too powerful to be overthrown. (This is a common strategy of nations. Just look at the scale of the architecture in Washington, D.C.) To enable its readers to envision a different reality, apocalyptic literature must present images of an even more powerful force for the good. The striking images in this literature want to shock its readers into perceiving a different reality.

Summary

Overall, then, the practical purpose of apocalyptic literature is to encourage readers to remain faithful in difficult times. The theological purpose of such writings is to defend and support belief in a God who is powerful, loving, and just. This literature assures its readers that God is who they say God is and that their suffering will receive a proper and loving response from God. It does not encourage readers to be passive but to do the work of God in the world bravely, even when doing so brings difficulty and suffering into their lives.

▶ The Book of Revelation

Author and Date

The Revelation to John in the New Testament is different from most apocalyptic works in that it is not pseudepigraphic; it comes to its readers under the real name of its author. The writer was a Christian prophet who was Jewish and well known to churches in western Turkey. Some early interpreters identified this John as the apostle John, but there is no evidence in the text for this identification. The author does not claim to be an apostle (though those who included it in the New Testament claimed he was) or to have known the earthly Jesus. His credibility stems from his acquaintance with the churches to which he writes, who recognize him as a prophet, not from being an apostle. We identify him as Jewish because he is familiar with Jewish writings.

Some scholars think John wrote Revelation near the end of the first century, between 90 and 95. They argue that it was written during the reign of **Domitian** (81–96), who organized a persecution against Christians. After all, the author of this book has been exiled to the island of Patmos because he is a Christian. There is, however, very little evidence that Domitian initiated an *empire-wide* persecution of Christians. In fact, the main evidence for such widespread persecution is the book of Revelation. This makes the argument for this date quite circular—one dates the book to the time of Domitian because he persecuted Christians, and one knows he persecuted Christians because one sees it in this book.

The circular nature of the argument that supports the date in the 90s has led many scholars to propose an earlier date for the book. These interpreters argue that Revelation was probably written in the 60s or 70s. The problem then is less state-sponsored persecution and more waning expectation of the end and a move toward assimilation to the culture in an attempt to avoid the social and economic consequences of the church's countercultural stance. The letters to the seven churches at the beginning of the book suggest that such assimilation has become a tendency for some in the church. Furthermore, since the church has now been waiting thirty to forty years for the end to come, many might well have begun to question its imminence and its reality. This book reaffirms both. Whichever of these views about the date is correct, Revelation was written in the second half of the first century to churches that are being harmfully disadvantaged by their allegiance to the movement and its lord, Christ.

The Purpose of the Book

Like all apocalyptic literature, Revelation wants to assure its readers that their suffering is not for nothing. It wants to encourage them to remain faithful and to continue to do those things (for example, worshiping only God) that make people reject and resent them because it will be worth it. God has not deserted them and those powers that oppress them are not stronger than God. These Christians need to hear that God will be victorious in the end. One can summarize the message of the book of Revelation with just two words: God wins! The slightly longer version is that God wins and you will participate in that victory if you remain faithful. Then all your suffering will have been worth it.

For readers who are in comfortable circumstances, this may sound selfish. But for people who are suffering and wondering if their sufferings show that they are wrong about turning to worship only God and about living for God, these words are necessary. They do offer a reward to the faithful, but more importantly they assure them that God is as powerful, loving, and just as they believe God is. Talk of rewarding the faithful in Revelation is not about greed but about justice and about God showing God's love for those who suffer, especially when that pain comes to them because of their faith in God.

A Series of Sevens

Seven seals. While Revelation's concern for justice plays a constant role in much of its narrative, John also addresses the issue explicitly in a few places. In the first in a series of sevens (seven seals, seven trumpets, and seven bowls), John has Christ open seals on a scroll (6:1). When Jesus opens the fifth seal, it reveals a picture of the souls of martyrs waiting under heaven's altar. These martyrs ask how long it will be until the powerful Lord who is holy and true passes judgment on those who had killed them. The response is that God will act soon and that those who killed the martyrs will get precisely what they deserve; just as they killed the martyrs, so they will be killed (6:9-10). The writer envisions the perpetrators receiving just what they did to others.

Seven bowls. In another series of sevens, John has angels pour out the contents of seven bowls. When the angel empties the third bowl the rivers and springs of the earth turn to blood (the writer is here drawing on the Exodus story of Moses turning the water of Egypt to blood, Exod. 7:14-25). Then another angel declares, "You are just, O Holy One," because this is a fitting punishment for those who have shed the blood of God's people. The angel concludes his pronouncement saying, "your judgments are true and just" (Rev. 16:4-7; see also 19:1-2).

Divine Retribution and Divine Love

In passages such as the series of sevens, Revelation has God show restraint in ways that we usually miss. Most ancient people thought

FIGURE 17.4 **PARTHIAN COIN**

A drachma from 2 B.C.E.–4 C.E. The distinctive culture of the Parthians is obvious from this coin. The Parthians were Persian, and so their cultural center was in what is today Iran. They represented the greatest threat to Rome on its eastern border. Thus, John envisions them as the power that God uses to bring down the Roman Empire. Art Resource

their gods were quite capricious and often overreacted to an offense in ways that wreaked undue havoc on the offenders. Revelation, on the other hand, is careful to note that God's wrath does not exceed what is just. The punishment the writer envisions is exactly what the offenders should receive. This is an important point because some modern readers see an angry, bloodthirsty, vengeful God in Revelation. It is true that the imagery is gruesome and beyond what we see as appropriate, but John still wants it to be clear that God does not go beyond what is just. God is not out of control as those other gods are. Is God angry? Of course—people have been hurting and killing God's people. What loving mother would not rightfully be angry? But this proper anger that comes from love does not lead God to act unjustly. The wicked are punished no more than they should be.

Such retribution does not mean that for John, God is finally not a God of love. Revelation interprets troubles in the world as the beginnings of God's judgment against evil. In John's telling about the series of bowls above, he patterns what happens after the plagues that came on Egypt when God freed God's people from oppressive conditions there. After the angel pours out the fourth bowl, John comments that even these plagues did not cause people to repent (16:9, 11). He says the same thing after the fifth bowl. John's amazement shows that one of God's goals at the beginning of the judgments God sends on the world was to lead the wicked to repent. Thus God's love potentially extends even to those who abuse God's people. If they would change their ways and turn to God, God would revoke their punishment. In some ways, John can hardly believe these people do not turn to God after these acts of judgment; in other ways he is sure they will not turn to God because of the advantages they accrue by being allies of the powers of evil (see ch. 18).

BOX 17.4

EARLY ARRIVALS AND JUSTICE

Who are the people who appear in heaven in Revelation 6:9-10? What do you think it suggests that these are the only humans in any scene in heaven in the book of Revelation. Other humans come to heaven only after the Second Coming of Christ. Also compare what these people want God to do with what the people say about God in Revelation 15:3. What do these passages suggest about the amount of punishment that will come on the wicked?

This understanding of God's goal in judgment also helps John explain why God is delaying the subjection of evil; that is, it gives a reason why it is taking God so long to act to relieve the suffering of God's people. While evil dominates, God's reactions to it and God's judgments against it show those who will see who God is and invite them to turn from evil. Thus the delay is an act of mercy on God's part; God delays to give more people time to repent.

John also helps his readers deal with the unexpected delay of the return of Christ and the end by the way he ends the first cycle of sevens. He has the action building through the opening of the seals on this scroll so that readers think he is about to describe a final act to establish God's reign, but instead "there was

BOX 17.5

FOOD EATEN AT TEMPLES

Compare the way the writer of Revelation deals with the issue of food sacrificed in a temple of a god in Revelation 2:14 with the way Paul deals with it in 1 Corinthians 8 and 10:1-22. Why do you think these writers are so concerned about where church members get their food?

silence in heaven for about half an hour" (8:1). The action just stops; there is an inexplicable delay. It seems everyone just goes on break. Once the action restarts, it is not the end but the beginning of a series of seven trumpets. This imagery and scenario acknowledge the delay of the end without giving an explanation. Still, it makes that postponement fit into God's scheme of things.

Seven Letters to Seven Churches

Revelation begins with an initial appearance of Jesus to John in which Jesus claims power over death and associates himself closely with God (1:17-20). The first thing Jesus does is dictate a letter to each of seven churches (2:1—3:22). Each has a problem or an issue to which Jesus wants them to give attention. Though there are differences, the main problems seem to center around rejecting false teachers and whether or how believers should accommodate themselves to cultural demands—and these two things may be related.

The churches these letters address are all located in western Asia Minor (the western part of Turkey). These are all churches that John has probably visited and so knows. Many scholars think the letters to these churches are intended for the whole church because there are seven of them. In apocalyptic literature, and more broadly in the ancient world, the number seven symbolized completeness or fullness. So addressing seven churches may mean that John intends Jesus to address the whole church with these letters.

Meals at pagan temples. A recurring question in these brief letters is whether Christians can attend meals at the temples of various gods (2:14, 20). Many business and social occasions were held at temples in the first century. Their dining rooms served the function of today's fellowship halls or activity centers in churches. When a group met at the temple, someone would offer the god a sacrifice. Fortunately, the gods usually only wanted the fat and the guts.

BOX 17.6

THE LETTERS OF REVELATION

After John's initial encounter with Christ, he relates a series of letters that the risen Christ addresses to seven churches in the western part of Asia Minor. Each letter begins with the formula: "To the angel of the church in [City] write," followed by a symbolic description of the risen Christ. Each letter has a message particularly suited to the things that city is known for. Many interpreters think there are seven of these letters to represent the church worldwide, because seven is a symbolic number for completeness.

FIGURE 17.5 **SANCTUARY OF ASCLEPIUS, PERGAMUM**

This theater is part of a sanctuary of Asclepius, a god of healing. Those seeking healing would often sleep at such an Asclepian sanctuary to receive a vision to tell them what they should do to be healed. Pergamum is one of the cities that John writes to in the letters in the opening chapters of Revelation. He warns them not to participate in activities at temples of other gods. *Cities of Paul*

This meant that the one who brought the sacrifice could keep most of the rest of the animal. Thus there would be plenty for a party or meeting that included a meal. Participants in the meal were under no obligation to attend the sacrifice or worship the god. Still, most people thought there was an advantage to having eaten such food, that one would thereby imbibe the power of that god.

Paul had told the Corinthians (1 Corinthians 8–10) that they could not go to such meals because it was too close to participating in the worship of another god. Other Christians, however, had taken the view that since the beings worshiped at those temples were not really gods, Christians could attend such meals and celebrations. The issue remains controversial when John writes. He is clear that participating in those meals violates the faith, so Christians must avoid them. This requirement could damage the business prospects of these Christians because they would miss business meetings. It could hurt their social lives because their neighbors would find it difficult to understand why their Christian neighbor refused to attend their child's wedding or some other celebration. To demand this separation from the rest of the world imposed a significant burden on some and put the countercultural beliefs of the church on display. Revelation says a believer must be willing to accept the consequences of this stance to remain one of God's people.

A Vision of Heaven

After the seven letters and as the prelude to the real action, John relates a vision of heaven (ch. 4). In this vision, John sees mighty beings surrounding God's throne proclaiming that God is holy and all-powerful. Furthermore, they proclaim that God is creator of the world (an affirmation that implies that other gods did not create it). The focus of this scene shifts at the beginning of chapter 5, when John sees that God is holding a scroll that no one is worthy or able to open. This scroll contains information John so desperately wants to know that he begins to cry when he hears that no one is qualified

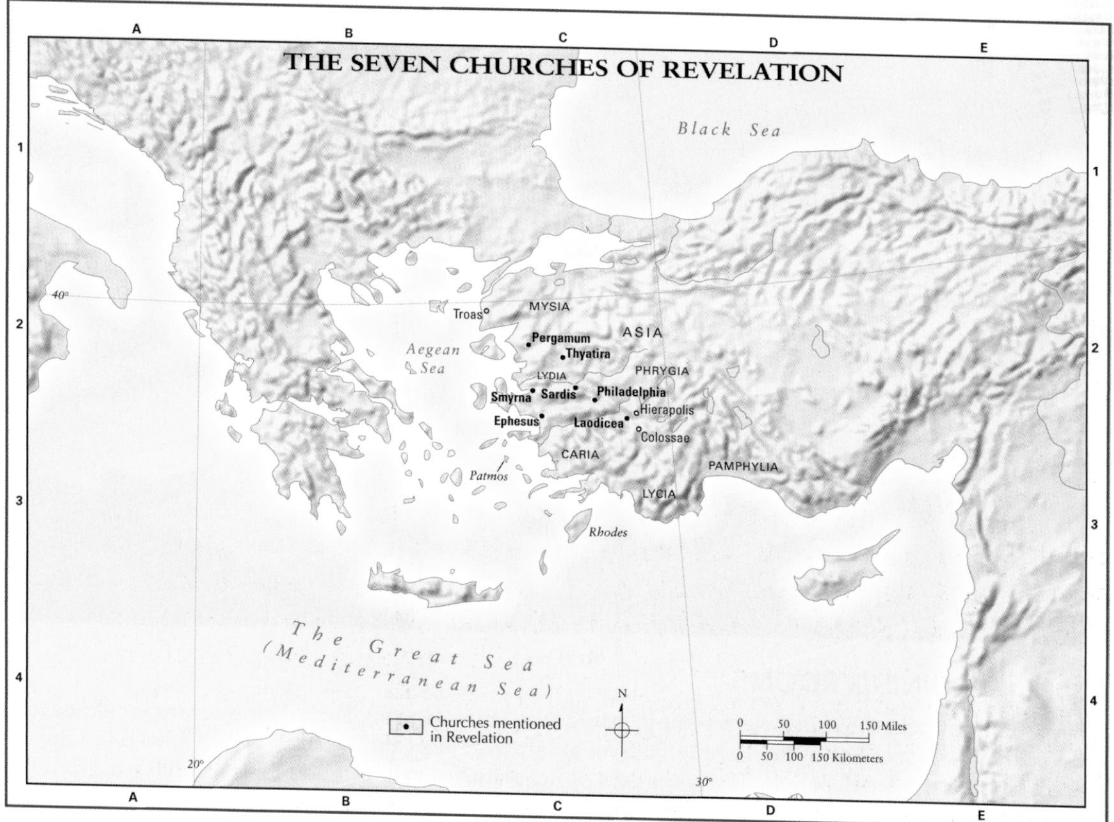

MAP 17.1

to open it. Then one of the powerful beings around God's throne assures him that there is one who is worthy, "the Lion of the tribe of Judah, the Root of David," who is a conqueror (v. 5). This description prepares readers for a powerful, kingly figure who could defeat anything. But when the "Lion" appears near God's throne it is "a **Lamb** standing as if it had been **slaughtered**" but now lives. This is perhaps the quintessential image of Jesus in Revelation. The most powerful being in heaven (other than God) has allowed himself to be killed and through that act becomes the conqueror. These images are intentionally paradoxical. The paradox becomes emphatic in the rest of the description of the Lamb: he also has seven horns and seven eyes. Horns represent strength and eyes signify knowledge in apocalyptic tradition; the number seven, as we have seen, denotes a full or perfect amount of whatever it appears with. So the slain

FIGURE 17.6 **DINING ROOMS**

Dining rooms attached to an ancient temple at Brauron (near Athens). Such dining rooms would have been used after a sacrifice at the temple. The meat left over after the sacrifice would have been the main course for the meal. John tells the readers of Revelation not to attend meals at such places because he believes that eating food that had just been offered to a god constitutes unfaithfulness to God. Jerry Sumney

Lamb has all power and all knowledge, and yet has been killed. And through that death he is the conqueror.

An example for those who suffer. This image violates all the cultural norms for evaluating power and status. How can the highest being have been defeated and even killed? Yet in this vision it is so. Jesus' power is seen in his willingness to accept humiliation, powerlessness, and death for others. This image also represents the experience of the churches to whom John writes. They have access to the only true God, and yet they suffer; they worship only the most powerful God, and still they are persecuted. The subsequent resurrection and assumption of power by this lamb assures such readers that God will take care of them when the suffering is finished.

This image intends to offer strength and comfort to people who are suffering because of their faith. It gives an interpretation of their suffering that helps them endure their problems. This image must not be a tool that people in power use to tell those in lower positions that they should accept abuse. Calls to imitate Christ by suffering abuse have often been used to tell women that they should remain in abusive situations. To use imitation of Christ to encourage acceptance of that sort of abuse misunderstands and violently misuses these texts. The New Testament's calls to imitate Christ by accepting suffering are never calls to submit to an abusive relationship. Instead, they offer encouragement when suffering for one's faith is inevitable. Whenever the more powerful person uses these texts to ask the less powerful person to suffer, these texts have been turned upside down. In this image of Jesus, the powerful one suffers for the less powerful. Imitating this example would require the more powerful person to intervene in a way that takes the abuse upon himself or herself, rather than sending the less powerful person into harm's way.

When this paradoxical lamb opens the first seal on the scroll, the action of the book gets underway. Now John starts relating flamboyant images of what happens when people violate the will of God. The action that begins here reaches its initial climax in the first account of the final judgment in chapter 11.

The Nearness of the End

Writing to a church that wonders why it is taking Christ so long to return to establish God's rule over evil, John asserts repeatedly that Christ will return "soon." He begins and ends the book with affirmations that the end is soon (1:1; 22:20). He shares this expectation with all apocalyptic writers. Part of the purpose of emphasizing the nearness of the end is to affirm its certainty. John does not give an outline of world history; he does not think the world will continue to exist as it is for long. Even if he thought it might be years, he probably did not think the end would be delayed by decades, and certainly not centuries. On the other hand, he did not think anyone could know just when the end would come. As in other New Testament books, John says that the end will come unexpectedly, like a thief sneaking into a house in the middle of the night (16:15). Since no one can know the timing, believers must always be ready for the end by remaining faithful.

Still, John emphasizes the nearness of the end. Without this emphasis, his book would not have been meaningful to those who were suffering. To tell people who are enduring pain or sending their children to bed hungry not to worry, because God will respond to their needs in two thousand years (or more), does nothing to help them endure. It is no comfort to be told that in two thousand years some big country they never heard of (whether Russia or Iran or whoever) would do something that would be a sign that the end was near.

People in the middle of suffering care nothing about distant history or events. They want to know how long their pain will last and what God is going to do about it. John assures his readers that God will act soon and that God's action will more than repay them for their suffering. After all, God despises this evil so much that God will not delay the required response much longer. Even as John tells them it will be soon, he acknowledges that he cannot say just when.

Not an outline of world history. Another indication that John does not intend to set out a map of world history for the following decades or centuries is the book's cyclical nature. We have already noted that he has the Lamb of God open seven seals, the seventh of which leads to seven trumpets. There are other such cycles within the book. After the opening of each seal and the blowing of each trumpet, John gives a description of God's judgment on the evil of the world. But these sketches do not set out a chronology that readers can trace to determine how long it will be before the end. Rather each seal and trumpet gives a different perspective on the consequences of the dominance of evil in the world; one might describe the social effects of ignoring God's will, another the military or economic effects of acting unjustly.

Cycles of symbols. That John intends these to be snapshots from different angles rather than a chronology is clear from the largest movement within the book. Once the action begins in chapter 6, John takes readers through the seals and trumpets. When the seventh trumpet blows John hears voices say, "The kingdom of the world has become the kingdom of our Lord," and now is "the time for judging the dead" (11:15-19). (This is the passage from which Handel drew when composing the "Hallelujah Chorus.") This is clearly the judgment day at the end of time. If John were giving a chronological account of things, the book would have to end here. But it does not. Instead, chapter 12 begins with a new set of symbols with the world going on as before. Chapter 11 clearly represents a climax that celebrates the coming victory of God, but it does not end the book. John has more to say about the defeat of evil and the difficulties God's people endure before that comes, so he simply starts with a set of new images. When people try to plot the course of history with the material in Revelation, they have failed to perceive its cyclical nature. The book does move toward another and final climax in chapters 21 and 22, but its cycles show that it does not give a chronology of events that lets a reader predict the date of the end.

Graphic Imagery

The Son of Man and the lampstands. Since this book is in the genre of apocalyptic, all its imagery and numbers are symbolic. John expects his readers to understand what the symbols stand for with very little trouble. When he thinks they may not grasp them immediately or clearly, he gives them a hint. The first example of this comes with his initial description of the Christ who appears to him. This Christ, who has white hair, eyes like fire, bronze feet, and a sword for a tongue, is standing among seven lampstands and holding seven stars (1:12-16). John thinks readers will understand most of this symbolism, but is concerned that they may not catch the meaning of the lampstands and stars. Since the meaning may not be clear, he tells them what they mean in verse 20. He says the lampstands represent the seven churches he is writing this book to and the stars are the angels of those churches, perhaps their heavenly representatives or guardians.

The prostitute. A second example is more startling. In 17:1-6 John describes a giant, drunk prostitute dressed in royal colors with extravagant jewelry who is riding on an enormous red animal that has seven heads and ten horns and blasphemous names written all over it. She is drunk because she has been drinking the blood of martyrs. After John sees this woman he says, "I was greatly amazed"—no kidding! But what could it mean? John knows this image goes beyond the common symbols in the tradition, so he needs to explain it. He signals that recognition in verse 9 with his understatement that interpreting this sign "calls for a mind that has wisdom." He explains that the seven heads of the animal that the woman rides are seven mountains. That may not seem like much help until we remember the nickname of the city of Rome: "the **City of Seven Hills**." The place this giant sits is the city of Rome, so she is the Roman

FIGURE 17.7 **THE GREAT ALTAR AT PERGAMUM**

This altar to Zeus, built in the second century B.C.E., is evidence of the city's great wealth. *Cities of Paul*

Empire (as his further explanation confirms because the heads also represent kings).

In paragraphs that follow his description of this woman and her mount, John describes the ways other governments and commercial enterprises are all related to this giant and will all be sad when she falls, which she is about to do. With this veiled language, John condemns the empire and predicts its fall, even celebrates its fall, because he and the church know it as the enemy of God and of God's people.

BOX 17.7

SEXUAL INFIDELITY AS A METAPHOR

Revelation often talks about the sin of fornication as one for which God will punish the evil empire and evildoers. This description of evildoers is metaphoric; it goes back to the Israelite prophets who described the Israelites' unfaithfulness to God as fornication. The most specific form of this unfaithfulness is worship of other gods. John takes up this language and even emphasizes it as he describes the evils of the Roman Empire (see particularly ch. 17). One of the chief evils the empire imposes is the demand that people venerate the emperor as one of the gods of Rome. Thus John sees fornication as the proper symbolic description of the demands of Rome.

Numerology

Just as these images are symbolic, so are all the numbers in the book. For example, when John says there are **twenty-four elders** around God's throne, he probably wants readers to think of the twelve tribes of Israel and the twelve apostles (who represent the church) so that these elders represent all of the people of God of all times. This way of using numbers, or **numerology**, also appears in chapter 7. At the beginning of the chapter, John uses the number 144,000 to designate the number of people who are faithful to God, and he describes them as members of the twelve tribes of Israel. John does not mean that only 144,000 people will end up with God (or that they will all be Jewish); rather, he uses numbers symbolically. The number 144,000 is 12 × 12 × 1,000. The first 12 clearly represents Israel, but he does not mean literally Jews. Israel represents the people of God and since all 12 tribes are there (remember 10 of them had been lost when the nation of Israel fell in 722 B.C.E.), it means the reconstituted whole people of God. It is that whole people of God times itself times 1,000 that we see being the faithful and the saved. He means to say that an amazing multitude will be saved. Verse 9 shows that John does not mean a literal number because when he looks again this crowd consists of people from every nation and they are innumerable.

A millennium. A number in Revelation that many people take literally appears in chapter 20. Here Satan and his minions are bound and cast into a pit, where they are kept for a thousand years before they are released. The image is a strange one, but we can be certain that the thousand is symbolic because all the other numbers in Revelation are symbolic (even the seven churches to which John writes probably represent the whole church). The number one thousand probably represents some kind of perfection. Perhaps John sees Satan's power limited during the ministry of Jesus or at some point in that ministry. After Jesus' ascension, the power of Satan is renewed and unleashed on the church. Perhaps he thinks the time of the limit to Satan's power is all of the time the church exists until the second coming of Christ. But he does not envision a time when God completely abandons the world to the powers of evil (or when people suddenly disappear). We should note that this text says nothing about a reign of Christ on earth and nothing about an antichrist. Some popular accounts of the end of time have to read these elements into Revelation to fabricate the scenario they envision.

Violence

Revelation contains a significant amount of violence. People are killed in wars, in plagues, in floods. Some people try to hide from terrible punishments, some are thrown into burning lakes. Jesus first appears in a frightening form with a sword for a tongue (1:16), and he appears elsewhere as a warrior (19:11-16). These are drastic images for desperate times. In the midst of all this violence, however, there is something important to note: the people of God never inflict a single act of violence or retaliation on anyone. All retribution is left to God and Christ, along with their heavenly entourage (for example, angels). It is never the business of God's people to injure others; they may ask God to do it, but they never raise their own hands to inflict it. Revelation does not authorize people who think they are God's people to impose their will through violence. In fact, Revelation regularly condemns human violence (for example, 6:9-10; 9:21; 11:7-10; 12:11-12; 13:7, 15; 16:4-6; 17:6).

▶ Conclusion

In the end, Revelation proclaims that God's justice and mercy will conquer the powers of evil and set in place a day of goodness in which the cosmos works as it should, reflecting the love, goodness, and justice of God. In that time, people live in direct fellowship with God and their will conforms to God's. All needs will be met and there is no suffering. Everlasting participation in this idyllic place and time is the promise John offers to help his readers who remain faithful to God, even when, or rather precisely when, faithfulness brings problems and pain. With this hope, John bolsters their resolve to live for God. With this vision, he asserts that God really is the God of justice, love, and power.

▶ LET'S REVIEW ◀

In this chapter we have learned about:

- The genre of apocalyptic
- The purpose of apocalyptic
  - —Reassurance to those suffering
  - —Apologetic for the character of God
- Narrative flow of Revelation
- Purpose of Revelation
  - —Reassurance to Christians enduring persecution
  - —Explanation of delay of the End
  - —Assurance of the certainty of vindication and of God's justice

▶ KEY TERMS ◀

Antichrist
Apocalyptic
City of Seven Hills
Cognitive dissonance
Domitian
Ex eventu prophecy
Numerology
Patmos
Pseudepigrapha
Relative deprivation
Slaughtered lamb
Theodicy
Twenty-four elders

▶ QUESTIONS FOR REVIEW ◀

17.1 What is the basic purpose of apocalyptic literature?
17.2 Why do apocalyptic writings use *ex eventu* prophecy?
17.3 Why does apocalyptic use such strange and extravagant imagery? How hard do the writers think this will be for their intended readers to understand?
17.4 What kind of persecution did most of the original readers of Revelation probably face?
17.5 What does the series of sevens (seals, trumpets, bowls) tell you about the way the narrative of Revelation works?
17.6 What characteristics of God does Revelation bring to expression in judgment? Why does the author welcome the exercise of those characteristics?
17.7 What are the functions of the image of Jesus as the slaughtered lamb in Revelation 5?
17.8 Why does John use such veiled images to deliver his message in Revelation?
17.9 What is the central message of Revelation?

▶ FOR FURTHER READING ◀

David L. Barr, *Reading the Book of Revelation: A Resource for Students*, Resources for Biblical Studies. Atlanta: Society of Biblical Literature, 2003.

Brian K. Blount, *Can I Get a Witness? Reading Revelation through African American Culture.* Louisville: Westminster John Knox, 2005.

John J. Collins, *The Apocalyptic Imagination: An Introduction to Jewish Apocalyptic Literature*, Biblical Resources Series. Grand Rapids: Eerdmans, 1998.

David A. deSilva, *Seeing Things John's Way: The Rhetoric of the Book of Revelation*. Louisville: Westminster John Knox, 2009.

Larry P. Jones and Jerry L. Sumney, *Preaching Apocalyptic Texts*, Preaching Classic Texts. St. Louis: Chalice, 1999.

Bruce Metzger, *Breaking the Code: Understanding the Book of Revelation*. Nashville: Abingdon, 1993.

Paul S. Minear, *New Testament Apocalyptic*, Interpreting Biblical Texts. Nashville: Abingdon, 1981.

Mitchell Reddish, *Apocalyptic Literature: A Reader*. Nashville: Abingdon, 1990.

Christopher Rowland, *The Open Heaven: A Study of Apocalyptic in Judaism and Early Christianity*. New York: Crossroad, 1982.

Christopher Rowland, "Revelation; Introduction, Commentary, and Reflections," in *New Interpreter's Bible*, vol. 12, ed. Leander Keck. Nashville: Abingdon, 2004.

D. S. Russell, *The Method and Message of Jewish Apocalyptic, 200 BC–AD 100*, Old Testament Library. Philadelphia: Westminster, 1964.

EPILOGUE: THE BIBLE TODAY

The Bible is a dangerous book—it always has been. It has been used to justify mass killings, executions of heretics, and enslavement of races, to scam people out of their life savings and for countless other egregious things. Such abuses are part of the reason everyone needs to know something about the Bible.

The Bible is also foundational for Western culture. Its influence on our culture and society has been incalculable. It has put its mark on the laws of most Western nations; it has shaped social policy, economic policy, and foreign policy. It has influenced writers from Shakespeare to Dostoyevsky, and allusions to it and echoes of its literary patterns continue to shape both the style and the content of political discourse, especially during recent U.S. presidential campaigns. Without knowledge of the Bible, we lack one of the tools required to understand our world.

The Bible has also been a book that has helped millions of people find meaning and significance in their lives, whether we think of saints from the past (Augustine, Aquinas), those who read religious self-help books now, or just the people in church on Easter. It has been a means of understanding and learning how to relate to the divine. Millions still look to it for guidance and for help in understanding God's will for them and the world.

Given all of these ways that the Bible exerts influence on our world, it is incumbent on us as informed and educated citizens to know what it contains and how to understand its content. This book has introduced you to the basic content of the Bible and to the primary methods scholars use to analyze and interpret it. I expect that some of what you have learned about the Bible is surprising, some of it comforting, and perhaps other things troubling.

This book also demonstrates that some of the ways the Bible is interpreted in the public square are not the only, or even among the better, ways to read it. Some readings, though intended to be faithful by being literalistic, are simply misunderstandings of the nature of the texts and so serious misunderstandings of what is being said. When we read poetry as if it were a scientific account, we not only get the wrong message but also miss the beauty of what is being expressed. When we isolate phrases or ideas from larger texts with little consideration of their historical and literary contexts, we will usually misunderstand them and often find in them (or insert into them, intentionally or unintentionally) nearly any meaning we want. Exploring the context and genre of the biblical texts helps readers arrive at more responsible and more respectful readings.

Learning how to recognize the various kinds of writings in the Bible can help us understand many of the arguments about the world's origin that have raged throughout the last century. If, for example, we recognize that the first chapters of Genesis are theological rather than scientific accounts of creation, we will be able to think about the discussion concerning "the Bible and evolution" in a very different way. Knowing that a central point of the Genesis creation stories is to argue that God alone, rather than a pantheon of gods, created the world helps us see the value of those stories as something other than an account that competes against a scientific investigation.

Indeed, the methods of science can never show that Genesis makes false claims, because scientific methods are not the tools we would need to make such an assessment regarding theological claims. Science can discover the structures of the physical world and so bring us wonderful advances in medicine and technology. We cannot, however, use those methods to assess the theological claim (for example) that God stands behind and supports those structures. Conversely, the theological claims of Genesis do not show that scientific observations and hypotheses concerning the origins of the world are wrong, because theological methods are not adequate for evaluating scientific discoveries. If we keep our scientific and theological discussions within their bounds and if we read Genesis as the kind of theological text it is, science and theology do not come into conflict. Rather, each approaches the discussion of the origins of the world from different perspectives. Only if readers of Genesis have too narrow an understanding of the kind of literature it is and of the message set out by its original authors might they see the theory of evolution as a threat to its message. Both evolution and Genesis can be true; they are different sorts of truth, but both true. There is no contradiction between saying theologically that God alone is responsible for the existence of the world and saying scientifically that the world evolved over millions of years. A reading of Genesis that is sensitive to its literary type and intended message can affirm both.

Such a recognition of the nature of the biblical texts, then, can move some of our cultural debates to a new place. We must take the same kinds of care when we see the Bible being used to support a particular war or a specific foreign policy stance, or to establish or oppose social policy. The Bible has been used extensively on both sides of many issues. Recall, for example, that both the Ku Klux Klan and those who marched for civil rights used the Bible to support their views! We all need to be prepared to assess whether people who make claims on the Bible for various sides of an issue represent a reading of the Bible that is sensitive to the type of literature they cite and thus to the kinds of messages the Bible could reasonably be taken to support. Of course, such assessment requires determining whether one or another reading of a biblical statement has taken seriously its literary and historical context. Nothing less will allow us to come to a responsible understanding.

For those who honor the Bible as an authority for their lives and beliefs, knowing these kinds of things about the Bible can help them understand where some very difficult kinds of texts (such as texts commanding the extermination of a city's inhabitants) come from. This kind of knowledge can also help them reach their own understanding of the Bible's important and central messages. Only careful study can bring out the depth and richness of biblical texts. Nothing we have seen in these texts or in any of the methods used here require us to conclude that God did not or cannot speak through the Bible, any more than they require us to conclude that God did speak through the Bible. My claim is that the best uses of the Bible will begin with the kinds of methods of study and interpretation introduced in this book. Using these methods will provide any community of interpreters the tools they need to test particular readings for their faithfulness to the message in the text. This way of approaching the Bible helps keep each interpreter honest and helps limit unintentional misunderstanding.

Once we have a better understanding of the concerns of the biblical authors and what they wanted to convey to their original readers, those of us who are believers can appropriate that knowledge to help us determine what to believe and how to live. Knowledge of the Bible alone will not be sufficient for determining what God might have us do today, because we face circumstances and issues the biblical authors never imagined. A better grasp of the biblical messages can, however, be a central element in helping us make judgments about what we should believe and do.

Many readers who approach the Bible from a stance of faith assume that it does the Bible the most honor to read it in a very literalistic fashion. But this assumption adopts a notion that is not in the Bible itself. Indeed, the varying kinds of literature in the Bible demonstrate that this approach to the Bible has serious problems. In some places it is easy for us to recognize this. Few read Genesis 3 and think God literally went on walks with Adam or could not find him one afternoon, for example. Or again, few insist that we read everything in the Psalms literally. It would be hard to find many people who think God is literally a rock. Yet the psalmist proclaims, "the LORD is my rock" (Ps. 18:2). Once we acknowledge that literalism gives us the wrong meaning in *some* places, we must take up the task of discerning how to approach *all* the biblical texts in the several ways appropriate to the kinds of writings they are. Only then, I suggest, will believing readers be able to arrive at ways to be faithful to the God Scripture reveals and the message it proclaims.

For those of us who do not grant the Bible such authority in our lives, it nevertheless remains a powerful force that shapes the world around us. We therefore need knowledge of the Bible to interpret the views of some of the people around us. We also need to be able to recognize uses of the Bible that do not correspond to what is actually in the text. Remembering that the Bible has been used on both sides of many debates does not suggest that it was represented equally well on both sides. Those who do not use the Bible as a religious authority will have to understand it to engage in some discussions about community standards and cultural models with those who do so use the Bible. Knowing what the Bible really is and what kinds of things it actually says may help us point out improper uses of the Bible in such deliberations. At least it will be possible to engage in such conversations knowledgeably and to make clear that there are alternative understandings of the Bible based on careful research and study.

In ancient Greece and the surrounding regions, the world-shaping literature was Homer. Every educated person knew Homer, indeed could quote him as "the poet." His writing, understood in many different ways, shaped Greek and Hellenistic culture. His work served as a cultural and social authority. In today's Western culture, the Bible holds that position. What you have learned about the Bible in this book will begin to help you understand it and to recognize the ways it shapes our world, the ways it serves as a cultural and social authority. Whether you grant it authority or not, knowing the Bible and how to read it prepares you to participate more fully in discussions about how we should understand and construct our world.

APPENDIX: ALTERNATIVE READING STRATEGIES

The kind of examination of the texts of the Bible that has been used throughout this book is known as **historical-critical reading.** That is, it analyzes (the meaning of "critical" here) a text in terms of its historical setting. That setting includes the political, cultural, and social situation in the relevant parts of the ancient world and the kinds of literary forms and religious beliefs that were present in that era and place. This method seeks to understand what the message of the text was and how it was heard by its original audience. But there are other ways to pursue this goal and some readers adopt different purposes in their reading.

Rather than focusing only on the specifics of the situation and beliefs of the writers and audience of the specific texts, **structuralist criticism** searches for the deep structures of the mind that influence the ways all people think and act. Being strongly influenced by the "History of Religions" school of thought, they assume that all of humanity shares the same mythic structures of thinking. Furthermore, these structures always appear in paired opposites (life/death; order/chaos; etc.). This method sees multiple layers of meaning in a text and seeks to uncover a text's underlying convictions by finding these structures. This enables better comparisons across religions. As its assumptions about the parallels in religions became less popular, so has use of this method. But it helped prepare the way for other methods that do not focus solely on the writer and original audience.

Canonical criticism shifts its focus so that it reads the biblical books primarily in the context of their place within the canons of Judaism and Christianity. Canonical critics are interested only in the final form of the text as it appears in the Bible. Rather than reading each book as though it were addressed to a specific ancient situation, canonical critics read the Hebrew Bible as a book addressed to all Jews and Christians and the New Testament as addressed to Christians. They assume a level of coherence of message across the canon that stands in tension with historical criticism's insistence that each text be read in its original context. For these readers, the order of the collection of the books in the canon provides more meaning than the original context. They analyze the text to discern its meaning in relation to the other books in the canon.

Narrative criticism developed in response to various methods (such as form criticism and redaction criticism) that analyzed various shorter units of a text, but paid less attention to the text as a whole. This method tries to interpret the text primarily in terms of the world that the narrative creates without examining the intentions of the author. It asks questions about how the text characterizes certain groups or individuals, about the role that the narrator plays, and how the text uses various kinds of rhetorical devices. It also asks how the world constructed in the story relates to the world of the readers. Does it confirm or subvert the way its readers see the world? This method looks for meaning by observing the world that the text's story creates.

Some interpreters who have used historical-critical reading assumed that they were able to be entirely objective in their reading. In response to that presumption, some twentieth-century interpreters began to emphasize the subjective role of the reader in making meaning. Interpreters who employ these methods argue that texts do not simply mean something that readers receive. Rather, readers are active in producing the meanings they find in their experience of the text. **Reader response criticism** recognizes that who the reader is and what her circumstances are shape the meaning found in the text. The reader must always fill in gaps left by the author. This is the case because the author cannot give a full background to his or her meaning for every word and phrase. Readers must fill in those gaps and readers in different social locations will fill them in different ways. This means that every reading overlooks or leaves out some elements that another reading sees. In this interactive process the text challenges the ways readers understand the world and so opens new possibilities of understanding.

Advocacy or **ideological readings** intentionally take on a particular perspective in their readings. While the Enlightenment privileged objectivity, these readings recognize the impossibility of that goal and so explicitly claim a particular experience and perspective that they argue allow them to see new things in the text. As a part of this intentional positioning, they also take up a particular agenda of social change. There are a number of different types of methods under this heading because each focuses on a different type of oppression. Some focus on economic issues, some on ethnicity, and others on gender or other social constructs. Some see these methods as quite different from historical-critical readings; others see them as a variation on that method. The central difference is that Advocacy readings commit themselves to a perspective with the intent of addressing the current circumstances with what they find.

Two of the foundational types of advocacy readings are **liberationist readings** and **feminist readings.** The former is rooted in liberation theology and focuses on social and economic oppression. Practitioners of this method try to read the text as it would be heard by the economically oppressed, that is, the poor. These interpreters often argue that working with this perspective is consistent with the view found in the Bible itself.

Feminist readings focus their attention on the oppression of women. They seek to expose the ways that cultural values that oppress women are embedded in some biblical texts, while working to reclaim other texts that might provide material that advances the cause of liberation of women. Further, they seek hints in the text that might reveal something to help them reclaim the lost voices of women.

Post-colonial readings are another type of advocacy reading. These interpreters draw their methods from observing the coping mechanisms employed by the subjects of nineteenth- and twentieth-century European colonial powers to support and legitimate their prior cultural identity and beliefs. These interpreters investigate how resistance literature supported and reinforced the identity of the colonized. Those who use these methods also examine the ways European scholarship has presented the colonized, exposing the prejudices of those characterizations. Within biblical studies, these interpreters emphasize questions about whether the biblical authors identify with those oppressed by the empire or with the empire and its values. They see many of the social circumstances of the biblical writers and their audience as a parallel with those oppressed by later European empires. Thus, we may expect that the biblical writers will employ some of the same coping mechanisms. Since this is the case we can gain new understandings of those texts by looking for how the biblical authors used those types of devices

Queer readings, another kind of advocacy reading, take on a derogatory term to give it a meaning that removes the stigma associated with it. These readers argue that sexual orientation comprises as much a part of a person's identity and social location as matters of gender and economic condition. They reject the either/or opposition of understandings of homosexuality and heterosexuality, emphasizing shifting boundaries and ambivalences. They refuse to accept heteronormativity as the perspective from which to understand existence. Thus, they analyze the ways biblical texts and their interpreters impose a normative heterosexism.

Advocacy criticisms have been more willing to point to perceived theological or ideological errors in the text than some other methods. They critique the message and assumptions of the biblical texts with the values their ideology affirms. For example, when feminist interpreters see elements in a text that do not support the rights and equality of women, they shine a light on them and reject their messages as unacceptable. At the same time, these methods reclaim some texts that have been thought to support the oppression of various groups. They demonstrate how the readers' assumptions gave the text an oppressive meaning that is not inherent in the text itself.

All of these methods recognize the religious and cultural power the Bible has and continues to exert. Some emphasize the struggle to understand the text in new ways in order to re-channel the power the Bible exerts so that it supports views it had earlier been used to oppose or to oppose views it had been used to support. Others accentuate the necessity of decentering the Bible as a religious and cultural authority. Either way, they acknowledge the ways the Bible shapes Western culture.

GLOSSARY

Abraham—The originating ancestor of Jews and Arabs in Genesis. God called him from his home region of Ur to travel to Canaan, which would become the homeland of his descendants.

Abram—Original name of Abraham.

Acrostic—A literary technique in which the first letter of each line (or alternatively the last letter) either follows the sequence of the alphabet or forms a word or phrase.

Alexander the Great—Macedonian king who conquers southern Greece and then all the territory east to the border of India, reaching as far north as the Black Sea and as far south as North Africa. This created the largest empire the world had seen. In all these territories he instituted the policy of hellenization to form a common culture based on Greek culture.

Allegory—A literary technique in which an extended metaphor or story draws parallels between elements in the story and nonfictional characters and events.

Amon-Re—Egyptian god of the sun.

Amos—Eighth-century Israelite prophet. He insisted that socioeconomic justice and personal morality must accompany worship of God.

Angelic worship—Worship that the angels offer to God in heaven.

Antichrist—This term does not appear in the book of Revelation. In the New Testament it appears only in 1 and 2 John, referring to someone who believes the wrong things. After the time of the New Testament it comes to refer to an end-time agent of Satan.

Antiochus IV—Syrian king who outlawed Judaism in Judea and defiled the temple in 167 B.C.E. His actions led to the Maccabean Revolt. He added the title Epiphanes to his name.

Antithetical parallelism—A literary technique used in Hebrew poetry that sets opposite ideas or statements in immediately successive lines.

Apocalypse, apocalyptic—A genre of literature (apocalypse) and a way of understanding the world. The genre has a heavenly being bring a message about God's actions to enact justice. Both the literature and the worldview envision this action happening soon. The fullest example of the genre in the New Testament is the book of Revelation.

Apocrypha—Books found in the Septuagint, but not in the Hebrew Bible. These books were never accepted as canonical by the Jewish community. They are given a secondary canonical status by the Roman Catholic and Eastern Orthodox churches.

Apostle—Most generally it means one who is sent. In the early church it comes to designate those who are recognized as the authorities in the church, particularly the Twelve (after they replace Judas), James, the brother of Jesus who becomes the leader of the Jerusalem church, and Paul. Others could be apostles in the sense that they were sent on missions by their churches, but these fourteen people were seen as sent by Christ and so as authoritative.

Apostolic—Related to an apostle or of apostolic origin.

Ark of the Covenant—Ornate box that symbolized the presence of God. It contained relics symbolic of particular divine acts (the tablets of the Law, Aaron's rod that bloomed, and a pot of manna).

Asherah—Important Canaanite goddess, consort of Baal or of El.

Assyrian empire—Empire that arose in the eighth century B.C.E. Its capital was in Nineveh, near today's Mosul in Northern Iraq (approximately 250 miles north of Baghdad).

Athanasius—Fourth-century bishop of Alexandria. He was one of the most powerful opponents of the theological position known as Arianism (which says that Christ was a created being). His Festal Letter of Easter in 367 contains the first listing of the 27 books now in the New Testament with his comment that these are the books that should be read in church.

Autograph—The original writing from the hand of the author. None of these exist for biblical books, only copies of copies are extant.

Baal—Popular Canaanite god who ranked high in their pantheon. He was also the storm god.

Babel—A place where Genesis says the people tried to build a tower to heaven. God responds by multiplying the languages the people speak so they are not able to understand one another. Thus, they must abandon their project.

Babylonian Empire—Empire that rises to regional dominance in the seventh/sixth centuries B.C.E. They replace the Assyrian Empire as the dominant power in the region. The capital of Babylon was near today's city of Baghdad, Iraq.

Balaam—A non-Israelite who was known for communicating with the God of Israel and other gods. King Balak of Moab called him to curse the Israelites who were advancing on his land, but God commanded Balaam to bless the Israelites. He obeyed God.

Baptism—The first initiation ritual for the early church. In the first century, it involved the immersion of the person in water. It was patterned on other ritual washings, particularly within Judaism. The church interpreted the act of immersion as a reenactment of the burial and resurrection of Christ, which symbolically also brought new life to the baptized person.

Bar-Kokhba—Leader of the Jewish revolt against Rome in 132–35 C.E.

Barnabas—Early member of the Jerusalem church who becomes a missionary of the Antioch church. From there he recruits Paul to be a missionary with him and they travel together in southeastern Asia Minor (Turkey) establishing churches that are made up primarily of Gentiles.

B.C.E.—"Before the Common Era" refers to the time when Judaism existed but before Christianity existed. That is, it covers the same time period as the older abbreviation B.C. (Before Christ).

Beatitudes—A list of aphorisms in the Sermon on the Mount in which Jesus sets out the attitudes his followers should adopt. These attitudes of the "blessed" are countercultural or contrary to any expectation of the way things are in the world.

Beloved disciple—The only name the Gospel of John gives for the disciple who sat next to Jesus in its account of the Last Supper. This Gospel also identifies him as the source of the material in that Gospel (John 21:24-25). He seems to be from Judea rather than Galilee because so many of the stories of Gospel of John that are not in the Synoptics occur in Judea.

Benedictus—Song/poem Zechariah recites when he gets his voice back at the naming of John the Baptist.

Biblical languages—The texts of the Hebrew Bible are written in Hebrew and Aramaic; the New Testament and the Apocrypha are written in Greek.

Birkat ha-Minim—The "Benediction against the Heretics" that eventually became a part of Jewish liturgical tradition. This line of a formalized prayer asks God to condemn heretics and the wicked. Many think this prayer was directed against Christians. It was probably added to the synagogue service sometime after all the books of the New Testament were written.

Body of Christ—A metaphor for the church that indicates the close relationship among members (because they are members of the same body) and that the church is the presence of Christ in the world. In early usage, it was applied only to individual congregations; as time passed, the image enlarged so that the church worldwide was identified as the one cosmic body of Christ.

Calvin, John—French leader in the Protestant Reformation (1509–1564). He took religious and political control of Geneva by 1555. His writings, especially his *Institutes* and his commentaries on biblical books, have been very influential. Churches in the Reformed tradition (which includes Presbyterians) have their roots in his work.

Canon—A group of authoritative writings. The Tanakh is the canon of Judaism, while the Hebrew Bible (Old Testament) and the New Testament make up the Christian canon.

Catholic—A term whose basic meaning is "universal" or "general." It is used with the Catholic Epistles to indicate that the audiences of these writings are broader than the original audiences of Paul's letters.

C.E.—The "Common Era" refers to the time when both Judaism and Christianity exist. It covers the same years as the older abbreviation A.D.

Chester Beatty Papyri—A collection of papyrus sheets (some in the Chester Beatty Library in Dublin, the rest at the University of Michigan) that date from about the year 200. They contain our earliest copy of many books of the New Testament.

Chronicler—The probably fourth-century author or authors of the books of 1 and 2 Chronicles. This group was also related to the authors of Ezra and Nehemiah. The Chronicler(s) presents the story of the Israelite nations in a way that conforms to the deuteronomistic pattern even more closely than the way it is told by the Deuteronomistic historians.

Chronicler's History—The way the books of Chronicles tells the story of the Israelite monarchies. After a brief account of ancestry from Adam to the kings of Israel, the books of Chronicles shape their story of Israelite kings stressing whether a monarch remained faithful to God. Even more than the Deuteronomistic historians, the Chronicler emphasizes the pattern Deuteronomy sets out for Israel's national life: the nation's and king's faithfulness brings blessings from God, worship of other gods brings disaster. When this pattern breaks down in the Deuteronomistic histories, Chronicles changes the account so that disaster comes on a king only as a result of unfaithfulness.

Circumcision—Removal of the foreskin. This is a sign of membership in the Mosaic covenant.

City of Refuge—A city established as a place to which those accused of murder could flee for protection until trial. If found not guilty they could remain under its protection.

City of Seven Hills—Nickname for the city of Rome in the first century. Revelation alludes to this name in one of its images as a sign to readers that it is talking about the empire.

Christology—The study of the nature and work of Christ. This field of study considers what it means to talk about Jesus Christ as human or divine (or both) and defines what the ministry and death of Christ accomplished.

Claudius, Edict of—*See* Edict of Claudius.

Classical prophecy—The designation for the kind of prophecy that begins in the eighth century B.C.E. The prophets of this era communicate with a wider circle of people, including average Israelites, and more of their messages were put into writing. These prophets are known for their message of the necessity of social justice and the worship of only God.

Codex—A manuscript in the form of a modern book. The codex has individual leaves for pages, rather than being a continuous roll as a scroll was.

Codex Aleph—Fourth-century codex of the Bible, also known as Codex Sinaiticus. Now in the British Library, it is one of the most reliable manuscripts for the books of the New Testament.

Codex Vaticanus—Fourth-century codex of the Bible housed in the Vatican. It is one of the most reliable manuscripts for books of the New Testament. However, books at both the beginning and the end of the Bible are missing from this codex.

Cognitive dissonance—A distressed mental state that occurs when a person's beliefs about the self or the world are significantly different from the way they actually experience the world or from other ideas about the world that they continue to hold.

Communion—A term used for the Lord's Supper that emphasizes that the participants are sharing the meal with one another, Christ, and God.

Concubine—A wife that has lower status than other wives.

Constantine—Roman emperor (died 337) who first granted toleration to the church and began to favor it because he thought the God of the church had granted him the victory that enabled him to take control of the empire. He also summoned the Council of Nicea.

Copyist—A person whose occupation is to replicate documents by hand so that multiple copies are available.

Cornelius—The Roman centurion, who in Acts 10–11 becomes the first Gentile convert to the church.

Council of Trent—Anti-Reformation Council (1545–63). This council rejected many Reformation doctrines and included the first official declaration about which books of the Bible were canonical.

Critical introduction—An analysis of a biblical book that deals with its authorship (who wrote it), date (when it was written), literary integrity (whether the book has been edited so that it is different from the way it was originally written), occasion (what situation led the author to write), purpose (what the writer hopes to accomplish), and theological themes.

Cultic purity—*See* Purity.

Cyrus—Ruler of the Persian Empire (539–530 B.C.E.) who allows the Judahites (the remaining Israelites) to return to their ancestral land (Judah). Isaiah calls him God's messiah, anointed one (Isa. 45:1-3).

D source—One of the traditions that came together to form the Pentateuch. This source advocates that if the nation is faithful, God will bless them; if they worship other gods, God will punish them for violating their covenant (agreement) with God. Most of the book of Deuteronomy comes from this source. It also influenced the books of Joshua, Judges, 1 and 2 Samuel, and 1 and 2 Kings.

Dagon—Patron god of the Philistines and sometimes seen as father of Baal.

Daniel—Leading character in the book of Daniel. He lived in the time of the exile and is an example of remaining faithful to God among the temptations and persecutions of life in a culture dominated by non-Israelites who worship many gods.

Day of the Lord—Originally it was a phrase prophets used to speak of the time when God would act on the behalf of the Israelites to bring them victory. Later prophets reverse its meaning to warn of the time when God would act against Israel and Judah because of their unfaithfulness to God. In the New Testament, it refers to the second coming or Parousia of Christ.

Dead Sea Scrolls—The manuscripts found in the caves around the Qumran compound at the northwestern end of the Dead Sea. Among the scrolls were numerous commentaries on biblical books. These scrolls provide some of the earliest evidence for the form of the text of the Hebrew Bible. They also give us information about the Essenes, the movement to which the authors of the scrolls belonged.

December 15, 167 B.C.E.—Date Antiochus IV desecrated the Jerusalem temple and outlawed Judaism. These acts led to the beginning of the Maccabean revolt.

Deuterocanonical—Books included in the Roman Catholic and Eastern Orthodox canons, but that do not possess quite as much authority as the other canonical books. These are also called the Apocrypha.

Deuteronomistic history—The telling of the story of the life of the nations of the Israelites from the perspective of the paradigm set out in

Deuteronomy (that is, faithfulness brings blessing to the nation and unfaithfulness will bring defeat and disaster). The books of Joshua, Judges, 1 and 2 Samuel, and 1 and 2 Kings are all written from this perspective and are called the deuteronomistic histories.

Deutero-Paulines—The writings in the New Testament that claim to be written by Paul, but that most scholars believe were written by someone else after his death. Those most likely to fall into this category are Ephesians, 1 and 2 Timothy, and Titus. Many scholars also think that Colossians and 2 Thessalonians were written after Paul died. These writings were intended to apply Paul's teaching to a new situation.

Diadochoi—The successors of Alexander the Great who broke up and ruled various parts of the empire he had established.

Diaspora—Designation for Jews who live outside Palestine. Since the Babylonian exile, more Jews have always lived outside Palestine than lived inside Palestine.

Diatessaron—The first extant synopsis of the Gospels, compiled by Tatian in about 170–175. It gives a running account of the material in the four canonical Gospels that smoothes over contradictions.

Didactic psalms—Psalms designed to teach about God and how God wants people to live.

Dispersion—Designation for Jews who live outside Palestine. *See* Diaspora.

Docetism—Belief that Jesus did not have a physical body, but was only a spiritual presence in the world.

Documentary hypothesis—Theory that holds that the books of the Pentateuch (or Hexateuch) were composed from sources written earlier (J, E, D, and P).

Domitian—Roman emperor 81–96 C.E. Some think he instigated the persecution of Christians that broke out soon after his reign.

Dynamic equivalence—A type of translation in which the translator tries to convey the original meaning of the originating text and does not concern him/herself with retaining much of the original wording. Its opposite is Formal Correspondence.

E source—One of the traditions that came together to form the Pentateuch. Its name derives from the characteristic way it refers to God; it calls God Elohim. Much of Exodus and Numbers come from this source.

Ecclesiastes—Name of a book of the Hebrew Bible. It is an example of the wisdom tradition in Israelite culture. This book questions whether life is meaningful.

Ecstatic experience—An experience during which a person thinks she or he is being controlled by another being.

Eden, Garden of—The ideal place where the first humans resided, according to Genesis.

Edict of Claudius—Edict in 49 (or perhaps in 41) by which the emperor Claudius expelled the Jews from the city of Rome because of problems arising about "Chrestus." Most New Testament scholars think this is a misspelling of Christ, so that the trouble arose in the Jewish community because of its debates about Jesus.

Elder, the—(1) Self-designation of the writer of 2 and 3 John. (2) It refers to a leadership position within the early church.

Election—Being chosen. In the Hebrew Bible, the Israelites are God's chosen people. New Testament writers also attach this designation to those who come to belief in Christ, in addition to those in the Mosaic covenant.

Eli—Eleventh-century Israelite priest and prophet at Shiloh who raised Samuel.

Elijah—Ninth-century Israelite prophet who performed many miracles and called the people to worship only God. He opposed the reign of Ahab and his dynasty because of their unfaithfulness to God. He was also the head of the "school of the prophets."

Elisha—Successor of Elijah. At Elijah's death he becomes the leader of the "school of the prophets" and continues Elijah's ministry of opposing Israelite monarchs who worship multiple gods.

Elizabeth—Mother of John the Baptist in Luke. She is a relative of Mary, the mother of Jesus.

Elohim—One of the ways the Hebrew Bible refers to God. This name for God is the plural of the Hebrew word El (god).

Enlightenment, the—The eighteenth-century movement that said humans should rely on reason and empirical knowledge for truth. Thus, proponents often discounted the value and validity of divine revelation and religious tradition.

Enuma Elish—A twelfth-century (or earlier) B.C.E. Babylonian text that gives an account of the creation of the earth by many gods.

Esau—Oldest son of Isaac who is excluded from the central promises to Abraham through the machinations of his younger brother, Jacob, and his marriage to a Canaanite.

Eschatology—Study of the end times, when it will be and what is to happen at that time. Often this area of study also includes discussion of the state of the dead in the present.

Essenes—A semimonastic interpretation of Judaism. They began as a protest against the way the Maccabeans were running the temple. Their eschatology fueled their expectation that God would intervene to put them in charge of the temple. They were probably the authors of the Dead Sea Scrolls.

Eucharist—From the Greek word that means thanksgiving, this word comes to designate the Lord's Supper in post–New Testament times.

Euodia—One of the leaders of the church in Philippi. Her dispute with Syntyche was one of the reasons Paul wrote the letter to the Philippians. Paul's mention of her and Syntyche provides clear evidence that women were among the leaders in Paul's churches.

Evangelist—(1) Author of a Gospel (for example, Matthew or Mark). (2) Someone who preaches the gospel.

***Ex eventu* prophecy**—A prophecy written after the event that fulfills it has already happened. Many pseudepigraphic works employ this technique so that they seem reliable when they predict what is truly still in the future.

Exhortation—Encouragement, in the New Testament it often means encouragement in ethical living.

Exile of Judah—When the nation of Judah suffered defeat at the hands of the Babylonians in 587 B.C.E. and the Babylonians forced the leaders and craftspeople of Judah to move to Babylon.

Exodus—The story of the Israelites escaping slavery in Egypt. This story becomes the foundational story for their understanding of themselves and God.

Exorcism—Getting a demon out of a person.

Ezekiel—Sixth-century prophet who was taken to Babylon in the first wave of exiles from Jerusalem in 597 B.C.E. There he has dramatic visions about the presence of God moving to be with the exiles. These visions contributed much to the development of apocalyptic thought and imagery.

Fall, the—Christian name for the story in Genesis of the first human sin. That sin results in the ejection of Adam and Eve from the Garden of Eden and in the introduction of the things that make life difficult.

Feast of Booths—A harvest festival that also commemorates the care God provided the Israelites while they were in the wilderness after the exodus and on the way to Canaan, the time they lived in booths (that is, tents).

Feast of Dedication—*See* Hanukkah.

Feast of Purim—*See* Purim, Feast of.

Formal correspondence—A type of translation in which the translator tries to stay as close to a word-for-word translation as possible. Its opposite is Dynamic Equivalence.

Fulfillment quotations—The way Matthew interprets the life of Jesus through passages taken from the Hebrew Bible. He introduces these quotations with the phrase, "This was done to fulfill what was spoken by the prophet ______."

Fundamentalism—A movement that originated in the nineteenth century in opposition to the use of Enlightenment methods and thought in the areas of theology and biblical studies. In the twentieth century, a conservative social agenda became part of the movement.

Genre—A literary form.

Gentiles—All non-Jews.

Gideon—One of the "judges" of the Israelites in the time before the Israelites were united as a single nation under a king.

Gilgamesh, Epic of—A document composed around 2000 B.C.E. in Sumerian that includes a story of Utnapishtim building an ark in which he and the animals survive a worldwide flood.

Glossolalia—*See* Speaking in tongues.

Gnosticism—Belief system that most scholars think develops in the second century C.E. that incorporates elements of mysticism and a radical rejection of the value of the material world. It seems to begin within Judaism and then quickly moves into Christianity. People who hold such views are called Gnostics.

Good Samaritan—Central character in a parable of Jesus. He helps a person who has been beaten and robbed. He is an example of the way Luke emphasizes outcasts because his ethnic identity made him objectionable as the story's hero to those in Jesus' audience.

Gospel—(1) A word that means "good news." (2) Books that tell of Jesus. In the New Testament, these are narratives of Jesus' life. Some extracanonical Gospels focus only on the sayings of Jesus (for example, the *Gospel of*

Thomas). (3) The message about what Jesus accomplishes for the relationship between God and humanity and for relations about fellow human beings.

Gymnasium—A central educational institution of classical Greece. Alexander the Great and his successors used it to spread Greek culture throughout the Ancient Near East.

Habakkuk—Late seventh- to early sixth-century Israelite prophet who questions God about why injustice flourishes and disasters are coming on Judah, particularly on the heels of the reforms of good king Josiah.

Hades—The abode of the dead in Greek mythology.

Haggai—Sixth-century prophet who encourages those who have returned to Judah from exile to rebuild the temple. He sees this rebuilding as a step toward peace and the establishment of God's kingdom.

Hanukkah—The Jewish feast that celebrates the retaking of the temple by Judas Maccabee in 164 B.C.E. It is also known as the Feast of Dedication because Judas rededicated the temple to God after it had been defiled by Antiochus IV.

Hasmonean—The family name of the Maccabean leaders.

Hebrew Bible—The books of the Bible that were written in Hebrew and Aramaic. They are the authoritative writings for Judaism and contain the same thirty-nine books as the Protestant Old Testament. The books, however, are in different orders in the two canons.

Hellenization—Making things Greek. The successors of Alexander the Great followed his lead in spreading Greek culture and the Greek language throughout the ancient Mediterranean world.

Herod the Great—Ruler of Judea, Samaria, Galilee, and the Decapolis from 37 to 4 B.C.E. In Matthew's Gospel he is still in power at the birth of Jesus. He was a ruthless and domineering ruler, but he also carried out a number of public works projects, including the enormous expansion of the temple in Jerusalem.

Historical Jesus—An image of what the actual person Jesus was like and what he did, without the interpretations of the church. Some present-day scholars work as though they were able to present the facts about Jesus' life without at the same time inserting their own interpretations. Thus, they present their "historical Jesus."

Holiness code—Leviticus 17–26, the section that defines the ways the people of Israel are to live so that they are holy. Thus, they please God and are different from the peoples around them.

Hosea—Eighth-century prophet whose message takes the form of an allegory. His unfaithful wife (Gomer) is given as the parallel for the Israelites' unfaithfulness to God that is seen in their worship of other gods and their oppressive social and economic systems.

Huldah—Woman recognized as a prophet who confirmed that the book found in the temple by workers during Josiah's reform was God's word (2 Kgs. 22:3-20).

Imprecatory psalms—Psalms that ask God to harm others and put curses on one's enemies.

Indictment-verdict pattern—A literary pattern the prophets borrow from the judicial and governmental (empire ruler to vassal) spheres in which the charges are set out and the declaration of a verdict follows. For example: "for three transgressions of Moab and for four, I will not revoke the punishment" (Amos 2:1).

Inerrant—Term used of Scripture to claim that it is without any mistakes of any kind (history, science, geography, and so on). Others use the term to signify that Scripture is without error in religious teaching, though it may not have all historical and scientific facts correct.

Inspiration—The belief that God was involved with the writing and/or the reading of the Bible.

Isaac—The long-awaited son of Abraham, who was to fulfill the promise that Abraham would have many descendants. In the Genesis story, Jews are the branch of Abraham's family that are descendants of Isaac.

Isaiah—At least three prophets write under the name of Isaiah. The first (also known as Isaiah of Jerusalem) is the eighth-century prophet who has a theophany of God in the temple as his call to a prophetic mission. The second Isaiah writes during the exile of Judah. The third Isaiah writes after Judah's return from exile. The messages of hope and restoration for the people found in these prophets were particularly important for the early church, which used them to understand the meaning of the ministry and death of Jesus.

Israel—(1) Name given to Jacob which becomes the designation for his descendants. (2) The name taken by the northern kingdom (whose capital was in Samaria) when the Israelites split into two nations following the reign of Solomon.

J source—One of the traditions that editors brought together to form the Pentateuch. It refers to God by God's name, Yahweh (or Jehovah in earlier renderings). Much of Genesis comes from this source.

Jacob—Younger son of Isaac who is the ancestor of Jews in Genesis. Even though he is an underhanded and unlikeable character, he is the one God chooses to work through in the Genesis narrative.

James—(1) One of the original Twelve disciples of Jesus. He became the leader of the Jerusalem church, but was executed in 44. (2) A brother of Jesus who becomes the leader of the Jerusalem church after the execution of the James who had been a disciple of Jesus.

Jehovah—The transliteration (that is, transferring the letters from one language to another) of the name of God into English that is found in older translations. This English form of the Name was influenced by the transliteration of the Name into German.

Jeremiah—Seventh- to sixth-century prophet of Judah who lives through the various stages of the exile in Jerusalem. He becomes the pattern for the persecuted and rejected but faithful prophet.

Jericho—First city the Israelites take in their conquest of Canaan.

Jerome—Biblical scholar who translated the Bible into Latin (324–420). His translation, called the Vulgate, becomes the church's standard translation for centuries.

Jerusalem—City in south central Palestine that served as the capital from the time of David. The temple is in Jerusalem and ancient Jews thought of it as the central place of the presence and acts of God.

Jerusalem Conference (Council)—In about the year 50, Paul and Barnabas go to Jerusalem to discuss with the leaders of that church (including James and Peter) whether Gentile members of the church had to be circumcised and begin to observe the Torah as Jews did. The basic question was whether Gentiles had to become full proselytes to Judaism in order to be full members of the church.

Jezreel—(1) The place of the bloody coup in which Jehu killed the descendants of Ahab and took the throne of Israel (2 Kgs. 9–10). (2) Name given to Hosea's first child to signal that terrible destruction was about to come upon Israel. After Israel repents, Hosea says the name will revert to its original meaning, "God plants."

Job—Leading character in the book of Job. God allows terrible things to happen to him and his family as a demonstration that Job is not faithful to God only because God blesses him. This book raises the issue of theodicy and questions the deuteronomistic scheme.

Joel—Prophet who is probably active in the late sixth century. With his vision of a locust plague he asserts that disaster can only be averted through proper worship of God, including proper temple services with prophets taking an important role.

John the Baptist—Cousin of Jesus who baptizes Jesus as Jesus begins his ministry. John acts as the one who prepares for the ministry of Jesus in the Gospels. Some scholars think that Jesus was a follower of John before Jesus began his independent ministry.

John Chrysostom—Bishop of Constantinople and theologian (347–407). He was a gifted preacher, and many of his homilies still survive. He advocated finding the "spiritual" meaning of biblical texts.

Jonah—Leading character in the story of the book of Jonah. This folktale questions important prophetic and deuteronomistic themes.

Joseph—(1) In Genesis, Joseph is one of the twelve sons of Jacob who are the progenitors of the twelve tribes of Israel. (2) In the New Testament, Joseph is the husband of Mary.

Josephus—First-century Jewish writer who was a general in the revolt of 66–70. After his capture he becomes the historian for the Roman general (who would soon be emperor) Vespasian. His writings give us important information about first-century Judaism and the war in which the Jerusalem temple was destroyed.

Joshua—Successor of Moses who leads the Israelites in the conquest of Canaan.

Judah—(1) One of the twelve sons of Jacob who are the traditional ancestors of the twelve tribes of Israel. (2) The name of the southern kingdom whose capital was in Jerusalem, when the Israelites divided into two nations (the other was called Israel). (3) The region around Jerusalem, known as Judea in New Testament times.

Judaizer—Name given to people in the early church who say that Gentiles must completely convert to Judaism (including being circumcised, keeping the Sabbath, and observing the Jewish food laws) to be fully members of the church. It is best to avoid this label for such people because it is anachronistic and because it is offensive to Jews, since it implies that to be Jewish is bad.

Judea—Name of the region around Jerusalem in the Greco-Roman period. In earlier times the same region was known as Judah.

Judges—A book in the Deuteronomistic Histories. It is named for the "judges," that is, the twelve people who on different occasions lead the Israelites in revolts against their neighbors after they had been subdued, the books says, because of their unfaithfulness to God.

Justification—A legal term that Paul uses to refer to the forgiveness of sins believers receive through Christ.

King James Version—Translation of the Bible into English in 1611. It becomes the standard English translation through the first half of the twentieth century.

Kingdom of Heaven—Matthew's way of referring to the kingdom of God. This expression shows Matthew's Jewish sensibilities because he is avoiding direct mention of God.

Kosher—The rules regarding food that Jews observe. These include regulations that prohibit eating certain foods (for example, camels and pigs) and rules for how to slaughter animals. Some rules concern what may be eaten together. Such observances are a part of what set Jews apart as a holy people.

Laban—Father of Rachel and Leah, father-in-law of Jacob. In Laban, Jacob had nearly met his match in deception and trickery.

Lament psalms—Psalms that mourn a personal or national loss or defeat.

Last days—The eschatological time. The New Testament writers assert that the rest of human history will take place in the "last days" because the death and resurrection of Jesus ushered in the last period of the way God is present in the world.

Legend—A literary form in which a narrative of earlier times is used to define a group's identity and place in the world, as well as to ground their morality.

Letter—Written form of communication intended to address the specific people named and usually to engage them personally and specifically.

Levirate marriage—A system designed to keep property within a clan. In this system, when a man dies without children, his brother is to marry the dead man's wife and have children in the name of the dead man so that there are heirs to inherit the family property.

Lex talionis—The Latin term for the law that restricts retaliation for a wrong done to a person by allowing the injured party to do to the perpetrator only exactly what he or she did to the injured. Its classic formulation is: "eye for eye and tooth for tooth" (Exod. 21:24).

Literary epistle—A formal letter intended to be read by a public audience.

Lo-Ammi—Name of one of Hosea's children. It means "not my people"; Hosea used it to signal that God would no longer have a special relationship with Israel because of the nation's unfaithfulness. After their judgment, however, this name will change to "Ammi," or "My people," to signal that God has restored them to their relationship with God.

Lo-Ruhamah—Name of one of Hosea's children. It means "not pitied"; Hosea used it to signal that God would no longer have pity on Israel. After they repent, however, the name will be changed to "Ruhamah," "Pitied," to show that God again looks with favor on Israel.

Lord—When the name of God appears in the Hebrew text, this way of writing the word Lord takes the place of the name of God. Replacing God's name with Lord is a way of respecting the name of God.

Lord's Prayer—Prayer Jesus teaches his disciples. In Matthew it appears in the Sermon on the Mount (6:9-13); a shorter version appears in Luke (11:2-4).

Lord's Supper—Ritual meal in the early church that commemorated and interpreted the death of Jesus. The Synoptic Gospels give an account of Jesus instituting this meal and remembrance on the night of his arrest.

Luther, Martin—German leader of the Protestant Reformation (1483–1546) who questioned a number of teachings of the Catholic Church at that time. After he was excommunicated, he translated the Bible into German and wrote an influential commentary on Romans, as well as books on many theological topics. He argued that Scripture was the only guide to what the church should believe.

Maccabean Revolt—Judean revolt that began in 167 B.C.E. against the decrees outlawing the practice of Judaism in Judea by Antiochus IV.

Magi—Astrologers and wise men. In Matthew a group of them follow a star to find the infant Jesus.

Magnificat—Song/poem Mary sings in Luke (1:46-55) when Elizabeth recognizes something special about her when Mary is pregnant with Jesus.

Malachi—Late sixth- to early fifth-century post-exilic prophet. He looks forward to a faithful leader who will call the people to repent so that God's blessings will come to them.

Man of Lawlessness—Person mentioned in 2 Thessalonians as evidence that the "Day of the Lord" had not yet occurred. Although he has been identified in many ways, we cannot be certain of his identity except to say that he was someone who lived in the late first century, otherwise the original readers of 2 Thessalonians would not have known who he is, which was necessary for the letter's argument.

Marcion—A native of Asia Minor who went to Rome in about 140 and tried to gain a position of leadership in the church. He argued that the Hebrew Bible came from a different god than the God seen in Jesus. He accepted as Scripture only ten letters of Paul and an edited version of Luke; he accepted none of the Hebrew Bible.

Marcionites—Originally those who follow Marcion. It comes to stand for anyone who questions the validity of the Hebrew Bible in comparison with the New Testament.

Mary—Mother of Jesus. She is a leading character in Luke's infancy narrative. Even though she appears only occasionally in the Gospel's narratives of the ministry of Jesus, she is present at the crucifixion.

Masoretic text—The standard text of the Hebrew Bible that comes from the scholars known as the Masoretes, who meticulously copied the text to preserve its integrity. They also added vowels and accents to make the text easier to read and understand.

Messiah—Anointed one. Various people throughout the Hebrew Bible were anointed, a way of appointing someone to perform specific tasks. The early church narrowed the definition of Messiah so that it designates only Jesus, the one who fulfills all proper expectations for the person God would send. To do this, they must radically redefine the tasks of the messiah.

Micah—Eighth-century Israelite prophet who emphasized the importance of social justice. He argued that God will not accept the worship of people who treat others unjustly.

Mishnah—The written account of the Oral Torah that was compiled in about the year 200 C.E. by Rabbi Judah.

Monotheism—Belief that there is only one god. No one in the ancient world was a monotheist because all believed that other powerful beings existed that most people worshiped. Israelites acknowledged the existence of such beings, but were called to worship only the God of Abraham.

Montanism—Apocalyptic movement of the second century with a rigorous ethic that expected renewed ecstatic manifestations of the Spirit in the church and thought those manifestations had begun among their numbers.

Mosaic covenant—Agreement between God and the Israelites that was given to Moses on Mount Sinai. God agreed to make the Israelites God's special people and the people agreed to make God their only god and to obey God's other laws.

Mount Sinai—Mountain on the Sinai Peninsula (in today's Egypt) where Moses received the Law from God. It is also known as Mount Horeb.

Muratorian Canon—A list of canonical writings set down probably in the late second century (180–200) in Rome.

Myth—A narrative that intends to reveal a truth about the meaning of life. This genre does not intend its narrative to be factual as it conveys its understanding of existence.

Nahum—Seventh-century prophet who writes an oracle against the Assyrians.

Naomi—Mother-in-law of Ruth. The non-Israelite Ruth follows Naomi back to Israel after the death of Ruth's husband, who was Naomi's son. Ruth adopts the religion of the God of Israel.

Nativity narrative—The story of the birth of Jesus; Matthew and Luke have very different stories about Jesus' birth.

Nephilim—Powerful and violent beings who are the offspring of human women and beings from the heavens (Genesis 6).

Nero—Roman emperor, 37–68. He accused the church of setting the fire that damaged much of the city of Rome in 64. This may be the first time that the Roman government officially identified members of the church as a group that was something other than simply a sect within Judaism.

New Testament—The collection of twenty-seven writings that the church added to the Hebrew Scriptures to complete their canon.

Nicodemus—Jewish teacher who came to see Jesus in the Gospel of John (John 3).

Nineveh—Capital of the Assyrian empire. This is the city to which Jonah was sent to preach. Its inhabitants are Ninevites.

Numerology—Use of numbers to represent letters (for example, 1=a, 2=b, and so on).

Obadiah—Prophet who writes oracles against the Edomites soon after the fall of Jerusalem.

Old Testament—A Christian designation for the Hebrew Bible.

Onesimus—Slave of Philemon whom Paul sent back to his master. Paul's letter to Philemon gives instructions about the treatment of Onesimus.

Oral Torah—The oral tradition of the Pharisees that recorded the various interpretations of the law from the sages of their tradition. In about 200 C.E., these oral traditions were compiled in written form in the Mishnah.

Oral tradition—The material about Jesus (both stories about what he did and remembrances of what he said) that were passed on by word of mouth before they were written down.

Origen—Biblical scholar and theologian (c. 185–250). He is known for seeing three levels of meaning in Scripture: literal, moral, and allegorical. He thought the allegorical meaning was more important than the literal.

Our Father—*See* Lord's Prayer.

P source—Probably the latest of the traditions that came together to form the Pentateuch. It has a priestly outlook that produced Leviticus and the first chapter of Genesis, among other parts of the various books.

Papyrus, papyri—An ancient writing material (much like paper) made from the stem of a thick wetlands plant, called papyrus. The earliest extant copies of New Testament books are written on papyrus.

Parallelism—A literary technique used in Hebrew poetry that thematically and structurally links two or more lines.

Parousia—Second coming of Christ at the end of things as the world knows them.

Partially realized eschatology—Belief that some of the blessings of the end time are now available to people. Members of the early church believed that the end had begun with the death and resurrection of Jesus. Thus, some of the end-time gifts of God were now available to them. Most prominently, they saw the presence of God's Spirit in their lives as the beginning of life in the intimate presence of God that comes fully at the end.

Passion—The last week of Jesus' life, the time that he suffers and dies (the word *passion* is derived from a Latin word for suffering).

Passover—The festival within Judaism that commemorates the exodus from Egypt. It is a pilgrimage feast that also celebrates the New Year. It is during the time of this festival that Jesus is crucified.

Pastoral Epistles—1 and 2 Timothy and Titus. They are called *Pastorals* because they give instructions about church leaders.

Patmos—Island off the western coast of Turkey where John had been exiled when he wrote Revelation.

Paul—A persecutor of the church who has an experience of the risen Christ on the way to Damascus that leads him to become a believer. He becomes the apostle and leading missionary to the Gentiles in the first generation of the church. His letters to his churches account for more books in the New Testament than any other author.

Pentateuch—The first five books of the Bible. These books are also known as the Torah.

Pentecost—A harvest festival within Judaism that also celebrates the giving of the Law to Moses. This pilgrimage feast comes fifty days after the Passover. In Acts, it is on this feast day that the church comes into existence.

Persecution—Unjust opposition experienced because of one's beliefs or identity.

Persians—Ancient people of what is today Iran.

Persian Empire—Empire that arises in the sixth century B.C.E. that displaces the Babylonian Empire. Its capital was in today's Iran.

Peter—Leader among the disciples of Jesus who becomes known as the apostle to the Jews.

Pharisees—One of the leading interpretations of Judaism in the first century C.E. They were know as the expert interpreters of the Law.

Philemon—Owner of Onesimus and primary addressee of one of Paul's letters.

Philo—First-century Jewish writer and philosopher. Known for his platonic and allegorical interpretations of the biblical texts, his many writings give important information about some Jewish thought in this period.

Phinehas—Grandson of the first Israelite high priest, Aaron. He is best known for killing an Israelite man and a Midianite woman who had married. In Numbers 25, such intermarriages had caused Israelites to worship foreign gods. In Numbers, his killing of the couple stops a plague.

Pilate—Roman procurator of Palestine who condemns Jesus to death.

Pious, the—The Judeans who joined the Maccabean Revolt. They rejected the hellenization of Judaism that Antiochus IV proposed before he outlawed Judaism in Judea.

Plenary inspiration—(1) In the early church, this was the view that Scripture is full of meaning, so a single text has multiple meanings (literal, allegorical, and spiritual). (2) In the twentieth century, plenary inspiration refers to the view that the words of the Bible come directly from God and so contain no scientific, historical, geographical, or any other sort of mistake.

Polytheism—The worship of many gods.

Pompey—The Roman general who was a member of the first triumvirate (with Julius Caesar and Crassus). He is the general who took control in Jerusalem in 63 B.C.E. Although he left a Hasmonean as ruler, Judea was no longer an independent nation.

Postexilic prophets—The Israelite prophets active in the time after the return of Judah from Babylonian exile to their ancestral homeland.

Preexistence—Belief that Christ existed with God before being born as Jesus.

Proselyte—A Gentile who converts fully to Judaism.

Proverb—A literary term that designates a brief wise saying; for example, "pride goes before a fall."

Providence—God's general guidance and care of the world as seen in the form of creation, the broad outlines of history, and perhaps even in events in the lives of individuals. This goodness of God supports human acts that lead to a world that more closely reflects what God wants.

Psalms of praise—These psalms praise various characteristics or acts of God.

Psalter—A term for the collection of psalms in the Hebrew Bible otherwise called the Psalms.

Pseudepigrapha—(1) Generically, any documents written under the name of someone other than their true authors. (2) A collection of about sixty-five writings (including the Apocrypha) by Jewish and Christian authors, often purporting to be written by ancestors of Jews or other prominent characters in the Hebrew Bible. Most of these books were written between 300 B.C.E. and 200 C.E. Although not truly pseudepigraphic, 3 and 4 Maccabees are grouped under this heading.

Pseudepigraphic—Claiming to be written by someone, but actually authored by someone else; for example, the book *1 Enoch* claims to be written by Enoch, but was not written for hundreds of years after the purported time of his life in Genesis.

Ptolemy—General of Alexander the Great. At Alexander's death he became ruler of Egypt and Coele-Syria (that is, much of the region once known as Canaan up through the Bekaa Valley).

Purim, Feast of—A nonreligious celebration in the Jewish month of Adar (February to March) that recalls the escape of the Jews from a pogrom in the fifth-century Persian Empire. The book of Esther serves to establish this as a feast Jews should keep.

Purity, ritual or cultic—The state of readiness to enter the presence of God. Its opposite is being unclean.

Q—Designation for the written source that contained the preserved sayings of Jesus; both Matthew and Luke used Q to supplement the material they found in Mark. No copies of this work have survived.

Qumran—Thought to be a settlement of the Essenes at the north end of the Dead Sea. The Dead Sea Scrolls were found in caves close to this compound.

Rachel—Second and favored wife of Jacob. She was the mother of Joseph and Benjamin.

Rahab—Woman of Jericho who agrees to help the Israelite spies if they will promise to spare her family when they take the city at the beginning of the Israelite conquest of Canaan.

Rebecca—Wife of Isaac and mother of Jacob and Esau. Her favoritism toward Jacob helped him attain the blessing of Isaac that was supposed to go to the firstborn son, Esau.

Reconciliation—A relational term that Paul uses to speak of the peace between believers and God that Christ effects. In other Pauline and New Testament contexts it can refer to the forced surrender of powers that are opposed to God

Redemption—A transaction in which persons or things are exchanged for some kind of payment. This includes buying slaves out of slavery. In the Bible it is used as a metaphor for national or personal salvation.

Red Sea—Traditional name of the place where the Israelites left Egypt at the Exodus. This name comes from the Greek found in the Septuagint. In the Hebrew of the book of Exodus, the name of the place may mean Sea of Reeds.

Reformation, the—Movement with roots in the early fourteenth century (with Wycliffe and Huss) that questioned the authority of the teaching and hierarchy of the Catholic Church. The movement gained significant momentum when Martin Luther publicly called for discussion of many issues in 1517.

Relative deprivation—The experience of not having things one thinks one is entitled to or deserves. Those who have this experience may not be impoverished, but only lack the things others around them have.

Resurrection experiences—Accounts of encounters with the resurrected Christ. These accounts in the canonical Gospels relate seemingly contradictory things about the nature of the resurrected Christ's body.

Ritual purity—*See* Purity.

Royal psalms—Psalms that deal with particular moments in a king's career, thanking God or asking God's blessing for the king's future.

Ruth—Moabite widow of an Israelite who returns to Israelite territory with her mother-in-law, committing herself to the God of Israel. Through the system of levirate marriage, she marries Boaz. Her great-grandson is King David.

Sabbath—Jewish holy day, Saturday. It is observed, in part, by refraining from work.

Sacrifice—Anything dedicated to or offered to a god.

Sadducees—One of the leading interpretations of Judaism in the first century C.E. This group had many priests as members.

Samson—One of the judges of Israel. He is known for his great strength.

Sarah—The originating female ancestor of Jews. She was the wife (and half sister) of Abraham and mother of Isaac.

Satan—A word that means opposer. In the book of Job this figure in the heavenly court serves as the prosecuting attorney in heaven. By the time of the New Testament, that term has become the name of the ruler of the demonic realm.

Saul—(1) First king of Israel who was eventually rejected by God for disobedience and taking the prerogative of a priest by offering a sacrifice. (2) Jewish name of the persecutor of the church who has an experience of the risen Christ on the road to Damascus and becomes the apostle Paul.

Second coming—Time when Christ returns to earth, bringing God's judgment, the resurrection of the dead, and the end of the world as it is now known.

Second Isaiah—Exilic prophet who wrote under the name Isaiah. His writings appear in Isaiah chapters 40–55.

Second Temple Judaism—The various forms of religious expression practiced by Jews in their worship of the God of Abraham in the time period beginning with the rebuilding of the Jerusalem temple at their return from Babylonian exile (c. 530) and ending with the destruction of the temple by the Romans in 70 C.E.

Seleucus—General of Alexander the Great. Upon Alexander's death, he became ruler of the area that included Persia, Babylonia, Syria, and part of southern Asia Minor.

Septuagint—The Greek translation of the Hebrew Scriptures that began coming together in the second–third century B.C.E.

Sermon on the Mount—First of five discourses (speeches) in Matthew. Matthew composes this discourse mostly from Q material. The material in the Sermon on the Mount includes: the Beatitudes, the Lord's Prayer (also known as the Our Father), and a series of Jesus' interpretations of the Law.

Servant Songs—A group of four songs in Second Isaiah (42:1-9; 46:1-6; 50:4-11; 52:13–53:12) that speak of a prophet who is part of a group that suffers for the good of the nation. His suffering leads to his exaltation by God in these poetic texts. From the time of the first century, Christians applied some of what was said about this prophet to Jesus to interpret the meaning of his ministry, death, and resurrection.

Sheol—Abode of the dead in Israelite thought. There were no distinctions between righteous and wicked people here, and the dead eventually faded out of existence.

Shema—The most basic confession within Judaism. It is taken from Deuteronomy 6:4, "Hear, O Israel: The Lord our God, the Lord is one" (this is an alternative translation in the footnote of the NRSV).

Shiloh—Place about twenty miles north of Jerusalem that had the central Israelite sanctuary to God before the time of David. In the time of David and Solomon, the sanctuary was moved to Jerusalem.

Slaughtered lamb—An image of Christ that appears in Revelation. A lamb represents both a helpless victim and a sacrificial gift. It signifies that the martyrdom of Jesus was not the last word. The resurrection has shown the power of God to be greater than the forces that killed Jesus.

Sodom and Gomorrah—Cities Genesis identifies as particularly wicked. Because of their wickedness, particularly their unjust treatment of the powerless, God destroys them.

Solomon—King of Israel after David. He is known for being wise and for building the first temple to God in Jerusalem.

Son of God—Claim made for Jesus in many New Testament writings. It asserts that Jesus has an extraordinarily intimate relationship with God.

Son of Man—Could be translated "son of a human." This ambiguous phrase could refer simply to a person or a mortal, but in the Gospels it designates Jesus as one who has an eschatological role. When these writers provide any clues about the phrase's meaning, it refers to the one who comes on the clouds bringing God's judgment. This understanding develops from the use of the expression in Daniel 7:13-14.

Speaking in tongues—*Glossolalia*. A phenomenon in which the participants believe they are taken over by the spirit of their god so that they say things they do not understand in languages they do not know. It is a kind of mystical experience that people in many religions experience. The early church saw this experience as evidence that the Holy Spirit had come into a person.

Stephen—First Christian martyr (Acts 7). He was also one of the first people appointed as a deacon in the Jerusalem church.

Super-apostles—Derisive name Paul gives to those teachers he opposes in 2 Corinthians.

He gave them this title because of their claims to have great powers that they get from God's Spirit, powers they say show that others should show deference to them.

Supersessionism—The belief that the church took the place of Israel as God's people. Even though this view has often been attributed to Paul, he was not a supersessionist; he believed that Israel remains in a special covenant relationship with God.

Synagogue—Place of worship and study, as well as a community center for Jews from the sixth or fifth century B.C.E. forward.

Synonymous parallelism—A literary technique used in Hebrew poetry that repeats in immediately successive lines the same idea using different language or imagery.

Synoptic Gospels—Designation for Matthew, Mark, and Luke, given because they are alike in so many ways. The *Synoptic Problem* is the question of how these Gospels are related to one another. Most interpreters think they have some literary relationship.

Synthetic parallelism—A literary technique of Hebrew poetry in which a second line expands on the idea of the first line.

Syntyche—One of the leaders of the church in Philippi. Her dispute with Euodia was one of the reasons Paul wrote the letter to the Philippians.

Tabernacle—Portable worship structure described in Exodus that served as the temple for God while the Israelites were in the wilderness.

Tanakh—A common name for the Hebrew Bible within the Jewish community. It is an acronym based on the three parts of those texts: the Torah (T); the Nebi'im (N), or Prophets; and the Ketubim (K), or Writings.

Teacher of Righteousness—The original leader of the Qumran community. They saw him as the authoritative interpreter of the law and as the rightful high priest.

Temple tax—The annual contribution of Jewish men to the operation of the Jerusalem temple. Jews all around the world sent their half-shekel offering each year to support the services in the temple.

Ten Commandments—The ten most basic instructions given to Moses on Mount Sinai. These set a basic religious and moral code that serve as an important element of God's covenant with Israel.

Textual criticism—The field of biblical studies that tries to establish the earliest possible wording of the biblical texts. This discipline also is able to trace the ways theological ideas developed as they note how they influenced copyists to make alterations in the biblical texts.

Textus Receptus—A Greek text produced in 1516 by the scholar Erasmus. It is based mostly on the Byzantine textual family, which most textual critics do not think is among the most reliable families of textual traditions. This edition of the Greek text, however, became the basis for the 1611 King James Version. Recent discoveries and the methods of textual criticism indicate that this text contains many errors and some major additions to the text.

Thanksgiving psalm—A psalm in which a person praises and thanks God for blessings or for being saved from some predicament.

Theodicy—The problem of the presence of evil and basic unfairness that exist in a world made by an all-good God. It is sometimes expressed by a person asking why bad things happen to good people.

Theophany—Visionary experience of the presence of God; see Isaiah 6:1-13.

Third Isaiah—Postexilic prophet who wrote in the name of Isaiah. His writings appear as chapters 56–66 in the book of Isaiah.

Torah—The name used in Judaism (and beyond) for the first five books of the Bible. These books are also known as the Pentateuch.

Transfiguration—An episode in the Gospels in which Jesus is transformed into a glorious (that is, shiny) state.

Twelve, the—The inner circle of followers that the Gospels have Jesus gather around him. There are twelve so they can represent the eschatologically reconstituted people of Israel, who represent the people of God.

Twenty-four elders—Powerful figures among the beings that surround the throne of God in the visions of heaven in Revelation 4–5. They represent the combination of the twelve tribes of Israel and the twelve apostles. Thus they represent the whole people of God.

Uncial—A manuscript written in all capital letters.

Universe of discourse—A distinctive way of reasoning that is appropriate within a particular way of analyzing and reasoning about a particular matter. Differing universes will understand things differently and allow different types of evidence. For example, the universe of scientific discourse uses evidence and some types of reasoning and evaluation that are not useful or appropriate in the universe of music composition.

Vanity—The idea that things have no purpose or meaning. Ecclesiastes uses this term to describe life, and various aspects of life.

Vulgate—The Latin translation of the whole Bible completed by Jerome in about 405 C.E. It becomes the standard translation of the church for several centuries.

Wellhausen, Julius—German biblical scholar (1844–1918). His hypothesis about multiple sources used to write the Pentateuch, called the Documentary Hypothesis (see above), had a great impact on the understanding of the Hebrew Bible.

Wicked priest—The name the authors of the Dead Sea Scrolls give to the Maccabean ruler who assumes the office of high priest in Jerusalem when they believed their leader (the Teacher of Righteousness) should have that post.

Widows—A group of women in the early church who were influential and engaged in a significant teaching ministry.

Wisdom literature—Books that reflect the literary forms and outlook of the Wisdom tradition. They rely more on observation and interpretation of the world than on direct revelation from God.

Word, the—A way John speaks of the identity of the preexistent Christ. Drawing on Israel's wisdom tradition, John has the Word assist God in the creation and sustaining of the world, as well as being the clearest revelation of God in the world.

Yahweh—The name of God as it appears in the Hebrew Bible. It is the most important name for God in the Hebrew Bible, the name revealed to Moses in the burning bush episode.

Zechariah—(1) Postexilic prophet who urges the people to complete the temple and treat the poor justly. (2) Father of John the Baptist.

Zephaniah—Seventh-century prophet who warned that the "Day of the Lord" would bring destruction on the nation unless the people stopped worshiping multiple gods. He also envisions restoration after the devastation.

INDEX

Leadership in the Church

The basic topic of all the letters of 2 Corinthians is the nature of Christian leadership. While the other teachers asserted that God enabled them to be powerful and impressive, Paul argued that the Spirit enabled him to give up rights and privileges for the good of his churches. We find in these letters that Paul had given up some of the kinds of status his rivals wanted to claim. For example, Paul supported himself by engaging in manual labor, in spite of the Greco-Roman cultural bias that said such work was demeaning, and even scarred one's soul. When he did this without having to, he intentionally lowered his social status so he could reach people of all parts of society. Paul argued that this is a proper model of leadership; Christian leaders must serve others, not expect deference and claim privilege.

Conform to the example of Christ. In some places Paul uses irony and sarcasm to convince his readers to abandon their infatuation with the

FIGURE 14.7 **REMAINS OF WORKSHOP, CORINTH**

Although this shop and its neighbors in a row were probably built a few decades after Paul's visit to Corinth, it is the typical size shop he would have worked in as he plied his trade, perhaps tentmaking (Acts 18:3), and preached to those passing by. Jerry Sumney